£35.00

Man & Music

THE EARLY
BAROQUE
ERA

Man & Music

THE EARLY BAROQUE ERA

From the late 16th century to the 1660s

EDITED BY CURTIS PRICE

150th YEAR
M
MACMILLAN

First published in the United Kingdom 1993 by
The Macmillan Press Limited
Houndmills, Basingstoke, Hampshire RG21 2XS
and London

Associated companies in Auckland, Delhi, Dublin, Gaborone,
Hamburg, Harare, Hong Kong, Johannesburg, Kuala Lumpur,
Lagos, Manzini, Melbourne, Mexico City, Nairobi, New York,
Singapore, Tokyo

ISBN 0-333-51600-1 (hardback)

British Library Cataloguing in Publication Data
Early Baroque Era: From the Late 16th Century to the 1660s. –
(Man & Music Series; Vol. 3)
    I. Price, Curtis Alexander II. Series
    780.9

Typeset by Florencetype Ltd, Kewstoke, Avon
Printed in Hong Kong

Contents

Illustration
Acknowledgments

The publisher would like to thank the following institutions and individuals who have kindly provided material for use in this book:

Maps by John Gilkes: J. M. Dent & Sons Ltd, from *Companion to Baroque Music*, compiled and edited by Julie Anne Sadie (London, 1990), reprinted with kind permission; National Gallery, London: 1; Trustees of the British Museum, London (Department of Prints and Drawings): 2(a), 4, 62; Devonshire Collection, Trustees of the Chatsworth Settlement/photo The Courtauld Institute of Art, London: 2(b), 66; Private Collection/photo Colnaghi, London: 3; Fratelli Alinari, Florence: 5; Biblioteca Reale, Turin/photo Chomon: 6; Metropolitan Museum of Art, New York (Elisha Whittelsey Collection, Elisha Whittelsey Fund, 1967): 7; Museo di Roma/photo Antonello Idini: 9; Theatermuseum, University of Cologne: 10; Kungliga Biblioteket, Stockholm: 11; Nationalmuseum Stockholm/photo Statens Konstmuseer: 13, 14; Biblioteca e Museo Correr, Venice: 15, 16, 20; Fotomas Index, Beckenham, Kent: 17, 69; Biblioteca Nazionale Marciana, Venice/photo Toso: 18; Library of Congress, Washington: 19; Archivio di Stato, Bologna: 21, 22, 23; Board of Trustees of the Victoria and Albert Museum, London: 25, 27, 56; Biblioteca Nazionale Centrale, Florence: 26; Istituto per le Lettere, il Teatro e il Melodramma (Raccolta Rolandi), Fondazione Giorgio Cini, Venice: 28; Österreichische Nationalbibliothek, Vienna: 29, 30, 31, 33; Kunsthistorisches Museum, Vienna: 32; Universitetsbibliotek, Uppsala: 34; Karl-Marx-Universität, Leipzig: 35; Kupferstichkabinett, Sächsische Landesbibliothek (Deutsche Fotothek), Dresden: 37, 38; Staatliche Landesbildstelle, Hamburg: 39; Bayerische Staatsbibliothek, Munich: 40; Stiftung Weimarer Klassik: 41; Museum für Hamburgische Geschichte: 42; Mercatorfonds: from *The Organ and its Music in the Netherlands 1500–1800* by F. Peeters and A. Vente (Antwerp, 1971): 43; National Gallery of Art, Washington (Widener Collection): 44; Cleveland Museum of Art, Ohio (Gift of the Hanna Fund, 51.355): 45; Bibliothèque Nationale, Paris: 46 and 50 (photo Giraudon), 49, 51; 53 and 54 (photo Bulloz); 55 (photo Larousse), 59; Musée du Louvre, Paris/photo Réunion des Musées Nationaux: 47, 48; École des Beaux-Arts, Paris/photo Giraudon: 52; Bibliothèque de Versailles/photo Larousse: 57; Musée Carnavalet, Paris/photo Bulloz: 58; The Marquess of Salisbury, Hatfield House: 60; Bibliotheek der Rijksuniversiteit, Utrecht (MS842, f.132r): 61; British Library, London: 63; Berkeley Castle/photo Courtauld Institute of Art, London: 65; Private Collection: 67; Nostell Priory (The National Trust): 68; National Portrait Gallery, London: 72; Museo Municipal, Madrid/photo Ayuntamiento de Madrid: 73; Gemäldegalerie, Berlin/photo Bildarchiv Preussischer Kulturbesitz: 74; Museo-Monasterio de San Lorenzo de El Escorial, Madrid/photo Ampliaciones Reproducciones MAS, Barcelona: 75; Houghton Library, Harvard University, Cambridge, Massachusetts (MS Typ. 258H): 76; Archivo Municipal, Madrid/Ayuntamiento de Madrid: from *Las Tarascas de Madrid*, by J. M. Bernáldez Montalvo (1983)

Abbreviations

AcM	*Acta musicologica*
AnMc	*Analecta musicologica*
EMH	*Early Music History*
Grove 6	*The New Grove Dictionary of Music and Musicians*
IMSCR	*International Musicological Society Congress Report*
JAMS	*Journal of the American Musicological Society*
JRMA	*Journal of the Royal Musical Association*
ML	*Music & Letters*
MQ	*The Musical Quarterly*
MR	*The Music Review*
MSD	Musicological Studies and Documents, ed. A. Carapetyan (Rome, 1951–)
MT	*The Musical Times*
NRMI	*Nuova rivista musicale italiana*
PRMA	*Proceedings of the Royal Musical Association*
RIM	*Rivista italiana di musicologia*
RMARC	*R[oyal] M[usical] A[ssociation] Research Chronicle*
RMFC	*Recherches sur la musique française classique*
RMI	*Rivista musicale italiana*
SIMG	*Sammelbände der Internationalen Musik-Gesellschaft*

Preface

The *Man and Music* series of books – eight in number, chronologically organized – were originally conceived in conjunction with the television programmes of the same name, of which the first was shown by Channel 4 in 1986 and distributed worldwide by Granada Television International. These programmes were designed to examine the development of music in particular places during particular periods in the history of Western civilization.

The books have the same objective. Each is designed to cover a segment of Western musical history; the breaks between them are planned to correspond with significant historical junctures. Since historical junctures, or indeed junctures in stylistic change, rarely happen with the neat simultaneity that the historian's or the editor's orderly mind might wish for, most volumes have 'ragged' ends and beginnings; for example, the Renaissance volume terminates, in Italy, in the 1570s and 80s, but continues well into the seventeenth century in parts of northern Europe.

These books do not, however, make up a history of music in the traditional sense. The reader will not find technical, stylistic discussion in them; anyone wanting to trace the detailed development of the texture of the madrigal or the rise and fall of sonata form will need to look elsewhere. Rather, it is the intention in these volumes to show in what context, and as a result of what forces, social, cultural, intellectual, the madrigal or sonata form came into being and took its particular shape. The intention is to view musical history not as a series of developments in some hermetic world of its own but rather as a series of responses to social, economic and political circumstances and to religious and intellectual stimuli. We want to explain not simply *what* happened, but *why* it happened, and why it happened when and where it did.

We have chosen to follow what might be called a geographical, or perhaps a topographical, approach: to focus, in each chapter, on a particular place and to examine its music in the light of its special situation. Thus, in most of these volumes, the chapters – once past the introductory one, contributed by the volume editor – are each devoted to a city or a region. This system has inevitably needed some modification when dealing with very early or very recent times, for reasons (opposite ones, of course) to do with communication and cultural spread.

These books do not attempt to treat musical history comprehensively. Their editors have chosen for discussion the musical centres that they see as the most significant and the most interesting: many lesser ones inevitably escape individual discussion, though the patterns of their musical life may be discernible by analogy with others or may be separately referred to in the opening, editorial chapter. We hope, however, that a new kind of picture of musical history may begin to emerge from these volumes, and that this picture may be more accessible to the general reader, responsive to music but untrained in its techniques, than others arising from more traditional approaches. In spite of the large number of lovers of music, musical histories have never enjoyed the appeal to a broad, intelligent general readership in the way that histories of art, architecture or literature have done: these books represent an attempt to reach such a readership and explain music in terms that may quicken their interest.

*

The television programmes and books were initially planned in close collaboration with Sir Denis Forman, then Chairman of Granada Television International. The treatment was worked out in more detail with several of the volume editors, among whom I am particularly grateful to Iain Fenlon for the time he has generously given to discussion of the problems raised by this approach to musical history, and also to Alexander Ringer and James McKinnon for their valuable advice and support. Discussion with Bamber Gascoigne and Tony Cash, in the course of the making of the initial television programmes, also proved of value. I am grateful to Celia Thompson for drafting the non-musical parts of the chronologies that appear in each volume and to Julie Anne Sadie for the musical part in the Baroque volumes, and to Elisabeth Agate for her invaluable work as picture editor in bringing the volumes to visual life.

London, 1993   STANLEY SADIE

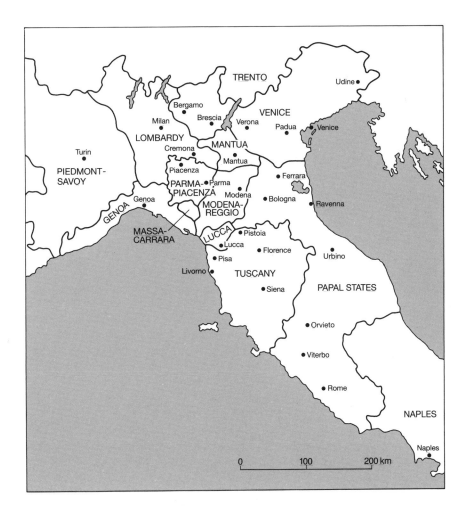

TRENTO

Udine •

Bergamo
•

Milan   Brescia   VENICE
•   •   Verona   Padua   Venice
                    •   •   •

LOMBARDY   MANTUA

Cremona
•

Turin
•   Piacenza   Mantua
                •   •

PIEDMONT-   Parma   Ferrara
SAVOY   PARMA- • Parma •
             PIACENZA   Modena   Bologna
         Genoa MODENA-   •   •   Ravenna
GENOA   •   REGGIO   •

MASSA-
CARRARA   LUCCA   Pistoia
                        •
                Lucca
                •   Florence   Urbino
         Pisa   •   •
         •
Livorno •   PAPAL STATES
              TUSCANY
                Siena
                •

                        Orvieto
                        •

                        Viterbo
                        •

                        Rome
                        •   NAPLES

                                        Naples
        0   100   200 km   •

The Early Baroque Era

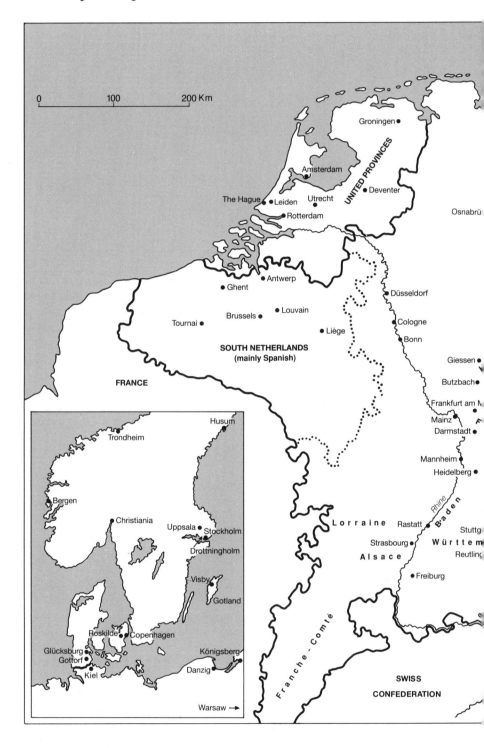

Groningen

UNITED PROVINCES

Amsterdam
Deventer

The Hague ● Leiden   Utrecht
Rotterdam

Osnabrü

● Antwerp
● Ghent

Düsseldorf

● Louvain
Brussels ●   Cologne
Tournai ●   ● Liège   Bonn

SOUTH NETHERLANDS
(mainly Spanish)

Giessen

Butzbach

FRANCE

Frankfurt am N
Mainz
Darmstadt ●

Husum

Trondheim

Mannheim
Heidelberg ●

Bergen

Christiania

Rhine

Uppsala ● ● Stockholm
Drottningholm

Lorraine   Rastatt Baden
Strasbourg ●   Stuttg
Alsace   Württem
                Reutling

Visby ●
Gotland

● Freiburg

Roskilde ● ● Copenhagen
Glücksburg ●
Gottorf ●   Königsberg
Kiel   Danzig ●

Franche-Comté

SWISS
CONFEDERATION

Warsaw →

0   100   200 Km

Chapter I

Music, Style and Society

CURTIS PRICE

The supplanting of the so-called *ars perfecta*, the equal-voice poly-phony of the late Renaissance, by the selfconsciously expressive vocal and instrumental music of the 'second practice', which happened about 1600, is one of the clearest watersheds in the history of Western music. This fundamental change in style does not appear to have been led significantly by the kinds of cultural, demographic or geographical forces and conditions to which this series of books is primarily devoted, but rather came from within music itself, with encouragement from its nearest sister art, poetry. Most music histor-ians now view this great style shift as the final bloom of Italian humanism, 'the main force for renewal in all the arts' during the late Renaissance,[1] the direct result of the search for ever more radical ways of setting expressive poetry. But whether the second practice was also a product of the Zeitgeist, the Mannerist movement in art, architecture and literature, is as debatable as the concept of Mannerism itself.

One historian has said that during the seventeenth century 'music followed a development all its own',[2] apparently disconnected spiri-tually and intellectually from the momentous scientific, political and philosophical movements of the period. So radical a change in the fabric of music – the invention of completely new textures – does not seem to have been closely paralleled in the other arts or indeed in any aspect of seventeenth-century intellectual thought, except per-haps in the writings of Thomas Hobbes. Yet it is tempting to con-struct a 'crisis' scenario for music in the early Baroque era, analogous to the 'general crisis in Europe' theory formulated by Eric Hobsbawm and Hugh Trevor-Roper in the 1960s, later qualified but not substantially challenged.[3] As with the pan-European political and economic scene during the first half of the seventeenth century, music was in disarray, with many stylistic dead ends and failed experiments: Gesualdo's ultra-chromatic madrigals, which had no immediate successors, and the desiccated early monodies in which virtually all contrapuntal interest was sacrificed to dramatic decla-mation of the text, are just two examples. The beginnings of the

1

resolution of the general crisis at about 1650, after the Thirty Years War, and a return to greater political and economic stability in the second half of the century, appear to parallel the 'normalization' of the new, wild art of music, the gradual reining in of excess. This was followed by the great levelling of style during the period 1680–1700 and the remarkable codification, after a century and a half of evolution, of the basic major/minor harmonic system that would serve composers from Corelli to Wagner.

But it is ultimately futile, if not dangerous, to construct such parallels, because upon closer examination the analogy breaks down or forces a distortion of the facts. For example, the change precipitated by the second practice did not affect all music; one style did not entirely supplant another. Indeed, the music of Palestrina, which epitomizes the *ars perfecta*, was studied and emulated well into the eighteenth century and beyond. This book does not aim to find or create connections between music and general historical trends, nor even between music and the other arts. But it does view the musical revolutions of the early Baroque era against the background of broad cultural issues: systems of government, political upheaval and evolution, philosophical developments in the wake of humanism, the Counter-Reformation, patterns of international travel, trade and diplomacy.

The etymologically slippery term 'Baroque' (originally a misshapen pearl) was expropriated by musicologists from art historians in the early twentieth century, first in the writings of Curt Sachs, to describe the music of the period 1600–1750. Though the application to music was asynchronous with art history, one of the eighteenth-century meanings of 'Baroque' – bizarre, irregular, uneven – does aptly describe much of the second practice repertory. The boldness of Luzzaschi, Monteverdi, Frescobaldi or d'India can still astonish audiences. Furthermore, a French critic had already applied the word 'Baroque' to music as early as 1734 (in a review of a Rameau opera in the *Mercure galant*), and in his *Dictionnaire de musique* (1768) Jean-Jacques Rousseau defined Baroque music as that 'in which harmony is confused, charged with modulations and dissonances'. As applied to style rather than to the period as a whole, 'Baroque' is obviously inadequate to describe the wide diversity of early seventeenth-century music, much of which eschewed the extremes of the second practice and gradually tempered the modal polyphony of the Renaissance into tonal counterpoint. Yet the most exciting and iconoclastic music of the era – that which helped make opera possible, that which brought the mature genius Heinrich Schütz back to Venice for a second period of study – is exquisitely Baroque.

One of the first manifestations of the new style that emerged about 1600 was the unorthodox, sometimes shocking use of certain dissonances which had been tightly controlled by long-established rules, rules evidently so necessary to musical order and coherence that they would have to be virtually re-invented many years later. The famous debate between Claudio Monteverdi, not the most adventurous of avant-garde composers, and the Bolognese theorist Giovanni Maria Artusi, hardly a reactionary, was triggered by a highly technical, even tedious disagreement over how far a composer could go in using 'unprepared' sevenths[4] to depict extreme emotions. But at the heart of the disagreement was the changing relationship between poetry and music. As Monteverdi's brother Giulio Cesare put it, clearly reflecting Claudio's own view: in the second practice 'the words are the mistress of the harmony' and not, as before, harmony the mistress of the words.[5] Acknowledgment of the composer's ability to fuse words and music into an expression of emotion greater than the sum of the parts is not of course unique to the Baroque period, but the three undisputed masters of the seventeenth century, including Monteverdi, are known primarily for their vocal music and each, like him, proclaimed the primacy of harmony over poetry. Schütz was imbued with the second practice as well as being a master of counterpoint, but his most original contribution was the discovery of how to set the German language in the Italian style, yet still capture the rhythm and meaning of the words. Like German, English was also supposed to be too lacking in open vowels, too clogged with consonants and diphthongs to lend itself to expressive musical setting. But Henry Purcell, after Monteverdi the most comprehensive musical genius of the century, was admired for possessing a peculiar ability 'to express the Energy of *English* Words, whereby he mov'd the Passions of all his Auditors'. Yet he, like Schütz before, looked to 'the most fam'd Italian masters' for guidance and inspiration.

THE DIFFUSION OF ITALIAN MUSICAL CULTURE

Italy was the source of most of the major innovations in music during the first half of the seventeenth century. It supplied court chapels, city churches, noble salons, theatres and publishing houses from Madrid to St Petersburg, from Edinburgh to Vienna, with music, composers, performers and instruments. It is important to understand how this potent musical culture was disseminated. The traditional model of the development of musical style during the Baroque era, with Italy as *fons et origo* of immensely attractive but rather insipid ideas which were later lent gravity and sophistication in northern countries, cannot fully account for the diversity of genres and styles at the beginning of the seventeenth century on both sides of the Alps. This model is somewhat analogous to the now largely discredited theory of the spread of civilization westwards from

3

Mesopotamia, a theory which was itself based anachronistically and probably subconsciously on the spread of Christianity westward from Palestine. The 'Mesopotamian' model assumes that influence flows mainly in one direction and that earlier, indigenous traditions are inherently inferior to imported ones. Yet France, the cities of the Hanseatic League, Dresden, Vienna, England and Spain each contributed something of their native musical styles to what was to become by 1700 the lingua franca. England and Spain, being the most remote and at times cut off from the mainstream (one by the Channel and the other by the worst roads in Europe), are perhaps the most susceptible to the 'Mesopotamian' theory, and scholars and critics have therefore tended to attribute innovation and excellence in seventeenth-century English and Spanish music to Italian influence. London, for example, attracted Italian musicians like a magnet after the Restoration of 1660, yet hardly any musicologist has considered the possible influence of English music on the foreigners, so conditioned are we by the traditional model.

Why did developments in early seventeenth-century Italian music gain such wide currency? To answer this question one must consider how musical ideas were transmitted. Italy has long held great fascination for northern Europeans, who are both attracted and repulsed by its art, religion, politics and especially its climate. During the war between England and Spain and until the peace treaty of 1604, communication between northern countries and Italy was difficult and at times impossible. But for the first two decades of the new century, travel throughout western Europe enjoyed a boom; Paris, Venice, Milan, Florence and Rome were by far the most popular destinations. Most documented trips were taken by diplomats and their entourages, wealthy merchants, and young aristocrats bent on pleasure, adventure or 'improvement'. Much less commonly did artists, writers or musicians travel independently of their royal or noble patrons; in fact, the majority of recorded visits of composers to foreign lands in the early seventeenth century – Schütz from Marburg and later Dresden to Venice, Nicholas Lanier from London to Florence, Filippo Piccinini from Bologna to Madrid – were at the behest or encouragement of princes. The English organist John Bull's tour of the Low Countries and the harpsichordist Johann Jakob Froberger's restless peregrinations to numerous cities, including Rome (where he studied with Frescobaldi), are among a small handful of instances of major composers travelling beyond frontiers at their own risk and expense during the early Baroque period. The fully international master of the Renaissance was not seen again until the eighteenth century.

While travel was a luxurious hardship available mainly to the upper classes, it was nevertheless routine and well organized and, by about 1620, held few surprises for the innocent abroad. Take for example the typical English aristocrat, among the most enthusiastic of pilgrims of the period, and with the furthest to go. He travelled on horseback, by public coach, mail packet, post-chaise and canal boat or on foot – often all on the same day. Depending on the winds affecting the Channel crossing, the journey from Gravesend to Rotterdam could take as little as 25 hours; London to Paris took four to eight days, the usual route being from Calais to Dieppe, Rouen, up the Seine to St Denis and Paris. The way then led almost invariably to Lyons. Merchants and other members of the lower ranks (including presumably musicians) would then make their way to Marseilles and sail for Genoa or Livorno (Leghorn). For the gentry and diplomats, the preferred route was by land, either over Mont Cenis, down into Piedmont and on to Turin, or over the Brenner Pass into the Veneto. The route over St Gotthard to Lugano and Milan was considered dangerous and generally avoided. In the early seventeenth century, English, as well as Dutch and German travellers, mostly confined themselves to Venice, Milan and Florence, with brief, incognito forays to Rome and, very occasionally, Naples. Besides viewing the 'treasures' and antiquities, attempting to learn the language and matriculating fashionably at the University of Padua, foreign travellers purchased books, paintings, music and musical instruments, artefacts, biological specimens, glass and other items, shipping them by sea from Livorno or Venice back to London, Amsterdam or Hamburg. The typical return journey was via Innsbruck, Augsburg or Strasbourg, then down the Rhine, ending with a period of recuperation at Spa (near Liège) or jaded wandering through the Low Countries.

The free flow of aristocratic and diplomatic traffic among Italian cities and across the Alps may have done little at first to encourage the transmission of musical compositions, but it created a demand in northern Europe for the one thing that returning travellers universally admired about Italy: the freshness, grandeur and virtuosity of the new music. For the final flowering of the magnificent polychoral style of the Gabrielis at Venice and the emergence of the *seconda prattica* coincided fortuitously with the vastly increased movement of music-consuming people across Europe. There can be little doubt that the eventual pervasiveness of the new Italian style is owing in no small part to the Grand Tour. Given the ease and frequency of travel after 1600, perhaps one should only be surprised that stylistic change was so slow to happen in some of the remoter musical centres.

With the outbreak of the Thirty Years War, the first of several epidemics of plague right across Europe and the economic crash – all of which happened about 1620 – Italy was temporarily isolated. But less than ten years later, travellers had found new routes which

1. Claude Lorraine: Seaport with the Embarkation of the Queen of Sheba, 1648

avoided infected cities and sieges and battles happening across Germany. All of Italy was opened up to foreign visitors, and the classical *giro* was firmly established along a route which would be followed with little variation for the next 200 years. This second, even more intense period of discovery coincided with the rapid development of public opera, first at Venice and then throughout Italy. Music, along with the treasures of Florence, the antiquities of Rome and the venial sins permitted in Venice, finally became one of the main attractions for the casual tourist.

With the preferred transalpine routes closed by the war, the traveller from France, the Low Countries or England embarked from Marseilles and hopped from port to port along the Riviera to Genoa or Livorno, where the *giro* properly began. Rome and Naples, now safe for northern Protestants, were added as winter and spring fixtures, while most travellers retreated to Venice or the Italian lakes as summer approached. Though they were not centres of major musical activity (and hence not represented by separate essays in this book), several cities along the route could offer excellent music: Genoa, Livorno (where opera was being produced in 1658), Lucca (especially admired for its fine music in the 1650s), Siena and Naples. Travel was no longer the exclusive privilege of the diplomat or heir-apparent, and many students, clergymen and writers joined the

Grand Tour. As John Stoye has remarked, 'They saw the same things, learnt what to think of them from books and the local inhabitants, tending to share a common and conventional outlook on the panorama around them'.[6] But music, especially concerted church music and opera, was the one aspect of the tour guaranteed to impress even the unmusical. The young poet John Milton, like countless other travellers, bought printed scores of Monteverdi at Venice and had them shipped home by sea. But what seemed to him and his compatriots ideal mementoes of the Lenten or Ascension extravaganzas at the Palazzo Rospigliosi and the Chiesa Nuova at Rome or St Mark's at Venice, must have looked like hieroglyphics when the packing-cases were opened back in London.

The printing of music at Venice and on a somewhat smaller scale at Rome was an important international business which depended on volume trade. Later in the century Antwerp and then Amsterdam joined the huge market for what was primarily Italian music. Strong trade and political links with Venice, upon which the Dutch Republic ostentatiously modelled itself, established Amsterdam as the main northern outlet of Italian instrumental music, a position it maintained well into the eighteenth century. Paris was also an important centre for music printing in the seventeenth century, but it was a privilege tightly controlled by the state and supplied a comparatively small domestic market, with the firm of Ballard producing fine editions fit more for the royal archives or presentation to diplomats than for practical use. Yet the international circulation of printed music, which is probably the surest index of the depth and influence of Italian musical culture (and thus is discussed in some detail in the following chapters), did not necessarily assure the transmission of the Italian *style*, especially in opera, which (after a few early examples) was rarely published. Unlike scientific discoveries, philosophical discourse or political theory, musical ideas could not be effectively transmitted through print or by itinerant tutors. The new basso continuo style was spread principally by a few exceptional performers and composers, *maestri* recruited at considerable trouble and expense to interpret the symbols of figured bass and to re-create Venetian splendour in northern climes; or, conversely, by native composers sent to Italy to learn the new art and bring it back home.

Today when one considers the deceptive simplicity of monody and early operatic recitative, the mechanical iterations of the *stile concitato* (Monteverdi's way of conveying extreme agitation) or the pseudo-counterpoint of some Venetian sacred concertos, it is difficult to appreciate just how little of the new style could be conveyed by the printed page or to imagine how wonderfully complex some at least of this music would have seemed to uninitiated northern musicians. As during the Renaissance, first-hand experience in Italy was con-

7

sidered essential for even the most gifted and resourceful northern composer, as exemplified by Heinrich Schütz, whose study at Venice, first with Giovanni Gabrieli (1609–13) and then most probably with Monteverdi (1628–9), is a *locus classicus* and too well known to need discussion in detail here. Schütz's trips helped to initiate Germany's musical dependency on Italy which would entice Handel, Hasse, Gluck, Mozart, Wagner and many others south for edification more spiritual than technical. Yet in a sense Schütz has become a victim of the 'Mesopotamian' model theorists, who would attribute too much of his genius to his Italian experience. His development of an essentially German style of word-setting took him far beyond the counterpoint learnt from Gabrieli or the lessons in opera that he may have had from Monteverdi. What he acquired in Venice were, first, a review of fundamentals and, second, the ability to be fashionable. But his own amazingly peripatetic career, forced upon him by the privations of the Thirty Years War and, later, by the wages of fame, illustrates that musical style was transmitted more effectively by charismatic practical demonstration than by printed scores, diplomatic traffic or osmosis between amateurs: the performance of major works in a new style required the presence of the composer himself, especially opera which, until Schütz introduced it in 1627, was by his own account completely unknown in Germany. But smaller-scale, non-theatrical works such as the *Symphoniae sacrae*, which might seem to us perfectly complete as published, also apparently needed the composer's presence for proper realization: according to Schütz (writing in 1647), German performers still did not understand music in the 'modern Italian manner'. Even if one allows for his endearing tendency to credit his Italian mentors with all his innovations, Schütz describes a Germany inquisitive about the new Italian style but lacking the resources or imagination to recreate it *in situ*.

The high value placed on Italian music and especially on Italian performers and composers assured the eventual domination of Italian as a lingua franca and was almost entirely responsible for the spread of opera. But the privileged, almost reverential position afforded the *maestri* in certain courts and cities became itself a hindrance to the development of musical style: at the court of Louis XIV, Jean-Baptiste Lully's brilliant transformation of Italian opera into *tragédie lyrique* soon ossified into an immutable classic; at the court of Ferdinand II in Vienna, Giovanni Valentini's similar domination of the imperial Hofkapelle created a virtual museum of the Venetian polychoral school, while during the later reign of Leopold I, Antonio Draghi established an operatic monopoly which allowed no competition and hence little development for most of the second half of the seventeenth century.

The musical geography of Europe during the Baroque era is thus paradoxical. Travel was routine and relatively painless for those who could afford it, but Italian music itself was slower to be assimilated into native traditions, as we have seen in the case of Germany. News of important musical events such as the operas at Florence and Venice spread rapidly; there was keen interest in the new style even in the furthest corners of the Continent, and printed music was widely available. That experiments in text setting were being conducted almost simultaneously by the Roman *compagnie*, the Florentine *accademie*, and Baïf in Paris, and only slightly later at the court of James I in London is no accident; nor is the contemporaneous development of the *intermedi* and opera in Italy, masques in England and ballet in France. Each was a manifestation of the growing awareness of the importance of theatrical spectacle as an impressive and instructive symbol of state power. There is little evidence that Italy was much aware or even interested in musical developments elsewhere in Europe, but she was not unaware of political events north of the Alps and of their potential for musical celebration and exploitation. Two examples will suffice. England naturally enjoyed warm relations with Rome after the accession of the Roman Catholic James II in 1685, and Queen Christina marked the event at her palace with a performance of Bernardo Pasquini's *Applauso festivo*, a huge work directed by Corelli.[7] The Duke of Monmouth's rebellion, which shortly thereafter gravely threatened James's position, was also acknowledged in Modena, home of his consort Queen Mary, with a bizarre oratorio by Giovanni Battista Vitali called *L'ambitione debellata, overo La caduta di Monmuth*.[8] These are isolated examples sparked by England's final experiment with Popery, but they serve to remind us that seventeenth-century Europe was a much smaller place than its geographical variety and political complexity might otherwise lead us to believe.

The general patterns of transmission described above can be more concretely illustrated by examining the spread of the basso continuo. The most pervasive and instantly recognizable characteristic of Baroque music, the basso continuo is nevertheless a difficult concept to grasp. On the one hand, it is a simple, efficient means of accompaniment; on the other, it is a sign of the fundamental change in texture and harmonic expression which Baroque music embodies. The practice gradually evolved during the second half of the sixteenth century as a means of accompanying madrigals and motets when the full complement of singers was unavailable or certain weak singers needed reinforcing. The organist, harpsichordist or archlutenist would play along from the score or, more usually, from the lowest voice part, filling out the texture where necessary. Given the growing concern for heightened poetic expression and the keen interest in solo singing, the logical extension of this practice of accompaniment was to have the instrumentalist play all but the top part, which could thus be rendered by a solo voice more expressively and with greater scope for ornamentation than when singing in consort with other voices. With the invention of monody, expressly designed for a single voice and devoid of supporting counterpoint, there was no need to write out a separate accompaniment, which could be reduced to a single line, the bass, with the now vestigial inner parts merely suggested by figures and accidentals to indicate which notes above the bass line should be sounded to produce a full harmony. With this system of shorthand ('figured bass'), the singer could even accompany himself, which is precisely what Giulio Caccini (one of the inventors of opera) recommended in order to achieve the closest possible union of music and poetry. Although the first publications of music with figured bass lines did not appear until 1600, the practice was already well known to those court and chapel musicians whose job it was to accompany singers.

But the basso continuo also signalled the arrival of the *seconda prattica* itself, a recognition that, in the new music, counterpoint had withered to the point that part-writing no longer needed staff notation. The sudden appearance of the basso continuo in Italian publications of 1600 might suggest an equally sudden acceptance and understanding of the new method of writing accompaniments. Monteverdi first used figured bass in his fifth book of madrigals (1605); but when he reprinted the fourth book (originally published in 1603) ten years later, he added a basso continuo, a retrospective conversion which probably reflects the manner of performance in 1603. But there are many indications that the basso continuo was slow to be understood outside north Italian courts and academies, even if similar methods of accompaniment must have been practised by musicians throughout Europe. The solo song, in the form of the *air de cour*, was a staple of French music during the first half of the seventeenth century, but the lute accompaniments were almost always given in tablature (a system of notation in which the exact location of every note is specified). The earliest examples of basso continuo in France are found in manuscripts dating from the 1640s, and the first print is Constantijn Huygens's *Pathodia sacra et profana* of 1647. In Spain, with its venerable tradition of guitar and vihuela accompaniment of solo song, the basso continuo was more quickly assimilated, though tablature was still the most convenient system of notation for plucked instruments. Thanks to Michael Praetorius's highly influential treatise *Syntagma musicum* (1614–18) and the force of his own advocacy of the Italian style, Germany quickly grasped the theory and practice of figured bass. In England, which was furthest from the source and, like Spain, long wedded to the lute family, the basso continuo remained largely an arcane practice until the last quarter of the century. Here, however, practice undoubtedly preceded theory, as lute intabulations of monody accompaniments appeared soon after 1600, and a set of anthems published in London as early as 1630 included a basso continuo.[9] But as late as the mid-century, English composers such as William Lawes were still writing out simple organ parts for consort music, accompaniments which in Italy would have been improvised at sight by any competent organist, given a figured bass. But we should not be guided entirely by the surviving sources: one gets the impression that northern keyboard players, upon having figured bass explained to them, discovered, like M. Jourdain, that they had, as it were, been speaking prose all their lives.

The different rates at which the basso continuo was absorbed into various native styles and traditions before its universal acceptance by about 1680 points to another important feature of the musical geography of seventeenth-century Europe. The old-style counterpoint, the *stile antico*, co-existed with the second practice and subsequent stylistic developments throughout the first half of the century and beyond. This was not merely a matter of pedantic veneration of Palestrina and the *ars perfecta*, which has featured prominently in the teaching of the rudiments of composition from 1600 to the present day with very few gaps in between. Rather, Palestrina was a living tradition in the Sistine Chapel and was occasionally performed at high feasts in many places throughout Europe. Two centres may be noted for their arch-conservatism. The Italian *maestri* who gradually replaced the old-guard Netherlanders at the Austrian Hofkapelle were, like Annibale Padovano, conservators of the old polyphonic style. While Venetian grandeur came to permeate the court of Ferdinand II, Vienna remained for the entire century a bastion of reactionary musical taste. It is no accident that Johann Joseph Fux, the eighteenth-century theorist and composer who helped to canonize Palestrina for generations of counterpoint students, spent most of his career at Vienna. The court music at Madrid was also a preserve of the old-style counterpoint, the source in this case being the Spanish Netherlands, which had strong historical and political connections with Spain. Flemings ran the chapel of Charles V, and his *maestro* Mateo Romero (born Mathieu Rosmarin) dominated Spanish art music during the first half of the seventeenth century as Lully and Draghi were later to tyrannize their respective adopted courts. But the extreme examples of Madrid and Vienna should not obscure the fact that in almost every city in Europe that maintained chapel choirs, including those in Italy itself, the *stile antico* played a key role in music education and in everyday worship.

The preservation of the style of Palestrina and in fact the works themselves, which formed the first musical canon, must be distinguished from a new style of counterpoint that was emerging simultaneously. This was a reaction against the excesses of the *seconda prattica* and arose from a need on the part of serious professional composers to invest the sophisticated part-writing which they had been trained to write with the new harmonic style of the basso continuo. The tension between the skilled contrapuntist and the natural melodist or radical amateur was the source of heated debate as well as some of the greatest compositions of the century. As mentioned above, Monteverdi seems effortlessly to have reconciled the two opposing forces and to have exploited them as a means of achieving coherence and maximum dramatic effect. For other composers, this reconciliation involved a greater struggle. Sigismondo d'India railed against the new melodists and never abandoned counterpoint.[10] Perhaps the clearest expression of this conflict of style and technique came in the famous dispute between Paul Siefert and Marco Scacchi of 1643–5. The Roman Scacchi, *maestro di cappella* to the King of Poland, attacked Siefert's psalm settings on two main counts: first, that he used certain modern techniques, such as the basso continuo and chromaticism, which Scacchi regarded as a violation of Counter-Reformation decorum; second, and much more telling, he criticized Siefert for contrapuntal incompetence.[11] Schütz, who was an outspoken advocate of solid contrapuntal training, was asked to adjudicate; in politely refusing, he nevertheless made it clear that his sympathies lay with Scacchi.

It is significant that the argument between Siefert and Scacchi as well as d'India's despair over the direction of modern music should centre on a genre which employed sacred texts – the motet. Here the conflict between the social function of music and the new contrapuntal style was most acute. *Cappelle*, even those of decadent Venice where the boundary between the sacred and the profane was all but erased during the seventeenth century, were inherently conservative institutions. At the heart of every *cappella* was a choir, which needed to sing in parts (that is, in counterpoint) and whose boy sopranos had to be trained, invariably in the traditional style. D'India, Scacchi and Schütz would certainly not have advocated more counterpoint in, say, opera, but at the same time they were talking at cross-purposes with their opponents. Siefert provoked the attack by claiming that Italian composers no longer knew how to write counterpoint, by which he meant the modal counterpoint of the *ars perfecta*, whereas Schütz and Scacchi were moving towards a new style of tonal counterpoint which would not be defined theoretically until the eighteenth century. The new counterpoint was shaped by the harmonic texture of the basso continuo, the major/minor tonal system, a more liberal policy towards the treatment of dissonance and a greater concern with figuration and contrast within movements. But, importantly, Schütz, Scacchi and other masters of contrapuntal vocal music actually believed that they were still writing in the style of Palestrina, only with a broader range of expression.[12]

The conflict was resolved much more amicably and naturally in instrumental music, unencumbered by text, sacred or secular. It, too, underwent a Mannerist phase in which traditional part-writing, which characterized the motet-like fantasia and ricercare, gave way to extreme expression, perhaps best exemplified by the superb toccatas of Frescobaldi. But the common thread which runs through the astounding variety of seventeenth-century instrumental music, including the later sonatas of Corelli, is counterpoint – fugal procedures rooted firmly in the *ars perfecta* and filtered through the incipient tonal system. Even late in the century northern composers who strove to emulate the latest Italian style and who saw themselves in competition with not just their own countrymen but with all modern Italian masters, continued to practise sixteenth-century counterpoint. Purcell is a good example of a composer who strove to be *à la mode* but was nevertheless steeped in tradition: he copied out madrigals by Monteverdi written 75 years earlier, transcribed the anthems of his Chapel Royal predecessors of two generations before, and wrote fantasias based on Renaissance models.

The last and most influential musical style to come out of Italy in the seventeenth century was created by a loosely knit school of instrumentalists trained at Modena and at the *conservatorio* and *duomo* of S Petronio in nearby Bologna, who then moved on to Rome, Naples or Venice to pursue careers as composer-performers. Unlike monody and other types of 'modern' vocal music, the new sonatas of the Rome-Bologna school were easily transmitted in printed collections and eminently exportable. The simple fugues, mechanical and highly engaging passage-work and addictive harmonic sequences of the new instrumental music became both the grammar and the clichés of the lingua franca. It is no exaggeration to say that by 1690 virtually all instrumental music composed anywhere in Europe sounded basically the same. There were of course regional accents, and in France much discussion of the relative merits of French and Italian taste. François Couperin tried later to reconcile the two in an international style; but this was more a question of aesthetics than technique, for the basic language of music was already thoroughly Italianate.

For two countries the levelling popularity of Italian music was ultimately devastating. After the death in 1621 of the great Dutch composer Jan Pieterszoon Sweelinck, who had no conspicuous successors, music in the Low Countries went into decline, reaching a low point with the closure of the court chapel of Archduchess Isabella at Brussels in 1633. A region that had once supplied Italian courts with generation after generation of consummate contrapuntists, where Amsterdam was an important cultural crossroads and, later, music publisher to all of northern Europe, the Netherlands so completely absorbed the Italian style that almost all traces of its Renaissance heritage were obliterated. By the end of the seventeenth century even the famed carillons were playing Corelli sonatas.[13] England, after the death of Purcell in 1695, was another country whose native music was largely overtaken by Corelli. Or rather, English composers so successfully imitated Roman sonatas and concertos that they lost their musical souls. Like Holland, England was never 'das Land ohne Musik', but it certainly became a musical society without a distinctive musical culture. Neither country fully recovered from the influence of 'the most fam'd Italian masters'.

OPERA: AN INTERNATIONAL PERSPECTIVE

Of all the institutions established during the early Baroque period, the one with the greatest consequences for the history of music was Italian opera. Some scholars have boldly suggested that during the seventeenth and eighteenth centuries opera formed the mainstream of music. If one considers opera as a cultural and political phenomenon, this claim is undoubtedly true. But the purely musical innovations that sprang from opera were minimal, except perhaps for recitative. Opera composers acquired what they needed from the madrigal, the cantata, the villanella and other popular song forms, the sonata and the concerto. Fundamental changes in musical structure happened first in chamber and instrumental works. Opera, in spite of its radical beginnings and voracious appetite for new and brilliant singers, was an intensely conservative institution which changed only gradually between 1640 and 1770. The music itself was renewed not by violent stylistic upheaval, rather 'by continual rotation of essentially similar materials'.[14] And some aspects – aristocratic auspices, management, finance and the social composition of the audience – changed hardly at all over nearly two centuries. Taken out of context, a secco recitative by Alessandro Scarlatti might conceivably be mistaken for one by Mozart.

Opera was a singular development of the early Baroque period in that it was consciously invented. That is to say, Jacopo Peri's setting of Ottavio Rinuccini's *Dafne* given under the patronage of Jacopo Corsi in his palace at Florence in February 1598 was immediately recognized as something new. Musicians and intellectuals belonging to several formal academies had long believed the creation of such a work was a theoretical possibility. The key ingredient of this new form, monody or the *stile rappresentativo* which allowed the actors to converse in music, had been carefully nurtured and tested in the neo-

2. (a) Design by Alfonso Parigi for Vulcan's Cave in the opera 'Le nozze degli dei', performed in Florence, 8 July 1637, as part of the celebrations on the marriage of Ferdinando II de' Medici and Vittoria, Princess of Urbino: etching by Stefano della Bella

(b) Design by Inigo Jones (copied from the above Parigi design) for The Way to the Throne of Honour for the masque 'Salmacida Spolia' performed at Whitehall, London, January and February 1640

15

Platonic hothouse and then pruned specially for grafting on to drama. But in another sense, opera had been naturally evolving in the Italian theatre for over a century, from at least the time of Angelo Poliziano's *fabula Orfeo* of about 1480.[15] Several genres – the *intermedio*, the mascherata and the spoken play itself – had already acquired many opera-like characteristics. But to say that all these developments, whether theoretical or practical, made the appearance of opera inevitable is a teleological fallacy, because Corsi, Peri and Rinuccini had at some point to decide that such a thing as a drama in continuous music was possible and would be acceptable to Duke Ferdinando de' Medici and his court. To have the courage of their convictions, they had to accept the high stylization – patent absurdity, even – of stage characters singing rather than speaking their way through a drama. This acceptance of the irrationality of dialogue through music, which happened in Early Modern Europe first in Italy, though its creators were assured that ancient Greek drama provided a striking precedent, is one of two key factors which determined the way in which opera spread to other countries. The other, closely related factor was the perceived suitability of various languages for setting as recitative.

That the myth of Daphne and Apollo should have been chosen as the subject of the first opera is somewhat surprising in that Ovid's story does not lend itself particularly to music, except that Apollo was patron of music and poetry and had thus long played an emblematic role in drama. As adapted by Rinuccini, however, the myth became a flattering allegory of the changing fortunes of the Medici dynasty itself.[16] This political function was merely borrowed from other kinds of courtly entertainment such as the *sbarra* and *intermedio*; it exactly paralleled the elaborate allegorical devices of the Stuart masque and *grand-ballet* of Louis XIII. Operas remained instruments of political statement throughout the seventeenth century, even after they were no longer occasional court entertainments designed specifically as gifts for princes but had become more widely observed public events.

The subject of the next Florentine opera was inextricably bound up with music itself. Rinuccini's *Euridice* was set by Peri in 1600 and then separately by Caccini shortly after, and these are the first operas whose music survives more or less intact. The story of Orpheus and Eurydice was a heaven-sent opera plot. Not only is the myth one of the most dramatic episodes in Virgil's *Georgics* (Rinuccini's main literary source), with a beginning, middle and end, but the drama is concerned with the power of music: the story of a Thracian musician whose song could influence both natural and supernatural forces required hardly any further suspension of disbelief to be represented entirely in music itself. An opera could literally be built round

Orpheus's powerful vocal displays, the first directed at Charon to gain passage across the Styx, and the second at Pluto, a plea for Eurydice's release from the Underworld. The myth naturally resurfaces as the plot of many operas throughout the seventeenth and eighteenth centuries. Significantly, it was the basis of some of the earliest examples of Italianate opera produced in various countries outside Italy, the story apparently being deemed an effective vehicle for overcoming any resistance to *dramma per musica*.

Peri's *Euridice* is so good a piece of theatre and Monteverdi's *Orfeo*, written only seven years later, so stunning a masterpiece that one might have expected Italian opera to sweep all other forms of theatre before it. Yet after the initial flourish in Florence and Mantua in the first decade of the seventeenth century, the development of opera was slow and halting. And opera did not displace the more frequently performed and, frankly, more popular forms of courtly entertainment, the *balli* and *intermedi*. The duchies of northern Italy, the very birthplace of opera, had little immediate sympathy for the new genre; a possible reason is the fact that opera erected an unwanted barrier between stage and audience.[17] Ballet allowed the courtiers to play an active role in the drama, but in opera the *dramatis personae* were professional singers, all of whose action was confined to the stage. There is an important parallel with the Stuart masque, in which the courtiers/players could emerge from the drama to interact with the audience during the revels, the highly formalized social dancing which was at the heart of every masque. The absence of any conceptual barrier between fantasy and reality was often given physical form by a ramp leading from the stage to the ballroom floor. For the courtiers the irresistible appeal of the ballet or masque was that, after dancing with members of the audience, the gods and goddesses and the nymphs and sylvans of the *dramatis personae* then returned to the fantasy world of the drama, thereby completing a circle of illusion. The danger which opera initially posed to audience gratification and self-glorification in France and England, as well as in Italy, was the necessary separation of these two worlds. This undoubtedly contributed to the strong resistance to opera outside Italy and retarded its development in Italy itself.

The kind of opera invented by Peri and modified by Monteverdi in *Orfeo* had no future except as an occasional grand accoutrement to princely weddings, coronations and other similar events of state. Opera did not become a significant international force until it was transformed or rather re-invented as a kind of glorified play at Venice in the late 1630s. The distinction between occasional, Italianate court opera, which found a function and an audience outside Italy only at Vienna, and the new public Venetian opera is considerable. The former was meant to overwhelm with sound and spectacle: choruses, dances, tableau-like scenes and lavish instrumentation. The latter was by comparison musically modest and rarely included ballets or chorus, relying instead on virtuoso solo singing supported by a small string orchestra and spectacular scenery. For Venetians, opera was as popular as the *commedia dell'arte* and just as idiomatic a means of dramatic expression. This was the kind of opera that diplomats and other foreign travellers were most likely to see on the Grand Tour and, in its sheer abundance and professionalism, made Venice the envy of courts and cities throughout Europe.

The impact of the new Venetian opera was felt first, of course, in Italy itself. While the idea of regional schools (Neapolitan, Roman, Venetian) is no longer supported by students of seventeenth-century Italy, the Venetian style was soon taken up throughout the peninsula and modified to suit local conditions. For example, in Naples, the largest kingdom in Italy, it became an instrument of royal propaganda; in Rome, during those periods when opera was not banned by papal decree, all roles had to be taken by males, a practice which did nothing to discourage the cultivation of the castrato. And in the northern cities, where court opera had begun, ducal theatres were remodelled or built from scratch and an impresario system established, whereby composers, singers and even whole theatre troupes travelled back and forth from Venice, which by the mid-century was the centre of a highly developed network. But how was Venetian opera received north of the Alps?

Pure, unadulterated Venetian opera was rarely heard outside Italy, except at Vienna, which had long-standing links with Venice and at whose court the polite language was Italian. As far as the early history of opera is concerned, Vienna was for all intents and purposes in north Italy. The introduction of *dramma per musica* elsewhere in Europe was much more complicated than the following model, an attempt to distil standard histories of opera, might imply. According to received opinion, ministers, diplomats and other aristocrats returning from the Grand Tour brought news of the lavish and enormously prestigious operas at Rome, which were mounted partly for the purpose of impressing foreign dignitaries; they also reported on the utter normality of opera at Venice. The travellers then persuaded their masters to establish opera houses to impress and entertain their fellow burghers or courtiers, many of whom had also been on the Grand Tour and had thus had their appetites whetted. Under heavy state subsidy, an Italian composer, a poet, singers and stage machinsts would be imported to inaugurate the court or municipal opera house. Knowledge of opera production was gradually absorbed by local artists, who could then wean the audience from an already uneasy dependence on Venetian opera.

The final result of this model was opera in the vernacular – *tragédie lyrique*, Singspiel, ballad opera and so on.

This model, though accurate in some respects for some countries, has two major flaws. First, it assumes that opera is at the end of an evolutionary chain, the most sophisticated and highly developed form of theatre. But, as we have seen, in the first two decades of the seventeenth century opera actually fed the development of the *intermedi*, not the other way round. A second weakness is that the model subordinates the importance of contemporaneous native drama. Most of the cities into which Italian opera was eventually introduced – Madrid, Lisbon, London, Paris, Amsterdam, Brussels, Hamburg, Dresden etc. – had their own traditions of music drama, whether the zarzuela, masque, pastoral, ballet or play with music, which were also becoming musically enriched during the course of the seventeenth century. The truth is that the export of Roman and Venetian opera to the rest of Europe was largely a failure, at least in terms of the music. In France, Cardinal Mazarin's fifteen-year attempt to ram a sharply modified form of Venetian opera down the throats of the courtiers fizzled out after a performance of Cavalli's *Ercole amante* in 1662. The first attempt at all-sung opera in Spain, *La selva sin amor* (1627), with a libretto in Spanish by no less a figure than Lope de Vega, was an abject failure. Amsterdam's flirtation with Venetian opera was confined to the 1680s. And in England the Italian opera company assembled at considerable expense by Charles II shortly after his restoration did not produce a single work, Venetian or otherwise. Perhaps, however, we should not regard these instances of rejection as evidence of failure or flashes in the pan but of the fact that the respective national traditions of France, Spain and England were remarkably vibrant and enjoyed a different kind of musical development. The reason why Lisbon was one of the last courts to introduce Italian opera may not therefore be owing to any backwardness or geographical isolation but to the importance of incidental music in Portuguese spoken drama.

The undeniable influence of Venetian opera was, firstly, theatrical rather than musical: changeable scenery, single-point perspective design and sophisticated stage machinery, though already in use by 1600, became routine aspects of Venetian production after 1640. The influence of the stage architects Giacomo Torelli and Cosimo Lotti on French and Spanish theatre, respectively, was far greater than that of any Italian opera composer. Secondly, Venetian opera houses helped establish the concept of state or aristocratic subvention necessary to sustain theatrical spectacle, including opera. Though there was no court at Venice and all her opera houses were open to the public and managed by impresarios who attempted to break even, the patrician landlords assumed responsibility for the deficit

19

that opera inevitably incurs. With only a few exceptions, notably London's thoroughly commercialized theatre, the noble or state-subsidized impresario system became the norm across Europe.

The key to the invention of opera in Italy, recitative, was also the greatest obstacle to its acceptance elsewhere, especially in the later, highly stylized secco form. All opera, which is chiefly concerned with the intensification of emotion to levels unattainable through dramatic speech and action alone, nevertheless needs some means of conveying narrative. The perceived differences in the suitability of various languages as recitative accounts in no small part for the radically different ways in which music drama developed outside Italy. France is the best example. Mazarin's failed attempt to establish a *théâtre italien* had nevertheless left the French courtiers with a strong taste for spectacular music drama. But the *surintendant* of the royal music, Lully, who had himself contributed Italian scenes to court ballets and, conversely, entr'acte ballets for Cavalli's *Xerse* and *Ercole amante*, declared the French language unsuitable for recitative. When Pierre Perrin and Robert Cambert apparently proved him wrong with their pastoral *Pomone* (1671), Lully manoeuvred to acquire their patent for the Académie Royale de Musique and quickly invented the *récit* which made French opera possible. Curiously, in granting the original royal patent to Perrin in 1669, Louis XIV's stated intention was to emulate 'the public performance of theatrical dramas in the manner of Italy, Germany and England'.[18] The mention of Germany and England would seem to betray an ignorance of the theatre in those countries. For example, opera was not introduced at Hamburg until 1678, along Venetian lines of management but initially with sacred plots inspired by Roman practice, mostly sung in German.

The countries which proved most resistant to Italian opera throughout the seventeenth century (apart from Portugal, which did not come into the operatic picture until the early eighteenth century) were Spain and England, which held strikingly similar attitudes towards music drama. This is surprising, given the different temperaments of the two peoples and general lack of artistic contact between them during the Baroque period, apart from English playwrights' heavy reliance on the plots of Spanish plays. Both countries developed so-called semi-operas, that is, grand, heroic spoken dramas with songs and whole musical scenes, best exemplified by the lyrical plays of Calderón de la Barca and the tragi-comedies of Sir William Davenant. Both included vernacular styles of recitative (more essential to Calderón than to Davenant), but somewhat different in function (for example, main characters rarely sing in English semi-operas) and utterly different in style from Italian secco recitative. The one serious attempt to establish opera on the Italian model in either country was Davenant's series of semi-private entertainments in the mid-1650s, which culminated in *The Siege of Rhodes*, the first all-sung opera in English (the music by various composers is lost). As in contemporaneous Roman opera, Davenant's purpose was to provide moral instruction, but instead of any Counter-Reformation tendencies, the guiding spirit behind this abortive attempt was Thomas Hobbes's *Leviathan*.[19]

The ultimate reason why all-sung opera did not take root in Spain or England in the early Baroque era was not, as John Dryden believed, because of the difficulties composers faced in setting their harsh and rugged languages to recitative music; for Hidalgo and Purcell were to show how this could be done in styles far removed from the Venetian secco recitative. The resistance to Italianate opera lay instead in an inability to accept the Orpheus gambit, the belief that one could speak in song. This attitude was succinctly expressed by Matthew Locke when defending his decision to call his semi-opera *Psyche* (1675) simply an 'opera', even though 'all the Tragedy be not in Musick'. He had carefully considered that, while 'Italy was, and is the great Academy of the World' for opera, 'England is not'. The mixing of music with spoken dialogue is 'more proper to our Genius'.

*

In spite of the cataclysmic musical events of the seventeenth century – the invention of opera and the emergence of tonal harmony – the early Baroque era remains the black sheep of music history. After the Middle Ages and the twentieth century, it is the least studied period of music history. The reasons are obvious. With only three or four composers of undisputed greatness, barely a handful of works in the modern standard repertory (Monteverdi's *Orfeo* and *Poppea*, Purcell's *Dido and Aeneas*, Pachelbel's Canon and perhaps Corelli's 'Christmas' Concerto), it is easy to regard the seventeenth century as transitional, a notion reinforced by general misunderstanding of how Italian musical culture was transmitted and by under-estimating the importance of music north of the Alps. This chapter has tried to put Italian influence in perspective. The following, more detailed studies of geographic centres will do little to help the reader form a coherent view of the early Baroque era. This is intentional. As Theodore K. Rabb wrote in summing up his scepticism about the 'general crisis in Europe' theory: 'One simply has to admit that regional variation was enormous, and that sharp patterns and well-defined waves of movement are unlikely to crystallize in the quicksilver experiences of Europe's localities'.[20]

It may be comforting to discover amid so much cultural and stylistic diversity that the seventeenth century also marks the beginning of what has been called modern music. Besides the almost unbroken traditions of opera and common practice harmony, one will find the emergence of professional women composers and musicians in significant numbers; the establishment of instrumental music as fully independent of vocal models and liturgy; the beginnings of the orchestra (as defined as a heterogeneous ensemble of instruments with doubling of some parts); the emergence of the concept of music as intellectual property, to be bought and sold for the benefit of the composer rather than for patron or employer; and the first public concerts. That these innovations do not appear to have been triggered by the deeper stylistic change which music underwent during the seventeenth century should further caution us against trying to find the source of that change outside music itself.

NOTES

[1] I. Fenlon, 'Music and Society', *The Renaissance: from the 1470s to the End of the 16th Century*, Man & Music (London, 1989), 1.

[2] A. Lossky, *The Seventeenth Century*, Sources in Western Civilization (London, 1967), 26.

[3] See *Crisis in Europe 1560–1660*, ed. T. Aston (London, 1965), 5–95.

[4] That is, dissonances formed when both parts strike the clashing interval simultaneously rather than when one part is introduced first and then the other sounds against it.

[5] For a revisionist view, see S. G. Cusick, 'Gendering Modern Music: Thoughts on the Monteverdi–Artusi Controversy', *JAMS*, xlvi (1993), 1–25.

[6] J. W. Stoye, *English Travellers Abroad 1604–1667* (London, 1952), 258.

[7] For further details, see p. 71 below.

[8] See S. E. Plank, 'Monmouth in Italy: *L'ambitione debellata*', *MT*, cxxxii (1991), 280–84.

[9] See L. Pike, 'Church Music I: Before the Civil War', *The Seventeenth Century*, ed. I. Spink, Blackwell History of Music in Britain, iii (Oxford, 1992), 66.

[10] For further discussion, see pp. 32–3 below.

[11] For further discussion, see L. Bianconi, *Music in the Seventeenth Century*, trans. D. Bryant (Cambridge, 1987), 47.

[12] For a detailed technical consideration of this issue, see E. Linfield, 'Modal and Tonal Aspects in Two Compositions by Heinrich Schütz', *JRMA*, cxvii (1992), 86–122.

[13] See p. 212 below.

[14] L. Bianconi and T. Walker, 'Production, Consumption and Political Function of Seventeenth-Century Opera', *EMH*, iv (1984), 212.

[15] As argued in N. Pirrotta and E. Povoledo, *Music and Theatre from Poliziano to Monteverdi*, trans. K. Eales (Cambridge, 1982), chap. 1.

[16] See pp. 135–6 below.

[17] This idea is further developed in Chapter II below.

[18] Translated in Bianconi, *Music in the Seventeenth Century*, 240–41.

[19] See J. R. Jacob and T. Raylor, 'Opera and Obedience: Thomas Hobbes and *A Proposition for Advancement of Moralitie* by Sir William Davenant', *The Seventeenth Century*, vi (1991), 205–50.

[20] *The Struggle for Stability in Early Modern Europe* (New York, 1975), 86–7.

Chapter II

The North Italian Courts

TIM CARTER

Italy is a Region, that, among many other advantageous Elogies, is
on all hands held to be the *Eden* of *Europe*, the Garden or Paradise of
this North-west part of the World. This *Peninsula* or Demi-Island,
formerly the absolute and redoubted Empress of the major part of
the then-known habitable World, yet may compare, as now it is,
nay exceed the most of the other Kingdoms of *Asia*, *Africa*, or
America. 'Tis situate in a most Temperate Clime; and [known] for
the amœnity of its Cities, the commodiousness for Commerce and
Negotiations, the deliciousness of its Fountains and Aqueducts, the
fertility of its well-cultivated Fields, insomuch that in some places
they have three Harvests in one year; the Uniformity and
Stateliness of Fabriques, and the rare Architecture and rich
Furniture and Ornaments of its Temples, and many other
Delicacies to gratifie the *gusto* as to Fruits and rare Wines, with
other Varieties too numerous to be crowded into the narrow confines of our intended Discourse.[1]

During the Renaissance, Italy had been a major political, economic
and cultural force: by the mid seventeenth century, it was more the
pleasure-garden of Europe, an essential stopping-point on the tourist
trail of the Grand Tour. The peninsula's political fate had been
sealed by the Treaty of Cateau-Cambrésis of 1559. Italy continued as
an agglomeration of separate states governed by a variety of political
systems, ranging from hereditary duchies through oligarchies to
republics. But the long years of internal strife and the harsh rewards
of being the pawn of the three European superpowers of Spain,
France and the Empire were tempered by the new political realism of
the late sixteenth century, by the increasing fiscal crises of the period,
and also by a sense that the Protestant reformation presented a more
important threat, transcending mere territorial disputes and requiring at least a semblance of cohesion in the Catholic world. The
task now facing the Italians was to put their house in spiritual order
by way of a Catholic reformation that was as essentially reactionary
as the Protestant reformation was iconoclastic.

Through Cateau-Cambrésis the French renounced, albeit temporarily, almost all claims to territorial rights in Italy. The military and diplomatic costs of their long presence in the peninsula were no longer feasible given the more immediate troubles now facing the kings of France at home. The papacy, too, was finally forced to realize the impossibility of a Holy Roman Empire centred on Rome as a temporal as well as a spiritual power. The Italian states broadly acknowledged the political facts of life: the peninsula was essentially a fiefdom of Spain and the Empire. Only the Republic of Venice succeeded in maintaining a semblance of independence by virtue of its strengths as a maritime and Mediterranean power. Elsewhere in Italy, the Spanish were well entrenched, at least until the mid seventeenth century. Spain ruled Naples, Milan and, less directly, Genoa; and the major duchies of northern Italy – Ferrara and Modena, Florence, Mantua, Parma and Piacenza, and Savoy – and the Papal States ignored their obligations to the 'Catholic King' of Spain and to the Emperor at their peril. To be sure, some of these duchies pursued with varying degrees of success a foreign policy of striking a balance between the European powers, seeking to maintain at least amicable relations with the 'Most Christian King' of France. Florence set an important example by the marriage of Grand Duke Ferdinando I to Christine of Lorraine in 1589, and then of Maria de' Medici to Henri IV of France in 1600. The dukes of Ferrara and Modena, Savoy and, later, Mantua also sought, or were obliged, variously to align themselves with the French, often by way of dynastic marriages. It is emblematic of Spanish pre-eminence in Italy, however, that Florence soon returned to the fold in 1608 with the wedding of Prince Cosimo, heir to the throne, and the sister of the Queen of Spain, Maria Magdalena, Archduchess of Austria. Venice, on the other hand, was losing its economic battle with the northern maritime powers, and it never achieved its desired status as a standard-bearer of Italian liberty. The notion of an independent, unified Italy remained as much a dream as it had been in the time of Petrarch.

The political stability fostered by Cateau-Cambrésis did not remain entirely untroubled. The papacy retained territorial ambitions beyond the confines of its state: witness the annexation of Ferrara in 1597–8 and of Urbino in 1631. Moreover, the War of Mantuan Succession between the French and the Habsburgs on the death of Duke Vincenzo II Gonzaga in 1627, culminating in the horrific sack of the city in 1630, demonstrated that a small Italian state was still hostage to fortune, subject to the whim of larger powers whose political and military strengths could scarcely be matched. Similarly, if less dramatically, the dukes of Savoy remained trapped between the Spanish and the French: Savoy controlled French access to Italy and also Spanish access (via Genoa and avoiding France) to the

Netherlands. Nor was Italy as a whole immune from natural disasters, such as the terrible plagues in northern Italy in 1630–33 and in central and southern Italy in the mid-1650s. But for the most part the peninsula acquiesced in its status as a backwater as the political and for that matter economic axis of Europe shifted beyond the Alps. Such a status no doubt had its advantages: the ravages of the Thirty Years War were felt far less acutely in Italy than in northern Europe. But world events were now being played on a different stage.

The gradual relegation of Italy to secondary status was exacerbated by the economic crisis affecting all of Europe in the early seventeenth century. It is generally assumed that the Italian states were particularly ill-equipped to handle this crisis, in which the carefully balanced mixed economies of the great mercantile and commercial powers of Renaissance Italy were replaced by a more land-based economy re-creating a polarization of landowners and peasants of almost medieval proportions. But in fact, many north Italian hereditary monarchies may have coped better with the economic tribulations of the period than has often been assumed; after all, an essentially regressive system of government, as a duchy undoubtedly was, need scarcely adapt to times of reactionary retrenchment. The return to a near-feudal economy may have caused problems for more modern proto-capitalist systems such as those developed in the Republic of Venice (and to a lesser extent in the not too distant Republic of Florence), but for the dukes of, say, Mantua, Parma or Savoy it meant little more than a retention of the status quo.

The 'crisis' scenario has also affected our thinking about the arts in the sixteenth and early seventeenth centuries. Even before the concept of crisis became fashionable among historians, students of the arts in this period had long accepted the notion of one or more stylistic revolutions at the end of the Renaissance: in the case of music, one need only point to the outpacing of the 'pure' polyphonic style of Palestrina and his contemporaries by the 'new music' of Florentine solo song and opera or by the *seconda prattica* madrigals of Monteverdi and his contemporaries. These stylistic changes have proved to be ripe for melding with notions of crisis, particularly now that Mannerism is increasingly recognized as a phenomenon affecting all the arts in late Renaissance Italy, whether painting (Parmigianino and Pontormo) and architecture (Giulio Romano) or – and somewhat later – poetry (Marino) and music (Gesualdo). The decline of Renaissance styles into Mannerist excess, and their eventual replacement by emerging Baroque styles, surely encourages the view that art and society were similarly affected by shifting political, economic, social and cultural emphases.

Often central to some historians' interpretations of the arts in the period is a nostalgic harking back to the glories of the High

Renaissance: things were generally changing for the worse. Certainly, by the second half of the sixteenth century contemporary critics were sensing a dangerous drop in artistic and intellectual standards. In poetry, witness the disputes over the relative merits of Torquato Tasso's *Gerusalemme liberata* and the older Ludovico Ariosto's *Orlando furioso*, or over the new pastoral dramatic genres promoted by Tasso's *Aminta* and, even more controversially, Giovanni Battista Guarini's *Il pastor fido*. Music theorists, too, attempted to stem the tide of change: Gioseffo Zarlino (1517–90) promoted a furious rebuttal of the new chromaticists, and his pupil Giovanni Maria Artusi (*c*1540–1613) pursued a systematic critique of the *seconda prattica* style of Monteverdi and other modern composers. For both Zarlino and Artusi, music was indeed in crisis.

Modern commentators tend to be more measured in their evaluations of the period, casting contemporary theorists as typically pedantic reactionaries: *a posteriori* historical perspectives generally support more favourable views of stylistic change. Nevertheless, critics of Mannerism, which seems to have been largely a courtly phenomenon, are often happy to associate the tendency with the political stagnation and cultural torpor that may certainly be detected in much of northern Italy in the second half of the sixteenth century. Even laying aside such aesthetic issues, the 'crisis' scenario surely has some relevance. For example, the musicologist Lorenzo Bianconi argues that economic crisis in the Italy of the 1620s had a significant effect on musical output, as demonstrated by the decline in music printing in the period: the Venetian presses were bringing out some 60 to 70 editions of music a year in the mid-1580s and less than a third of that in the 1630s.[2] In consequence, the position of the composer in the musical market-place would appear different in the 1630s compared with, say, the 1580s.

The question to be addressed by this chapter is the extent to which these undoubted changes affected musical activity in the courts of northern Italy. Here we enter relatively uncharted terrain: music historians, like most historians, have tended to ignore these courts in favour of ostensibly more exciting musical centres. Nevertheless, the answer appears to be simple: the effect of these changes was probably less marked than elsewhere in the peninsula. Just as the retention of feudal systems, once a potential limitation, became a strength in the new economic light of the seventeenth century, so too did the traditional and still functioning requirements of court patronage shelter the arts from the vagaries of shifting circumstances. Business carried on as usual.

This is not to say that the north Italian courts were insensitive to changing musical styles in the late Renaissance and early Baroque periods: indeed, some were in the vanguard of current musical de-

velopments. The point remains, however, that these musical developments were subject to, and indeed a result of, patronage systems
predicated upon requirements other than the purely artistic. The
musical demands of the late sixteenth- and seventeenth-century duke
were little different from those of his forebears a century or more
before. Musicians were employed essentially to protect and display
the secular and sacred magnificence of the state (the two are inter-
twined, especially in the age of the Catholic Reformation). This they
did by fulfilling predominantly functional requirements, with music
for theatrical entertainments, dances and banquets and also for the
liturgy. In all cases, the message to be conveyed by this music
depended less on originality and quality, although that could be
important, than on articulating the greater glory of the duke and the
stability of his dominion.

An example is the attempt of Duke Guglielmo Gonzaga of Mantua
(ruled 1550–87) to establish a new ducal chapel for his state in the
church of S Barbara. Here he was creating precisely the devout
image required of a Counter-Reformation prince, and indeed
Mantua was second only to Milan (and in many ways well ahead of
Rome) in its enthusiasm for the Catholic reforms. Guglielmo's
expense on the construction of the church (built between 1562 and
1565) was matched by his attempts to staff it with the leading
musicians of Europe. He brought to Mantua as his new *maestro di
cappella* the Fleming Giaches de Wert (1535–96), demonstrating a
preference for northern talent that had long been typical of
Renaissance princes. He also created a new liturgy (consequently
requiring a new set of plainchants) unique to the church, again
displaying a self-conscious independence that was important for
ducal prestige. The duke, himself a talented composer, recruited
some of the best musicians in Italy to write for his chapel, including
Giovanni Pierluigi da Palestrina.[3] Indeed, under Duke Guglielmo
and, later, Duke Vincenzo I (ruled 1587–1612), Mantua became one
of the most exciting musical centres in Italy. The list of musicians
employed there reads almost as a roll-call of the principal composers
of the time: Wert as *maestro di cappella* of S Barbara (until 1592) and
of the private ducal chapel (until his death in 1596), Francesco
Soriano (*maestro* of the ducal chapel, 1581–6), Giovanni Giacomo
Gastoldi (*maestro* at S Barbara, 1592–1608), Girolamo Cavazzoni
(organist at S Barbara, 1565–77), Francesco Rovigo (organist at S
Barbara, 1590–97), Benedetto Pallavicino (*maestro* of the ducal chapel, 1596–1601), Salamone Rossi (1570–*c*1630, associated with the
court instrumental music), Lodovico Grossi da Viadana (*maestro* at
the cathedral, 1593–7) and Claudio Monteverdi (*maestro* of the ducal
chapel, 1601–12). Wert's imposing motets for S Barbara, perhaps the
last in the great Franco-Flemish tradition of sacred polyphony, trans-

cend their liturgical function to make powerful political statements. So, too, do Monteverdi's flamboyant settings for Vespers (the introit, psalms, antiphon substitutes and two *Magnificat* settings) published in 1610, even if we do not know when they were first performed (if indeed they were). Here Monteverdi combines what he seems to perceive as Roman and Venetian styles (intricate counterpoint over a cantus firmus; rich vocal and instrumental writing; polychoral textures) with traits of the Florentine 'new music' (solo song, duet) to produce sacred music unrivalled in splendour and magnificence.

If one moves from the Gonzaga court to Ferrara, which was closely linked to Mantua by political and cultural ties, one finds similar messages conveyed by somewhat different means. The musical interests of Duke Alfonso II d'Este were more secular in focus. He was presumably motivated by the emphasis on music as an essential attribute of the courtier in Baldassare Castiglione's important manual on etiquette, *Il libro del cortegiano*. Alfonso fostered at his court a new style of secular music based on his *concerto di donne*, a performing group concentrating on female voices. Composers in the Ferrarese ambit such as Luzzasco Luzzaschi (?1545–1607), Lodovico Agostini (1534–90) and Paolo Virchi (c1550–1610), and some foreigners deemed worthy of the honour, were selected to write music for the group. Their works were intended to remain a 'secret music' (*musica segreta*) used only for private entertainment or to honour visiting dignitaries: it was indeed a privilege to be granted an opportunity to hear the *concerto*. The 'secret' nature of this music attracted a number of musical spies sent to Ferrara to discover the nature of the Ferrarese style in the hope of copying it for home consumption: both the Medici in Florence and the Gonzagas in Mantua created their own *concerti di donne* in imitation of Ferrara. These imitations reveal the extent of competition between Italian courts that placed a premium on artistic innovation within certain well defined limits. Such rivalry had helped foster the Renaissance and must have provided a crucial security of employment for artists in the period, or at least for those willing to toe the courtly line.

The Ferrarese style is reflected in a number of publications written by, or in imitation of, Ferrarese composers in the 1580s, particularly the two madrigal anthologies *Il lauro secco* (1582) and *Il lauro verde* (1583). However, the music that can perhaps be most closely identified with the actual repertory of the *concerto* was published only in 1601 – in Luzzaschi's *Madrigali per cantare a una, doi e tre soprani* – some three years after the death of Duke Alfonso in late 1597 and Ferrara's subsequent loss of independence to the papacy (the Estense court moved to Modena). One result of the soprano-dominated textures of the *concerto di donne* was to alter the traditional emphasis on balanced polyphony, where all the voices have an equal contribution, in favour

3. Geronimo Valeriani, lutenist to the Duke of Modena: portrait by Ludovico Lana (1597–1646); for all the emphasis on vocal virtuosity, instrumentalists also played a significant part in court life

of a style emphasizing the harmonic relationship of upper parts (often two high voices moving in thirds) and the bass (which in Luzzaschi's 1601 volume is played on a keyboard). This led to a more vertical, rather than linear, orientation that significantly affected the new musical techniques emerging over the 1600s. But more important, in the case of the *concerto* the emphasis was less on the music *per se* than on the singers' performance:

> They moderated or increased their voices, loud or soft, heavy or light, according to the demands of the piece they were singing; now slow, breaking off with sometimes a gentle sigh, now singing long passages legato or detached, now groups, now leaps, now with long trills, now with short, and again with sweet running passages sung softly, to which sometimes one heard an echo answer unexpectedly. They accompanied the music and the sentiment with appropriate facial expressions, glances and gestures, with no awkward movements of the mouth or hands or body which might not express the feeling of the song. They made the words clear in such a way that one could hear even the last syllable of every word, which was never interrupted or suppressed by passages and other embellishments.[4]

We have moved into the age of the virtuoso – the singing ladies of

29

Ferrara, Adriana Basile of Naples, Francesca Caccini of Florence and Virginia Andreini of Mantua – who could command far higher rewards than even the best composers.

Artists certainly benefited from the security of court employment, but they paid the price of being essentially functionaries employed by the duke and subject to his whim. Monteverdi (1567–1643) is a good example. Born in Cremona, he studied with the cathedral choirmaster Marc'Antonio Ingegneri, whose solid teaching in the traditional polyphonic style made itself apparent in his pupil's earliest publications: indeed, all Monteverdi's works display a consummate craftsmanship and compositional integrity that contrast with the more dilettante tendencies of many exponents of the 'new music' over the 1600s. In 1590 or thereabouts, Monteverdi moved to Mantua to join the court musicians of Duke Vincenzo Gonzaga. Although employed as a string-player, he continued to publish madrigals. Indeed, his third (1592), fourth (1603) and fifth (1605) books of madrigals represent the epitome of the genre. Many influences upon them are apparent, not least those of his two senior colleagues in Mantua, Wert and Pallavicino – Wert was perhaps the leading madrigalist of his generation – and Monteverdi also shows that he was well acquainted with the soprano-dominated textures of the Ferrarese style newly taken over by the Mantuan *concerto di donne*. These textures led him to take the logical step already made by Luzzaschi of abandoning unaccompanied vocal polyphony in favour of new styles of writing for solo voices and an instrumental basso continuo (which becomes obligatory in the last six madrigals of the fifth book). Monteverdi also assumes the new literary emphases characteristic of the Ferrarese school of the 1590s: the Ferrarese *concerto di donne* was on the decline by the mid-1580s, and in their secular music Ferrarese composers began to focus on other qualities, particularly under the influence of Carlo Gesualdo, Prince of Venosa, whose marriage to Leonora d'Este in 1594 brought him into close contact with the Estense court.[5] Thus Monteverdi increasingly set the best poets of the age, Tasso and Guarini,[6] and he attempted to find new musical idioms to match the emotional intensity of their verse.

This search for new idioms involved Monteverdi in a dispute with the Bolognese theorist Artusi over his allegedly extravagant treatment of dissonance: Artusi had heard Monteverdi's madrigals performed in Ferrara several years before they were published.[7] Monteverdi claimed that such dissonances were entirely logical in a style devoted to expressing emotional texts, and the notion of music's subservience to words became a central tenet of the so-called *seconda prattica*, which Monteverdi contrasted with the 'first practice' of traditional polyphonists where music reigned supreme. This text-orientated 'second practice', with its obvious humanist implications, was founded, Monteverdi said, by Cipriano de Rore (1515 or 1516–65), a Franco-Fleming who had worked largely in Ferrara. Monteverdi fully explored the implications of his second practice in the intense settings of his fourth and fifth books of madrigals. The literary orientation of these settings, together with their subtle allusions to other composers (including Marenzio, Wert, Pallavicino and Gesualdo) and indeed their sophisticated musical play,[8] emphasizes their function as a courtly art for cultivated listeners.

By the mid-1590s, Monteverdi was accompanying Duke Vincenzo Gonzaga on trips outside his kingdom – to Hungary and Flanders, and perhaps to Florence for the wedding celebrations of Maria de' Medici and Henri IV of France in October 1600 – and in 1601 he gained a long-sought-for appointment as the head of the duke's musical establishment, with responsibility for fulfilling his requirements in sacred, secular and theatrical music (witness his opera *Orfeo* of 1607). But Monteverdi increasingly found court service oppressive and his employers unappreciative of his talents. The situation came to a head in 1608 with the festivities for the wedding of Prince Francesco Gonzaga and Margherita of Savoy. Monteverdi was already afflicted by the death first of his wife and then of his favourite pupil Caterina Martinelli (who was to have sung the title role in his opera *Arianna*, which was staged during the festivities). He also found himself overworked, underpaid, and ignored in favour of foreign artists brought to the city for the celebrations, particularly the Florentine Marco da Gagliano. Monteverdi began to look elsewhere for work – his *Sanctissimae Virgini missa . . . ac vespere* (the 'Vespers') of 1610 clearly advertises his availability – and on 19 August 1613 he was appointed *maestro di cappella* at the basilica of St Mark's, Venice.

Monteverdi now enjoyed the fame, responsibility and security of the leading musical position in Italy. Perhaps more important, he was working for a republic rather than a court. His former employers continued to press him for music for operas, ballets and tournaments, but many of these requests remained unanswered. Monteverdi blamed the pressures of time and his duties at St Mark's, but clearly he now disliked catering for court tastes, where entertainments had to be peopled with mythological, allegorical and supernatural characters. As he wrote to the Mantuan court secretary Alessandro Striggio in 1616 about one such entertainment, *Le nozze di Tetide*: 'I have noticed that the interlocutors are Winds, Cupids, little Zephyrs and Sirens . . . [but] how can I, by such means, move the passions? Ariadne moved us because she was a woman, and similarly Orpheus because he was a man, and not a wind . . . *Arianna* led me to a just lament, and *Orfeo* to a righteous prayer, but this fable leads me I don't know to what end.'[9] Monteverdi did provide some entertainment music for Mantua, including *Tirsi e Clori* (printed in his seventh book of madrigals in 1619) and part of a *sacra rappresentazione*, *La Maddalena* (1617). But he had left the court far behind.

Monteverdi, then, grew to resent the requirements of court service. Other composers, however, preferred, or were required, to stay within the system. Sigismondo d'India was born in Palermo, Sicily, about 1582 and spent the first years of his professional career as a touring singer and composer, passing through Florence (?1600), Mantua (1606), Florence (1608), Rome and Naples (?1608), and then Parma and Piacenza (1610), where he provided music for court festivities. In 1611, he was appointed director of chamber music at the court of Carlo Emanuele I, Duke of Savoy, a post he held until May 1623, when he was forced to leave Turin owing to malicious gossip at the court. He resumed his perambulatory career around Italy for some five months, was employed at the Estense court in Modena between October 1623 and April 1624, and then moved to Rome under the patronage of Cardinal Maurizio of Savoy (son of Carlo Emanuele I). In early 1626, d'India was again in the service of the Estensi, to whom he dedicated his eighth book of five-part madrigals (the dedication notes that Modena supported a 'gathering . . . of the best singers to be heard in Europe'). D'India was also involved in plans for the entertainments to celebrate the wedding of Duke Odoardo Farnese of Parma and Margherita de' Medici in 1628. He may then have sought an appointment at the court of Maximilian I of Bavaria, but he seems to have remained in Modena until his death (before 19 April 1629).

Like any court composer, d'India needed to adapt his style to meet the requirements of the various royal patrons who figure prominently in his dedications. He published secular songs and polyphonic madrigals, theatrical music and sacred works, revealing a flexibility which in some ways exceeded what Monteverdi achieved. More than Monteverdi, he was open to the new experiments in solo song developed in Florence by Giulio Caccini and his contemporaries, and the songs and duets of d'India's *Le musiche* of 1609 are perhaps the first examples to place the 'new music' on the map of serious musical endeavour. Unlike Caccini, he was a professional composer well skilled in the art of expressing a text while at the same time providing the large-scale structural coherence necessary for any successful musical setting. Significantly, he was equally at home in both polyphonic and solo-voice writing, and he enriched the solo song with many expressive and technical devices first developed within the polyphonic madrigal.[10]

D'India's music, which deserves serious study, ranks among the best of its time and exemplifies the artistic quality that could emerge from a court system. But it also reveals a limitation of that system: despite his skill and flexibility, d'India was eventually unable or unwilling to avail himself of the new styles developing in other more innovative musical centres. Although the 'new music' of the early 1600s was an essentially courtly phenomenon, the trend in the 1620s was to move away from the intense madrigal, whether for five polyphonic voices or for solo voice and basso continuo, towards more lyrical arias often exploiting new, more expansive kinds of triple-time writing. This new style, which was important for future musical developments in the Baroque period, is particularly apparent in the arias and cantatas of Venetian composers. However, although d'India made some attempt to come to terms with such writing – his aria 'Torna il sereno Zefiro' (published in 1623) is an important forerunner of the multi-sectional cantata[11] – his working environment clearly fostered an innate conservativism that prevented the wholesale adoption of newer trends. Indeed, the most striking feature of d'India's overall output is its stylistic consistency, and by the 1620s his music was fast becoming outdated. Not surprisingly, in the preface to his first book of four-part motets (1627) he decried the modern tendency towards facile melody instead of serious counterpoint. But the tide had turned.

The careers of composers such as Monteverdi and d'India show the ease with which a celebrated artist could move between the north Italian states. Such mobility has a bearing on the transmission of musical styles in this period, especially given the increasingly uncertain status of printing as an effective means of musical dissemination. It also emphasizes the community of artistic discourse in northern Italy, the complex cultural webs linking the activity of different centres along political lines of communication. Finally, these careers reveal at least some of the strengths and weaknesses of courtly patronage systems through which composers had to fulfil requirements that could often conflict with their own artistic sensibilities. The point is particularly apparent in court entertainments.

Entertainments provided a focus for the life of a ducal court which showed the interaction of art and politics at its clearest. It was through such entertainments that the court projected its sense of social identity and cohesion. The birth of an heir to the throne, the wedding of a prince or the death of a duke were all key moments in courtly life that required due emphasis on both private and public platforms. The cohesiveness of the political and social fabric depended upon the articulation and consequent control of moments of both celebration and crisis as manifestations of the glory and, perhaps more important, permanence of the ducal state.

Again, Mantua provides a telling example. Duke Vincenzo Gonzaga, more of a hedonist than his father, seems to have been anxious to establish for himself and for his state a pre-eminence in theatrical entertainments. He worked for almost a decade to secure

DISEGNO DEL GRANDE ET MARAVIGLIOSO APPARATO DE FVOCHI TRIONFALI

4. Celebration with fireworks in the Piazza S Pietro, Mantua (the Palazzo Ducale is on the right), for the wedding of Eleonora Gonzaga and Emperor Ferdinand II in January 1622; the entertainments included a play with intermedi, 'Le tre costanti' (music in part by Monteverdi): engraving

for his court one of the first full-scale stagings of Guarini's *Il pastor fido* (an early version of the play had already been performed in part in Turin for the wedding of Carlo Emanuele I of Savoy and Catalina, Infanta of Spain, in 1585). *Il pastor fido* exploited newly developed pastoral conventions in a manner controversial enough to prompt extensive and often bitter debates in Italian academies. Therefore a staging of the work was clearly a matter of some prestige. Vincenzo initiated his plans for the work in the early 1590s – he originally seems to have hoped for a performance in 1592 – but technical problems, in particular the difficulties of matching the choreography, declamation and music of the central scene of Act 2, the 'Giuoco della cieca' (a game of blind-man's buff), caused delays. Eventually, the court staged three performances in 1598, one on 22 November before the visiting Margherita of Austria on her way to marry Philip III of Spain. By all accounts, it was a spectacular success.[12]

Less then a decade later, Mantua again entered the battle for theatrical prestige in Italy, this time concerning another new genre that had created some controversy at its inception, opera. The through-composed music drama had been developed in Florence in the 1590s and had taken pride of place at the festivities for the wedding of Maria de' Medici and Henri IV of France in October 1600, which included Ottavio Rinuccini's *Euridice*, set by Jacopo Peri

– the first opera to have survived complete – and also Gabriello Chiabrera's *Il rapimento di Cefalo*, with music by Giulio Caccini and others.[13] The 'invention' of opera was clearly designed as a propaganda coup for the city, emphasizing its position as the leading centre of humanist enquiry in Italy. Mantua responded with Monteverdi's *Orfeo*, to a libretto by the court secretary Alessandro Striggio, which was first performed before the Accademia degli Invaghiti under the sponsorship of Prince Francesco Gonzaga on 24 February 1607. Duke Vincenzo had been in Florence in October 1600 (so, too, had Striggio and, probably, Monteverdi), and no doubt he encouraged his eldest son to support a Mantuan response to these Florentine claims: the fact that Francesco did so within the confines of an apparently neutral academy should not obscure the opera's clear political intent.

Orfeo obviously derives from Peri and Rinuccini's *Euridice*. The subject matter is the same, and clearly Striggio knew its libretto, although significantly he avoids much of Rinuccini's self-indulgent artistry in favour of a more concise dramatic presentation (a comparison of their respective narrations of Eurydice's death is instructive). Monteverdi, too, must have known Peri's score (it was published in early 1601), and he follows Peri's use of the new dramatic recitative for solo voice and basso continuo. *Orfeo* also refers back to other Florentine traditions, particularly that of the *intermedi*: witness the spectacular stage effects depicting scenes from mythology, the allegorical figures, the use of the instruments and the extended choruses. There are also obvious connections with classical tragedy and, perhaps most important, the recent pastoral dramas of Tasso and Guarini. Similarly, Monteverdi's music is redolent of sixteenth-century techniques: for example, even in the 'new' recitative, he exploits expressive devices first explored in his 'traditional' five-part madrigals, including carefully crafted vocal lines, dissonances and chromaticism.

These backward-looking, 'Renaissance' aspects of the opera are reinforced by its various humanist messages concerning the power of man and music. But *Orfeo* also looks forward to the Baroque era. Monteverdi demonstrates his openness to the new styles developed by his contemporaries, particularly in his use of recitative and new kinds of aria and duet writing. Another novel aspect of his score is the detail with which he sets out precise instructions in matters of scoring and ornamentation. *Orfeo* (like, for that matter, the 1610 Vespers) thus contains an intriguing mixture of old and new elements. Rather than rejecting previously perfected techniques in an iconoclastic search for novelty, Monteverdi reinterprets the old in the light of the new (and vice versa) to produce a powerful synthesis of undeniable dramatic force. Moreover, and unlike the Florentines,

Monteverdi is unquestionably a masterly composer. His attention to the drama, to large-scale structure and to expressive detail demonstrate his skills to the full. They also produce the first great opera.

Clearly, *Orfeo* was intended to emphasize Mantua's cultural rivalry with Florence. Exchanges between the two cities are scarcely surprising: Duke Vincenzo's wife, Eleonora, was a Medici princess, and Prince Ferdinando spent a good deal of his early life in Florentine circles (he studied at the university in Pisa) and was closely involved with musicians there.[14] Similarly, the wedding festivities for Prince Francesco Gonzaga and Margherita of Savoy, held after some delay in May–June 1608, also drew on a number of Florentine archetypes to articulate the significance of an occasion intended to glorify the Gonzaga court and to emphasize its place in the Italian political arena. As the Florentines had long realized, wedding entertainments were important as propaganda, presenting an image of strength and stability designed for both national and international consumption. The Mantuans learnt their lesson well. Margherita made her triumphal entry into the city on 24 May 1608; on the 28th the opera *Arianna*, by Monteverdi and Rinuccini, was staged (another opera planned for the festivities, Marco da Gagliano's *Dafne*, was eventually performed in advance of the event); the 31st saw a grand naval battle on the lagoon; on 2 June came the centrepiece of the festivities, a performance of Guarini's *L'idropica*, with spectacular entr'acte *intermedi* by Chiabrera; and on the 4th, Monteverdi's dramatic ballet *Il ballo delle ingrate* was staged (a revised version was later published in his *Madrigali guerrieri, et amorosi*, Venice, 1638). The festivities also included other comedies, ballets and tournaments.

The two main entertainments of the festivities, *Arianna* and *L'idropica*, were great successes. The audience at the performance of *Arianna* were particularly moved by Ariadne's lament at her desertion by Theseus, the only section of the opera to survive. According to later commentators, including the composer and writer Severo Bonini, this lament became one of the most popular works of its time. *L'idropica*, on the other hand, made its effect by its spectacular staging, particularly of its splendid *intermedi*: indeed, Federico Zuccaro reported that although the play 'was beautiful and well performed . . . however it served merely as *intermedi* to the *intermedi*'.[15]

Crucial to the spectacle of the *intermedi* was the emphasis on the political supremacy of the Gonzagas and their state. Indeed, Mantua provided the setting for the performance, as the official account of the festivities describes:

> The invited cardinals, princes, ambassadors and ladies took their
> places in their assigned seats, and once the torches were lit in the

theatre, the usual trumpet fanfare was given from behind the stage. At the third statement of the fanfare, the large curtain which concealed the stage disappeared with such speed, at the blink of an eye, that although it rose upwards few could see how it had been removed. With the stage revealed to the spectators, one saw on its sides many palaces and towers standing out, partitioned by loggias and porticos done with such realism that everyone quickly recognized the scene for the city of Mantua, which was illuminated in such a way that without seeing any light lit therein was revealed the splendour not of torches or other illumination but of the pure rays of the sun . . . One saw in the air three most beautiful enclosed clouds, constructed with such artifice that they appeared no different from those made in the sky by the vapours of the earth, and with the stage floor covered by pleasant waters it was so like reality that indeed it seemed that there lay a most placid lagoon. One saw the lagoon bubble in the middle and from it emerge the head of a lady who, rising little by little, revealed herself through her costume and attributes to be Manto, daughter of Thyresia and founder of Mantua, who was raised up in so measured a fashion that by the time the trumpets had finished sounding she stood on a little island bathed by those waters; and pausing among some reeds that were placed thereupon, to the sound of several instruments which were behind the stage she sang the following words [not quoted here], which enraptured the minds of all the audience.[16]

Setting the performance both literally and figuratively in Mantua obscured any distinction between reality and scenic artifice. In all these entertainments, courtly art imitated life (and vice versa) in a continuum overriding conceptual and perceptual boundaries.

The essentially encomiastic function of court entertainments remained constant throughout the period, despite occasional differences in interpretation caused by varied local circumstances. These entertainments relied on long-established archetypes that still retained their potency: indeed, what is most notable in all these entertainments is less their individuality than the consistency of their treatment of themes of power and sovereignty. Just as the Mantuan festivities of 1608 differed little in essence from the famous Florentine wedding festivities of 1589 (one of their models), twenty years on in the Duchy of Parma and Piacenza, we find precisely the same messages conveyed by remarkably similar means. In 1628, Duke Odoardo Farnese of Parma married Margherita de' Medici of Florence. The celebration of the event was somewhat soured by the long diplomatic battle which had preceded it.[17] But to emphasize his political and cultural supremacy in northern Italy, Duke Odoardo forced his Florentine guests in Parma to endure a long succession of entertainments.

5. The Teatro Farnese, Parma, designed by Giovanni Battista Aleotti in 1618 and opened in 1628 with the tournament 'Mercurio e Marte' for the wedding of Odoardo Farnese and Margherita de' Medici; originally, as in many court theatres (see fig. 27 below) there were steps from each side of the stage to the auditorium

Pride of place in the festivities in Parma was taken by a spectacular performance of Tasso's *Aminta* with grand *intermedi* (performed on 13 December 1628) and a full-scale tournament, *Mercurio e Marte*, staged in the Teatro Farnese eight days later. Both had music by Monteverdi, despite Sigismondo d'India's attempts to gain the commission for the events. The subjects of the *intermedi*, emphasizing the power of love, were typical in their articulation of a courtly ethos: Bradamante and Ruggiero (from Ariosto's *Orlando furioso*); Dido and Aeneas; a scene on Olympus; the Argonauts; and a final assembly of the gods. The thematic content and scenic conventions of the *intermedi*, including heaven scenes, pastoral scenes, sea scenes and inferno scenes, had changed little since those staged in Florence in 1589. Moreover, the tournament, which marked the official opening of the splendid Teatro Farnese (built, in fact, some ten years earlier; *see* fig. 5), adopted similar thematic and scenic devices. Duke Odoardo himself took part in the contest and its associated action (with celestial and sea gods in profusion), which was staged with spectacular effects magnified to display the glories of the new theatre. The opening was particularly striking, as Aurora (played by Settimia Caccini, Giulio's daughter) appeared on a chariot driven by the winged horse Pegasus:

While the horse, gently beating its wings, drew the chariot from the waves, and as the sea and the rocks were illuminated little by little at its ascent, a distinguished singer, singing the following verses [not quoted here] with superhuman grace and an angelic voice, made the air resound and filled the entire theatre with sweetest accents . . . As soon as Signora Settimia, representing Aurora, began to sing, all conversation among the spectators ceased on account of the amazing illumination of the scene produced by Aurora's rays, and of the representation of the aforesaid sea, and all eyes were amazed by the divinity manifest in the countenance and garments of the goddess, in the chariot and in the skilful motion of Pegasus. Similarly, all ears were so consoled by the sweetness of the voice and the divine quality of the song, that among the 10,000 people seated in the theatre, there was no one . . . who did not grow tender at the trills, sigh at the sighs, become ecstatic at the ornaments, and who was not stupefied and transfixed by the miraculous beauty and song of a heavenly siren.[18]

The description of Aurora's entrance emphasizes that music played a vital role in conveying and enhancing the magic and splendour of these theatrical occasions. But the most striking aspect of the festivities in Parma is the absence of one genre that seemingly had been developed to display the power of music at its best, opera. At its birth, opera was directly associated with court wedding festivities – witness the Peri–Rinuccini *Euridice* (Florence, 1600) and the Monteverdi–Rinuccini *Arianna* (Mantua, 1608) – but in fact they were strange bedfellows. For example, *Euridice* was a private entertainment supplied by an individual, Jacopo Corsi, for a public ceremony intended to glorify the Medici. The resulting conflict was not entirely resolved. *Euridice* may have suited Corsi's personal tastes and requirements, and also broader academic and humanist criteria, but, at the same time, it did not quite meet the standards required by the court.[19] The work was not particularly successful – at least one eyewitness account ignored it completely – and the new dramatic recitative introduced in both *Euridice* and in *Il rapimento di Cefalo* was generally judged to be rather tedious ('like the chanting of the Passion' was one comment). Moreover, neither work provided the kind of spectacle and imagery required of a true court entertainment, and the subtle humanist programme behind *Euridice* was inappropriate for a celebration intended primarily to extol the Medici in the national and international arena. The Florentine court seems to have acknowledged all this in its next wedding celebration in 1608, when it put aside opera and reverted to the old-fashioned but expedient formula of a comedy with *intermedi*.

Mantua might appear to have offered a more welcoming climate for the new genre: witness the performances of Monteverdi's *Orfeo* in

1607 and *Arianna* in 1608. However, current views of *Arianna* are misleading. The opera is called a 'tragedia in musica', and the only section of the opera that survives, Ariadne's lament, certainly conveys a tragic spirit commensurate with the serious ideals of early opera. Significantly, however, when Rinuccini first presented his libretto of *Arianna* to the Duchess of Mantua (in February 1608), she found it 'rather dry', and he was ordered to 'enrich it with some action'.[20] As a result, the surviving libretto has more in common with the *intermedi* than with high-minded opera – for that matter, there is only a scant dramatic thread – and indeed the opera ends in a triumphal apotheosis as Bacchus descends from heaven to rescue Ariadne from her despair and to celebrate hymeneal bliss. If this is a tragedy, it is emphatically one with a happy ending, which had been typical of court *intermedi* for well over 50 years. To be sure, Mantua was not averse to opera. *Orfeo*, for example, was a notable success, but significantly, this success was achieved within the confines of an academy, an institution better suited to the intellectual and cultural pretensions of early opera. When it came to court festivities, however, new types of entertainment were fundamentally ill-equipped to cope with traditional modes of princely celebration. The apparent problems of reconciling early opera with courtly requirements goes a good way to explaining its fluctuating fortunes in the first half of the seventeenth century.

Italian princes focussed on other ways of presenting the messages to be articulated by court celebration. A survey of entertainments sponsored by the dukes of Savoy perhaps suggests why. Duke Carlo Emanuele I (ruled 1580–1630) worked hard to rescue his dominion from medieval feudalism and to raise it to the level of a true Renaissance state. He became a major patron of the arts, particularly poetry (he offered significant support to Tasso, Tassoni, Chiabrera and Marino), and not surprisingly he relied extensively on court festivities to establish his princely authority. As an anonymous chronicler recounted:

> It is easy to judge the ordinary expenses of His Highness, but the extraordinary expenses cannot be reckoned precisely. [These expenses] involve presents, which he offers more liberally than any other prince of his condition, and also battlements, fortifications, furniture, and rare ballets and other magnificences, more beautiful and more frequent in his court than in any other.[21]

Such moments of celebration centred broadly on two types of entertainment, the tournament and the court ballet. The duke himself was frequently involved in devising these festivities, although he also made use of prominent courtiers, notably Lodovico d'Aglié and, after

1627, Lodovico's nephew, Filippo (1600–67), as producers of perhaps the most spectacular entertainments to be seen in seventeenth-century Italy.

Although Carlo Emanuele died in 1630, a Savoyard tradition of entertainments was continued and indeed enhanced by the new Duchess of Savoy, Christine (the sister of Louis XIII), who had married Prince Vittore Amedeo (later Vittore Amedeo II) in 1619. She made her entrance into Turin in early 1620, and the occasion was celebrated by a grand tournament, *Il giudizio di Flora* (text by Lodovico d'Aglié, music by Sigismondo d'India), performed on 18 February 1620 with the participation of the royal family (some of d'India's music for the festivities is included in his *Le musiche e balli*, Venice, 1621). Christine continued to encourage court entertainments with passionate enthusiasm throughout her reign as duchess and (after 1637) as regent for her son Carlo Emanuele II: she regularly sought news from her native France about entertainments staged in Paris so as to imitate them in Turin. She relied extensively on the talents of Filippo d'Aglié, who became her chief counsellor (and majordomo from 1650). His brilliant political career was matched by his artistic abilities: according to Claude-François Ménestrier, whose treatises on theatrical representations provide important evidence of Savoyard court practice, d'Aglié was 'versed in a knowledge of history, antiquity, politics and of all the *belles-lettres*. He wrote excellently in Latin, Italian and French verse, played all types of instruments, composed in music, and was without difficulty the first master of all those ingenious entertainments.' D'Aglié devised over 30 entertainments for Savoy between 1624 and 1660, all revealing the 'ingéniosité' and 'esprit' that were highly prized by the court. However, these entertainments are characterized less by any search for novelty than by their repeated use of standard formulae. The only 'evolution' was in the stage machinery, which became ever more elaborate as the century progressed. Even the apparent distinction between outdoor tournaments and indoor ballets was lessened by the fact that both entertainments adopted very similar formats, fusing all the arts in a succession of grand *entrées* involving spectacular extravaganzas, allowing dance to articulate the order and magnificence of the state. Clearly, the Turin court felt that it had found a successful formula for glorifying the duke and his dominion. There was no reason for change.

The most spectacular of these Savoyard entertainments were the festivities for the wedding of Princess Margherita of Savoy and Ranuccio II Farnese, Duke of Parma, on 29 April 1660. Margherita was to have married Louis XIV, but plans fell through. Nevertheless, the Turin court sought to make the best of the new match, celebrating it with a splendour all the more emphatic because

6. *Musicians perform during the festivities for the wedding of Princess Adelaide of Savoy and Prince Ferdinand Maria of Bavaria, 11–16 December 1650: engraving from Tomasso Borgonio, 'Gli Hercoli domatori' (Turin, 1650)*

of the Duke of Parma's well-known love of lavish entertainments. The festivities, which also included firework displays and French comedies, were crowned inevitably by a tournament, *La gloria delle corone delle Margherite* (staged on 2 May), and a ballet, *L'unione perla peregrina margherita reale e celeste* (11 May). In the case of the tournament, the court historian Guichenon enthused: 'Never had anything so beautiful been seen, whether for the skill of the combatants and the dancers, whether for the richness of their costumes, whether for the rarity of the machines, whether for the invention of the descriptions and devices, whether for the beauty of the verses'. Its theme, and the inevitable play on 'Margherita' (=flower, =pearl), was taken up again in *L'unione perla peregrina* (designed by Count Amedeo de Castellamonte). The ballet dealt with how the pearl gains its perfection. Hercules, Juno, Neptune and Venus appeared, plus a rhinoceros, an elephant and ostriches, and the action also included a naval battle of rival pearl-fishers plus a final apotheosis involving the appearance of the city of Turin.

Certainly music was prominent in *L'unione perla peregrina*, and perhaps more so than in previous Savoyard entertainments, but it remained subordinate to the main focus of the entertainment, the spectacle. This, of course, offers one clue to the evident reluctance of Duchess Christine, and for that matter other north Italian courts, to embrace opera, where music had a much more crucial role to play. But these entertainments also suggest other factors that militated against the general acceptance of opera in a courtly environment. Tournaments remained popular not just because of their spectacular elements or because they provided convenient outlets for princely aggression. Abbé Tesauro offered a revealing comment on Duchess Christine, whose 'magnificence . . . has not been limited to fortifications; it has also appeared in the sumptuous ceremony for the weddings of her sons with an infinite number of surprising spectacles, and with tournaments which, although feigned and simulated, have caused terror in our enemies'. Military tournaments issued clear messages for both internal and external consumption. The point was reinforced by the participation of members of the royal family. When Christine entered Turin in February 1620, the British ambassador, Sir Isaac Wake, noted the 'continual Feasts, Banquetts, Musik, Mascks, and divers other Carnival recreations' and also the provision by Carlo Emanuele I of '4 several Tournies, and Tiltings, wherein himselfe, and the 3 princes his Sonns, are the principal Actors and Leaders of several squadrons'.

The active participation of the court was also a characteristic of Savoyard ballets, in which the royal family and their courtiers again took prominent roles. Opera, however, prevented such participation by erecting a conceptual and physical barriers between the stage action and the audience. This detachment, however crucial for the aesthetic development of the genre, meant that yet again opera failed to meet the demands of courtly entertainment. The proscenium arch of the theatre, the conceptual unity of the plot and also the musical focus of the dramatic action negated the merging of reality and fantasy that was so central to court celebration. Other European centres, notably Versailles under Louis XIV, were more successful in adapting opera to a courtly context. However, it is not surprising that on the whole the duchies of northern Italy felt little sympathy with the new musico-dramatic experiments of the early seventeenth century.

Still less did these duchies accept the 'public' opera developed in the Republic of Venice from 1637 onwards. To be sure, touring companies such as the Febiarmonici occasionally brought Venetian operas to the courts: for example, the Febiarmonici performed Francesco Sacrati's *La finta pazza* (first produced in Venice in 1641) before the Duke of Parma in Piacenza in 1644. Similarly, two leading Venetian opera composers, Francesco Manelli (*b* 1595–7, *d* 1667 or before) and Benedetto Ferrari (1603 or 1604–81), eventually swapped the financial precariousness of free-lance careers for the

7. *Theatre constructed in Modena in 1652 for the performance of 'La gara delle stagioni'*
('The Battle of the Seasons') on the visit of Archduke Ferdinand Karl, his wife Anna de'
Medici, and his brother Sigismund Franz: etching by Stefano della Bella

security of court employment (in Parma and in Modena respectively). Significantly, however, on taking up their posts Manelli and Ferrari effectively dropped their associations with Venice, and the occasional theatrical endeavours they now promoted retained the mythological–pastoral ethos crucial to courtly celebration. The more fashionable Venetian public opera, dependent upon newer patronage systems and generally focussing on other, often 'historical', subjects, found its home in different political institutions and cultural environments. Only after several decades were such operas generally accepted in the courts of northern Italy.

All this would seem to reinforce the notion of the innate conservatism and political restraints of court patronage. One can see why historians tend to look elsewhere for exciting musical developments in the seventeenth century. However, this shift of attention surely reflects a now outmoded evolutionist ethic for historical enquiry. It also misses several crucial points. Other Italian or European centres may be more 'interesting' in terms of their musical activity because of their apparent modernity, but the place of music in the north Italian courts emphasizes a continuity from the Renaissance, and also a precise socio-political context for the arts, that cannot be ignored. No less significant is the fact that these courts provided a major source of income for a large number of seventeenth-century Italian musicians.

NOTES

[1] W. Crook, *A Discourse of the Dukedom of Modena* (London, 1674), 3–4.

[2] See L. Bianconi, *Music in the Seventeenth Century*, trans. D. Bryant (Cambridge, 1987), 1–7, 28–33. Fuller statistics are provided in A. Pompilio, 'Editoria musicale a Napoli e in Italia nel Cinque–Seicento', *Musica e cultura a Napoli dal XV al XIX secolo*, ed. L. Bianconi and R. Bossa (Florence, 1983), 79–102; T. Carter, 'Music Publishing in Italy, c.1580–c.1625: some Preliminary Observations', *RMARC*, no. 20 (1986–7), 19–37.

[3] See K. Jeppesen, 'The Recently Discovered Mantova Masses of Palestrina: a Provisional Communication', *AcM*, xxii (1950), 36–47.

[4] V. Giustiniani, *Discorso sopra la musica de' suoi tempi* (1628), in Hercole Bottrigari, *'Il Desiderio . . .'; Vincenzo Giustiniani, 'Discorso sopra la musica'*, trans. C. MacClintock, MSD, ix (1962), 69.

[5] See A. Newcomb, 'Carlo Gesualdo and a Musical Correspondence of 1594', *MQ*, liv (1968), 409–36.

[6] For Tasso, see *Tasso, la musica, i musicisti*, ed. M. A. Balsano and T. Walker (Florence, 1988). A similar set of essays on Guarini – *Battista Guarini e la musica*, ed. P. Fabbri and A. Pompilio – is forthcoming.

[7] See C. V. Palisca, 'The Artusi–Monteverdi Controversy', *The New Monteverdi Companion*, ed. D. Arnold and N. Fortune (London, 1985), 127–58. Some additional remarks are offered in T. Carter, 'Artusi, Monteverdi, and the Poetics of Modern Music', *Musical Humanism and its Legacy: Essays in Honor of Claude V. Palisca*, ed. N. K. Baker and B. R. Hanning (New York, 1992), 171–94.

[8] See G. E. Watkins and T. La May, '"Imitatio" and "Emulatio": Changing Concepts of Originality in the Madrigals of Gesualdo and Monteverdi in the 1590s', *Claudio Monteverdi: Festschrift Reinhold Hammerstein zum 70. Geburtstag*, ed. L. Finscher (Laaber, 1986), 453–87.

[9] Monteverdi to Striggio, 9 December 1616, *The Letters of Claudio Monteverdi*, trans. and ed. D. Stevens (London, 1980), 115–18.

[10] See the remarks in T. Carter, *Music in Late Renaissance & Early Baroque Italy* (London, 1992), 193–6.

[11] The piece is discussed in N. Fortune, 'Italian Secular Monody from 1600 to 1635: an Introductory Survey', *MQ*, xxxix (1953), 171–95; Carter, *Music in Late Renaissance & Early Baroque Italy*, 251–2.

[12] For the performances and critical fortunes of *Il pastor fido*, the basic text remains V. Rossi, *Battista Guarini ed 'Il pastor fido': studio biografico-critico con documenti inediti* (Turin, 1886). The Mantuan productions are discussed in I. Fenlon, *Music and Patronage in Sixteenth-Century Mantua* (Cambridge, 1980–82), i, 146–57. For the performance before Margherita of Austria, see also Anon., *A Briefe Discourse of the Voyage and Entrance of the Queene of Spaine into Italy* [trans. from the French and Dutch by 'H. W.'] (London, n.d.), 10:

> The morrow after being Sunday, the 22. of Nouember [1598] there was done nothing except at night: about 5. of the clocke there was vpon a great round Theater (wherein every one might stand) played an excellent Comedy, which dured from the said five of the clocke vntill 3. houres after midnight, without any one beeing wearied with seeing or hearing, for the great singularities of inexplicable artificies which were shewed in the same: which vnto all seemed so admirable, so rare and so excellent, that in the iudgements of them all, it should seeme impossible, (as long as the world shal stand) to represent a Comedy more excellent and pleasant, where (over and above the said artificies and admirable rarieties,) there was betweene every enter-lude, heard most rare musicke of many partes, with divers instruments, accomp-anied with angelical & delicate voyces, insomuch that it seemed rather a divine, the[n] humane thing, or at least wise, that the voices of heauen had intermixed themselues with the entire perfection of that of men, and the spirits of this age. Being in fine a thing so rare, that it is impossible to set the same in writing, except the author therof, or the inventor of the artificies should doe it himselfe: The said comedy, besides the castle of artificial fireworkes, and besides the triumphall arkes which were in good number excellent well made, and over and aboue the present of the litter, did cost aboue 25000. crownes of gold . . .

[13] For a full discussion of the early Florentine operas, see below, pp. 135–8.

[14] See E. Strainchamps, 'New Light on the Accademia degli Elevati of Florence', *MQ*, lxii (1976), 507–35.

[15] F. Zuccaro, *Il passaggio per l'Italia* (1608), given in A. Solerti, *Gli albori del melodramma* (Milan, 1904), iii, 240.

[16] F. Follino, *Compendio delle sontuose feste fatte l'anno MDCVIII nella città di Mantova, per le reali nozze del serenissimo prencipe d. Francesco Gonzaga con la serenissima infanta Margherita di Savoia* (Mantua, 1608), given in P. Fabbri, *Monteverdi* (Turin, 1985), 134–5 (my translation).

[17] For the circumstances surrounding the wedding, see T. Carter, *Jacopo Peri (1561–1633): his Life and Works* (New York and London, 1989), 96–102. S. Reiner, 'Preparations in Parma – 1618, 1627–28', *MR*, xxv (1964), 273–301, slightly confuses the issues, for all its value in terms of documentation.

[18] M. Buttigli, *Descritione dell'apparato fatto per onorare la prima et solenne entrata in Parma della serenissima d. Margherita di Toscana duchessa di Parma e Piacenza* (Parma, 1629), given in Fabbri, *Monteverdi*, 279 (my translation).

[19] Again, see below, pp. 135–8. These issues are further discussed in T. Carter, 'Music and Patronage in Late Sixteenth-Century Florence: the Case of Jacopo Corsi (1561–1602)', *I Tatti Studies: Essays in the Renaissance*, i (1985), 57–104; idem, '*Non occorre nominare tanti musici*: Private Patronage and Public Ceremony in Late Sixteenth-Century Florence', ibid., iv (1991), 89–104.

[20] See Solerti, *Gli albori del melodramma*, i, 92.

[21] This and the following quotations are taken from M. M. McGowan, 'Les fêtes de cour en Savoie: l'œuvre de Philippe d'Aglié', *Revue d'histoire du théâtre*, xxii (1970), 181–241 (my trans-lations), which is the main source for this discussion of Savoyard entertainments.

BIBLIOGRAPHICAL NOTE

General

The Italian courts in the late sixteenth century and the seventeenth are poorly covered both by historians and, at least for the latter part of the period, by musicologists. Recent historical studies of the 'crisis' of the seventeenth century take their origin from *Crisis in Europe, 1550–1660: Essays from 'Past and Present'*, ed. T. Aston (London, 1965): the essays of E. Hobsbawm and H. Trevor-Roper are particularly significant for the initial development of the 'crisis' scenario. The issues have been further explored, and in part reconsidered, in *The General Crisis of the Seventeenth Century*, ed. G. Parker and L. M. Smith (London, 1978). This volume includes an important essay by R. Romano ('Between the Sixteenth and Seventeenth Centuries: the Economic Crisis of 1619–22', pp. 165–225) and also an intriguing exploration of the 'crisis' in terms of climactic changes (J. A. Eddy, 'The "Maunder Minimum": Sunspots and Climate in the Reign of Louis XIV', pp. 226–68). Revisions of the 'crisis' scenario appear in T. K. Rabb, *The Struggle for Stability in Early Modern Europe* (New York, 1975), where the emphasis is more on the reconfiguration of European institutions, and in the Marxist interpretations advanced in V. G. Kiernan, *State & Society in Europe, 1550–1650* (Oxford, 1980). Important for an economic historian's view of the seventeenth century is J. de Vries, *The Economy of Europe in an Age of Crisis, 1600–1750* (Cambridge, 1976), and more intriguingly, R. A. Goldthwaite, 'The Economy of Renaissance Italy: the Preconditions for Luxury Consumption', *I Tatti Studies: Essays in the Renaissance*, ii (1987), 15–39. For primary source material on the north Italian courts in the late sixteenth century, the ambassadorial reports transcribed in E. Albèri, *Relazioni degli ambasciatori veneti al senato* (Florence, 1839–63), remain indispensible.

The arts

Some important issues in art history are raised in F. Haskell, *Patrons and Painters: a Study in the Relations between Italian Art and Society in the Age of the Baroque* (London, 1963), and M. R. Maniates, *Mannerism in Italian Music and Culture, 1530–1630* (Manchester, 1979). The literary debates in the late sixteenth century are surveyed in B. Weinberg, *A History of Literary Criticism in the Italian Renaissance* (Chicago, 1961). Court theatre is discussed in C. Molinari, *Le nozze degli dèi: un saggio sul grande spettacolo italiano nel Seicento* (Rome, 1968), and A. M. Nagler, *Theatre Festivals of the Medici, 1539–1637* (New Haven, 1964) – Nagler also covers the festivities in Mantua, 1608, and in Parma, 1628 – while a contemporary viewpoint can be gleaned from C.-F. Menestrier, *Des représentations en musique anciennes et modernes* (Paris, 1681), and, with particular reference to Savoy, Menestrier's *Traité des tournois, joustes, carrousels et autres spectacles publics* (Lyons, 1669).

Music

There are a number of reasonable surveys of styles and genres in the period, including *The Age of Humanism, 1540–1630*, ed. G. Abraham, New Oxford History of Music, iv (London, 1968), C. V. Palisca, *Baroque Music* (Englewood Cliffs, NJ, 2/1979), and T. Carter, *Music in Late Renaissance & Early Baroque Italy* (London, 1992). G. Stefani, *Musica barocca: poetica e ideologia* (Milan, 1974) suggests a broader cultural view, but the most successful attempt at placing music in context is L. Bianconi, *Music in the Seventeenth Century*, trans. D. Bryant (Cambridge, 1987): Bianconi is remarkably sensitive to social issues, his unashamedly Italian focus offers a welcome corrective to earlier historical trends for this period, and his remarks on early opera are of vital significance.

The main composers discussed in this chapter are covered in D. Arnold, *Monteverdi* (London, rev. 3/1990 by T. Carter); *The New Monteverdi Companion* ed. D. Arnold and N. Fortune (London, 1985); J. J. Joyce, *The Monodies of Sigismondo d'India* (Ann Arbor, 1981); C. MacClintock, *Giaches de Wert (1535–1596): Life and Works*, MSD, xvii (1966); *The Letters of Claudio Monteverdi*, trans. and ed. D. Stevens (London, 1980);

The Early Baroque Era

Claudio Monteverdi: 'Orfeo', ed. J. Whenham (Cambridge, 1986); and, more contro-versially, G. Tomlinson, *Monteverdi and the End of the Renaissance* (Oxford, 1987). For opera, A. Solerti, *Gli albori del melodramma* (Milan, 1904) remains crucial for its documentation, although important modern interpretations are presented in N. Pirrotta and E. Povoledo, *Music and Theatre from Poliziano to Monteverdi*, trans. K. Eales (Cambridge, 1982), and in two major studies by L. Bianconi and T. Walker, 'Dalla *Finta pazza* alla *Veremonda*: storie di Febiarmonici', *RIM*, x (1975), 379–425, and 'Production, Consumption and Political Function of Seventeenth-Century Italian Opera', *EMH*, iv (1984), 209–96. The madrigal and solo song are covered in A. Einstein's brilliant *The Italian Madrigal* (Princeton, 1949), although the remarks here need updating in the light of recent scholarship, and in N. Fortune, 'Italian Secular Monody from 1600 to 1635: an Introductory Survey', *MQ*, xxxix (1953), 171–95. For oratorio, see H. E. Smither, *A History of the Oratorio*, i: *The Oratorio in the Baroque Era: Italy, Vienna, Paris* (Chapel Hill, 1977); V. Crowther, *The Oratorio in Modena* (Oxford, 1992) also provides important material (but for a period later than that covered in this chapter) on the genre in a specific court context. For sacred music, see L. Lockwood, *The Counter-Reformation and the Masses of Vincenzo Ruffo* (Venice, 1970), and J. Roche, *North Italian Church Music in the Age of Monteverdi* (Oxford, 1984). Useful contemporary views of musical developments can be seen in *Hercole Bottrigari, 'Il Desiderio . . .'; Vincenzo Giustiniani, 'Discorso sopra la musica'*, trans. C. MacClintock, MSD, ix (1972).

For specific north Italian courts, the following titles are particularly useful. Ferrara: E. Durante and A. Martellotti, *Cronistoria del concerto delle dame principalissime di Margherita Gonzaga d'Este* (Florence, 1979); A. Newcomb, *The Madrigal at Ferrara, 1579–1597* (Princeton, 1980). Mantua: I. Fenlon, *Music and Patronage in Sixteenth-Century Mantua* (Cambridge, 1980–82); C. Gallico, 'Guglielmo Gonzaga, signore della musica', *NRMI*, xi (1977), 321–34; S. Reiner, 'La vag'Angioletta (and others): i', *AnMc*, no.14 (1974), 26–88. Parma: S. Reiner, 'Preparations in Parma – 1618, 1627–28', *MR*, xxv (1964), 273–301; A. Yorke-Long, 'The Duchy of Parma', *Music at Court* (London, 1954), 1–40. Savoy: S. Cordero di Pamparato, 'I musici alla corte di Carlo Emanuele I di Savoia', *Biblioteca della società storica subalpina*, cxxi (1930), 31–142; M. M. McGowan, 'Les fêtes de cour en Savoie: l'œuvre de Philippe d'Aglié', *Revue d'histoire du théâtre*, xxii (1970), 181–241.

Chapter III

Rome: Sacred and Secular

SILKE LEOPOLD

The musical life of Rome in the late sixteenth and early seventeenth centuries was shaped by political and social conditions different from those in all other European capitals: nowhere else was the tension between spiritual and temporal influences so obvious. The peculiarity of the situation lay not so much in the fact that the head of state was an ecclesiastic – after all, an ecclesiastic ruled every diocese – nor in the fact that the ruler was elected, for so were those of the European city republics. But the lord of Rome did not merely rule the Papal States; he was also the guardian of religious and moral traditions that were supposed to serve as a model for the entire Catholic world. The power of the Pope was not limited to the political and military power of his state; in his capacity as Christ's representative on earth, he also had spiritual authority over the emperors and kings of Europe.

While the rulers of the city republics were elected from the old-established city families, few sixteenth- and seventeenth-century popes were members of the Roman aristocracy.[1] Most of them came from outside, and found themselves confronting city nobles who were far from inclined to accept their claims to leadership without question. They were obliged on the one hand to create links with the old-established families by contracting a wide variety of family alliances, on the other to bestow high office on the people they trusted, chiefly members of their own families; this in turn aroused the suspicion and rivalry of the Roman nobility. As there was no family continuity in the papal succession, the Pope's kinsmen too had to make all the use they could of his reign to further their own interests; once he was dead, the Vatican's horn of plenty would cease to overflow, since the new pope in his turn would fill influential and lucrative posts with persons he himself trusted. Nepotism flourished in seventeenth-century Rome – and, as it happens, the nephews of various popes gave the greatest stimulus to the musical life of the city: Scipione and Marcantonio Borghese, Francesco and Antonio Barberini, Benedetto Pamfili and Pietro Ottoboni all, as cardinals, had staggering sums of money at their disposal and willingly disbursed them to promote the arts. In the palaces of the papal nephews, operas were produced, oratorios performed, cantatas composed and sung, and instrumental music played. Not until the art-loving Queen Christina of Sweden settled in Rome did the city boast a non-clerical household whose cultural significance could compete with that of the cardinals' establishments.

The Pope's claim to moral leadership was reflected in the musical life of the city. The history of the Roman opera, for instance, is one of permissions and prohibitions.[2] Thus, women were sometimes forbidden and sometimes allowed to appear in opera; opera houses were sometimes closed and then reopened by papal decree; there were times when public performances of opera were banned but private performances allowed, and then again all performances, private as well as public, would be forbidden. All this was done in the name of propriety and morality, and it shows how great was the tension between the temporal and the spiritual in the capital of Christendom.

The church music of Rome in the sixteenth and seventeenth centuries was also beset by decrees and prohibitions. Since the Council of Trent had moved against the secularization of church music, declaring the pure *a cappella* style mandatory for all time, the popes had been conducting a campaign as tenacious as it was hopeless against the intrusion of secular elements into church music. Yet the ruling on pure *a cappella* style was strictly observed only in the papal chapel itself, the Cappella Sistina; its choir was one of the biggest and best in Europe, and its performances for the great church festivals became a legend that even outlasted the decline of the choir in subsequent centuries. In other Roman churches – and there were over 200 of them – the banned instruments were played, even the most sacred words of the liturgy were set to cheerful dance rhythms, and liturgical texts were replaced by non-liturgical ones, so that in the middle of the seventeenth century the Vatican several times had to remind the faithful that the Benedictus was to follow the Sanctus and the Offertorium the Credo. Constant control by the Curia and the imposition of a style that was becoming increasingly outdated were not calculated to promote the interest of composers in church music; no wonder, then, that the seat of the Catholic Church seemed unable to inject new life into church music in the seventeenth century.

Innovation in sacred music was concentrated in two institutions founded within a short time of one another and bearing the stamp of their founders' wholly different personalities: the Jesuits and the Oratorians. At an early stage the Jesuits had recognized both the educational and the propagandist qualities of music, in particular of musical drama, and they introduced it into their educational establishments in Rome: the Collegio Germanico, the Collegio Romano and the Seminario Romano. The Jesuits, the crack troops of the Counter-Reformation, knew that people are more easily reached through the senses than the intellect. Music was employed by Filippo Neri's Oratorians for quite different ends; it was a basic component of their daily meetings for communal devotions, and was also intended to attract the faithful to houses of prayer, not to educate them but to give them a sense of community and joy. It is no coincidence that the history of musical theatre in Rome begins with the work of an Oratorian and with a didactic musical drama at the Jesuit College.

It was also in the colleges that a great many of the musicians who actively shaped the musical life of Rome were trained. More than any other city, Rome offered the professional musician a variety of opportunities to work within the framework of both Church and society. Many churches besides the Sistine Chapel employed not only the obligatory organist but their own choirs, particularly the cardinal churches of St Peter's, St John Lateran and S Maria Maggiore. Musicians were much in demand in the religious fraternities, particularly for the great church festivals, donations from patrons and members of the religious orders providing the necessary funds. And the numerous cardinals and prelates, princes and margraves employed their own musicians in their palaces. When opera became established, even more musicians were required, for Roman operas made much use of choruses. There was no strict division into the sacred and the secular: the same musicians came together to perform for the various different institutions. Court musicians in the service of cardinals or noblemen sang in their employers' titular churches, musical directors of churches were brought in to improve princely dance ensembles, singers from the papal chapel appeared in operas. From 1566 onwards Roman musicians were organized into a company, or congregation, an association which oversaw musical training, music publishing and appointments to musical posts.[3]

The Roman festival calendar too differed from that of other capitals: rather than family events such as weddings, birthdays, births or christenings, those occasions chiefly celebrated in Rome were the enthronement of the Pope, canonizations and religious festivals. In Rome, as elsewhere, Carnival was a time of much festivity, particularly when great princes from abroad were staying in the city on state visits, but even during Lent there were opportunities for magnificent productions in the centres of sacred music. Indeed, in Holy Week itself, when no music outside the churches was allowed, musical performances on a large scale took place in the oratories. Moreover, the popes made a point of celebrating the festive occasions of the whole Catholic world: the birth of the heir to the French throne in Paris, the coronation of the Habsburg emperor in Vienna, the accession to the throne of the Catholic Stuart king in London. In the century of the Counter-Reformation, ceremonial glorifying the Church was seen as being of far from secondary importance: foreign guests and ambassadors reporting every successful festival back to their native lands heightened the Church's prestige. The more the political influence of the Vatican and the Curia declined in Italy and elsewhere in Catholic Europe, the more the popes turned to their task of religious leadership: in the century of Catholic revival every event at a Catholic court of Rome could become a public manifesto of the strength and importance of the papacy.

1580–1600: CHAPELS AND CONGREGATIONS

The musical history of Rome in the late sixteenth century was shaped by the movement to renew the Catholic Church, which had begun with the Council of Trent and was vigorously promoted by Popes Gregory XIII (1572–85) and Sixtus V (1585–90). Reformation of church music was part of this movement. On the one hand, music was to be purged of secular influences, including instrumental accompaniment and the embellishment of compositions by diminutions; on the other, the structure of the composition was not to impair the comprehensibility of the text; the sacred words should stand at the centre of a work. This second requirement was to have a particularly decisive influence on the development of church music in the last third of the sixteenth century.

The Roman churches led the way in this reform, first and foremost the Cappella Sistina, which at the time of Gregory XIII employed one of the greatest choirs in the world, with 24 permanent choristers. However, as mentioned above, an important part was also played by the considerably smaller choirs of St Peter's (the Cappella Giulia) as well as of S Maria Maggiore (the Cappella Pia) and St John Lateran (the Cappella Liberiana), not to mention the choirs of smaller churches such as S Maria in Trastevere, S Luigi dei Francesi, S Spirito in Saxia and S Lorenzo in Damaso. For while the Sistine Chapel engaged famous professional singers from all over the world, using falsetto singers, generally of Spanish origin, for the high voices,[4] the other chapels, where the high parts were sung by choirboys, also undertook the musical education of these boys, who generally came from Rome or the surrounding area. The influence these chapels exerted not only on the musical life of Rome but, in their capacity as models, on the musical culture of the whole of Europe, is clearly demonstrated by Giovanni Pierluigi da Palestrina, the outstanding musician in Rome in the second half of the sixteenth century: Palestrina, himself trained as a choirboy at S Maria Maggiore, was choirmaster successively at St Peter's, St John Lateran and S

Maria Maggiore; he was also connected with the Sistine Chapel first as singer and later as composer.[5] He composed many of his works specifically for these chapels. If one remembers that after his death Palestrina was declared (in the first instance by Agostino Agazzari and Adriano Banchieri in 1609) the 'saviour of church music' and his personal style of composition proclaimed as the model for all church music, the full significance of Rome's church choirs for European musical history becomes clear.

The members of the papal chapel, appointed for life and strictly organized by statutes, were the most respected and best-paid musicians in the city. They had a say in deciding what works were worthy of performance in the Sistine Chapel and which should be taken into repertory; papal choristers were engaged to perform on special occasions in other Roman churches, in the oratories and in the palaces of the nobility. From the 1580s onwards the chapel's soprano falsettist singers were gradually replaced by castratos, whose voices were stronger and had a wider compass. Gregory XIII, in a papal bull, had forbidden castration, but those soprano singers who by some strange chance had fallen off horses in childhood, the horses then kicking them in a manner as painful as it was well aimed, and who had subsequently made the best of their mutilated condition by training their voices, were soon the most highly prized singers of the papal court, and were frequently called upon for the musical adornment of the Pope's private entertaining. By 1600, the Sistine Chapel was engaging no more soprano falsettists, and under Urban VIII the last of them was finally replaced by a castrato.

Though Roman musical life was dominated by church musicians who were often in holy orders themselves, a lively secular musical culture was also developing. In 1585 Pope Sixtus V gave the company of Roman musicians permanent status, with its own privileges, which were principally to do with education and publishing. Initially, papal choristers were not allowed to belong to this Vertuosa Compagnia dei Musici, which survives in Rome today in the form of the Accademia di S Cecilia. Soon, however, they too joined the influential company of musicians, which included instrumentalists as well as singers. In 1589 the Compagnia published a collection of secular madrigals by its members, with contributions from Palestrina and three papal choristers, as well as Luca Marenzio, Ruggiero Giovannelli and the Neapolitan Giovanni de Macque, Gesualdo's teacher. The founding of the Vertuosa Compagnia marked the beginning of the concept of music as a profession; the musician was no longer merely a servant employed to glorify God or his secular lord but an independent artist who served music itself.

In spite of the demand of the Council of Trent for greater textual comprehensibility in vocal music, Palestrina always remained faithful to polyphony. But the musical intellectuals of Florence hoped to replace counterpoint with a new method of solo singing derived from the declamation of ancient times, while the Roman Compagnia were striving for a better understanding of the text by employing longer homophonic sections in the polyphonic style.[6] After decades of adhering to a method of composition in which the text might be a point of departure for musical invention but in which the art of composition had to conform to certain rules, musicians began once again to pay attention to the forms of the text they were setting, not just their content. In 1585 Giovanelli published *Gli sdruccioli*, a madrigal collection whose title refers to the particular metrical form of the words and not to the music.[7] Marenzio, first as court musician to Cardinal Luigi d'Este and later in the service of Virginio Orsini and Cinzio Aldobrandini in Rome, gave this new kind of madrigal (in which the text began to dominate the counterpoint) its classic form; mostly written in Rome in Compagnia circles, Marenzio's madrigals were as widely disseminated as Palestrina's sacred music and as influential in the secular sphere during his own time and the following generation.

Through the close links between Rome and the Medici court in Florence, experiments with accompanied solo singing reached Rome long before the first works in this new style of writing were printed. Marenzio contributed to the Florentine *intermedi* of 1589,[8] in which this style first appeared. The director of these performances was the Roman nobleman Emilio de' Cavalieri (*c*1550–1602), who was active at the Medici court from 1588 but who never severed his close ties with Rome and Roman musicians.[9] Another contributor to the *intermedi*, the singer and composer Giulio Caccini, was a native of Rome and court singer to Ferdinando de' Medici. He had made his reputation in the noble houses of Rome with a style of decorated solo singing long before his works of this kind was published in *Le nuove musiche* in 1602.

1600–23: JESUITS AND ORATORIANS

At the end of the sixteenth century and the beginning of the seventeenth, a period regarded as one of the great turning-points of musical history, Rome seemed to have been deprived of its leading composers: Palestrina, guardian of the purist style, had died in 1594, and Marenzio, whose madrigals and villanellas went into hundreds of editions in his lifetime, died in 1599. New creative impetus came not from the established musical institutions but from the Oratorians and Jesuits. Cavalieri, who was choirmaster of the Arciconfraternità del SS Crocefisso for several years before he left for Florence maintained close with Filippo Neri (1515–95) and his brotherhood. Tired

8. The Chiesa Nuova (formerly S Maria in Valicella; right), with the associated Oratory of St Philip Neri (built to designs by Maruscelli and Borromini, 1637–50; centre): engraving by Giuseppe Vasi from 'Delle magnificenze di Roma antica e moderna', vii (1756)

of the quarrels of the Medici court and the intriguing of his rival Caccini, Cavalieri moved permanently back to Rome at the end of 1600; in the carnival season of 1599–1600, his *Rappresentatione di Anima, et di Corpo* was performed in the oratory of the Chiesa Nuova, in the presence of high-ranking clerics and nobles. The *Rappresentatione* is, by a few months, the first printed musico-dramatic work, although Cavalieri had in fact been experimenting with theatrical music in the 1590s, as had Peri and Caccini.[10]

Musicologists have long debated the question of whether the *Rappresentatione* is the first opera or the first oratorio. This is a moot point, for the simple reason that at this early stage there was no clear distinction between the two genres. The *Rappresentatione* was certainly performed without scenery, despite a number of suggestions for staging offered in the preface to the printed edition; however, the work contains all the dramatic and musical elements found in the mythological *favole in musica* of the period: sung dialogue in the new solo style which Cavalieri called 'recitar cantando'; aria-like forms; dance music; choruses. Even the echo scene typical of the pastoral is incorporated as a series of questions and answers between Anima and Heaven. The action of the *Rappresentatione* is allegorical: Anima (the soul) and Corpo (the body), in search of true happiness, are torn between the temptations of Mondo (the world) and Vita Mundana (worldly life) and promises of Heaven. When Corpo and the guar-

55

dian angel tear the glittering garments from the bodies of Mondo and Vita Mundana, disclosing the ugliness of the tempters, and when they see the torment of the damned souls in Hell and the joy of the blessed in Heaven, they choose the way of faith. The drama closes with the rejoicing of the heavenly hosts.

The *Rappresentatione*, ushering in a new age of music drama, is also firmly linked to the tradition of the Oratorians. The central dialogue between Anima and Corpo, 'Anima mia che pensi', had already appeared in an oratorian collection of *laude* in 1577. Dialogues with an allegorical, hagiographic or biblical content were among the most popular musical presentations in the oratories even in the sixteenth century. In the *Rappresentatione* Cavalieri combined aspects of the Florentine pastoral, to which he himself had made considerable musical contributions, with the divine service of the Roman oratories, which had abandoned Latin in order to aid comprehension. Filippo Neri had thus attracted believers of humble origin to the oratories. A devotional service normally began with silent prayer, followed by a series of lessons and homilies and a piece of music; music was more prominent at Vespers; and from November to Easter the musical part of these *oratori vespertini* was even further extended. Neri favoured the popular *lauda*, a simple syllabic composition in whose singing the congregation could join.

The *Rappresentatione* had no immediate successors in the oratories. With Cavalieri's death in 1602, the interest in such lavish theatrical productions was temporarily extinguished. However, the new musical style of solo singing over a bass was also suitable for the composition of ordinary *laude*. Roman composers published a great many collections of sacred works in Italian during the first two decades of the seventeenth century; intended for use in the oratories, they included the *Affetti amorosi spirituali* (1617) of Paolo Quagliati, organist of S Maria Maggiore, and the Jesuit Giovanni Francesco Anerio's *Teatro armonico spirituale* (1619).[11] Both collections contain a number of dialogues, similar in style to Caccini's madrigals in *Le nuove musiche*. Anerio also suggested pieces from the *Teatro armonico*, predominantly madrigals, which would be suitable for Sundays and feast days between November and Easter. Considering how far dramatic recitative had developed in the years between the *Rappresentatione* and the collections of Quagliati and Anerio, particularly in Monteverdi's Mantuan operas, one is struck by the conservatism of these Roman works. No one in Palestrina's city saw any reason to declare war on counterpoint.

Anerio provides a good example of the close connection that had existed between the Jesuits and the Oratorians from the time of Ignatius Loyola and Filippo Neri onwards. Besides his work for the oratories and as organist of various Roman churches, Anerio had also been musical director of the Seminario Romano for several years. The Jesuit educational establishments had also reacted to the stimuli to music drama provided by Cavalieri in his *Rappresentatione*, though in a different way: while the Oratorians at first resisted the infiltration of magnificent theatrical effects into the music of their houses of prayer, the Jesuits regarded these same theatrical possibilities as highly suitable for the propagation of their ideas.[12] Six years after the *Rappresentatione*, Agostino Agazzari, a native of Siena, author of an important treatise on thoroughbass and musical director of the Collegio Germanico, composed an opera entitled *Eumelio*, which was performed by the students of the college in Carnival 1606 and later published. This opera, although wholly different in conception, cannot conceal its relationship with the *Rappresentatione*: it too is a mixture of pastoral play and allegory, a struggle between earthly and heavenly powers, in which the heavenly powers, here personified by Apollo, finally win the day.[13] And Agazzari's music also has conservative features: what at first appears to be declamatory recitative like that of Peri or Caccini turns out, on closer inspection, to be in effect polyphonic music reduced to the top vocal part and an instrumental bass; moreover, the dialogues are strophically devised – unlike Cavalieri's, but in a way similar to the old dialogue *laude* – and the various characters in the drama have their own musical patterns.

Whether *Eumelio* was the only sacred opera of this kind performed by the Jesuits it is not known; many manuscript works of this period are lost. But in any case, the Jesuits, like the Oratorians, certainly encouraged the new genre of dramatic music in Rome. Among their students were many of the composers who were later to establish opera in Rome, the most notable being Stefano Landi (1586/7–1639), whose career was typical of those of Roman musicians in the early Baroque period. Accepted as a choirboy at the Collegio Germanico, he later graduated from the Seminario Romano, taking minor orders in the household of first an art-loving relative of the Pope and then of a rich cardinal. He then became *maestro di cappella* at one of the Jesuit churches in Rome and finally in 1629, he was appointed a singer in the papal chapel – the climax of a Roman musician's career.[14] His creative output is also typical in its diversity, since it includes polyphonic madrigals and solo arias as performed in private circles, as well as a strictly polyphonic mass and concerted psalms. Landi also helped to establish a specifically Roman type of opera, distinguished from the Florentine and Venetian varieties mainly by its conservatism: while in north Italian opera the few choral passages were set in a simple and unpretentious homophonic style, in Roman opera the chorus, often polyphonic, played an increasingly important part.[15] Landi's first opera, *La morte d'Orfeo* (1619), is an example of this new style, with its extensive choral passages at the end of each act which,

9. *Carousel in the courtyard of the Palazzo Barberini, 28 February 1656 in honour of Queen Christina of Sweden (who had just arrived in Rome): painting by Filippo Lauri and Filippo Gagliardi*

being only vaguely related to the action, take on the character of interludes. Although the work was actually written in northern Italy, Landi was at this time in the retinue of the Pope's nephew Cardinal Scipione Borghese. The opera may never have been performed: until the Barberini built a theatre in their palace (it opened in 1632), opera in Rome was only an occasional private entertainment, without the scenic and musical splendour lavished upon it in the court theatres of Florence or Mantua. *La morte d'Orfeo* was followed by Filippo Vitali's *Aretusa* (1620), performed in the house of the prelate Ottavio Corsini, who also wrote the libretto, and by Giacinto Cornacchioli's *Diana schernita*, given in the house of Johann Rudolph, Baron of Hohen-Rechberg. Domenico Mazzocchi's *La catena d'Adone* (1626), which was performed in the Palazzo Conti in the presence of the Pope's nephews Francesco and Antonio Barberini, is noteworthy for its cast of well-known singers and its great scenic splendour. Carnival remained the only time of year when Rome allowed itself such worldly pleasures.

The popes gave no stimulus of any consequence to the musical life of Rome in the first two decades of the seventeenth century. Paul V, who reigned from 1605 to 1619, was a great patron of the visual arts, but does not seem to have been particularly knowledgeable about music. He did, however, employ as organist at St Peter's, Girolamo Frescobaldi, the most important and innovative keyboard player and composer of his time, whose pupils took his style back to other European countries.[16] But when Claudio Monteverdi came to Rome in 1610 with his Vespers, dedicated to the Pope, he was not even granted an audience, let alone a post. Not until Maffeo Barberini succeeded to the papal throne in 1623, as Urban VIII, did the papal family take over the spiritual, political and cultural leadership of Rome.

1623–56: THE BARBERINI

Awkward and not very successful in Vatican politics, Maffeo Barberini was nonetheless able to represent his own interests so skilfully that the influence of his pontificate (1623–44) is visible in Rome to this day. As Urban VIII, he chose the young Gian Lorenzo Bernini as his favourite artist, offering him the chance to give the city a new image.[17] The Pope himself wrote poetry and loved music; several composers from his entourage, among them Domenico Mazzocchi and Johann Hieronymus Kapsberger, set his poems. He appointed scholars and men of letters as his closest colleagues, including Giulio Rospigliosi of Pistoia, whose librettos were to mould the shape of Roman Baroque opera.[18]

But Urban VIII's particular skill was in putting his three nephews into key positions in every area of sacred and secular life in Rome. He made the eldest, Francesco (*b* 1597), a cardinal in the year of his enthronement; he married the second, Taddeo (*b* 1603), to a member of one of the oldest and wealthiest families of Rome and made him the city's prefect and military leader; and the youngest, Antonio (*b* 1607) was also made a cardinal when he was only twenty. He also gave Francesco and Antonio the most lucrative posts in the Curia, thus creating the financial basis for their lavish patronage. The Barberini palace, the Palazzo alle Quattro Fontane rebuilt by Bernini between 1625 and 1632 (*see* fig. 9), where Taddeo and at times the two cardinals lived, became the cultural centre of Rome. The Pope was also to be seen there attending all important events; he supplied not only considerable funds but his own Vatican musicians for certain particularly extravagant productions. Under Urban VIII the choir of the Sistine Chapel again became 30 strong; it included singers such as the castrato Loreto Vittori, whom the Pope himself had discovered as a child and whom he subsequently raised to the nobility. Vittori was to have a great influence on early opera, singing the main roles in most of the Roman operas; in addition he was engaged for operatic performances in Florence and Parma. The chapel also employed important composers such as Gregorio Allegri, whose *Miserere* (1638) is the most enduring sacred work of the era.

From the beginning of Urban VIII's pontificate, the Barberini family had provided particularly lavish spectacles during Carnival. The wedding of Taddeo to Anna Colonna at the end of 1627 was also celebrated with great pomp. And with the operatic performances at the Palazzo alle Quattro Fontane, which continued with occasional interruptions until 1656, a new and important era in Roman opera began. Carnival 1632 saw the first production in the so-called Teatro Barberini, a great hall in the palace where a stage and all the necessary machinery could be installed as required. This theatre did not, as a contemporary report claimed, hold 3000 people, but only a few hundred privileged spectators.

The inaugural opera at the Teatro Barberini, *Sant'Alessio* (*see* fig. 10), is in every respect a typical work of the period; its score has come down to us in the extended version of 1634. The libretto was by Giulio Rospigliosi who, after a meteor-like career furthered by Urban VIII, became Pope in 1666. Rospigliosi had acquired a broad education at the Jesuit Seminario Romano; he distinguished himself in jurisprudence, philosophy and, particularly, literature. On a journey to Spain in the retinue of Francesco Barberini he became acquainted with the plays of Calderón, which were later to influence his own writing. His librettos united literary and dramatic traditions of widely differing provenance. *Sant'Alessio* contains elements of classical

10. Scene from Act 1 of Stefano Landi's 'Sant'Alessio' (Palazzo Barberini, Rome, c1632): engraving by F. Collignon after a design (attributed to P. da Cortona, G.L. Bernini or F. Buonamici) for the 1634 production

tragedy, comedy, Jesuit drama, the *sacra rappresentazione*, the pastoral and *intermedi*.[19]

The action, a combination of allegory and legend, is both pious and entertaining: the Roman citizen Alexis, having left his betrothed wife and his family years previously in order to renounce worldly pleasure, is living incognito and in self-imposed asceticism under the steps of his father's house. His mother, believing him far away, mourns his loss; pages mock the ragged beggar, and the Devil tries to entice him from the path of virtue. Alexis withstands all temptations until death finally releases him; the Devil is sent straight back to Hell, and Religion, amid the heavenly hosts, praises the saint, dedicates a temple to him and urges mankind to follow his example. The moralizing theme of the legend, which had already been used in a sixteenth-century *sacra rappresentazione*, was combined most felicitously in Rospigliosi's hands with the theatrical spectacle of the Jesuit drama, as is most evident in the allegorical figure of Religion and the vanquishing of the Devil. Alexis also faces a moral dilemma, when he sees his betrothed wife preparing to travel to distant lands in search of him. In a long monologue Alexis struggles with himself over whether to reveal his identity to her. Helping to take the edge of this central didactic theme are comic scenes for the pages. The opera celebrates not only the glory and grandeur of the Eternal City but, most important of all, Rome as the centre of the Catholic faith. In the Prologue, Rome appears in person, releasing slaves from their chains.

The music of *Sant'Alessio* is by Stefano Landi. He found the right tone for all the literary levels: wide declamatory sweeping phrases for the tragic monologue, harsh dissonances for the scenes in which the women lament, busy chattering music for the pages, smooth, lyrical phrases for the arias. He paid particular attention to the demons: the Devil is a bass part with a wide compass, and his associates sing dark-toned choruses in ponderous rhythms. Landi also provided three instrumental symphonies, one at the beginning of each act, and closed the acts with ballets and polyphonic choruses, typical of the Roman style. For the first time in the history of opera, high voices predominated,[20] and the male lead, the saint himself, was sung by a soprano castrato. It is impossible to explain the preference for the high male voice which dominated *opera seria* until the nineteenth century; possibly, however, Rospigliosi and Landi wanted, in this special case, a voice that sounded naturally neither male nor female to represent the saint who had already withdrawn from the world and was hardly an 'earthly' man any longer. In the next Barberini opera, *Erminia sul Giordano* by Michelangelo Dossi, performed in 1633, the male lead was sung by a tenor.

The cast list of *Sant'Alessio* is typical of Rome at the time: most of the parts were sung by singers from the papal chapel, some of whom were also employed in the private houses of the Barberini. For the final rehearsals all these singers were released from their duties in the Sistine Chapel by order of the Pope, causing considerable discontent in the choir. Boys from the Cappella Giulia, the choir of St Peter's, sang the parts of the pages and Taddeo's pages danced the ballets at the ends of the acts.

Sant'Alessio which was revived in 1634, started a trend. Legends of the saints, embellished with moral teachings, were found to be particularly suitable for legitimizing the secular pleasures of opera. Rospigliosi wrote no fewer than four such librettos. However, he also took themes from narrative literature (*Chi soffre speri*, after Boccaccio) and from epic poetry, making use of Tasso's *Gerusalemme liberata* for *Erminia sul Giordano* and of Ariosto's *Orlando furioso* for *Il palazzo incantato*. *Il palazzo* was set to music by Luigi Rossi (1597/8–1653), a musician who had already made a name in Rome with his cantatas.[21] It was the first opera produced under the patronage of Antonio Barberini, in 1642, and its spirit is quite different from that of the operas on the lives of the saints. The tale of the rescue of Ruggiero from the enchanted palace is told in a convoluted manner, no fewer then seven pairs of lovers being involved in misunderstandings and confusion until all is righted at the end. This medley of comic and tragic scenes tinged with magic, a mixture typical of later Venetian opera, was ideal for Rossi's talents. Although the action is sometimes grotesque, he wrote tender arias and tragic laments for his characters. In its choice of musical forms *Il palazzo* shows how far Roman opera had come in the decade since *Sant'Alessio*: whereas before recitatives predominated, arias – short, often dance-like pieces – now occupied much more time. *Il palazzo incantato* was enthusiastically received, and contemporaries agreed that its success was due largely to the music. Criticism was mainly directed at the length of the performance, which went on for eight hours, too long even for the patient audiences of the seventeenth century.

In this opera the trend away from artistic unity and towards a varied mosaic, anticipated in the literary forms of Rospigliosi's librettos, affected the music too. In his chamber cantatas Rossi had already tried using a multiplicity of styles: recitatives both conversational and pathetic, arias both mournful and joyful, large- and small-scale musical forms. In the service of the Borghese family until 1636, he had composed many smaller-scale vocal pieces for private occasions in their palace. Nearly 400 such compositions are known: declamatory recitatives, strophic songs, dance-like arias, cantatas with a free sequence of recitative and aria sections, and serenatas in several movements. His political laments are particularly noteworthy. Shortly after 1632, Rossi commemorated the death of King Gustavus II Adolphus of Sweden (at the Battle of Lützen) with a dramatic lament supposedly from the mouth of his daughter, the new Queen Christina,[22] in spite of the fact that Christina was only five years old at the time. Other political laments, which became popular outside Rome, dealt with affairs at the court of the Osman ruler Murad IV, whose reign of terror included the assassinations of his brothers Mustafa and Bayezit and their families.[23] It is significant that these laments referred to events in both the Protestant and Islamic worlds: the power of Catholicism could thus be illustrated not only by celebrating the grandeur of Rome but also by depicting the sufferings of those who did not follow the true faith.

Il palazzo incantato was the last of the operas performed in the Palazzo Barberini during the pontificate of Urban VIII, who died in 1644. His successor, Innocent X, who ruled until 1655, was a suspicious and avaricious man who did not care for art. He reduced the papal chapel by a third, and the production of opera ceased. Rospiglioli went to Spain as papal nuncio, and the Barberini fled to France. The Palazzo alle Quattro Fontane, once the brilliant centre of Roman musical life, was left deserted.

The Early Baroque Era

1644–55: INTERREGNUM

In spite of Innocent X's lack of interest in art, the musical life of Rome continued, though on a much more modest scale. With the decline of the Palazzo Barberini, Carnival in Rome emerged from the shadows: masquerades, tournaments, balls – events in which music played an important part, though hardly any of it has survived. In 1647, for instance, a *carro*, a decorated wagon with a stage on it, went through the streets, and an opera entitled *Il premio della fatica* was performed on it. The tradition of these small, travelling operas had begun with Paolo Quagliati's *Il carro di fedeltà d'Amore* as early as 1606, the year in which Agazzari's *Eumelio* was performed at the Seminario.

While secular music in Rome was on the wane, a new sacred style was developing, although its origins lay in northern Italy, particularly Venice: polychoral technique. The great churches of Rome, such as St Peter's, St John Lateran and S Maria Maggiore, all with their own choirs, were an invitation to expand the polyphonic *a cappella* style to fill the large spaces with music to the glory of the Church.[24] At the end of the pontificate of Urban VIII, composers had begun experimenting with the possibilities of multiple choirs or *cori spezzati*: Virgilio Mazzocchi, younger brother of Domenico, was one of the first to make use in his works of the vast space inside Roman churches. About 1640 he wrote a mass for twelve choirs for St Peter's, one choir singing an echo part up in the dome. These early works for multiple choirs, however, have not survived: they were regarded more as functional music than as art worth preserving and circulating. And few churches could have found enough performers for such works. Only after the death of Urban VIII, when attention was once again concentrated on church music, was it possible to establish the *cori spezzati* style firmly in Roman musical life. Works for four, eight or twelve choirs, distributed all over a church, were no longer a rarity; such works were printed and thus made available to other musicians. Among the most important composers of this music were Antonio Maria Abbatini, who later set librettos by Rospigliosi and Orazio Benevoli; Ottavio Pitoni continued this tradition into the eighteenth century. In these works the time-honoured Palestrina style was combined with the new concerted forms. No longer was the pure *a cappella* style obligatory: for a performance of a work by Virgilio Mazzocchi in the Collegio Romano, the six choirs were accompanied by trumpets and drums.

The musical splendour of multiple choirs also found its way into the oratories, for here too, under the protection of the Barberini cardinals, a more exuberant and festal kind of music had won the day. Three such brotherhoods were now at the forefront: the oratories of S Girolamo della Carità, of the Chiesa Nuova (rebuilt in 1640) and of the Arciconfraternità del SS Crocefisso at S Marcello. The last-named had moved furthest from the ideas of Filippo Neri, reverting to the use of Latin. From the very beginning, the Arciconfraternità del SS Crocefisso, founded in the early sixteenth century and thus long before Neri's oratorian brotherhoods had catered for nobles, scholars and high-ranking clerics. No wonder, then, that Latin, which was still the language of the educated classes in seventeenth-century Rome, was preferred. Since the end of the 1630s, this oratory had provided lavish music for Good Friday services, especially a Latin *historia* (history) presented by a narrator, a choir and various soloists. A biblical text such as the story of Jephtha or Jonah was freely retold in prose and set to music in a manner close to opera. A history seldom lasted longer than 20 minutes, since, unlike Cavalieri's *Rappresentatione*, it had to fit in with the devotions, lessons and homilies. Domenico Mazzocchi's Latin dialogues, based on the New Testament stories of Lazarus, Joseph and Mary Magdalene, belong to the genre of oratorian devotions in SS Crocefisso, as do Marco Marazzoli's Latin oratorios.

The most important composer of such histories, however, was Giacomo Carissimi (1605–74).[25] Born near Rome, he became a teacher at the Collegio Germanico and *maestro di cappella* of the collegiate church of S Apollinare in 1629, and he held both posts until his death. Under his direction the music of the Jesuits in Rome reached a high point; inevitably, he neglected his real task, the musical education of the college students, for he engaged so many professional musicians for the performances, that there were several calls for him to be reprimanded. However, it was the college students themselves, mostly of German or Hungarian origin, who made Carissimi's works known beyond the borders of Italy. His European fame was enormous. His style differed from that of Luigi Rossi, who was only a few years older, in its greater uniformity of both form and mood; where Rossi sometimes alternated rather abruptly between sentimental and expressive sections, Carissimi composed great sweeping declamatory phrases full of dramatic pathos.

Even during the lifetime of Urban VIII, the oratories had always offered good music to pilgrims and to the Roman middle class, who were generally excluded from the palaces. During the reign of Innocent X, the oratories were even grander, for lack of competing musical events. The exile of the Barberini lasted for ten years; then, at the end of the reign of Innocent X, they returned to Rome and were reconciled with the Pope. Giulio Rospigliosi had come back from Rome shortly before, and in 1654, under the influence of the Spanish cloak-and-dagger play, he wrote the libretto of *Dal male il bene*, the wedding opera for Taddeo's son Maffeo Barberini and the

11. *Queen Christina riding into Rome, flanked by Cardinals Orsini and Costaguti on 23 December 1655 (the vignettes below show her meeting with the cardinals outside the Porta del Popolo, with the clergy of St Peter's outside the basilica and the Pope in consistory): etching by Oratio Marinari*

Pope's great-niece. In 1656 the Teatro Barberini had a final moment of glory. To welcome Queen Christina of Sweden, it mounted a performance of an allegorical and didactic opera entitled *La vita humana, ovvero Il trionfo della pietà*, whose subject resembled that of Cavalieri's *Rappresentatione*.

1656–89: QUEEN CHRISTINA OF SWEDEN

The conversion of Queen Christina of Sweden, who had abdicated in 1654 and embraced the Catholic faith in 1655, was an event of particular importance for the Curia, which had declined into political insignificance. It was a political and diplomatic success upon which the newly elected Pope Alexander VII could congratulate himself at the very beginning of his pontificate. The queen's arrival in Rome, astutely delayed until Carnival 1656, was celebrated with great pomp. The musical institutions of Rome vied with each other in festive productions. The Collegio Germanico gave performances of a *sacra rappresentazione, Il sacrificio d'Isaacco,* with its *intermedi, Giuditta;* the music was by Carissimi. In the oratories where Christina attended the Holy Week services, the celebrations were particularly magnificent; the palaces of the Roman nobility presented dramatic spectacles, with and without music, and there were ballets and banquets with musical accompaniment. However, the greatest attractions were to be found at the Palazzo Barberini, where Giulio Rospigliosi had yet another chance to display the breadth of his art: in the two operas *Dal male il bene* and *Le armi e gli amori* he offered the literary fruits of his years in Spain. The first of these was set to music by Antonio Maria Abbatini and Marco Marazzoli, the second by Marazzoli alone. The brilliant climax, however, was the performance of Rospigliosi's opera *La Vita humana,* with music by Marazzoli.[26] The final scene was a view of Rome with the Castel Sant'Angelo as the backdrop for a firework display given by the queen's hosts, the Barberini, to honour her and the city of Rome (fig. 12). Yet again, this opera dealt with the struggle between the powers of good (Innocence and Understanding) and evil (Guilt and Pleasure), with Vita (Life) almost crushed between them until finally the powers of good triumph.

With a few interruptions, Christina stayed in Rome until her death in 1689, her household becoming the centre of the city's intellectual and artistic life. Her patronage continued through four pontificates, so that the disruption created in Rome by the death of a pope was hardly felt in its musical life. Alexander VII (1655–66) and Clement IX (1666–8) certainly gave music far more support than Clement X (1669–76) and Innocent XI (1676–89), to whom opera was a particular thorn in the flesh. But even these two niggardly popes, with their hostility to the arts, could influence only public functions: the productions Christina presented in her palaces were beyond their control. Her fortune was by no means as large as the Barberini's, but she succeeded in continuing the tradition they had begun in a manner more suited to the times. In the Barberini era, opera in Rome had been a pleasure exclusively reserved for invited guests, nobles, and high-ranking ecclesiastics. Opera in Venice, however, had by now become a commercial enterprise; travelling operatic troupes were beginning to take Venetian operas all over Italy. The subjects of these works were neither sacred nor didactic, and the singers could lay no claim to membership of church choirs, especially as half of them were women. But these public performances opened up opera to those classes of society barred from such pleasures in Rome. By the early 1650s we find a mention of a performance in Rome of Cavalli's Venetian opera *Giasone,* which anyone with money could attend. When Rospigliosi was elected Pope in 1666 he tried to resist

12. Set for the final scene and firework display from Marazzoli's opera 'La Vita humana', performed in the Teatro Barberini, Rome, 31 January 1656: etching by G. B. Galestruzzi after Giovanni Francesco Grimaldi's design

this trend, and during Carnival 1668 he presented, in the theatre of his palace, *La comica del cielo*, which deals with the conversion of an actress to a life of pious asceticism; the music was by Abbatini. In accord with the changing times, he invited not only persons of rank but ordinary monks and nuns as well as the people. However, although this opera was a great success, even Rospigliosi could not halt the total secularization of opera. Queen Christina set up the first public opera house in Rome in 1671, the Teatro Tordinona, in which were presented not pious works but operas that had already been successful in Venice: Cavalli's *Scipione affricano*, Antonio Cesti's *Tito* and Antonio Sartorio's *Massenzio*, on subjects from Roman history but not of a kind that would serve as propaganda for the moral grandeur of Rome as Rospigliosi would have wished. Christina even ventured to allow women singers to perform, thus setting off a dispute that would preoccupy Rome up to the end of the century. Time and again new popes tried to call a halt to alleged immorality on the stage and in the boxes of the opera; but even in Rome such pleasures triumphed over the Curia's ideas of morality. In 1679, despite the protests of the Church, the second commercial opera house, the Teatro Capranica, was opened.

Besides supporting the opera, Christina also gave financial aid to the oratories and commissioned large-scale compositions. A fourth oratory had joined the three which were already of musical importance: the Oratorio dei Fiorentini,[27] for which Alessandro Stradella (1644–82) composed his most famous work, *S Giovanni Battista*, in the Holy Year of 1675. Stradella's works are typical of the development of Roman oratorio after Carissimi and Luigi Rossi; as well as narrative oratorios with a *testo* – the *historicus* or narrator of the Latin oratorios – Stradella also set librettos with dramatic action, differing from the operas of the time in that they represented stories from the Bible or the lives of the saints without these entanglements, disguises and sub-plots typical of Venetian opera. The fact that these oratorios were not staged forced Stradella to provide music which characterized the actors more strongly than would have been necessary in opera, with its stage effects. For instance, in *S Giovanni Battista*, Stradella provided Salome with dance rhythms in nearly all her arias, thus suggesting stage effects in the music.

13. Performance before a courtly audience: drawing by Pierre Paul Sevin (1650–1710)

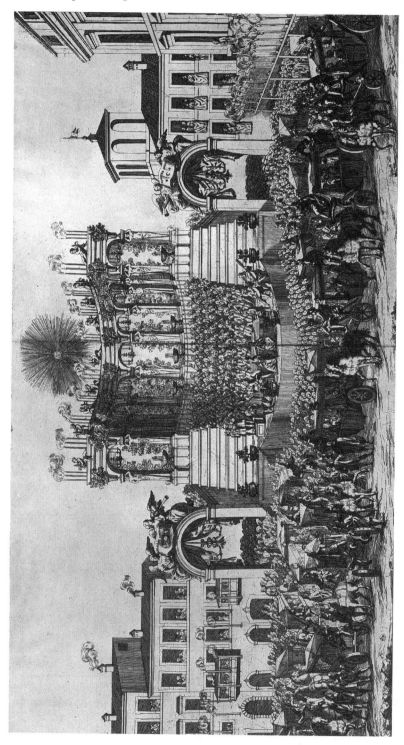

14. Serenata (*Applause musicale*) by Pasquini on a specially erected stage in the Piazza di Spagna, performed in celebration of the name-day of Maria Luisa Bourbon, Queen of Spain, August 1687 (the instrumentalists are probably under the direction of Corelli): engraving by Christopher Schor after his own design

Stradella was one of several Roman composers whom Christina sponsored. Scarcely six months after her arrival in 1656 and despite her growing dislike of the Jesuits, she made Carissimi musical director of her chamber; she took singing lessons from Loreto Vittori, who had performed in *La catena d'Adone* in 1626; she also patronized Bernardo Pasquini and Arcangelo Corelli and was one of the first to recognize the talent of the young Alessandro Scarlatti (1660–1725), whom she appointed her musical director in 1679. After her support for the eighteen-year-old Scarlatti's second opera, *Gli equivoci nel sembiante*, in that year, he composed a series of operas and cantatas for her until he left for Naples in 1683.

The private gatherings to which Christina regularly invited artists and scholars influenced more than just music history. It had been a long time since any Italian academy had provided a venue for discussion of contemporary issues of science and culture. In the time of Urban VIII, the scholars who met in the house of the Barberini concerned themselves chiefly with literature and music, in accordance with the tastes of the Pope and his nephews. Rospigliosi belonged to this circle, as did the classicist Giovanni Battista Doni, whose numerous writings in the 1630s on monody, Greek drama and modern dramatic music were a first attempt at reforming the young genre of opera. Doni's criticism was directed principally at the tendency towards a musically closed aria form, to the detriment of recitative declamation, which had been perceptible in Luigi Rossi's *Il palazzo incantato*. Such conservative criticism had in fact aroused defenders of the modern style of music, among them Vincenzo Giustiniani in his *Discorso sopra la musica* (1628) and Pietro della Valle, who defended those same little arias or entertaining canzonets condemned by Doni in his treatise *Della musica dell'età nostra che non è punto inferiore, anzi è migliore di quella dell'età passata* (1640).[28]

Yet Christina of Sweden, called 'the Pallas of the north' by her admirers, invited to her 'conversationi della Regina' not only musicians and men of letters but also archaeologists and classicists, mathematicians and alchemists. In 1674 these informal gatherings gave rise to the regular meetings of the Accademia Reale. According to the statutes of the newly founded academy, every meeting had to begin with an instrumental work and close with a vocal one. The part played by the Accademia Reale in the development of the cantata on the one hand and the concerto grosso and trio sonata on the other cannot be overestimated, for here was an audience which could take an active and critical part in the development of style. A great many of Scarlatti's early cantatas must have been composed for meetings of the academy. The fact that Corelli dedicated his op.1 trio sonatas (1681) to Christina leads one to suppose that these works too were written for the Accademia Reale. Its part in developing large-scale musical genres is clearly shown by the festivities Christina held in her palace to celebrate the accession to the English throne of the Catholic James II, though they took place two years after the event, when the English ambassador was staying in Rome in 1687. After a speech in honour of James II, a monumental work entitled *Applauso festivo* by Bernardo Pasquini was performed. According to contemporary accounts, it called for five soloists, a hundred choral singers, and an orchestra of 150 instrumentalists; Corelli directed the performance.

This 'Accademia solenne per festeggiare l'Assunzione al trono' was the last great event held in Christina's palace, for she died two years later at the age of 62. However, her influence on the cultural and intellectual life of Rome continued to be felt. In 1690 the Accademia Reale became the Accademia dell'Arcadia;[29] besides discussing many other matters, it again attempted to reform opera – not by criticizing the music, as Doni had done, but by urging reform of the libretto as a starting-point. The fact that Scarlatti and Corelli were later accepted as members of the Accademia dell'Arcadia shows the regard in which music was held by men of letters.

Rival patrons to Christina during the last decade of her life, Cardinals Benedetto Pamphili and Pietro Ottoboni, were to dominate the musical life of Rome at the end of the seventeenth century.[30] After Christina's death all the musicians whom she had sponsored moved to serve the two cardinals. Thus, whereas the flight of the Barberini from Rome had caused a painful break in the city's musical life, the continuity of musical activity was on this occasion ensured.

NOTES

[1] For the history of the papacy during the period discussed here, see L. von Pastor, *Geschichte der Päpste seit dem Ausgang des Mittelalters* (Freiburg, 9/1958–), vols. x–xiii.

[2] A basic work on the theatrical history of Rome in the seventeenth century is A. Ademollo, *I teatri di Roma nel secolo decimosettimo* (Rome, 1888).

[3] For an account, see R. Giazzotto, *Quattro secoli di storia dell'Accademia nazionale di S. Cecilia* (Milan, 1970).

[4] See especially H. Hucke, 'Die Besetzung von Sopran und Alt in der sixtinischen Kapelle', *Miscelánea en homenaje à Monseñor Higinio Anglés* (Barcelona, 1958), 379–96.

[5] See J. Roche, *Palestrina* (London, 1971).

[6] The significance of this stylistic development was already being emphasized by contemporaries: see, for example, Vincenzo Giustiniani in his *Discorso sopra la musica de' suoi tempi* (1628), in *Hercole Bottrigari, 'Il Desiderio . . .'; Vincenzo Giustiniani, 'Discorso sopra la musica'*, trans. C. MacClintock, MSD, ix (1962).

[7] Cf. S. Leopold, 'Madrigali sulle egloghe sdrucciole di Jacopo Sannazaro: struttura poetica e forma musicale, *RMI*, xiv (1979), 75–127.

[8] On Marenzio, see H. Engel, *Luca Marenzio* (Florence, 1956), and D. Arnold, *Marenzio* (London, 1965).

[9] For biographical information about Cavalieri, see W. Kirkendale, 'Emilio de' Cavalieri, a Roman Gentleman at the Florentine Court', *Quadrivium*, xii (1971), 9–21.

[10] See N. Pirrotta, 'Temperaments and Tendencies in the Florentine Camerata', *Music and Culture in Italy from the Middle Ages to the Baroque: a Collection of Essays* (Cambridge, Mass., 1984), 217–34.

[11] On Anerio, see H. E. Smither, *A History of the Oratorio*, i: *The Oratorio in the Baroque Era: Italy, Vienna, Paris* (Chapel Hill, 1977), 118–44.

[12] See T. D. Culley, *Jesuits and Music*, i: *A Study of the Musicians connected with the German College in Rome during the 17th Century and of their Activities in Northern Europe* (Rome, 1970).

[13] There is an account of *Eumelio* in A. A. Abert, *Claudio Monteverdi und das musikalische Drama* (Lippstadt, 1954), 164–7.

[14] Comprehensive source material on Stefano Landi may be found in Gerda Panofsky-Soergel, 'Nachträge zu Stefano Landis Biographie', *AnMc*, no.22 (1984), 69–129.

[15] Cf. D. J. Grout, 'The Chorus in the Early Opera', *Festschrift Friedrich Blume* (Kassel, 1963), 151–61.

[16] On the reception of Frescobaldi in the seventeenth century, see A. Silbiger, 'The Roman Frescobaldi Tradition c. 1640–1670', *JAMS*, xxxiii (1980), 42–87.

[17] Cf. T. Magnusson, *Rome in the Age of Bernini* (Stockholm, 1982–6).

[18] The operas to texts by Giulio Rospigliosi are extensively discussed in M. Murata, *Operas for the Papal Court* (Ann Arbor, 1981).

[19] Cf. the chapter on *Saint'Alessio* in S. Leopold, *Stefano Landi: Beiträge zur Biographie – Untersuchungen zur weltlichen und geistlichen Vokalmusik* (Hamburg, 1976), 278–309.

[20] Abert, op cit, 180.

[21] See A. Ghislanzoni, *Luigi Rossi* (Milan and Rome, 1954).

[22] See G. Masson, *Queen Christina* (London, 1968).

[23] See S. Leopold, booklet with the recording *Luigi Rossi, Canzonette amorose*, Deutsche Harmonia Mundi 1C 165–99 950/51 T (Freiburg, 1982).

[24] See F. Testi, *La musica italiana nel Seicento* (Milan, 1972), ii, 242–62.

[25] G. Dixon, *Carissimi* (Oxford, 1986).

[26] On the preparation and performance of *La Vita humana*, see W. Witzenmann, 'Die römische Barockoper *La Vita humana ovvero Il trionfo della pietà*', *AnMc*, no.15 (1975), 158–201.

[27] See A. Morelli, *Il tempio armonico: musica nell'oratorio dei Filippini in Roma (1575–1705)*, *AnMc*, no.27 (1991).

[28] Printed in A. Solerti, *Le origini del melodramma* (Turin, 1903), 148–79.

[29] *Tre secoli di storia dell'Arcadia*, ed. A. Greco (Rome, 1991).

[30] On cultural life in Rome at the end of the seventeenth century, see L. Montalto, *Un mecenate in Roma barocca: il cardinale Benedetto Pamphili (1653–1730)* (Florence, 1955).

BIBLIOGRAPHICAL NOTE

A general survey of the history of Rome is given in L. von Pastor, *Geschichte der Päpste seit dem Ausgang der Mittelalters* (Freiburg, 9/1958–60), encyclopaedic and still unsurpassed. Rome in the later seventeenth century is also vividly described in G. Masson, *Queen Christina* (London, 1968), and from the viewpoint of art history in T. Magnusson, *Rome in the Age of Bernini* (Stockholm, 1982–6). For up-to-date views of aspects of music in early seventeenth-century Rome, see L. Bianconi, *Music in the Seventeenth Century*, trans. D. Bryant (Cambridge, 1987), and T. Carter, *Music in Late Renaissance & Early Baroque Italy* (London, 1992). Musical life in Rome during the later seventeenth century is a focal point in L. Montalto, *Un mecenate in Roma barocca: il cardinale Benedetto Pamphili (1653–1730)* (Florence, 1955). At present the history of the papal choir of the Sistine Chapel is mainly to be found in monographs on individual musicians; on Palestrina, see J. Roche, *Palestrina* (London, 1971). Daily records of the choir are published in 'Das Diarium des sixtinischen Sängerkapelle in Rom für das Jahr 1596', ed. H.-W. Prey, *AnMc*, no. 22 (1984), 129–204 – a little before the period covered in this volume but useful nevertheless. The most up-to-date study of the Roman oratorio is contained in H. E. Smither, *A History of the Oratorio*, i: *The Oratorio in the Baroque Era: Italy, Vienna, Paris* (Chapel Hill, 1977). On the importance of the Jesuits, in particular the German College, to Roman musical life, see T. D. Culley, *Jesuits and Music*, i: *A Study of the Musicians connected with the German College in Rome during the 17th Century and of their Activities in Northern Europe* (Rome, 1971). Three of the most important oratorio composers of the seventeenth century are discussed in L. Bianchi, *Carissimi, Stradella, Scarlatti e l'oratorio musicale*, (Rome, 1969), and see also the short study by G. Dixon, *Carissimi* (Oxford, 1986).

F. Hammond gives a full account of the part played by the Barberini family in the musical life of Rome in two articles: 'Frescobaldi and a Decade of Music in Casa Barberini: 1634–1643', *AnMc*, no. 19 (1979), 94–124, and 'More on Music in Casa Barberini', *Studi musicali*, xiv (1985), 235–61. There has been much interest in opera in seventeenth-century Rome for over a century. Important recent studies include M. Murata, *Operas for the Papal Court* (Ann Arbor, 1981); A. Ghislanzoni, *Luigi Rossi* (Milan and Rome, 1954); S. Leopold, *Stefano Landi: Beiträge zur Biographie – Untersuchungen zur weltlichen und geistlichen Vokalmusik* (Hamburg, 1976); and W. Witzenmann, *Domenico Mazzocchi, 1592–1665: Dokumente und Interpretationen*, *AnMc*, no. 8 (1970) [whole vol.].

Chapter IV

Venice, 1580–1680

ELLEN ROSAND

The period of Venetian music history with which this essay is concerned falls neatly into two parts. The first, closely linked to the past, is dominated by music at the Basilica of St Mark's. The second, representing a fundamental change of focus, and very much looking to the future, is dominated by opera. These two formidable institutions, the one essentially sacred, the other secular, were quintessentially Venetian, helping to promote the reputation of the Serenissima at home and abroad.

ST MARK'S: INTRODUCTION

In 1581 Francesco Sansovino, son of the great sculptor and architect Jacopo, made his own monumental contribution to the mythology of the Venetian republic. The very title of his book *Venetia città nobilissima et singolare* (which enjoyed two major enlargements in the seventeenth century – in 1604 and 1663) confirmed an image of the city on the lagoon that would remain intact (though repeatedly or increasingly buffeted by destructive winds) until the very end of the eighteenth century, when the republic ceased to exist. The book was both a physical and a conceptual guide to the city, describing its monuments and its political and social institutions and customs. Present and past mingle in the narrative as Sansovino sought to enrich his portrait of the churches and palaces, the public and private buildings, by providing a sense of their function within both the Venetian political system and contemporary life.

Especially relevant for the present purpose is the peculiar interpenetration of the sacred and the secular that characterized the institutions and customs of the Serenissima. Since at least the eleventh century, religious feast days had been linked with significant events in Venetian political history, epitomized by the traditional identification of the Feast of the Ascension with the Marriage of Venice to the Sea. The tradition of such double celebrations was continually enriched, and three new feasts were added during the sixteenth century: Sta Marina, commemorating the recapture of Padua in

15. *Ducal procession ('andata in trionfo') into St Mark's: engraving from Giacomo Franco, 'Habiti d'huomini' (Venice, 1609). Following the standard bearers are six heralds playing trumpets, followed by the 'piffari' (the Doge's wind and brass players); the Doge can be seen, centre foreground, walking under his special gold-cloth umbrella*

1509; Sta Giustina, celebrating the victory at Lepanto in 1571; and the Festa del Redentore, in thanksgiving for the cessation of the plague of 1576. Several others were added in the seventeenth century, including the feast of Sta Maria della Salute (coinciding with the feast of the Presentation of the Virgin) to commemorate salvation from the plague of 1630. These annual ceremonies involved the entire city, and most included the full ducal procession, the *andata in trionfo*, which made its way through Venice to the church proper to the feast, ending up in the piazza before entering St Mark's.

Beyond these specially constituted historical–religious occasions, similarly elaborate celebrations also accompanied the highest holy days of the Roman rite, such as Christmas and Easter, as well as a number of days in the standard church calendar that had particular Venetian implications, notably those associated with St Mark and the Virgin Mary. By 1663 the number of such annual celebrations involving *trionfi* had reached 22 (Sansovino had originally listed fourteen). Added to these were the special events such as coronations, funerals, state visits and military victories, which likewise called for the display of the full panoply of Venetian celebratory resources.

MUSIC AT ST MARK'S

Of central importance on all these occasions was the musical establishment of the church at St Mark's. Distinguished from the cathedral of Venice (S Pietro in Castello, which was located in the easternmost part of the city), St Mark's was in essence the ducal chapel. It had its own liturgy, based on the Gradese rite, which differed from that of Rome in a number of particulars.[1] The connection between church and state is symbolized in the physical proximity of St Mark's to the ducal palace; the doge could enter the church through his private entrance, directly from the palace. And the significance of the connection is emphasized by the location of the two buildings in the Piazza S Marco, at the very centre of the city.

In the 1580s St Mark's chapel was enjoying the fruits of expansion and improvement that were the legacy of several doges. Gioseffo Zarlino, one of the most respected musicians in Europe, was in the final decade of his nearly 40-year tenure as *maestro di cappella*. Having succeeded two illustrious composers, Adrian Willaert and Cipriano de Rore, he was to be followed during the course of the seventeenth century by a number of renowned musicians, the most important of whom was Monteverdi. The organists serving under Zarlino were equally prominent: Claudio Merulo (1557–86), Andrea Gabrieli (1566–86) and his nephew Giovanni (1585–1612). And the chapel membership rolls included not only a standard complement of singers but instrumentalists as well.

The Early Baroque Era

The number of musicians employed at St Mark's had increased considerably since the fifteenth century, when eight regular singers apparently fulfilled all the necessary musical functions. By 1600 that number had risen to 30, and they were joined by six regular instrumentalists, who were supplemented by an additional fifteen or twenty, hired on an ad hoc basis for special occasions. By 1614 the regular, salaried orchestral ensemble was expanded to sixteen members.[2] This growth in the size and complexity of the performing forces, evidently a result of the increased number of occasions for which elaborate musical partipation was required, brought with it a corresponding expansion in the number of administrative positions: in 1557 a *maestro de' concerti* had been appointed to take charge of instrumental music (the position was taken by Giovanni Bassano in 1601) – he was also required to conduct from the organ loft where the instrumentalists were located, relaying the beat of the *maestro di cappella* from the floor of the basilica);[3] in 1588 the two organists, whose participation was established in the late fifteenth century, were joined by a third, who played a portative organ;[4] and in the late 1580s a *vice-maestro di cappella* was appointed to conduct the choir and to substitute for the *maestro* when he was absent.[5] Finally, in 1596, a *maestro di canto* was hired to take charge of teaching the boys.[6] These extra musicians were required not only to perform on an increased number of occasions but also to ensure an adequate supply of new music for these performances, for most of the administrators were also composers.

The publications of the composers at St Mark's during the late sixteenth and early seventeenth centuries illustrate the nature and variety of the music performed by the ducal chapel. For instance, the *Concerti di Andrea et di Gio: Gabrieli . . . libro primo et secondo* (Venice, 1587), in addition to several madrigals, contains a large number of motets, four mass movements and a *Magnificat*. The overwhelming predominance of motets over music for the Mass is characteristic of later Venetian publications as well: each of Giovanni Gabrieli's two main volumes, the *Sacrae symphoniae* (Venice, 1597) and *Symphoniae sacrae* (Venice, 1615) contains only a single set of mass movements but well over 40 motets. Moreover, Monteverdi's *Selva morale e spirituale* (Venice, 1640) contains, among its multiple sacred compositions, only one complete mass and two mass movements.[7] Cavalli published only one mass, in his *Musiche sacre* (Venice, 1656); and masses represent only a tiny fraction of Giovanni Rovetta's and Alessandro Grandi's sacred publications. These masses, moreover, frequently lack the Sanctus and Agnus Dei.[8] The preponderance of motets over masses in the published sources and the incidence of individual mass movements or incomplete masses suggest that in St Mark's services ceremonial aspects were emphasized at the expense of the traditional items of the Roman rite. This is confirmed by documentary evidence indicating that on special occasions elaborate motets – often called *concerti* – were used as liturgical substitutes for items of the Mass Proper at the Gradual, Offertory, Elevation and Communion.[9] For example, a mass for the investiture of a new Procurator is described as follows: '*Concerti* were sung by the church musicians at the Offertory as well as at the Elevation of the Most Holy Host and at Post-Communion'.[10]

Most Venetian motets of the time are quite elaborate, embodying the Venetian polychoral style with multiple choirs of voices and instruments – the so-called *cori spezzati*. Evidently the most splendid of them were designed to be performed on the major Venetian festivals that included *trionfi*, since their texts are taken from the liturgy for Christmas, Easter, Ascension, St Mark's Day and Corpus Christi. (Among its 40-odd motets, Giovanni Gabrieli's 1597 volume contains three different large-scale settings of the liturgy for the Feast of St Mark.) But the mass movements, too, were often also scored for multiple choirs and thus were probably also intended for special occasions rather than for everyday use. Andrea Gabrieli's sixteen-part Gloria, for example, may have been written for a special mass to celebrate the visit of the Japanese ambassadors in 1585.[11] And the Gloria and Credo in Monteverdi's *Selva morale*, scored for an ensemble containing four trombones ('trombe squarciate'), were probably written for the mass celebrating the founding of Sta Maria della Salute in 1631.[12]

The resources available – instrumental as well as vocal – and variety of occasions requiring elaborate ceremonial music encouraged composers to experiment with the polychoral style, with the number and make-up of the individual sound bodies and with their relationship to one another. Giovanni Gabrieli, in whose works the polychoral style reached its apogee, used two, three and even as many as four distinct groups comprising from two to eight voices and/or instruments in various combinations, most of them harmonically self-sufficient. Contrast between the groups, which alternated in dialogue, was variously heightened by means of tessitura (higher against lower groups), scoring (instruments against voices) and texture (solo against tutti). Gabrieli exploited such contrasts to enhance the structure and drama of the texts he set as well as to create dynamic, large-scale formal shapes, in some cases producing grand rondo-like structures in which full choral refrains recur between episodes for few voices or even one voice accompanied by basso continuo; *In ecclesiis* is a good example.

There were evidently some occasions for which simple pieces of the kind introduced in Lodovico Viadana's *Cento concerti ecclesiastici* (Venice, 1602), would have sufficed. Scored for solo voice and continuo, such motets appeared with increasing frequency during the early decades of the seventeenth century. Perhaps they were intended to be used at some of the less elaborate services at St Mark's for which the presence of the full choir was not required or else for services in churches that lacked large choirs. Nor did all the important St Mark's feasts require elaborate music. Some of them seem to have called specifically for music in an austere, almost retrospective, style. This is suggested by a special genre of Vespers publication, the so-called *Vespri delle cinque laudate* ('Vespers of the Five Laudate'), which were designed for the ceremony when the most important liturgical object in the church of St Mark's, the Pala d'Oro, was displayed. In settings by such diverse composers as Giovanni Croce (1597), Giovanni Rovetta (1662), Francesco Cavalli (1675), Natale Monferrato (1675) and Antonio Sartorio (1680) these psalms were uniformly scored for eight voices arranged in two four-part choirs with no solo writing, a style that evoked the venerated manner of Willaert's *salmi spezzati*.[13] Unlike the elaborate polychoral *concerti* of Gabrieli, in which the various groups were positioned far from one another, in the choir-lofts on either side of the nave and on the floor, the sound bouncing from side to side and from dome to dome of the ancient basilica, the more austere *salmi spezzati* emanated from a single place, usually the small pergola on the floor of the church known as the *biogonzo*, just in front of the main altar.

The publications of Venetian composers during the sixteenth and seventeenth centuries also included a large number of independent instrumental compositions such as canzonas, ricercares and toccatas for organ and, especially, for instrumental ensemble. These range from the organ *intavolature* of Claudio Merulo, Annibale Padovano, Andrea Gabrieli and others to the four-voice canzonas and ricercares of Giovanni Gabrieli and various four-, five-, and even six-part sonatas by Cavalli and Rovetta 'for every kind of instrument'. These works, too, formed part of the elaborate ceremonies, perhaps functioning as preludes or postludes, and must often also have been performed during processions. The dynamic variety and subtlety of a piece like Gabrieli's *Sonata pian e forte* indicates the state of development of these pieces. The function of independent instrumental music within the service was analogous to that of the motets. In addition to adding lustre to the occasions on which it was heard, such music often substituted for liturgical items.

The development of an elaborate instrumental group exploited the brilliant tradition of organ playing at St Mark's that went back to the late fifteenth century. Competition for the positions of first and second organists was keen and extremely taxing. Although the sixteenth-century organists left a large and important repertory of

16. Ceremony at the high altar of St Mark's, possibly the installation of a doge: painting (late 17th century) by an unknown artist (note the musicians in the balconies, which were probably only used on rare occasions)

music, including canzonas, ricercares and toccatas, it is clear from the requirements of the entrance examination for the position, and from various descriptions of organ playing at the basilica, that the St Mark's organists were remarkable above all for their skills of improvisation. Thus, it is likely that their publications represent only a fraction of the music they performed during the services. In any event, as well as alternating with the choir in individual items of various Offices, such as psalms, the *Magnificat*, the *Te Deum* and the hymn, independent organ music also functioned within the Mass. At least until the late sixteenth century, organ toccatas were heard during the Introit and at the Elevation, canzonas during the Gradual and Communion, and a ricercare at the Offertory. Eventually, many of these were replaced by music for instrumental ensemble, usually canzonas or sonatas.[14]

Much more was required of the St Mark's musicians than participation in services at the basilica. They were frequently called upon to perform at special occasions elsewhere: on the doge's ceremonial barge, the *bucintoro*, for example, particularly during the celebration of Ascension or on the occasion of a royal visit or at ceremonial dinners at the ducal palace. On these occasions they performed madrigals, such as those in Andrea Gabrieli's *Concerti* (for the visit of Archduke Karl of Carinthia to Venice in 1569), or what Monteverdi called 'cantatas' (in a letter of 21 April 1618).[15]

CHURCHES AND 'SCUOLE'

Although it was the leading musical institution in Venice during this period, the ducal chapel was not the only institution to employ musicians. According to visitors' reports, nearly every Venetian church – parish or monastic ('each with its fine organ') – employed an organist,[16] and the monastic churches at least employed *maestri di cappella*. Several of the most illustrious musicians at St Mark's began their careers as organists at smaller churches. Cavalli, Carlo Grossi and Massimiliano Neri, among others, served first at SS Giovanni e Paolo; and Pietro Andrea Ziani was employed at S Salvatore some 30 years before his appointment as organist of St Mark's in 1669. More often, however, these peripheral positions were filled by musicians already in the service of the ducal chapel, a state of affairs facilitated by the relatively few responsibilites of the church organist and the availability of a substitute at St Mark's. Such 'moonlighting' evidently proved a serious problem at St Mark's, however, for the Procurators instituted a number of measures designed to eliminate, or at least regulate, it.[17]

The monastic churches were occasionally the scene of elaborate special services, such as two notable ones at SS Giovanni e Paolo: a requiem mass for Cosimo II de' Medici in May 1621, to which Monteverdi contributed, and a celebration of the French Peace of the Pyrenees in 1659, for which Cavalli wrote a mass and a *Te Deum*. And a number of others were described by foreign visitors to Venice: in 1608, Jean-Baptiste Du Val, secretary to the French ambassador, observed a mass at the Frari in which 'the music was most satisfying and well done . . . accompanied by trombones, spinets, bass viols, violins, lutes, and shawms'.[18]

Aside from the ducal chapel, however, the most significant musical performances of the period took place at the six *scuole grandi*, the major confraternities of Venice. These charitable institutions, whose spectacular public image was mandated as well as strictly regulated by the state, used music to emphasize the splendour as well as the solemnity of a number of important occasions. According to the English traveller Thomas Coryat, 'their main halls were for devotion and religion, therin to laud and praise God and his Saints with Psalmes, Hymnes, spirituall song and melodious musicke upon certaine daies dedicated unto Saintes'.[19] Such occasions included the installation of officers and the governing board, the first Sunday of the month and Palm Sunday.[20] The other chief celebrations were their feast days. That of S Rocco was memorably described by Coryat in 1608:

> This feast consisted principally of Musicke, which was both vocall and instrumental, so good, and delectable, so rare, so admirable, so super-excellent, that it did even ravish and stupifie all those strangers that never heard the like. . . . Sometimes there sung sixteen or twenty men together, having their master or moderator to keepe them in order; and when they sang, the instrumentall musitians played also. Sometimes sixteene played together upon their instruments, ten Sagbuts, foure Cornetts, and two Viol-de-gambaes of a extraordinary greatness; sometimes tenne, six Sagbuts and foure Cornets; sometimes two, a Cornet and a treble violl. Of these treble viols I heard three severall there, whereof each was so good, especially one that I observed above the rest, that I never heard the like before. Those that played upon the treble viols, sung and played together, and sometimes two singular fellowes played together upon Theorboes, to which they sung also, who yeelded admirable sweet musicke, but so still that they could scarce be heard but by those that were very neare them. These two Theorbists concluded that nights music, which continued three whole hower at the least. For they beganne about five of the clocke, and ended not before eight. Also it continued as long in the morning: at every time that every severall musicke played, the Organs, whereof there are seven faire paire in that room, standing al in a rowe together, plaied with them. Of the singers there were three or foure so excellent that I think few or none in Christendome do excelle them, especially one, who had such a peerless and . . . supernaturall voice . . . that I think there was never a better singer in all the world. . . . I alwaies thought that he was a Eunuch, which if he had beene, it had taken away some part of my admiration, because they do most commonly sing passing well; but he was not, therefore it was much the more admirable. Againe it was the more worthy of admiration, because he was a middle-aged man, as about forty years old. . . . Truely, I thinke that had a Nightingale beene in the same roome, and contended with him for the superioritie, something perhaps he might excelle him, because God hath granted that little birdie such a privilege for the sweetnesse of his voice, as to none other; but I thinke he could not much. To conclude, I attribute so much to this rare fellow for his singing, that I thinke the country where he was borne, may be as proude for breeding so singular a person as Smyrna was of her Homer, Verona of her Cattullus, or Mantua of Virgil. But exceeding happy may that Citie or towne, or person bee that possesseth this miracle of nature.[21]

At about the same time, the celebration of the saint's day at another *scuola* attracted the attention of the Frenchman Du Val. He described the Vespers ceremony on the Feast of S Teodoro, which was celebrated at the neighbouring church of S Salvatore: 'A concert was performed by the best musicians there were, both singers and instrumentalists, primarily on six small organs, apart from the one belonging to the church itself, which is very good, and trombones or sackbuts, oboes, viols, violins, lutes, trumpets, recorders and flutes.'[22]

The most important civic function of the *scuole*, however, was their participation in processions – the ducal *trionfi* – for which they were all required to provide a company of singers and instrumentalists. In the last decades of the sixteenth century the government had sought to assure an equally high level of performance at all the *scuole* by assigning to each of them a specific group of St Mark's musicians. Baldassare Donato was to direct those at the Misericordia, S Marco and S Giovanni Evangelista; Giovanni Croce was responsible for the other three *scuole*, S Maria della Carità, S Rocco and S Teodoro. Furthermore, the St Mark's instrumentalists were divided into three companies each of which was responsible for playing at two *scuole*. These regulations gave way to greater freedom by the end of the century, with each *scuola* evidently making its own arrangements; each employed a choir of four or five singers, most from St Mark's, and an ensemble of five or six instrumentalists, including violinists.[23] No expense seems to have been spared in the attempt to attract the most illustrious musicians from St Mark's. Monteverdi reported that the *scuole* were so anxious to employ the *maestro di cappella* of St Mark's that they were willing to pay 'up to fifty ducats for two Vespers and a Mass', that is, an eighth of his entire yearly salary at St Mark's.[24]

Although the *scuole* seem to have maintained elaborate musical establishments into the seventeenth century – witness the descriptions quoted above – by 1622 signs of decline were apparent to the English traveller Sir Henry Wotton, who reported an amazing fact ('one great solecism'): 'a St Rocco's day uncelebrated with music'.[25] This decline certainly accelerated at the end of that decade and into the next, when the plague of 1630–31 took its toll on all the resources of Venice.

ORPHANAGE–CONSERVATORIES

Although the musical fame of the four so-called *ospedali* or orphanages (establishments for destitute or abandoned young women) reached its height only in the eighteenth century, some activity can be documented as early as Giovanni Gabrieli's time.[26] A few of them employed *maestri di musica* who later moved on to St Mark's; and their curricula must have included instrumental instruction, since several inventories of their holdings from the late seventeenth century list a variety of instruments. Music was certainly taught at the *ospedale* of the Mendicanti during the seventeenth century, where first Rovetta (from 1639), then Monferrato (from 1642) and later Giovanni Legrenzi (from 1676) served as *maestro di musica*.[27] At the Derelitti the list is even longer; it includes Donato, Bassano, Rovetta, Neri, Legrenzi and Grossi.[28]

By the mid seventeenth century, developments at St Mark's had begun to taper off. A decline in the quality of the music-making, which had begun even during Monteverdi's tenure, intensified in the years following his death. The focus of musical interest in Venice had shifted away from the state-sponsored civil ceremony centred around the Piazza S Marco to the widely dispersed opera houses. Travellers' reports were increasingly concerned with operatic productions. And the most important Venetian musicians, once closely linked to St Mark's, had become more and more involved in the burgeoning operatic industry. Composers and singers, and probably instrumentalists as well, now divided their time between chapel and theatre. Although the location may have shifted, music nevertheless continued to play a major role in the public image of the Republic.

OPERA: INTRODUCTION

The performance of *Andromeda* by Benedetto Ferrari and Francesco Manelli at the Teatro S Cassiano during Carnival 1637, before a paying audience, has been accorded almost mythic significance as the beginning of opera as we know it today. Although the importance of that moment cannot be overemphasized, it must be seen in context, as the result of developments that had begun much earlier. A long tradition of dramatic entertainments with music was firmly in place in Venice more than a century before the opening of the first opera house. These entertainments took place in three distinct, though often overlapping spheres, controlled, respectively, by the state (initially through the *Compagnie della calza*), by aristocratic *privati* (academies, the patrician élite) and by professional actors (the *comici dell'arte*).

PUBLIC ENTERTAINMENTS

The state entertainments – *rappresentazioni* or *favole pastorali* – which were usually designed to celebrate special occasions, such as the visit of a foreign dignitary, a military victory or a ducal coronation, had a clear political function. Encomiastic in character, they were marked by repeated reference to the glories of the Venetian republic presented in an allegorical or mythological context; and they were well documented through publication. Responsibility for whatever music they required generally devolved on the St Mark's musicians.[29]

Two of the best documented *rappresentazioni* were linked with the celebration of the victory at Lepanto in 1571 and the visit of Henri III of France in 1574. The first, a verse drama by Celio Magno entitled *Trionfo di Cristo per la vittoria contr'a' Turchi*, may have included music by Zarlino;[30] the second, a tragedy by Cornelio Frangipani, certainly included music – not only in the choruses but in the dialogue as well – by the then second organist of St Mark's, Claudio Merulo.[31] It was performed by the Gelosi, a troupe of professional actors.

Towards the end of the sixteenth century, such spectacles came to be performed regularly in the ducal palace on four of the most important feast days in the Venetian calendar: S Marco, Ascension/Marriage to the Sea, S Vito and S Stefano. The subjects of these spectacles were chosen for their general relevance to the rather abstract mythology of Venice as a haven of liberty and model of good government. Whatever music they required, none of it extant, was apparently provided by the current *maestro di cappella*.

Earlier in the sixteenth century, seasonal performances of another kind, at carnival had been prepared by special groups of young noblemen who operated under the direct supervision of the Council of Ten. These *compagnie della calza*, so called because they wore identifying hose, took complete charge of the entertainments, writing, producing and performing in them. Among the more than 40 such groups active between 1487 and 1565, most were dissolved after the single season for which they were constituted. In keeping with the raucous nature of the carnival celebrations, their productions were generally quite popular in appeal. The *compagnie della calza* sponsored performances of the comedies of Plautus and Terence as well as appearances in Venice of the popularizing actor and playwright Ruzante.[32] Although more varied in theme, geared to a broader audience and less overtly iconographic than the state-sponsored *rappresentazioni*, the productions of the *compagnie* nevertheless had a political purpose: a splendid, opulent carnival, attracting crowds of foreign visitors, was as important to the image of the Serenissima as the pomp and ceremony of the celebrations in St Mark's.

PRIVATE PATRONAGE

Not all theatrical activity in Venice was so overtly political or state-orientated. During the second half of the sixteenth century a number of theatrical endeavours were organized and supported by private academies of noblemen. While they resembled the *compagnie della calza* in several respects, such as their restricted membership – initially only patricians were admitted – the academies were more solidly founded institutions. Their theatrical activities, moreover, were not confined to the carnival season but took place all the year round. Audiences were primarily limited to the members themselves and thus represented a relatively narrow spectrum of society. As a result, their entertainments were on a generally higher level and included a preponderance of works in the classical genres, particularly tragedies, as well as tournaments and ballets of various kinds.[33] Like the *compagnie della calza*, the academicians not only organized their productions but often performed in them as well.

Surely the best-known academic production of the late sixteenth century that involved music took place in Vicenza, some 50 miles west of Venice. There, in 1585, under the auspices of the Accademia Olimpica, Palladio's great Teatro Olimpico was inaugurated by a performance of *Edipo tiranno*, an Italian translation of Sophocles by the academician Orsatto Giustiniani. As well as an instrumental prelude and an *intermedio*, the musical portion of the production included four choruses by Andrea Gabrieli.[34] The academy had intended to produce such entertainments regularly, for the benefit of a heterogeneous public, but their plans failed to materialize. Their subsequent productions were sporadic, their audiences remained restricted to the élite members of Vicentine society, and their music was limited to *intermedi* between the acts of spoken plays.

In Venice itself, however, the theatrical activity of the academies was much more consistent and regular; eight different academies combined to produce some seventeen plays between 1595 and 1634, many of them featuring musical *intermedi* and prologues. These entertainments were performed in the meeting rooms of the academies themselves, in the private palaces of individual members or in temporary theatres built for the occasion. Their staging was occasionally quite elaborate. Whatever music was included seems to have been provided by musicians from St Mark's. These academic performances shared many features, and even some personnel, with those sponsored by individual patrician families to celebrate private occasions, such as Monteverdi's *Combattimento di Tancredi e Clorinda* and *Proserpina rapita*, at the Palazzo Mocenigo in 1624 and 1630 respectively, the latter in honour of a Mocenigo wedding.

Several artists besides Monteverdi participated both in private entertainments and in opera, such as the poet Giulio Strozzi, author of the text of *Proserpina rapita*, and the painter Giuseppe Alabardi, who designed the scenes for *La Rosilda*, a tragedy produced in 1625 by the Accademia dei Sollevati, and *Proserpina rapita*, as well as for *La maga fulminata*, the second opera performed in Venice. And Felicita Ugo, who sang the prologue of an academic tragedy, *Solimano*, in 1634, became a well-known opera singer; she appeared in several works in the late 1630s, including *La maga fulminata*, and she eventually assumed an impresarial role within the society that was formed to produce operas at the Teatro S Cassiano from 1639 on. It is worth noting that the society was actually called an 'academia', though it was more a business association than a literary group. The most significant and influential connection between academy and opera, however, was forged somewhat later. In 1641 the Accademia degli Incogniti, probably the most powerful such group in Venice, assumed the management of an opera house.

THE 'COMICI DELL'ARTE'

Companies of professional actors, *comici dell'arte*, travelling up from the south, had performed regularly in Venice during Carnival, the period between S Stefano and Lent traditionally reserved for diverse popular entertainments; they also acted sporadically during the rest of the year. Opposed by the Jesuits and temporarily banned in 1581 (until after a papal interdict some 30 years later), these groups became increasingly active during the course of the century. As many as three different companies often appeared at the same time.[35] Although they were sometimes entrusted with state productions (such as Frangipane's tragedy performed by the Gelosi on the occasion of Henri III's visit), their repertory comprised mostly improvised plays with music, which they performed either out of doors in the *campi* (as illustrated by Giacomo Franco; fig. 17) or in temporary theatrical structures (as described by Coryat and Girolamo Priuli) built for the purpose, for which they sold tickets.[36]

At the end of the sixteenth century, two permanent theatres were built at S Cassiano for the sole purpose of hosting the *comici dell'arte*; one of them was to become the first public opera house. Their patrician proprietors, the Michiel and Tron families, contracted with individual troupes, the Gelosi and the Confidenti, providing a model for the first opera company. That company, a group of what might be called *musici dell'arte*, headed by Benedetto Ferrari and Francesco Manelli, signed a contract with the Tron brothers to produce an opera for Carnival 1637. Thus at the Tron theatre at S Cassiano, rebuilt after a fire in 1629 specifically to house 'opere in musica', was Venetian public opera born.

Unlike academic plays, which had considerable literary pretensions, the entertainments produced by the professional actors were designed to appeal to large, heterogeneous, paying crowds, rather than small groups of intellectuals. They were controlled by a well-established set of theatrical conventions – a scenario – within which the actors could improvise freely, each one playing his accustomed role or mask.

17. Comici dell'arte actors performing on an open-air stage in St Mark's Square: engraving from Giacomo Franco, 'Habiti d'huomini' (Venice, c1609)

All the earlier types of entertainment – the state-sponsored *rappresentazioni* and *favole pastorali*, the academic *favole pastorali* and tragedies with musical *intermedi* and, especially, the improvised scenarios of the *commedia dell'arte* troupes – left their mark on opera. Although all three types persisted for some time after the introduction of opera in Venice, their influence gradually diminished. But their most fundamental elements nourished the new genre.

What may be regarded as the final step in the establishment of opera took place in Padua in 1636 with a performance of *Ermiona*, a mythological pastoral with political allusions to Venice's mastery of the seas. Planned under patrician auspices (Pio Enea degli Obizzi) for a mixed audience of aristocrats, foreigners, citizens and students in a specially constructed theatre, it was performed by a travelling troupe from Rome augmented by some local musicians borrowed from St Mark's. This was basically the same company that signed the contract with the Tron brothers for Carnival of the following year.

The Early Baroque Era

OPERA

From shortly after 1637 until the end of the century, opera was the focus of Venetian cultural life. All the attention lavished on sixteenth-century ceremonial – the elaborate pageantry at St Mark's, the theatrical extravaganzas of the academies, even the popular frenzy of Carnival – became concentrated in the new genre.

Opera also demonstrated to the world at large the power and wealth of the Serenissima, even if that power was under siege. Its public function is made explicit in the remarks of a foreigner, the Florentine Francesco de' Pannocchieschi, coadjutor of the Papal nunzio in Venice from 1647 to 1652:

> What struck me most was to see how they lived in those days in Venice; how always full of riches and luxuries the city was, involved in almost continual festivities, public as well as private, which not only seemed inappropriate to a city fighting a war, but even for another quieter and more peaceful place would have seemed super-fluous. . . . And as for the theatres, or, as they call them, the 'opere in musica', they are presented in Venice in the fullest and most exquisite form, competing to make them ever more exceptional not only the industriousness of the people, but the resources of the city itself, from which it appears they [operas] originated, and, suffice it to say, that they do it more for business purposes than for entertainment.[37]

The influence of the state on opera was both metaphorical and practical. Many of the early operas drew their plots from the supposed pre-history of Venice, the Troy–Rome succession; and many of the early operatic prologues were delivered by mythological and allegorical figures familiar from the ducal *rappresentazioni*: Venus, Mars, Astrea, each important in Venetian iconography as representing, respectively, its birth from the sea, its military prowess and its personification of justice. The close connection between the State and operatic spectacle in these years is illustrated by the prologue to *Bellerofonte* (1642), in which the stage designs of Giacomo Torelli, the most important scenographer of the time, featured an image of Venice itself as background (fig. 18).

On a more practical level, the political connection was reinforced by co-operation between the ducal chapel and the theatres. The early opera companies borrowed singers from St Mark's, and later the chapel co-opted singers who had come to Venice specifically for opera. Claudio Monteverdi himself, as *maestro di cappella* of St Mark's, was a major operatic presence during the early 1640s; and several other important opera composers, including Cavalli, G. B. Volpe, P. A. Ziani and Antonio Sartorio, were employed mainly at the ducal chapel. Finally, direct government control of opera was exercised through the offices of the *Provveditori di Comune*, which supervised the inspection and licensing of theatres before productions could be advertised, determined opening and closing times and even regulated the price of the librettos sold at the door.[38]

Although the Venetian state stood behind opera in a myriad of specific, observable ways, it was the particular political structure of that state, the unique relationship between the public and private domains, between politics and economics, and the sharing of political power among a large group of patricians, that gave special impetus to the Venetian operatic venture. The new art form provided an ideal arena in which patrician families, competing for political and economic standing, could exploit the presence in Venice of a large, diverse audience, drawn to the city by the fame of its carnival celebrations and its reputation for freedom and excitement. This combination not only assured the success of the genre but deeply affected the very nature of the works themselves. The success of opera was virtually instantaneous. The pioneering Teatro S Cassiano, whose productions of *Andromeda* and *La maga fulminata* in successive years were highly publicized through the printing of their librettos, along with detailed descriptions of their staging, was joined in 1639 by two more theatres: the Teatro Giustinian at S Moisè, converted from a spoken theatre, and the Teatro Grimani at SS Giovanni e Paolo, also converted (actually rebuilt and moved) from brief use as a spoken theatre; and 1641 witnessed the opening of yet another house, the Novissimo, the first to be built expressly for opera. In 1642 alone these four theatres produced seven different operas.[39] Although Venice could boast seven opera houses by the end of the century, it was rare for more than four to operate at the same time; the more usual number, in fact, was two. Operatic activity thus practically reached its height within five years of its inception.

By 1640 the basic organization which characterized operatic production in Venice for the next two centuries was essentially in place: patrician proprietors, aided in the construction or refurbishing of their theatres by other noble families (who provided initial subscriptions for boxes, which they then rented on an annual basis), negotiated impresarial arrangements with individually constituted, self-sufficient companies. The original company of Ferrari and Manelli that had come to S Cassiano from Padua moved to SS Giovanni e Paolo after two seasons; it was replaced by the already mentioned 'accademia' headed by a composer (Cavalli), a poet (Persiani) and a singer (Felicita Ugo), formed for the express purpose of producing operas at S Cassiano. A third troupe, headed by Francesco Sacrati from Rome, was in charge of productions at the Novissimo. By producing one or two operas per season in competition with other

companies, these troupes were forced to fashion an entertainment that would sell tickets by appealling to the tastes of the unusually diverse Venetian audience. The productions also had to be portable, since these troupes, like the *commedia dell'arte*, regularly augmented their carnival earnings by travelling round Italy, producing operas wherever they were welcome. Travelling companies, bearing Venetian operatic wares, were a common phenomenon for several decades, until opera was accorded a permanent place in practically every Italian city.

Three phases of development can be distinguished for opera in Venice during the half-century under consideration here: (*i*) the establishment of conventions; (*ii*) the enthusiastic exploitation and extension of conventions; (*iii*) the period of decay.

(*i*) Between 1637 and *c*1650 the genre was established by the activity of two distinct but interactive groups. The initial efforts of professionals – Ferrari (poet, composer, theorbist) and Manelli (composer, singer), first at S Cassiano and then at SS Giovanni e Paolo – were exploited, and justified theoretically by a group of academic amateurs, members of the Accademia degli Incogniti. The activities of these academicians centred on the theatre they founded and ran, the Novissimo; but they were also involved in productions at SS Giovanni e Paolo. Among the Incogniti were the librettists Giulio Strozzi, Gian Francesco Busenello and Giacomo Badoaro, all of whom collaborated with Monteverdi.

Most of the composers active during these crucial years were novices who cut their teeth on the new genre. Only Monteverdi was an experienced composer of opera. In lending the enterprise his experience and prestige as Italy's leading musician, Monteverdi undoubtedly helped to ensure its success. In his two surviving Venetian operas, *Il ritorno d'Ulisse in patria* (1640) and *L'incoronazione di Poppea* (1643), he realized the full potential of his *seconda prattica*, bringing all his experience to bear in the musical imitation of words and in the portrayal of human characters in dramatic interaction with one another.

Yet Monteverdi's Venetian operas are exceptional. They alone among the operas of this period have earned a secure place in the canon; but rather than inaugurating a new tradition, they represent the culmination of Monteverdi's own personal development as a dramatist: they are magnificent peaks in the history of opera rather than the specific impetus for local developments. More important for the shaping of a new tradition were the works of Monteverdi's

18. Stage designs by Giacomo Torelli for the Prologue (above) and Act 2 scene iii (below; a deserted island, with the Temple of Venus in the sky) from Sacrati's opera 'Bellerofonte', first performed at the Teatro Novissimo, Venice, in 1642

19. Title-page (with a portrait of Monteverdi) of G. B. Marinoni's 'Fiori poetici', a collection of poetry and a eulogy published in Venice after the composer's death in 1644

younger colleague – and possible pupil – at St Mark's, Francesco Cavalli (1602–76). Of the 50-odd operas produced in Venice between 1637 and 1650 by more than a dozen composers and librettists, nearly a quarter (thirteen) were composed by Cavalli, most of them to librettos by Giovanni Faustini (1620–51).[40] These almost yearly collaborations between Cavalli and Faustini dominated the period and established the conventions of *dramma per musica*.

For the plots of his librettos Faustini generally eschewed the most common sources of his predecessors, namely, mythology and ancient history and Renaissance epic poetry. Relying instead on more overtly theatrical models, the pastoral and *commedia dell'arte*, he created a series of tragi-comedies of similar stamp – fourteen in all. *Ormindo* (S Cassiano, 1644) is a typical example. It is set in an exotic Near Eastern land, and its pseudo-historical plot is buttressed by elaborate inventions which follow the adventures of two pairs of nobly-born lovers (Erisbe and Ormindo, Sicle and Amida) attended by comic servants (the page Nerillo; the nurse Erinda; the maid Melide) who, through a series of complications and coincidences borrowed from classical comedy and the pastoral (disguises, sleeping potions, overheard conversations, mis-delivered letters), are separated and finally reunited.

Faustini's poetic language is as conventionalized as his plots, consisting primarily of *versi sciolti*, that is, irregularly rhymed verses of seven and eleven syllables, which are interrupted occasionally by groups of rhymed verses in various metres, often organized in multiple stanzas. To the composer, the *versi sciolti* generally signalled speech-like recitative and the rhymed verses lyrical aria, but Cavalli's settings, like Monteverdi's before him, are admirably flexible. His music, lyrical or dramatic, is more a response to the meaning than to the form of the text: not all the aria poetry is set lyrically, and many recitative lines are expanded musically for emphasis.

The wide social spectrum represented by Faustini's characters, the comfortable aura of spoken comedy exuded by his plots and the varied expressive range of Cavalli's musical settings evidently appealed to audiences from the beginning. A set of dramatic and musical conventions was quickly established: the love duet, the prison scene, the invocation, the lullaby, the lament. These conventions, keenly anticipated and therefore enjoyed even in the breach, became the norms of the genre after 1650.

(*ii*) The period *c*1650–70 is characterized both by the enthusiastic exploitation of the conventions established in the 1640s and by a growing sense of suffocation by the past. Several new theatres were opened, including the tiny S Apollinare in 1651 and the much more imposing and enduring Teatro Vendramin at S Salvatore, whose inauguration in 1661 initiated a decade of intense and extremely fruitful competition with SS Giovanni e Paolo. The period is spanned by the impresarial career of Marco Faustini, who, after his brother Giovanni's sudden death in 1651, assumed the management of S Apollinare; he moved to S Cassiano in the late 1650s but his career ended in failure at SS Giovanni e Paolo in 1668. As the first impresario in operatic history, Faustini was responsible for hiring librettists, composers, ballet masters and scene and costume designers, and for assembling casts.

With as many as six theatres running simultaneously, some of which mounted two new productions each season, there was both a demand for new works and a growing supply of old ones. This led to the exploitation of a widening array of sources for plots, new transformations of old sources, and reuse of old material – either disguised or not. Librettists now reached out beyond Greco-Roman history to exploit the exotic possibilities of the Orient. Once historically-based librettos became increasingly fictionalized, to the point where, in some works, all that remained of history was the characters' names.

Two librettists were pre-eminent: Nicolò Minato (*c*1630–98) and Aurelio Aureli (*c*1630–*c*1708), both of whom had begun their careers by collaborating with Cavalli. Cavalli had achieved international recognition, but by the late 1660s his style was patently old-fashioned, and he eventually yielded to the more melodious, less ascetic style of younger, more facile composers like Pietro Andrea Ziani (1616–84), Antonio Boretti (1620–73), Antonio Cesti (1623–69), Antonio Sartorio (1630–81) and Carlo Pallavicino (*d* 1688).

The more relaxed style was largely determined by the singers, who had gained prominence over all the other participants in operatic productions, a fact reflected by an astronomical rise in their salaries. There was a corresponding increase in the number of arias in the operas (from around twenty in *Ormindo* to at least twice that number in Ziani and Aureli's *Ercole e Deianira* of 1662, and a third as many again in Sartorio and Aureli's *Orfeo* of 1673). The elevation of the singers is signalled not only by the growing proportion of aria to recitative but in the placement, form and setting of the arias themselves. While most of the arias written during the 1640s are brief strophic refrain forms – each strophe forming a closed bipartite structure – and often occur at beginnings of scenes, the arias of the 1660s are generally longer, non-strophic and musically more expanded with enclosing refrains. These characteristics encouraged vocal ornamentation and elaboration. Arias now occur frequently at the ends of scenes and are followed by the exit of the character – thus encouraging applause.

Librettists, particularly Aureli, complained about the increasing demand for new works and the growing prominence of singers. They lamented the decline of aesthetic standards and justified aria-laden librettos as necessary responses to the demands of an ignorant and spoiled public obsessed with novelty and with the displays of favourite singers. Indeed, compared with the fluid unfolding of a work like Monteverdi's *Poppea* or Cavalli's *Ormindo*, many of the operas of the 1660s appear static and formulaic. Emotions that were once expressed in a wide variety of musical styles – from recitative to arioso, arietta or more elaborate musical shapes – are now more clearly channelled into recitatives of conversation and action and formal arias expressing emotion. These developments, which undermined the original Venetian musico-dramatic values, reached a climax during the third period, the 1670s.

(*iii*) In 1674 an event occurred that signalled the end of an era: the Teatro S Moisè, which had been closed for nearly 30 years, reopened under the management of a relative newcomer to the Venetian operatic scene, Francesco Santurini. In order to compete with the established, larger and better equipped theatres of SS Giovanni e Paolo and S Salvatore, Santurini reduced the price of admission, which had

20. *The Teatro Grimani a S Giovanni Grisostomo, built by Tomaso Bezzi for Giovanni Carlo and Vincenzo Grimani, and opened in 1678: engraving*

remained constant at 4 lire in all theatres since the 1640s, by more than 50 per cent to a quarter of a ducat (a ducat was worth 6 lire, 4 soldi). The other theatres were eventually forced to lower their prices as well. Cristoforo Ivanovich, the first historian of opera, regarded this as the final step in the decline of opera. By opening the theatres to the lower classes, operatic decorum, he argued, had been fatally undermined:

> The entrance fee, which is the basic source of profit, instead of increasing, is falling with obviously negative consequences, endangering the continuation of this most noble entertainment. The low price reduces the capital available to meet the considerable cost of display, facilitates the entry of ignorant and tumultuous crowds, and leads to the loss of decorum of that virtuous undertaking, which is conspicuous no less for the delight it causes than for the profit it earns.[41]

There was more concrete evidence of decay within the operas themselves, which Ivanovich also noted: a tendency towards obscenity in librettos of the 1670s and 1680s, Adriano Morselli's *Candaule* (1679) and Aureli's *Alcibiade* (1680) being typical examples; the departure from historical sources and extensive rewriting designed to provoke the audience's surprise and amusement; the loss in stature of historical heroes who were forced to undergo rapid emotional shifts dictated by their numerous arias (Orpheus shed his traditional identity as a mythical musician and became merely a jealous husband in Aureli's *Orfeo* of 1673); the absence of dramatic coherence caused by the wholesale transfer of arias from one opera to another; and the erosion of musico-dramatic language signalled by the use of arias for purposes served more naturally by recitative, such as conversation.

The need for reform articulated by Ivanovich culminated in significant stylistic changes towards the end of the century, spearheaded by the group of critics known as the Arcadians, who were based in Rome. But the issues had already crystallized in Venice with the opening of S Angelo and SS Giovanni Grisostomo in the late 1670s. These two theatres, the first 'new' opera houses to be built in Venice since the Novissimo nearly 50 years before, represented the two poles in the ever-increasing dichotomy between the original aesthetic aims of opera as *dramma per musica* and ever more decadent popular taste. The Teatro S Angelo, owned by the Marcello family, opened in 1677 under the stewardship of Santurini with his infamous admission policies. By contrast, the Teatro S Giovanni Grisostomo, the second Grimani theatre, which opened in 1678 (fig. 20), was built specifically as a place where high standards, and high prices, would be maintained. Here the burgeoning Arcadian values were aired for the first time early in the 1690s in works based on French models and in those by the renowned 'reformers' Apostolo Zeno and Domenico David.

Thus, the two great institutions of music in Venice had lost their momentum. St Mark's had ceased to be a creative musical centre by the middle of the century, although its influence gave rise to an important tradition of polyphonic music in Germany, which lasted well into the eighteenth century. Venetian opera likewise was further developed beyond the confines of the lagoon. The political and social conditions in Venice that had contributed to the establishment of opera there were not necessary for its continuation elsewhere. Thanks in part to the travelling troupes emanating from Venice, opera had become pan-Italian, even international. Nonetheless, Venice remained an important operatic capital, with more theatres than any other city in Europe. Thanks to the opera houses and the *ospedali*, with their instrumental music and oratorios, Venice retained its importance as a musical centre well into the eighteenth century and beyond.

NOTES

[1] The Gradese rite was also to be used in any church that the doge visited on a *trionfo*. For an outline of the differences, see J. H. Moore, 'The *Vespro delli cinque laudate* and the Role of *salmi spezzati* at St. Mark's', *JAMS*, xxxiv (1981), 255.

[2] See E. Selfridge-Field, *Venetian Instrumental Music from Gabrieli to Vivaldi* (Oxford, 1975), 15.

[3] See D. Bryant, 'The "Cori Spezzati" of St Mark's: Myth and Reality', *EMH*, i (1981), 182.

[4] There was a second portative organ, but a fourth official organist was not hired until 1645; see Selfridge-Field, op cit, 296.

[5] Baldassare Donato, by at least 1592, seems to have been the first *vice-maestro*, though the documents apparently do not award that honour until 1607, to Bartolomeo Morosini; see J. H. Moore, *Vespers at St. Mark's: Music of Alessandro Grandi, Giovanni Rovetta and Francesco Cavalli* (Ann Arbor, 1981), i, 109; and Selfridge-Field, op cit, 293.

[6] F. Caffi, *Storia della musica sacra nella già cappella ducale di S. Marco in Venezia (dal 1318 al 1797)* (1853); rev. E. Surian (Venice, 1987), 410.

[7] These were the *Messa a quattro voci* and the concertato Gloria and Credo; see J. H. Moore, '*Venezia favorita da Maria*: Music for the Madonna Nicopeia and Santa Maria della Salute', *JAMS*, xxxvii (1984), 328, 348.

[8] In 1623 it was observed that Venetian Sanctus and Agnus Dei movements were typically short, to provide time for a concerto at the Elevation and a sinfonia at Communion; see J. H. Moore, 'The Liturgical Use of the Organ in Seventeenth-Century Italy: New Documents, New Hypotheses', *Frescobaldi Studies*, ed. A. Silbiger (Durham, North Carolina, 1987), 367.

[9] Motets, organ music and instrumental music thus functioned similarly at St Mark's.

[10] See D. Bryant, 'Andrea Gabrieli e la "musica di stato" veneziano', *Andrea Gabrieli: 1585–1985* (Venice, 1985), 39, quoted from Sansovino, *Venetia città nobilissima et singolare* (Venice, enlarged 2/1604), 211–12.

[11] See D. Arnold, 'The Significance of Cori Spezzati', *ML*, xl (1959), 7; also Bryant, 'Andrea Gabrieli', 38–9, for a description of the mass quoted from Sansovino: 'cantata in quattro chori con quella solennità che si ricerca'.

[12] See Moore, '*Venezia favorita*', 342–8.

[13] The first double-choir settings of these psalms for Venice appeared in Croce's *Vespertina omnium solemnitatum psalmodia* (1597); see Moore, 'The *Vespro delli cinque laudate*', 252–3. There were many other double-choir vesper psalms that were not designed for the *Cinque laudate* service; see Bryant, 'The "Cori Spezzati"' 167–8, but even they called for at least one group of four singers against all the others.

[14] See S. Bonta, 'The Uses of the *Sonata da Chiesa*', *JAMS*, xxii (1969), 54–84; Selfridge-Field, *Venetian Instrumental Music*, 23, table; and Moore, 'The Liturgical Use of the Organ'.

[15] Gabrieli's madrigal was 'Felice Adria'. See I. Fenlon, '*In destructione Turcharum*: the Victory of Lepanto in Sixteenth-Century Music and Letters', *Andrea Gabrieli e il suo tempo*, ed. F. Degrada (Florence, 1987), 313. For Monteverdi's letter, see *The Letters of Claudio Monteverdi*, trans. and ed. D. Stevens (London, 1980), no. 29.

[16] According to T. Coryat – *Coryat's Crudities* (London, 1611), i, 426 – Venice had '143 paire of organs' at the end of the sixteenth century.

[17] See Moore, *Vespers at St. Mark's*, 75–80.

[18] See A. Pirro, 'La musique des italiens d'après les Remarques Trienniales de J. B. Duval (1607–1609)', *Mélanges offerts à M. Henry Lemonnier* (Paris, 1913), 180, reprinted in *Mélanges André Pirro*, ed. F. Lesure (Geneva, 1972), 81–91.

[19] Coryat, op cit, i, 370.

[20] See D. Arnold, 'Music at the Scuola di San Rocco', *ML*, xl (1959), 233, and J. Glixon, 'A Musicians' Union in Sixteenth-Century Venice', *JAMS*, xxxvi (1983), 392–421.

[21] Coryat, op cit, i, 389ff; quoted in Arnold, 'Music at the Scuola di San Rocco', 236–7.

[22] See D. Bryant, 'Alcune osservazioni preliminari sulle notizie musicali nelle relazioni degli ambasciatori stranieri a Venezia', *Andrea Gabrieli e il suo tempo*, 181–2.

[23] Glixon, 'A Musicians' Union'.

[24] Letter of 13 March 1620 to Alessandro Striggio in Mantua; *The Letters of Claudio Monteverdi*, no. 49.

[25] Quoted in Arnold, 'Musica at the Scuola di San Rocco', 240.

[26] The four were the Mendicanti and Derelitti, or Ospedaletto, both at SS Giovanni e Paolo; the Pietà; and the Incurabili.

[27] Oratorios were performed here by 1640; see Selfridge-Field, *Venetian Instrumental Music*, 45.

[28] See G. Ellero, J. Scarpa and M. C. Paolucci, *Arte e musica all'Ospedaletto: schede d'archivio sull'attività musicale degli ospedali dei Derelitti e dei Mendicanti di Venezia (sec. XVI–XVIII)* (Venice, 1978).

[29] For a catalogue of these celebrations, see A. Solerti, 'Le rappresentazioni musicali di Venezia dal 1571 al 1605', *RMI*, ix (1902), 503–58.

[30] Possibly not only the choruses were set to music; see A. L. Bellina and T. Walker, 'Il melodramma: poesia e musica nell'esperienza teatrale', *Dalla controriforma alla fine della repubblica: il Seicento*, Storia della cultura veneta, iv/1 (Vicenza, 1983), 409. For a full account of activities before the seventeenth century, see I. Fenlon, 'Venice: Theatre of the World', *The Renaissance: from the 1470s to the End of the 16th Century*, ed. idem, Man & Music (London, 1989), chap.III.

[31] According to the published description. On Lepanto, see Fenlon, '*In destructione Turcharum*', 293–318.

[32] See E. Muir, *Civic Ritual in Renaissance Venice* (Princeton, 1981), 171.

[33] See E. Povoledo, 'Una rappresentazione accademica a Venezia nel 1634', *Studi sul teatro veneto fra rinascimento ed età barocca*, ed. M. T. Muraro (Florence, 1971), 119–69; also idem, 'Scène et mise en scène à Venise: de la décadence des Compagnie de la Calza jusqu'à la représentation de l'*Andromeda* au théâtre de St-Cassian (1637)', *Renaissance, Maniérisme, Baroque: XI Stage international du CESR de Tours, 1968* (Paris, 1972), 87–99.

[34] Gabrieli's music for these choruses is published in L. Schrade, *La représentation d'Edipo Tiranno au Teatro Olimpico* (Paris, 1960). See N. Pirrotta, 'I cori per l'*Edipo Tiranno*', *Andrea Gabrieli e il suo tempo*, 272–93.

[35] See N. Mangini, *I teatri di Venezia* (Venice, 1971), 34.

[36] For Coryat's and Priuli's comments, see ibid, 34–5; one of the most frequently reprinted of Franco's illustrations, originally published in his *Habiti d'huomini et donne vinitiani* (Venice, 1610), can be found in C. Molinari, *La commedia dell'arte* (Milan, 1985), 78.

[37] 'Quello che più mi faceva restare attonito era il vedere come si vivesse in quel tempo in Venetia; come piena sempre di ricchezze e di lussi se ne stesse quella Città involta per lo più in continue feste si pubbliche come private, che non solamente pareva disconvenissero ad un paese che haveva all'hora la guerra, ma che ad ogn'altro più quieto etiandio e più pacifico haverebbero semprato superflue. . . . E quanto alli teatri, overo come essi dicono le Opere in musica, si rappresentano in Venetia in ogni più ampia et esquisita forma, concorrendo a renderli più riguardevoli, oltre l'industria della gente, l'opulenza del proprio Paese, d'onde pare che habbino tratto l'origine et ove parimente basterà di dire, che le si fanno quasi più per negotio che per trattenimento' (Pannochieschi, quoted in Mangini, *I teatri di Venezia*, 29–30).

[38] See C. Ivanovich, *Minerva al tavolino* (Venice, 1681), 405–7.

[39] See E. Rosand, *Opera in Seventeenth-Century Venice: the Creation of a Genre* (Berkeley and Los Angeles, 1991), Introduction.

[40] See T. Walker, 'Cavalli, Francesco', *Grove 6*, iv, 24–34.

[41] 'L'utile della porta, ch'è fondamento principale dell'interesse, in vece di crescere si và diminuendo con evidente pregiudizio, e pericolo di tralasciarsi la continuazione di questo nobilissimo trattenimento. Il poco prezzo lieva il modo alla spesa considerabile delle pompe, introduce più facilmente il Volgo ignorante, e tumultuario, e fà perder il decoro à quella Virtù, che comparisce non meno per diletto, che per profitto' (Ivanovich, *Minerva al tavolino*, 411–12).

BIBLIOGRAPHICAL NOTE

Historical background

Convenient surveys of Venetian history are offered in F. C. Lane, *Venice: a Maritime Republic* (Baltimore, 1973) – which, as its title suggests, views that history from an appropriately maritime perspective – and J. J. Norwich, *A History of Venice* (London, 1982), a more general and popular account. Specific studies of relevant aspects of that history are: W. J. Bouwsma, *Venice and the Defense of Republican Liberty: Renaissance Values in the Age of the Counter Reformation* (Berkeley and Los Angeles, 1968); B. Pullan, *Rich and Poor in Renaissance Venice* (Oxford, 1971), a pioneering study of the structure and role of the *scuole grandi*; and E. Muir, *Civic Ritual in Renaissance Venice* (Princeton, 1981), an excellent discussion of the pageantry of Venice. Particular aspects of the economic history of Venice are considered in *Crisis and Change in the Venetian Economy in the 16th and 17th Centuries*, ed. B. Pullan (London, 1968). O. Logan, *Culture and Society in Venice: 1470–1790* (London, 1972), offers a broad survey of aspects of

Venetian culture in their historical context; the richest consideration of the complexities of culture and society can be found in the various contributions to *Dalla controriforma alla fine della repubblica: il Seicento*, Storia della cultura veneta, iv/1 (Vicenza, 1983).

Visual arts

For developments in late Renaissance painting, see D. Rosand, *Painting in Cinquecento Venice: Titian, Veronese, Tintoretto* (New Haven and London, 1982), and, for the seventeenth century, R. Pallucchini, *La pittura veneziana del Seicento* (Milan, 1981). Architecture is best surveyed in D. Howard, *The Architectural History of Venice* (London, 1980). The iconography of the ducal palace is the subject of two important monographs: S. Sinding-Larsen, *Christ in the Council Hall: Studies in the Religious Iconography of the Venetian Republic* (Rome, 1974), and W. Wolters, *Der Bilderschmuck des Dogenpalastes: Untersuchungen zur Selbstdarstellung der Republik Venedig im 16. Jahrhundert* (Wiesbaden, 1983).

Literature

There is an unfortunate paucity of material in English on Venetian literature of this period. The most useful general survey in Italian is the essay by G. Getto, 'Letteratura e poesia', in *La civiltà veneziana nell'età barocca* (Florence, 1959). Several excellent essays in *Dalla controriforma alla fine della repubblica: il Seicento*, Storia della cultura veneta, iv, treat individual aspects of the literature in greater detail: M. L. Doglio, 'La letteratura ufficiale e l'oratoria celebrativa', F. Erspamer, 'Petrarchismo e manierismo nella lirica del secondo Cinquecento,' G. Baldassarri, '"Acutezza" and "ingegno": teoria e pratica del gusto barocco', and G. Auzzas, 'Le nuove esperienze della narrativa: il romanzo'. For dramatic literature in particular, see N. Mangini, 'La tragedia e la commedia', and E. Povoledo, 'I comici professionisti e la commedia dell'arte: caratteri, tecniche, fortuna', in the same volume. Two further essays by Povoledo provide important background concerning the pre-operatic theatrical tradition in Venice: 'Una rappresentazione accademica a Venezia nel 1634', *Studi sul teatro veneto fra rinascimento ed età barocca*, ed. M. T. Muraro (Florence, 1971), 119–69, which contains a chronological list of academic spectacles covering the period 1593–1642, and 'Scène et mise en scène à Venise: de la décadence des Compagnie de la Calza jusqu'à la représentation de l'*Andromeda* au théâtre de St-Cassian (1637)', *Renaissance, Maniérisme, Baroque: XI Stage international du CESR de Tours, 1968* (Paris, 1972), 87–99. The best survey of theatres is N. Mangini, *I teatri di Venezia* (Turin, 1971), which brings together much of the available documentation on their history.

Music

For a general discussion of the importance of music to the Venetian political image, see E. Rosand, 'Music in the Myth of Venice', *Renaissance Quarterly*, xxx (1977), 511–37. The classic survey of music at St Mark's is F. Caffi, *Storia della musica sacra nella già cappella ducale di S. Marco in Venezia (dal 1318 al 1797)* (1853), rev. E. Surian (Venice, 1987). Two recent scholars have made particularly important contributions to an understanding of music at St Mark's: J. H. Moore, in a book, *Vespers at St. Mark's: Music of Alessandro Grandi, Giovanni Rovetta and Francesco Cavalli* (Ann Arbor, 1981), and three articles, 'The *Vespro delli cinque laudate* and the Role of *salmi spezzati* at St. Mark's', *JAMS*, xxxiv (1981), 249–78, '*Venezia favorita da Maria*: Music for the Madonna Nicopeia and Santa Maria della Salute', ibid, xxxvii (1984), 299–355 and 'The Liturgical Use of the Organ in Seventeenth-Century Italy: New Documents, New Hypotheses', *Frescobaldi Studies*, ed. A. Silbiger (Durham, North Carolina,

1987), 351–83; and D. Bryant in, among other articles, 'The "Cori Spezzati" of St Mark's: Myth and Reality', *EMH*, i (1981), 165–88. D. Arnold's numerous studies of music in Venice cover a wide variety of important topics, in particular the *scuole* ('Music at the Scuola di San Rocco', *ML*, xl (1959), 229–41), the two Gabrielis (*Giovanni Gabrieli and the Music of the Venetian High Renaissance* (London, 1979)) and some of their successors at St Mark's, including Monteverdi (*Monteverdi* (London, rev. 3/1990 by T. Carter)). More recently, music at the *scuole* has been exhaustively treated by J. Glixon in, among other articles, 'A Musicians' Union in Sixteenth-Century Venice', *JAMS*, xxxvi (1983), 392–421. The most recent and useful survey of music at the *ospedali* is a catalogue: G. Ellero, J. Scarpa and M. C. Paolucci, *Arte e musica all'Ospedaletto: schede d'archivio sull'attività musicale degli ospedali dei Derelitti e dei Mendicanti di Venezia (sec. XVI–XVIII)* (Venice, 1978). Much information on music at St Mark's as well as at the other institutions is also found in E. Selfridge-Field's important book *Venetian Instrumental Music from Gabrieli to Vivaldi* (Oxford, 1975). Two of the most interesting recent books on Monteverdi are P. Fabbri, *Monteverdi* (Turin, 1985), and G. Tomlinson, *Monteverdi and the End of the Renaissance* (Berkeley and Los Angeles, 1986).

The most comprehensive study of opera is E. Rosand, *Opera in Seventeenth-Century Venice: the Creation of a Genre* (Berkeley and Los Angeles, 1991). Excellent briefer treatments of the material may be found in L. Bianconi, *Music in the Seventeenth Century*, trans. D. Bryant (Cambridge, 1987), and A. L. Bellina and T. Walker, 'Il melodramma: poesia e musica nell'esperienza teatrale', *Dalla controriforma alla fine della repubblica: il Seicento*, Storia della cultura veneta, iv/1 (Vicenza, 1983). An important socio-historical study that compares opera in Venice with that in two other, different social contexts is L. Bianconi and T. Walker, 'Production, Consumption and Political Function of Seventeenth-Century Opera', *EMH*, iv (1984), 209–96. The best book on Venetian scenography is P. Bjurström, *Giacomo Torelli and Baroque Stage Design* (Stockholm, 1961). Venetian opera is the subject of important articles by N. Pirrotta in *Music and Culture in Italy from the Middle Ages to the Baroque: a Collection of Essays* (Cambridge, Mass., 1984): 'Monteverdi and the Problems of Opera', 'The Lame Horse and the Coachman' and '*Commedia dell'arte* and Opera'. Another of his major contributions to the field, 'Early Opera and Aria', first published as an article in 1968, was revised and published as Chapter 6 of N. Pirrotta and E. Povoledo, *Music and Theatre from Poliziano to Monteverdi*, trans. K. Eales (Cambridge, 1982).

Facsimiles of a representative sample of Venetian opera scores and librettos may be found in two series: *Italian Opera: 1640–1770*, ed. H. M. Brown (New York, 1978–82); and *Drammaturgia musicale veneta* (Milan, various dates).

Chapter V

Bologna, 1580–1700

ANNE SCHNOEBELEN

The city of Bologna experienced its golden age of music in the seventeenth century. Under its distinctive arcades and in its sumptuous palaces and churches a lively, innovative musical culture suddenly sprang up. Imaginative composers and skilful performers were drawn to its celebrated musical institutions, and influential new musical ideas appeared. Nurtured by its vigorous artistic and intellectual spirit, which dates from the founding of its famous university, Bologna emerged as one of Italy's most important musical centres, along with Venice and Rome.

In the late Renaissance, Bologna as the 'second city' of the Papal States was rich and populous. Its economic power resulted from its position as an agricultural and commercial centre at the edge of the fertile plain of the Po. Thriving silk mills and dyers made it a significant industrial city too. In the early decades of the seventeenth century, however, great changes occurred in Italy's economy.[1] As already mentioned in Chapter II, foreign competition and the ravages of war brought economic disaster to its urban centres. The silk industry declined severely at Bologna, as at Venice, Florence and Como.[2] In addition, unfavourable climatic conditions produced two great cycles of drought and disastrous harvests. Grain prices rocketed, as health suffered and disease spread. Plague in 1630 reduced Bologna's population from 67 000 to 50 000. The disastrous effects of the Thirty Years War, the collapse of the Spanish Empire and the aggressive mercantile policies of France continued to affect urban economies adversely throughout the century. As a papal city, Bologna also felt the declining power of the Church. With the decrease of Spain's political and military power, the traditional axis of Spain and Rome was clearly crumbling. By an intimidating use of force, France gravely damaged Rome's prestige. The venality of the popes and curia only increased the already bleak conditions in the Papal States.

In spite of these events, however, Bologna maintained an active cultural life. The visual arts flourished with the followers of the celebrated Carracci, Guercino and Guido Reni.[3] And in the middle of the century, the city was to reach the apogee of its musical life. What particular factors, then, enabled the Bolognese to thrive in these adverse circumstances?

An explanation may be found in the character of Bolognese political life, in its intellectual traditions and in the institutions, both religious and secular, that shaped its cultural life in the seventeenth century. Politically, Bologna nurtured a fierce spirit of independence, stemming from 1228, when it declared itself a free commune and created a form of senate to govern itself. Under papal rule, it managed to maintain a unique duality of governance by both senate and papal legate. Renaissance popes and their successors recognized that the only practical way to rule Bologna was to placate its noble senatorial families. Such an uneasy alliance, the balance changing with each pope, resulted in a vigorous civic pride, always jealous of their prerogatives of self-government. Bologna's relative inaccessibility from Rome only served to heighten its sense of independence.

Papal authority in Bologna was personified in the cardinal legate and his vice-legate. Both lived in richly decorated apartments in the Palazzo Pubblico, a symbol of Rome's presence in civic as well as church affairs. Local government was administered by the senate in a type of republic. Nine senators, called Anziani della Signoria, were chosen from the Bolognese aristocracy for a two-month term. As chief executive, the cardinal legate frequently engaged in a more or less subterranean conflict with the Anziani. Though papal rule weakened their power, the Anziani still exercised a dynamic role in civic affairs and in relations with the various dukes of the region. Their attitudes were notably supple, which helped to maintain their delicate position within the territory of a declining papal power.[4]

The ecclesiastical/secular duality that marked government also characterized the patronage of its culture. Though the Church was a major supporter of the arts, it was not the only one. There was no court, and patronage was divided among the many families who shared in the government of the city. Bologna's cultural life did not bend to the taste of the reigning pope, nor to that of a single ducal family. Rather, it thrived on the healthy rivalry among its nobility, its professional and merchant families and the legate himself. Families and individuals – the Albergati, Aldrovandi, Ercolani, Ghisilieri, Pepoli and others – competed in building palaces and theatres and in providing sumptuous entertainments. They sponsored performances of dramas, comedies, operas and oratorios, both public and private. The proliferation of rival households vying for pre-eminence provided frequent employment for many musicians. These families were also the collectors of contemporary Bolognese paintings, and under their auspices, academies were founded to stimulate enlightened discussions. Bologna's independent spirit was kept alive by the presence of its university, already prestigious in the twelfth century. The influx of students and teachers brought an international character to the city and encouraged a lively exchange of ideas. Its intellectual reputation as the mythic Alma Mater Studiorum, lasted into the seventeenth century, especially in the natural sciences.

Yet another source of energy in Bologna was its vigorous religious institutions. By 1700 the city could boast nearly 150 churches, numerous monasteries and convents, and several confraternities of lay persons. Major religious orders – Dominicans, Franciscans and Jesuits – formed musical organizations and built churches and libraries, decorating them with commissioned art-works and thus giving employment to artists and musicians.

This duality of sacred and secular, ecclesiastical and civic, is vividly represented in the historic centre of the city. Its two famous leaning towers, survivors of the many noted by Dante in the *Divine Comedy*, memorialize the fierce rivalries among medieval noble families. Surrounding the Piazza Maggiore, Bologna's central square, are handsome civic buildings dominated by the imposing church of S Petronio, itself a joint symbol of civic and religious pride. Begun in 1390, it was intended to be one of the largest churches in Italy.

21. *Festival of S Petronio in the Piazza Maggiore, Bologna in 1701: miniature from 'Le insignia degli Anziani del comune', xi (1696–1710)*

The Early Baroque Era

Though later plans included transepts equal to the length of the nave and a grandiose cupola, they were never built. The church remains a magnificent Italian Gothic nave, its façade never completed, and only in the 1660s was the apse enclosed (*see* fig. 22 below). The architecture and acoustics of S Petronio undoubtedly affected the evolution of Bolognese instrumental forms, as will be seen later. Unusual if not unique in Church history, the affairs of the basilica were governed by a vestry-board of lay persons who were also members of the Anziani.

Ecclesiastical and civic authorities came together in the yearly celebration of the name-day of St Petronius on 4 October. Account books reveal the importance of the occasion. The vestry-board spent large amounts of money on silk and taffeta hangings, commissioned special music for Mass and Vespers, and hired extra musicians. Trumpets and trombones accompanied processions in the piazza (fig. 21). Special platforms were built for the musicians and extra organs were moved in.[5] The cardinal legate officiated at Mass and Vespers in splendid vestments, his authority underlined by the solemn and joyous music that accompanied the ritual. From the piazza originated two of Bologna's major institutions: the civic wind band, called the Concerto Palatino della Signoria, and the *cappella musicale* of S Petronio. Both served their respective sponsors as important symbols of power and prestige in distressed times for city and papacy.

The Concerto Palatino, documented as early as 1250,[6] had a nucleus of eight trumpeters, to which trombones, fifes, timpani, lutes and harps were eventually added. The group provided ceremonial music for public occasions, often from balconies on the central square, and at Mass in the basilica on principal feasts. It also played an important role in such popular events as the Festa della Porchetta, when a suckling-pig was thrown down to the crowd from a balcony on the Piazza Maggiore to celebrate the taking of Faenza by the Bolognese in 1228, an incident initiated by the theft of a pig. In 1627 the Anziani, wishing to give particular lustre to this celebration, commissioned the esteemed leader of the Concerto Palatino, Camillo Cortellini, to compose canzonettas and instrumental dances. Cortellini fitted the pieces of music into a set of 'azioni' – five separate scenes reflecting Bolognese life, which included singing, dancing, and actions symbolic of the ideal relationship of citizens and government, each ending with the distribution of food, wine and gifts to the populace.[7]

The *cappella musicale* of S Petronio was founded by Pope Eugene IV in 1426 as a school of singing. Gradually professional musicians, both singers and instrumentalists, entered the group, and the *cappella* separated from the school. By 1600 there were 36 singers, and the instrumental ensemble in 1610 consisted of seven trombones, two cornetts and one violin. Strings gradually became a regular part of the ensemble: violins, alto and tenor viols, theorbos, and various sizes of bass viols and violoncellos.

Like the basilica itself, the *cappella musicale* inspired immense pride in Bologna's citizens. Early in 1696, however, it entered a period of crisis, both financial and artistic. The vestry-board disbanded the regular musical organization, retaining only the *maestro*, his assistant and two organists, and liturgical singing was carried on by the beneficed priests and by other musicians hired only for special occasions. The dissolution of the *cappella* was significant in that, with many musicians forced to seek employment elsewhere, the Bolognese style was transmitted throughout northern Italy and across the Alps. Only in 1701 did the vestry-board restore the *cappella musicale*, returning it, in the words of a contemporary chronicle, to 'its pristine dignity and its splendid primacy'.[8]

Perhaps the most influential of Bologna's musical institutions was a third professional body, the Accademia Filarmonica, formed in 1666 by Count Vincenzo Maria Carrati. It was the most important of several such academies established during the century. The first of these to include professional musicians was the Accademia dei Floridi, founded in 1615 by the Olivetan monk and composer Adriano Banchieri. Its frequent concerts gave opportunity for performances of members' compositions. Among its distinguished visitors was Claudio Monteverdi in 1620. From 1622 to 1628 the group, renamed the Accademia dei Filomusi, met in the house of Girolamo Giacobbi, *maestro di cappella* at S Petronio. In 1633 another group was to emerge, the Accademia dei Filaschisi, which prospered for more than three decades.

The Accademia Filarmonica brought together as charter members 50 of the city's most prestigious composers, instrumentalists and singers. Through its stringent entrance requirements and its weekly meetings at which music was played, the academy fostered a high level of performance. Twice-weekly lessons in composition elevated the contrapuntal skills of its composers. Its compositional ideals always remained conservative, focussing largely on vocal polyphony. A powerful president, who served a one-year term, and a pair of censors elected from the membership approved the compositions to be performed and judged their adherence to the academy's traditional standards. They exercised a decisive role in determining taste and in codifying a uniform musical style among Bolognese musicians. Even though the academy's compositional ideals were conservative, its pragmatic modern ways of applying traditional rules encouraged both solid craftsmanship and remarkable inventiveness. As its prestige grew, and benefited from the financial support of the city fathers, virtually all the professional musicians in Bologna became members.[9]

In 1657 an event occurred that was to prove of central musical importance in Bologna: the election of Maurizio Cazzati (*c*1620–76) as *maestro di cappella* of S Petronio. Throughout his fourteen-year tenure Cazzati was a pivotal figure. Despite hostility from within, he reformed the regular *cappella musicale*, issuing rules that governed both the duties and the conduct of its members. He increased the number and quality of performers for the patronal feast, bringing in excellent instrumentalists as well as singers, made important innovations in sacred music and in the genre of the instrumental sonata, and introduced to S Petronio its distinctive repertory of music for trumpet and strings. Often at the centre of controversy, he is significantly absent from the roster of the Accademia Filarmonica. Possibly because of conflicts within the musical community, he was dismissed from S Petronio in 1671.[10]

Shortly after Cazzati's arrival, a musical polemic erupted over one of his published compositions. One of a series of such debates from the fifteenth century onwards, the dispute illuminates the traditionally practical side of Bolognese music theory. To appreciate its significance, it might be useful to examine the famous polemic between Giovanni Maria Artusi and Claudio Monteverdi around 1600. Artusi, a canon at S Salvatore, Bologna, strongly defended the traditional rules of counterpoint while criticizing some of Monteverdi's madrigals. The ensuing controversy highlighted the generational differences between the followers of the *prima prattica*, rules and standards set by Gioseffo Zarlino and practised by most late Renaissance composers and the adherents of a freer use of dissonance championed by Monteverdi. Such innovations as the combination of voices and instruments in the concerted style of church music, ornamented singing and the use of dance rhythms were viewed by Artusi as encroachments on the art of composition, practised by unskilled composers. The polemic forced Monteverdi, through the pen of his brother Giulio Cesare, to enunciate the tenets of the new or second practice. Though Artusi represented the traditional ideals, he was not the arch-conservative he was once thought to be. An eminent theorist, his own writings advocated the importance of dissonance in composition, relaxing what he saw as unnecessarily strict rules. He was also among the early supporters of equal temperament as a standard tuning of keyboard instruments. His attitude towards counterpoint, fixed in traditional principles but not unyielding, was reaffirmed later in the century by the composers of the Accademia Filarmonica.[11]

The same pragmatic attitudes inform the theoretical writings of the Bolognese composer Adriano Banchieri (1568–1634). A lively figure, he was active in many different areas: theatre, academies, church music, theory and composition. Fully cognizant of the old style, he was at the same time favourably disposed towards new ideas. Above all he was interested in the practical: his music was among the earliest to be published with a printed organ bass and the dynamic indications *piano* and *forte*; and what may be the earliest instructions for organ registration appear in his *L'organo suonarino* (2nd edn, 1611). Most important for this discussion is his approach to the teaching of the modes and *tuoni* (psalm tones), set forth in *L'organo suonarino* and in the *Cartella musicale* of 1611. Rather than defining them traditionally by ranges and octave species (scales), he codifies them in terms of their finals and alternative cadential notes. He writes that the modes are to be used in compositions (including concerted works for voices and instruments) 'which have nothing to do with plainchant'. He acknowledges the difficulty in preserving the ancient monophonic psalm tones in polyphonic music and established a new set of *tuoni* to meet contemporary performance requirements.[12] Banchieri intensified the central theoretical problems of the seventeenth century: how to grapple with the confused state of the traditional modal system, and how to reconcile it with the growing tendency towards major-minor tonality permeating modern compositions. These same concerns are still reflected in the Cazzati controversy, which began in 1659.

The debate revolved around a mass Cazzati published in 1655, two years before he arrived at S Petronio. Written for full choir without soloists, it was nominally in the archaic *a cappella* style – ostensibly in imitation of Palestrina. The work was severely criticized by Lorenzo Perti, a beneficed priest at S Petronio, and by Giulio Cesare Arresti, organist at the basilica. They attacked Cazzati's contrapuntal technique, which, because of his modern reinterpretation of the traditional modal system, was more suited to the *seconda prattica*. However, while Perti demanded strict adherence to the old rules, Arresti, by far the more influential of the two, allowed some practical modifications. While the details of the controversy are too complex to be examined here, it is significant that Arresti, a charter member and later president of the Accademia Filarmonica, represented the mainstream of Bolognese theoretical thinking – a conservative pragmatism soon to be reflected in the academy.

One of the most interesting terms which surfaced in the controversy is 'harmonic tones', which seems to indicate an undefined but clearly understood concept of the modes acceptable for use in *a cappella* composition. These modes, or tones, differed from those defined by Zarlino but had strong connections with those described by Banchieri and in later treatises by Lorenzo Penna and Giovanni Maria Bononcini (both members of the Accademia Filarmonica).

Perhaps the most significant characteristic of these modes is the emphasis on the first, third and fifth notes, making in modern terms a complete tonic triad. When used in a polyphonic composition, initial entries of fugal subjects had to begin on either the first or fifth note of the mode, and all important sections must finish on one of these two notes. As a result, a strong sense of tonality was affirmed within the contrapuntal structure. Furthermore, a system of both real and tonal answers to fugue subjects was recognized. Implicit in this discussion of the rules of imitation in the 'harmonic tones' are the basic principles of the mature Baroque fugue.[13]

Such modern concepts, seemingly well understood by Accademia composers, were essential to the rapid rise of Bolognese instrumental music in the 1660s. Elegant counterpoint and secure tonality characterize many movements of the string sonatas by the Bolognese school. Its composers were leaders in the establishment of major-minor tonality as an architectural resource, especially in concerto form. In the development of the mature Bolognese sonata, Cazzati served as a transitional figure as the influence of the prevailing Venetian style weakened. Starting from the ensemble canzona, a multi-sectional form based on vocal models, he expanded its sections into fast imitative movements, dances in triple metre, and slow chordal movements as introductions or transitions. He was among the earliest composers to use tonal answers in his imitative movements. He introduced to Bologna the sonata for solo violin, accompanied by harpsichord and violone. His trio sonatas are cohesive works of three to five movements, held together by close tonal relationships.

Using Cazzati's formal model and maintaining the individual character of the movements, Giovanni Battista Vitali (1632–92) unified his sonatas by a consistent application of counterpoint throughout, especially in works intended for church performance. He distilled the art of instrumental counterpoint in his canons published in 1689, the *Artifici musicali*, forerunners of Bach's *Musical Offering*. In his chamber sonatas, which consist of diverse dance movements, he achieves unity by employing the principle of variation. The elegant, restrained lyricism of his slow movements illustrates the growing influence of vocal music on instrumental works. This characteristic is predominant in the sonatas of Pietro degli Antoni (1648–1720), who was also an opera composer. His opp.4 (1676) and 5 (1686) include several movements with such titles as 'Aria grave'. Slow movements often resemble recitatives, embellished by ornaments similar to vocal appoggiaturas.

The development of the Bolognese concerto style owes much to the architecture and acoustics of S Petronio. With the completion of the apse in the 1660s, music was performed from the *cantoria*, a narrow balcony which lines the walls above the canons' choir-stalls (fig. 22).

22. *The apse of S Petronio with musicians performing from the 'cantoria' (balcony) during the visit of James III of England (the 'Pretender') to Bologna on 4 October 1722: miniature from 'Le insignia degli Anziani del comune', xiii (1716–41)*

Two organs face each other at the same level. At the rear of the apse the *cantoria* is wider and more commodious and thus suitable for holding instrumentalists. Though the apse is a nearly perfect sound-chamber which amplifies but does not blur overtones, music performed from there emerges as a mass of echoes as it moves through the vast nave. Choral polyphony is all but obscured. Though large numbers of people and the silk and damask hangings used for festive occasions undoubtedly absorb some of the echo, serious acoustical problems remain. Only the brilliant sounds of the trumpet and the solo voice penetrate with clarity.

It was Cazzati who initiated the unique repertory for trumpet and strings at S Petronio, perhaps influenced by a renowned trumpeter at the ducal court of Sabbioneta, where he had earlier been employed. Finding excellent trumpeters in the Concerto Palatino, Cazzati incorporated the instrument into his sonatas for strings, emphasizing their contrasting timbres. In 1665 he published his op.35, instrumental sonatas which included the first printed works for trumpet and strings. Indiscriminately called sonata, sinfonia or concerto, similar works by other S Petronio musicians – Petronio Franceschini, Domenico Gabrielli, Giacomo Antonio Perti, Giuseppe Jacchini and, especially, Giuseppe Torelli – quickly followed, also written for use in the liturgy.

The Bolognese concerto took significant shape in the hands of Torelli (1658–1709), who wrote 33 such works. When he came to the S Petronio *cappella* in 1686 he found several conditions favourable to its development. Besides the acoustic, the well-established practice of hiring extra instrumentalists for special occasions meant the presence of not only virtuosos but also less skilled performers for whom suitable music had to be provided, giving rise to a musical distinction between the soloists (concertino) and the larger group (ripieno). The discrete placing of the organs on either side encouraged the separation of two distinct groups of musicians. Indeed, in the late seventeenth century the two organs came to be differentiated according to function. The newer organ (completed in 1596) was known as 'the organ of the concerto', while the older organ (from 1476) had two of its registers coupled to be used for ripieno parts.

Virtuosity, an essential feature of the concerto style, was furnished by the Bolognese school of violin playing. It was established in the early seventeenth century by Ercole Gaibara, and it flourished later under Leonardo Brugnoli and Giovanni Benvenuti. Probably among its outstanding performers was Arcangelo Corelli (1653–1713), who spent several years in Bologna from the age of thirteen. This sustained activity resulted in an advanced string style, which found a natural place in the concerto.

The sources of the Bolognese concerto style may also lie in the Venetian opera sinfonia and the ritornello design of opera arias, both well known to Torelli. The highly charged opening statement, the 'hammer-stroke', came from the opera sinfonia, where it was often performed by trumpets. The application of these compact openings to a ritornello design is the most significant formal development of the Bolognese composers.[14] Tentatively, Torelli applied the timbral contrasts of trumpet and strings, already explored at S Petronio, to works for strings alone, assigning the solo role to a violin rather than a trumpet. As the ritornello design evolved, he made clear thematic distinctions between the music of the ritornello, played by the large group, or ripieno, and the virtuoso passages of the solo violin. Eschewing contrapuntal writing, he combined these ideas with techniques for defining major-minor tonality and effecting a larger-scale design based on related keys. With these developments Torelli gave final shape to the eighteenth-century concerto.

The architecture of S Petronio may well have affected the origins of another distinctive Bolognese repertory – works for solo violoncello. The acoustics of the church demanded heavy bass reinforcements to counterbalance echoes that magnify higher notes. Trombones had largely fulfilled that role until the middle of the seventeenth century, when increasing numbers of lower strings appeared. Surviving orchestral parts of concerted masses from the 1680s indicate a large component of bass instruments, including violoni, contrabasses and violoncellos. Violoncellists appear on the S Petronio rosters as early as 1664. Among them were three of the performer-composers who produced the earliest solo literature for the violoncello: Giovanni Battista Vitali, Domenico Gabrielli (1651–90) and Giuseppe Jacchini (*c*1670–*c*1727). Virtuosos themselves, and almost certainly inspired by the excellent violinists around them, they wrote partitas (variations), ricercares and sonatas for the cello, liberating it from its traditional basso continuo role.

Vitali, who performed at S Petronio from 1664 to 1674, wrote several sets of partitas which probably date from this period. In 1687 the Bolognese organist Giovanni Battista degli Antoni (*b* 1660) wrote an important set of ricercares for cello with multilinear textures, probably intended as studies. Gabrielli contributed seven ricercares for cello alone and two sonatas for cello and continuo, which, with their florid scale passages, multiple stops and active string crossing, reflect his own advanced performing technique and awareness of the instrument's sonority. The strong tonality is reinforced by sequential passages and frequent secondary dominants. Both Gabrielli and Jacchini, (a pupil of his, incorporated the cello in their trumpet sonatas, often in imitative dialogue with the trumpet. A sonata for cello solo by Jacchini incorporates Gabrielli's techniques, with the addition of repeated arpeggios.

The emphasis in Bologna on instrumental music enhanced its liturgical music as well. Splendid combinations of voices and instruments in the concerted style characterize the festive music at S Petronio. As is well known, the concerted style cultivated in Venice from the end of the sixteenth century emphasized the contrasting timbres of several choirs, solo voices, groups of instruments and organ. Early in the century Girolamo Giacobbi, *maestro di cappella* from 1604 to 1628, brought the style to S Petronio in his psalm settings for solo voices, several choirs and organ. Banchieri, writing in 1609, described a concerted mass he composed for four choirs which included violins, viole da gamba and three trombones, plus a large group of continuo instruments.[15] Camillo Cortellini, leader of the Concerto Palatino during its most distinguished period, published masses in 1617 and 1626 that included trombones.

Under Cazzati, instruments became a distinctive feature in liturgical music at S Petronio. For the patronal feast he wrote vesper psalms for two choirs, solo voices and orchestra, including two trumpets. He carried the concerted style into festive mass settings and published several sets of masses and psalms for voices and instruments. His love of contrasting timbres was carried on by the *maestri*

23. *Concert in S Petronio by members of the Accademia dei Gelati for the festival of S Antonio of Padua, 1676, in the presence of the major ecclesiastical and civic authorities and their guests: miniature from 'Le insignia degli Anziani del comune', ix (1668–80)*

who succeeded him, Giovanni Paolo Colonna (1637–95) and Giacomo Antonio Perti (1661–1756). From his Roman training Colonna brought an elegant polyphonic vocal style to the concerted mass, which was continued by Perti in his early years at S Petronio.

In the Bolognese festive masses only the Kyrie and Gloria (and occasionally the Credo) received elaborate concerted settings. The Sanctus and Agnus Dei were often replaced by motets or even instrumental works. Each of the mass movements is divided into sections of large proportions, set in a variety of textures. Preceded by an instrumental sinfonia which sometimes included trumpets, solo voices initiate finely crafted fugal sections for chorus, reinforced by strings. For contrast, two choirs alternate in chordal antiphony, often punctuated by brief instrumental passages. Virtuoso solo passages with obbligato instruments reflect the pervasive influence of opera on all vocal forms. These mass settings are significant milestones, early precursors of the orchestral masses of Haydn and Mozart.

The evolution of opera was significant for both vocal and instrumental music in seventeenth-century Bologna. One of its important predecessors, the madrigal comedy, was cultivated there from 1597. Banchieri wrote several madrigal comedies modelled on works by Orazio Vecchi which married polyphonic madrigals to a loosely contrived plot. The music aptly describes the humorous situations and characters of the *commedia dell'arte*. Meanwhile, the new ideals of musical expression embodied in the *seconda prattica* and the emotional musical declamation of Florentine composers led to the first experiments in opera, brought to maturity in Monteverdi's *Orfeo* of 1607. With their passion for theatre, the Bolognese quickly embraced *dramma in musica*, and Giacobbi was the first local composer to write in the new style. In 1608 his *intermedi L'Aurora ingannata*, intended for performance between acts of a play, were cast in intense, affective recitatives and strophic choruses. Two years later, his opera *Andromeda*, in a similar style, initiated a love for the genre that has persisted in the city to the present day.

Until the later decades of the century, Bologna's operatic repertory was largely imported. In 1616 a performance of Peri's *Euridice* in the palazzo of a patrician family introduced the Florentine style. A few operas from the Roman repertory, notably Domenico Mazzocchi's *La catena d'Adone*, were staged in the 1620s. Works by Giacobbi and another local composer, Ottavio Vernizzi, were largely focussed on *intermedi*, often performed at academic functions. The city was also served by travelling companies of singers, often from Rome. These itinerant singers, formed in the *commedia dell'arte* tradition, came to be known as 'Febiarmonici'.[16] Such a company in Venice, in 1637, produced the first public opera, *Andromeda*, composed by its leaders Benedetto Ferrari and Francesco Manelli. The same company brought subsequent Venetian productions to Bologna, beginning with Monteverdi's *Il ritorno d'Ulisse* in 1640. Working between the seasons of Venetian opera, they were largely responsible for the diffusion of the Venetian style in the 1640s. Operas staged by travelling mercenary companies alternated with local and academic productions. The role of academies, especially the Accademia dei Gelati, was vital in the early support of opera in Bologna. Its most enthusiastic promoters were the *principi* of the Gelati, notably Cornelio Malvasia. A patrician who frequently sponsored grandiose musical and theatrical spectacles, he served as agent for the comic troupes of the Duke of Modena and procured ducal singers for operatic productions in Bologna.[17]

Two important theatres were now inaugurated in Bologna: the Teatro Formagliari (1641) and the Teatro Malvezzi (1653). In addition to dramas and comedies, they presented the operas of Ferrari and, especially, Francesco Cavalli, the leading Venetian opera composer after the death of Monteverdi. His name dominates the rosters well into the 1670s, along with such men as Antonio Cesti, Pietro

The Early Baroque Era

Andrea Ziani and Carlo Pallavicino.

Only in the late 1670s were operas by Bolognese composers staged regularly at its theatres. Among the first were two works by Petronio Franceschini in 1676. Perhaps to establish their credentials in the Venetian style, Gabrielli and G. A. Perti both composed for Venetian theatres before writing their first operas for Bologna in the 1680s. The Bolognese adapted Venetian opera to their particular tastes. Not surprisingly, instrumental music played a prominent role in their operas. Basing their works on the Venetian formula – arias for solo voice and continuo, separated by recitatives and varied by occasional duets or trios – they enriched and varied their arias with virtuoso obbligato parts for solo violin, cello, trumpet, theorbo and mandolin. Important arias were surrounded with concerto-like ritornellos for full orchestra, with instruments punctuating vocal phrases. Their introductory sinfonias, occasionally borrowed from the repertory at S Petronio, often featured the concerto contrasts of trumpets and strings. Such works point up the mutual influence of concerto and aria and the growing role of instrumental music in opera.

It is not clear what, if any, connection Bolognese opera composers had with the Neapolitan school. An opera by Alessandro Scarlatti, *Gli equivoci nel sembiante*, was performed in Bologna in 1679, but it is an early work from his Roman days. It is interesting, however, that an opera by the Bolognese Giuseppe Aldrovandini (1672–1707), *Semiramide*, was performed in Naples in 1702 with florid arias added by Scarlatti.[18] Aldrovandini, one of the most original Bolognese opera composers, also contributed to the history of regional comic opera. Catering to the Bolognese penchant for earthy humour, he composed three comic operas, beginning with *Gl'inganni amorosi scoperti in villa* in 1696. Written largely in Bolognese dialect, its rustic *doubles entendres* offended the church authorities, who insisted on their excision before the first performance was allowed. Though the works were very successful, Bolognese comic opera lay dormant until the late eighteenth century, perhaps because of restrictions imposed by the ecclesiastical authorities.

Closely related to opera was oratorio, actively cultivated by Bolognese composers from 1659, when Cazzati's *La morte di San Giuseppe* was performed. Based on biblical stories, though not staged, oratorio was substituted for opera during Lent. However, in Bologna more than elsewhere, oratorios were performed throughout the year for religious, civic, academic and private ceremonials. They took place in churches, oratories, halls of religious confraternities, and private residences. In these last, they assumed the function of entertainment, often enhanced by elegant food and drink. At the performance of an oratorio by Colonna in 1690, the dancing and general levity resulted in the composer being put in gaol. The centre of oratorio activity was the church of the Madonna della Galliera, belonging to the Oratorians of St Philip Neri, an order of priests founded in Rome. Though many Roman oratorios were performed there, Bolognese composers were well represented. Writing both oratorio and opera, they readily used the same styles and forms in both genres, and the brilliance of the instrumental ensembles in their oratorios distinguished their works from the Roman repertory.

In the 1660s Bolognese composers began to structure their oratorios in two parts (divided by a sermon) on subject matter from the Old or New Testament and the lives of saints. The story was sung in recitative by a narrator or *testo*, alternating with arias and recitatives for three to five vocal soloists portraying the characters. Ensembles and choruses made up of soloists varied the texture. In varying proportions the text combined narrative, dramatic and, sometimes, meditative elements. As the century progressed, oratorios became increasingly dramatic, and the meditative elements and use of the narrator decreased. The works of Colonna best represent the mature Bolognese style of the 1680s and 1690s. Though not known to have composed operas, he conceived his oratorios along operatic lines. His later works show an increasing preference for ternary arias and duple metres, as in contemporary developments in opera. Flexible structures and a rich harmonic vocabulary express the dramatic and emotional content of the text. Like oratorios by Franceschini and Gabrielli, his works require an instrumental group in four to six parts, larger than those for oratorios written outside the Bologna-Modena orbit. Instruments were used for introductory sinfonias and ritornellos, as well as obbligato accompaniments for arias and ensembles.[19]

Aria and recitative dominate two other genres favoured in Bologna: cantatas and motets for solo voices and continuo. Cazzati was the first important Bolognese composer in both genres. Written in a fully lyrical style, with occasional florid passages burgeoning from the simple melodies, his solo cantatas are often charming settings of texts celebrating the joy, cruelty and whimsicality of love. Solo motets, which differ from cantatas only in their religious or devotional texts, were written by all the S Petronio *maestri* of the era. Though polyphonic motets for four to six voices and organ prevailed in the first half of the century, after 1650 the preferred texture was a smaller combination of one to three voices and continuo, occasionally with two violins added. Solo motets by Colonna and Perti, intended for use in the basilica, often have a full complement of string instruments as well as florid vocal lines.

The music printing firms established in the city were significant for the wider dissemination of Bolognese music. The first volume of music from a Bolognese press appeared in 1584, a set of madrigals by

Camillo Cortellini printed by Giovanni Rossi. Giacomo Monti was Bologna's leading publisher of music. He founded his publishing house in 1632 and began issuing music in 1639; he was especially active from 1662 to 1689, when the firm passed to his son Pier Maria. Marino Silvani had established a music press by 1665 and edited several Bolognese anthologies issued from the Monti firm. Cazzati published several of his own works from a private press.

Finally, the rich archives and libraries of modern Bologna offer ample evidence of its robust musical life. Manuscript scores and parts preserved in the archives of S Petronio give scholars opportunity to study not only the music but the manner in which it was performed. Carefully kept account books and memoranda permit reconstruction of the musical ambience. Equally important are the early music prints and manuscripts collected in the eighteenth century by Padre Martini, which form the nucleus of the renowned music library, the Civico Museo Bibliografico Musicale. With such complete resources, one can view the entire panorama of Bolognese music in the seventeenth century, its most splendid epoch. In the context of the city's proud independence and cultural energy, music thrived in an unprecedented manner. Its performers, composers and institutions bestowed notable vigour upon Italian Baroque music.

NOTES

[1] See the relevant chapters in *The New Cambridge Modern History*, iv (Cambridge, 1970): *The Decline of Spain and the Thirty Years War 1609–48/59*, especially J. P. Cooper, 'General Introduction', 1–66; F. C. Spooner, 'The European Economy 1609–50', 67–103; v (Cambridge, 1961): *The Ascendancy of France 1648–88*, especially D. C. Coleman, 'Economic Problems and Policies', 19–26; A. Whiteman, 'Church and State', 128–30; G. Spini, 'Italy after the Thirty Years War', 461–73. More detailed discussions can be found in specialized studies such as G. Parker, *Europe in Crisis, 1598–1648* (Ithaca, 1980), and *The General Crisis of the Seventeenth Century*, ed. idem and L. M. Smith (London, 1978).

[2] C. M. Cipolla, 'The Decline of Italy: the Case of a Fully Matured Economy', *Economic History Review*, ser. 2, v (1952), 179.

[3] For a useful survey of Bolognese art, see E. Waterhouse, *Italian Baroque Painting* (London, 1962), 85ff.

[4] L. Avellini, 'Tra "Umoristi" e "Gelati": l'Accademia Romana e la cultura emiliana del primo e del pieno Seicento', *Studi secenteschi*, xxiii (1982), 119–20.

[5] A. Schnoebelen, *The Concerted Mass at San Petronio in Bologna ca. 1660–1730: a Documentary and Analytical Study* (diss., U. of Illinois, 1966), 38–46.

[6] O. Gambassi, 'Origine, statuti e ordinamenti del Concerto Palatino della signoria di Bologna (1250–1600)', *NRMI*, xviii (1984), 264–5.

[7] R. Dalmonte, *Camillo Cortellini madrigalista bolognese* (Florence, 1980), 22–6.

[8] Schnoebelen, op cit, 74–8.

[9] J. G. Suess, 'Observations on the Accademia Filarmonica di Bologna in the Seventeenth Century and the Rise of a Local Tradition of Instrumental Music', *Quadrivium*, viii (1967), 51–62.

[10] A. Schnoebelen, 'Cazzati *vs.* Bologna: 1657–1691', *MQ*, lvii (1971), 26–39.

[11] C. V. Palisca, 'The Artusi–Monteverdi Controversy', *The New Monteverdi Companion*, ed. D. Arnold and N. Fortune (London, 1985), 127–8. See also pp. 30–31 above.

[12] C. Cranna, *Adrian Banchieri's 'Cartella musicale' (1614): Translation and Commentary* (diss., Stanford U., 1981), 1–7, 475, 489.

[13] This discussion is based on U. Brett, *Music and Ideas in Seventeenth-Century Italy: the Cazzati-Arresti Polemic* (New York and London, 1989).

[14] S. Watts, *The Stylistic Features of the Bolognese Concerto* (diss., Indiana U., 1969), 181–4.

[15] A. Banchieri, *Conclusioni nel suono dell'organo* (Bologna, 1609), 50.

[16] See L. Bianconi and T. Walker, 'Dalla *Finta pazza* alla *Veremonda*: storia di Febiarmonici', *RIM*, x (1975), 379–454.

[17] ibid, 429.

[18] In this discussion of Bolognese opera I am indebted to Charles Rowden for the use of his unpublished notes.

[19] J. A. Griffin, *The Oratorios of G. P. Colonna and the Late Seventeenth-Century Oratorio Tradition in Bologna and Modena* (diss., U. of North Carolina, Chapel Hill, 1978), 266–73.

BIBLIOGRAPHICAL NOTE

General

For books on the general crisis in Italy in the seventeenth century, the reader should consult the bibliography for Chapter II. In addition, C. M. Cipolla, 'The Decline of Italy – the Case of a Fully Matured Economy', *Economic History Review*, ser. 2, v (1952), 178–87, gives a useful summary from an economic viewpoint. For discussions of music as a social and political power, see G. Stefani: 'Musica e festa nell'Italia barocca', *AnMc*, no. 12 (1973), 143–68, and 152ff; *Musica barocca: poetica e ideologia* (Milan, 1974); and *Musica e religione nell'Italia barocca* (Palermo, 1975). Essential to the understanding of the social context of Italian music of this period is L. Bianconi, *Music in the Seventeenth Century*, trans. D. Bryant (Cambridge, 1987).

The only books in English on the history and culture of Bologna date from the early twentieth century, both enjoyable narratives in the history-cum-guidebook tradition: E. James, *Bologna: its History, Antiquities and Art* (London, 1909); and A. Wiel, *The Story of Bologna* (London, 1923). Artistic life is well surveyed in E. Waterhouse, *Italian Baroque Painting* (London, 1962), which devotes a chapter to the Carracci and their Bolognese successors. Urban life is treated in L. Frati, *La vita privata di Bologna dal secolo XIII al XVII* (Bologna, 1900). For valuable information on theatres and dramatic presentations, see C. Ricci, *I teatri di Bologna nei secoli XVII e XVIII* (Bologna, 1888).

Music

Several pioneering studies on the history of music in Bologna were written by G. Gaspari. Originally appearing in fascicles in the series *Atti e memorie della r. deputazione di storia patria per le provincie della Romagna*, they have been brought together and reprinted under the title *Musica e musicisti a Bologna: ricerche, documenti e memorie risguardanti la storia dell'arte musicale in Bologna* (Bologna, 1969). Two useful early contributions are F. Vatielli, *Arte e vita musicale a Bologna* (Bologna, 1927), and L. Frati, 'Per la storia della musica a Bologna nel secolo XVII', *RMI*, xxxii (1925), 544–66. Modern studies in English began with H. Mishkin, 'The Solo Violin Sonata of the Bologna School', *MQ*, xxix (1943), 92–112, which drew attention to this important repertory. J. Berger performed a similar service for the trumpet/string repertory in 'Notes on some 17th-Century Compositions for Trumpets and Strings in Bologna', *MQ*, xxxvii (1951), 354–67. D. L. Smithers, *The Music and History of the Baroque Trumpet before 1721* (London, 1973), devotes a substantial chapter to the

Bolognese trumpet repertory. Cazzati's instrumental music is explored in J. G. Suess, 'The Ensemble Sonatas of Maurizio Cazzati', *AnMc*, no.19 (1979), 146–85.

Aspects of sacred music by composers at S Petronio are discussed in J. Berger, 'The Sacred Works of Giacomo Antonio Perti', *JAMS*, xvii (1964), 370–77, and in P. Smith, 'Girolamo Giacobbi and his *Salmi concertati* of 1609', *Studies in Music from the University of Western Ontario* (London, Ontario, 1978), 15–21. Two articles are concerned with various aspects of music at S Petronio: A. Schnoebelen, 'Performance Practice at San Petronio in the Baroque', *AcM*, xli (1969), 37–55; and idem, 'Cazzati *vs.* Bologna: 1657–1691', *MQ*, lvii (1971), 26–39. O. Gambassi, *La cappella musicale di San Petronio* (Florence, 1987), is an excellent archival study of the musicians at S Petronio from 1436 to 1920.

Bolognese opera has been little studied. L. Bianconi and T. Walker have investigated the history of the 'Febiarmonici' in 'Dalla *Finta pazza* alla *Veremonda*: storia di Febiarmonici', *RIM*, x (1975), 379–454. Their article 'Production, Consumption, and Political Function of Seventeenth-Century Italian Opera', *EMH*, iv (1984), 209–96, contains information on the role of academies in Bolognese opera. The history of the oratorio in Bologna is treated in H. E. Smither, *A History of the Oratorio*, i: *The Oratorio in the Baroque Era: Italy, Vienna, Paris* (Chapel Hill, 1977).

F. Vatielli's early study of the Concerto Palatino, *Il concerto palatino della signoria di Bologna* (Bologna, 1940), is amplified in O. Gambassi, 'Origine, statuti e ordinamenti del concerto palatino della signoria di Bologna, I, 1250–1600; II, 1600–1797', *NRMI*, xviii (1984), 261–83, 469–502, and especially in idem, *Il concerto palatino della signoria di Bologna: cinque secoli di vita musicale a corte (1250–1797)* (Florence, 1989). For biography and analysis of the music of its leading composer, see R. Dalmonte, *Camillo Cortellini madrigalista bolognese* (Florence, 1980).

My discussion of the Cazzati–Arresti polemic is based largely on U. Brett, *Music and Ideas in Seventeenth-Century Italy: the Cazzati–Arresti Polemic* (New York and London, 1989). A pioneering study of the Accademia Filarmonica is N. Morini, *La R. Accademia Filarmonica di Bologna* (Bologna, 1930). J. G. Suess, 'Observations on the Accademia Filarmonica of Bologna in the Seventeenth Century and the Rise of a Local Tradition of Instrumental Music', *Quadrivium*, viii (1967), 51–62, points up the influence of the academy on the development of the Bolognese instrumental repertory. For a recent documentary study of the Accademia Filarmonica, see O. Gambassi, *L'Accademia Filarmonica di Bologna: fondazione, statuti e aggregazioni* (Florence, 1992).

Chapter VI

Florence: Musical Spectacle and Drama, 1570–1650

JOHN WALTER HILL

Music in Florence during the decades around 1600 has assumed for us, as for Europeans of that time, an importance out of proportion to the city's size, wealth and power. The population of Florence during the period in question remained at about 60,000 (59,216 in 1562; 63,143 in 1630) until the plague of 1630–33 reduced it by about 10,000, after which it rose to about 70,000 (70,352 in 1674). These figures show that it was only the sixth largest city in Italy, after Milan, Venice, Rome, Naples and Palermo. And it was far smaller in extent than any of these, enclosed as it was within walls little more than five miles in circumference.

Earlier, in the fourteenth and fifteenth centuries, Florence had risen to prominence because of its wealth, derived from wool and silk trading, goldsmithing and, above all, banking. The economy had recovered during the reign (1537–74) of Grand Duke Cosimo I de' Medici after the ruin caused by 35 years of political chaos, culminating in the siege of 1529–30, by which Pope Clement VII (Giulio de' Medici), in alliance with Emperor Charles V (who was also King of Spain), had returned his exiled mercantile family, now as absolute rulers of their city. After a serious decline during the reign (1574–87) of Francesco de' Medici, another recovery marked the period of his brother, Ferdinando I (ruled 1587–1609). The early death of Cosimo II (ruled 1609–21) and the regency of his mother, Christine of Lorraine, and widow, Maria Maddalena of Austria, coincided more or less with the onset of a financial collapse that involved all of Europe. And the emergence of Ferdinando II as a ruler in his own right (1621–70) was overshadowed by the last great Italian plague, from which the economy of Florence never fully recovered.

The power claimed by the Medici grand dukes was absolute in Florence. Florence claimed to rule Tuscany. But Tuscany could claim no more than its independence. Medici politics aimed at preserving these three claims: it was, like the prevailing character of their city's people, largely conservative.

The Early Baroque Era

Italy as a whole, however, was hardly independent. With the defeat and capture of François I by Charles V at Pavia in 1525, Spain won her struggle with France over domination of Italy (conceded to Spain in the Treaty of Cambray in 1529), and Pope Clement had no choice but to bestow the imperial crown to the victor at Bologna, where the political map of Italy was redrawn, as it would be at various times during the next three and a half centuries, in accordance with the balance of power in northern Europe. After conceding the Papal States, Charles placed his viceroys in Milan and Naples and took control of several minor principalities, including Siena and two important enclaves on the Tuscan coast. After Siena, with French help, briefly expelled the Spanish in 1552, Cosimo I was allowed to lead its reconquest for Charles and to rule it as his fief until, in 1557, by cancelling Spain's enormous debt to Florentine bankers, he purchased full title to it from Philip II, to whom Charles had meanwhile abdicated the Spanish throne. Even though Cosimo I had created a territorial state extending roughly from Carrara at the beginning of the Ligurian coast, along the Appennine watershed to Sansepolcro at the border with the Marche in the east, and down to the region of Castro on the Tyrrhenian coast at the frontier with the Papal States, he ruled under the hegemony of Spain; Spain maintained coastal enclaves surrounding the peninsulas of Monte Massoncello (with the city of Piombino and the island of Elba) and Monte Argentario (Port Ercole, Talamone and Orbetello), through which she could easily invade whenever the need arose and other distractions and alliances permitted. The pretext for an invasion could always be found. Future Medici grand dukes would be descendants of Spanish rulers. Charles V had named Cosimo's wife, Eleonora of Toledo, daughter of his viceroy in Naples, while Cosimo's eldest son, Francesco, married Charles's niece, Giovanna of Austria. One of the chief aims, then, of grand-ducal policy was to hold off the Spanish through appeasement and counterpoising alliances, while holding the territories and potentially rebellious cities of Tuscany in thrall. The most important counterpoises to Spanish hegemony were France and an independent papacy.

The other chief aim of grand-ducal policy, of course, was to retain power at home. Florence had a history of civil war, anarchy and rebellion; the Medici family had been forced from the city twice during the four decades before Cosimo's seizure of power. Florentine exiles, always a threat, had assembled an army of invasion at Montemurlo, just north of Prato, during the first summer of Cosimo's reign. A series of recent, abrupt changes of constitution, rivalries and conspiracies among patrician families, and a long tradition of republican egalitarianism among the guild tradesmen made the Florentines potentially difficult to rule. And the underclass of disenfranchised and underfed *sottoposti* of the cloth industry, amounting to nearly a quarter of the population, had a history of rioting. In times of trouble, the ultimate recourse would be to Spanish military power, which, however, would put Tuscany's independence at risk. Locally, therefore, Cosimo and his successors assumed absolute control of the councils, magistracies and bureaucracies of Florence, built two fortresses to command the city, hired foreign militiamen to keep order, installed a neighbourhood spy network to discover threats to their authority, imposed heavy taxes, punished their enemies with prison, and rewarded their friends with patronage. 'The citizen has submitted, friends have become servants, and the latter have been changed into slaves', wrote the Florentine Giovanvettorio Soderini, who was arrested for sedition one month later (January 1588) and sentenced to death by Ferdinando I (but later pardoned). Two further, more remarkable, and related means of local control were the refeudalization of the Florentine patriciate and a mythology supporting divine right created through deliberate control over the visual and performing arts.

The refeudalization of Florence was a policy begun by Cosimo I as a means of securing the loyalty of the city's powerful élite and fostering social and cultural values supportive of an absolutist regime. The first steps in that direction included Cosimo's creation in 1562 of the new crusading order of S Stefano, which conferred the coveted prestige of knighthood on those wealthy enough to help finance the grand duke's galley fleet. For the same purpose, Cosimo and his successors granted or sold innumerable fiefs conferring the title of marquis or count of some remote outpost of Tuscany or the kingdom of Naples. Cosimo II even rehabilitated the feudal rights of the older, pre-republican nobility in their ancestral lands. At the symbolic level, Cosimo I introduced Spanish etiquette, which controlled in minute detail court protocol and access to the grand duke's person, and an elaborate series of public spectacles, with singing, dancing and allegorical staging, that revolved around mock jousts, dramatized acts of chivalry in defence of honour, staged attacks upon costumed Turks, miniature naval battles in courtyard ponds, theatres or rivers, choreographed displays of horsemanship, or even ceremonial football matches, in any of which the scripted results were intended to confer upon his sons and favourites a mythic heroism that meant to clothe in legitimacy their otherwise naked power. The aristocracy, new and old, were required to participate in these pageants, to act out in public the roles of fealty that Cosimo and his descendants wished them to take on in real life.

For the visual images of a Medicean mythology, Cosimo turned to the leaders among the 70 members of the Accademia del Disegno (45 of whom were employed in the grand-ducal household), of which

The Early Baroque Era

Cosimo himself was the founder (in 1563) and first *principe*. Some lasting results of this programme can be seen on the walls of the Palazzo Vecchio (or Signoria), which Cosimo had transformed into a pictorial Medici genealogy on a colossal scale. More typical, however, were the ephemeral designs for public pageants, for which the concepts, scripts and poetry were provided by members of the Accademia Fiorentina, which Cosimo had founded earlier (in 1541).

The outdoor street pageants that resulted from collaborations between these two academies were intended for local consumption and included the most blatant elements of political propaganda. Typical of these was the entrance procession, based on the extensive research report of the historian Vincenzo Borghini, for the arrival of Giovanna of Austria to marry Prince Francesco de' Medici in 1565. The underlying programme was the foundation, restoration, victories and royal destiny of Florence depicted in a series of triumphal arches. The first of these was dedicated to the history of Florence as a progress to the royal present. The second celebrated previous Medici marriages. Statues on the Ponte S Trinità presented Cosimo Vecchio and Cosimo I as founders of the present age. The third arch depicted the bride's family. Later in the procession, Cosimo I and his grand duchess, Eleonora, were shown as golden statues. The decoration before the Palazzo Vecchio showed Cosimo crowned grand duke by Pius V, Francesco enthroned amid his court and magistrates, and the allegorical figure of Tuscany arrayed in the grand-ducal mantle, her crown being taken away from her by the pagan Etruscan king Porsenna, while Cosimo leans forward to crown her again. Thus were the Medici presented as heirs of ancient kings and preordained patrons of restoration and rebirth.

Slightly more subtle suggestions of the Medici social and political agenda were woven into the outdoor or tent-covered pageants designed for a still large but somewhat more select audience of local patricians, courtiers, foreign visitors and ambassadors. Representative of these was the *sbarra* that celebrated Francesco's second marriage, to Bianca Cappello, in 1579. It consisted of mock combat between three men costumed as Persian knights and a series of Florentine *cavalieri*. Several days before the *sbarra*, heralds announced that the Persian knights claimed that the ladies of their country were the most beautiful and that they would defend their claim in combat. At the pageant itself, the duels were preceded by the entrances of twelve small groups of knights in armour – not actors but actual Florentine noblemen – carried by allegorically decorated parade floats (*carri*) that emerged one by one from a papier-mâché Mount Parnassus. On the first *carro*, the Persians appeared on a giant throne drawn by two elephants, with loud music played by drums, shawms (coarse-sounding double-reed instruments) and other 'barbaric' instruments. From inside Mount Parnassus a group of pilgrims sang in sweet harmony of their devotion to Apollo. A beautiful maiden approached the grand duchess to declaim her story of the aggrieved damsels of Dalmatia, to the accompaniment of vocal and instrumental music composed by the head of the grand duke's *cappella*, Alessandro Striggio (1536 or 1537–92), an important and prolific composer of polyphonic madrigals.

The second *carro*, pulled by two lions, represented enthroned Apollo, who sang five stanzas of *ottava rima* (a verse form traditionally used for semi-improvised solo singing based on harmonic and melodic formulae) to the accompaniment of his own 'lyre' (probably the *lira da braccio*, a bowed instrument capable of producing chords, which had become a Renaissance symbol of ancient bards) reinforced by other instruments hidden inside Mount Parnassus. Suddenly a cruel witch appeared on a dragon. Apollo told the damsel to remove the crown from the head of the animal. This done, the dragon spread its wings, and the damsel's beloved Uliterio, one of the Florentine knights, emerged. Third came the *carro della notte* pulled by two black animals and carrying the figure of Night seated on a large rock that seemed to be emerging from a swamp, in accordance with Homer's description. When the *carro* arrived before the grand duchess, the figure of Night awoke and began to sing, again to the accompaniment of his own bowed instrument, together with others hidden inside the *carro*:

> Out of my watery den, with my prophetic band of phantoms, dreams and illusions, I am Night, who come to your shores, O most majestic royalty, to give thanks for such joyful, lofty pageants and such decorations. These wise warriors who now do battle will show you, O famous heroes of the Tuscan plain, that Love concedes beauty, noble bearing and all his other honours only to their ladies, as the more worthy recipients.

This 'madrigal' in praise of Medici court festivities was sung by Giulio Caccini (1551–1618), a virtuoso singer in the grand duke's household who would emerge two decades later as one of the most significant composers of the time. The music was by Piero Strozzi (*c*1550–*c*1609), a member of one of the largest and most prestigious noble families in Florence.

The next *carro*, pulled by swans, carried Venus on a throne surrounded by cupids, one of whom sang a madrigal in praise of the bride. After the unexpected appearance of a monster, the sixth *carro* brought forth two ladies, representing Europe and Africa, along with their knights, who were to defend them against their enemy, Asia (i.e., Persia). Their float took the form of a giant shell floating on the

24. Sixth float ('carro'), with ladies representing Europe and Africa (with attendant knights) from the 1579 'sbarra' which formed part of the celebrations for the marriage between Francesco I de' Medici and Bianca Cappello: engraving from 'Feste nelle nozze. . .' (Florence, 1579)

sea, drawn by two men costumed as tritons (*see* fig. 24). One of the ladies accompanied the other with her archlute in a song by Vincenzo Galilei (*d* 1591; the father of Galileo Galilei), in which the eyes of her beloved are compared with two stars that are never eclipsed by the sun, which dims the brightness of Venus, the single morning star of Love. Other knights arrived afterwards on a mountain, on the back of a dolphin, on a giant conch shell, in a galley etc., each accompanied by a vocal solo or ensemble related to the theme of their *carro*. In the end, each of these knights performed mock combat with the Persian *mantenitori*. Although the personages depicted in this and scores of similar pageants are drawn from mythology rather than Medici family history, as they were in the processional decorations, the essential message of the restoration, victory and royal destiny of Florence are equally present, along with the courtly virtues of chivalry and fealty – all of it enacted by the same Florentine noblemen who were intended to receive this message.

The third type of pageant with which the Medici grand dukes celebrated births, weddings and the like were the *intermedi* that had been traditionally performed between the acts of plays in Italy since the later fifteenth century. The eleven especially elaborate Florentine court *intermedi* produced from 1539 (for the wedding of Cosimo I) to 1589 (for the wedding of Ferdinando I), described and analysed repeatedly in the scholarly literature, consisted of rather static vignettes. The focus of attention was on spectacular stage effects and scenic transformations. The themes of the *intermedi* might or might not be linked together and with the play. Such dialogue as took place in them was sung by soloists accompanied by instrumental ensembles (occasionally by the singer's own archlute) or by the singing of an ensemble of dramatic personages, who were invariably drawn from Graeco-Roman mythology. The scenario was normally designed so as to amalgamate Medici pretensions with ancient mythology. For the 1586 wedding of Virginia de' Medici to Cesare d'Este, Duke of Ferrara, for example, Giovanni de' Bardi (1534–1612) wrote the poetry and scenario and Bernardo Buontalenti designed the staging for six *intermedi* for Bardi's play *L'amico fido*: (1) Jupiter and the gods celebrate the return of the Golden Age (a cliché of Medici eulogy since the time of Lorenzo *magnifico*), conventionally identified with the return to Florence of the Medici family and the restoration of the city's former greatness, (2) infernal demons (enemies of the regime) lament their resulting defeat, (3) the perpetual spring of the Golden Age is depicted, (4) the seas are calmed, (5) Juno, goddess of marriage, showers her blessings, and (6) the happiness of earth and heaven are celebrated by Tuscan shepherds and shepherdesses dancing in triumph. In this case, the engineering feats of the staging and the virtuosity of the singers impressed the select audience of courtiers and ambassadors, who were also expected to understand the finer allegorical points. These points included, according to Roy Strong,[1] references, in the four central *intermedi*, to the elements – fire (inferno), earth (spring), water (seas) and air (Juno) – of the magical hermetic universe as it was known to the Florentine neo-Platonists from Ficino onwards. The message was that, under the natural order of Medici rule by divine right, Florentines had set themselves in tune with and achieved conquest over the elements, so that the latter could pour forth their riches.

Parallel to the two academies (the Accademia del Disegno and Accademia Fiorentina) whose members provided the visual and literary materials for these three types of pageant, there was an academy in Florence whose members provided at least some of the music for these events. This one began, like the Accademia Fiorentina, as a private, unofficial group that met informally. But unlike the Fiorentina, it never achieved official recognition, probably because of court politics. Its leader was the playwright of 1586 and scion of old Florentine nobility, Giovanni de' Bardi, Count of Vernio, a humanist scholar and amateur composer in whose palace the group met weekly during the 1570s and 80s. As far as we know, it never had an official name, but one of its central members, Giulio Caccini, refers to it as Bardi's 'Camerata' in the prefaces to his opera *Euridice* (1600) and to *Le nuove musiche* (1602), where he claims that it included 'not only a large part of the nobility but also the best musicians, most learned men, poets, and philosophers of the city'. Bardi's son Pietro repeats Caccini's word *camerata* ('club, society') and also calls the group an *accademia* in a letter (1634) describing its activities. Although Pietro de' Bardi mentions Caccini, he names Vincenzo Galilei as its principal musician. Piero Strozzi, who collaborated with Caccini and Galilei in the 1579 *sbarra*, can be identified as another member because he and Bardi are the interlocutors in Galilei's *Dialogo della musica antica, et della moderna* (1581), the central statement of the Camerata's historical and aesthetic discussions of music. This *Dialogo* relies heavily on a series of letters written to Galilei by the Florentine expatriate humanist Girolamo Mei (1519–94), which formed the basis of the Camerata's weekly meetings from about 1572 to 1578. At the end of that period, Bardi made a practical summary of Mei's findings, in the form of a *Discorso mandato a Caccini sopra la musica antica e'l cantar bene* (1578),[2] much of which was also incorporated into Galilei's *Dialogo*. Many of the same ideas and phrases recur in the prefaces of Giulio Caccini and of two other Florentines who may well have been among the young boys educated by the preceptors in Bardi's Camerata: the court poet and librettist Ottavio Rinuccini (1562–1621) and the singer and composer Jacopo Peri (1561–1633), who were to collaborate during the 1590s in writing the earliest operas.

Given the Medici court's heavy reliance on classical mythology and carefully researched Greek and Roman models of pageantry, it is not surprising that the central quest of Bardi's Camerata was to discover the nature of Greek music and to reform modern music in accordance with ancient practice in order to recapture its legendary miraculous effects. It sought, in other words, a new Golden Age in music to complement and to accompany the court pageantry and propaganda of return, revitalization and apotheosis.[3] The principal findings and recommendations of Bardi's group were that Greek music (which was in fact vocal music) derived its effects from a rhythmically accurate and dramatically emphatic intoning of a poetic text, which, in turn, was the source of the passions to be magnified by the single declamatory melody of a soloist or of a chorus singing in unison. The defects of modern music are that it combines several melodies in counterpoint, which cancel the expressive effects of individual, limited voice ranges (*tonoi*), and that, with contrapuntal motifs and many notes to single syllables (melismas), it destroys the integrity of the poetic metres. Although Mei maintained that the ancient Greeks sang their melodies without accompanying harmony, Bardi, Galilei and the other musicians in the Camerata were unwilling to base their own compositions on a model so austere and unfamiliar.

Florence: Musical Spectacle and Drama, 1570–1650

Since no actual examples of Greek music were known to Bardi's group, the music they produced was necessarily based on the existing repertory of solo singers, which, at that time, included principally (1) light-hearted, dance-like canzonettas, which tended to employ mechanical, musically generated (rather than poetically determined) rhythms; (2) musical recitation formulae, called *arie*, consisting of two or three phrases of vocal melody with narrow range and exactly eleven notes each (matching the eleven-syllable lines of verse) repeated in patterns suited to the most common poetic forms – *ottava rima*, sonnet, capitolo – to the accompaniment of distinctive chord progressions (often themselves subject to standardization); and (3) freely composed settings of *madrigali* (which used an unpredictable series of setterns and hendecasyllables with open rhyme schemes) in a syllabic, homophonic style that imitated some of the distinctive features of the *aria* formulae and, accordingly, were often called *madrigali ariosi*. All three types had been found among the accompanied solo songs in the first of the Florentine court *intermedi* (1539). Bardi himself composed exclusively *madrigali ariosi*, to which category also belong the songs by Piero Strozzi and Vincenzo Galilei for the *sbarra* of 1579, which, as we have seen, also included several musical recitations of *ottava rima* stanzas, undoubtedly using *aria* formulae.

All three types of solo song are found among the early compositions of Giulio Caccini, written about 1585 but revised and published along with newer compositions in *Le nuove musiche* (1602) and *Le nuove musiche e nuova maniera di scriverle* (1614). Caccini's innovations, compared with the older repertory, involved indicating the accompaniment to the vocal melody by means of an abbreviated chordal notation instead of composing individual lines for ensemble instruments. This chordal notation, later called basso continuo, consisted of notes on the bass-clef staff supplemented by occasional figures or accidentals that suggest the harmonies to be added by the archlutenist, harpsichordist or organist above the bass notes. Since archlutenists, like Caccini, had been in the habit of improvising chordal accompaniments while reading from the bass book of a partsong collection, Caccini's minimal innovation involved omitting the superfluous notation of the inner accompanying voices. This, of course, would eliminate the possibility of using the harmonization of an instrumental ensemble instead of the chords of the archlute, but Caccini intended only accompaniment by one chordal instrument, preferably played by the singer himself, in order to free the performer from the restraints of the metronomic rhythm that is generally necessary in ensemble performance. In addition, some of Caccini's settings of *ottava rima* stanzas and of strophic canzonettas attempt to capture in notation improvisational aspects of the solo singer's art. In the stanza settings, instead of repeating the same two phrases of music for every couplet of poetry, as we see in the written form of the older reciting-formula *arie*, Caccini wrote out a different variation of the *aria* for each two lines. (I believe that earlier singers improvised these variations, as they improvised their own accompanying chords.)

The same variation technique is shown in the notation of the strophic canzonettas as well. Furthermore, Caccini's notation attempts to convey some of the rhythmic freedom (*sprezzatura di canto*, 'nonchalance in singing') and florid ornamentation that was part of 'the noble manner of singing learned from [his] famous master Scipione del Palla',[4] whose music for some *intermedi* performed at Naples in 1558 was described as 'in a style midway between singing and reciting', although its notated form in print looks as rhythmically rigid as any early sixteenth-century reciting-formula *aria*.[5] In other words, many features of Caccini's music consist in codifying and capturing in notation the previously spontaneous and individualistic features of an improvising singing style with strong associations to noble manners and values: Baldassare Castiglione's neo-Platonic book *Il cortegiano* of 1514, the indispensable guide to courtly etiquette and virtue, popularized *sprezzatura* as the foundation of aristocratic grace and manners while it extolled self-accompanied improvisational singing of stanzas as an important noble accomplishment. What better style to emblematize classically inspired absolutist control of individuality through creation of a refeudalized class of dependent and loyal courtiers?

Most innovative, however, are Caccini's settings of madrigal texts, in which the bass part (i.e., the guide for the chordal accompaniment) occasionally holds a long note while the singer declaims the text, sometimes on one note or to a few notes within a narrow range, using rhythms that are quite free of the restraints imposed by regular bars. Later, Caccini would proudly pretend that this style was copied by those who claimed to have written the first musical dramas.

Caccini's early solo songs seem to reflect the last phase of discussions in Bardi's Camerata, the gist of which are apparently preserved in Vincenzo Galilei's late unpublished treatises (*c*1590). Galilei suggests eight specific melodies as modern examples of the narrow range and fidelity to verse form that characterized ancient Greek singing: four are popular dance-songs and four are well-known *aria* formulae. As a modern parallel to what Plato called *proschorda*, Galilei recommended accompanying the solo voice with one simple chord (a root-position triad) on the lute (archlute or similar instrument) for each note of the melody, from whose scale the notes of each chord will be drawn, except when the expression of the text is harsh. In that case, dissonances can be used, the bass and the melody can form a sixth, and notes from various modes (i.e., scales) and genres

(diatonic and chromatic) can be used. The notes of the accompanying chords should not form distinct counter-melodies, and
the traditional rules of counterpoint need not be observed. The goal
of this style of singing, as stated by Girolamo Mei in his first letter to
Galilei in 1572, was

> to express completely and with force everything that speaking com-
> municates, by means [, however,] and with the aid of the inflections
> of that voice which [the Greeks] called diastematic, in distinction to
> the continuous [voice], with which they otherwise ordinarily spoke
> in their language – diastematic, as if to say intervallic, [that is,]
> occasioned by the regulated adjustment of fast and slow [in order]
> to pronounce the syllables of the words according to the one and
> the other quality [i.e., accented and non-accented], each according
> to its special nature and accommodated to some determined affect.[6]

Galilei's distillation of this idea led him to conceptualize a style that
he called 'singing with attention to the words', which 'has to be
different from speaking only in that which suffices to distinguish the
one from the other' (i.e., musical pitch).[7] Galilei concluded that it
was with this style that the ancient Greeks sang their dramas
throughout, thus concurring with Mei's findings.

By the time Galilei connected his *cantare nel ricercare delle voci* with
singing dramas throughout, however, Bardi's Camerata was a thing
of the past. Some time during the 1580s the activities of the
Camerata and of at least some of its members were transferred to the
patronage of one of the wealthiest noblemen in Florence, Jacopo
Corsi (1561–1602), an amateur composer who had studied with Luca
Bati (*c*1550–1608), the master of the grand duke's *cappella* from 1599
to 1608. Corsi maintained close ties with Bardi throughout the 1580s
and may have attended the last of the Camerata's meetings. But he
seems to have lured away Bardi's protégés with generous patronage.
Corsi's household account books record a series of significant gifts to
Caccini between 1578 and 1595.[8] In 1584 Galilei dedicated the
reprint of his *Fronimo* to Corsi with the remark that in his *Dialogo*
there were many things that Corsi had heard directly from him.
Galilei and Piero Strozzi had begun receiving money from Corsi
early in the 1580s. Later, Jacopo Peri placed Piero Strozzi among
Corsi's circle in the early 1590s; and indeed Strozzi collaborated with
Corsi's chief poet, Ottavio Rinuccini, in the *Mascherata degli accecati*
(25 February 1596). In his *Discorso intorno all'opere di messer Gioseffo
Zarlino* of 1589, Galilei uses the past tense with reference to Bardi's
Camerata, when he says that his 1581 *Dialogo* was written 'only to
demonstrate [methods of dividing the octave] to some gentlemen
with whom I then found myself'.

We may hypothesize that Bardi and his coterie parted company perhaps partly because Corsi, in a spirit of rivalry, bribed Caccini, Galilei and Strozzi away from Bardi's patronage. But this shift may also have occurred partly or even mostly because the younger members and, to some extent, Galilei had drifted toward an Aristotelian aesthetic point of view at odds with Bardi's neo-Platonism.

If this is so, the decisive moment may have come in the summer of 1584. In June, Bardi, fresh from a visit to Ferrara, reported enthusiastically to the Accademia degli Alterati on Francesco Patrizi's *Della poetica*, which was then nearing completion. On 10 July the Alterati's leading figure, Lorenzo Giacomini, launched a major rebuttal against Patrizi's (and Bardi's) neo-Platonic ideal of ethical music. Against it he proposed that the highest purpose of music was the same as that of tragedy: emotional purgation or catharsis through the composer's heartfelt expression of the strongest passions. In his *Discorso*, on the other hand, Bardi asserted that the aim of music was to dispose our minds to virtue and that its aesthetic ideal was sweetness; it contributed to the expression of the text principally through fidelity to the structure of the poetic verses sung. The attack on Bardi's position continued in meetings of the Accademia degli Alterati until Giacomini's final discourse on the subject, 'Del furor poetico', was delivered in 1587. By that time, the membership of the academy included Corsi and Rinuccini, both of whom joined in 1586.[9] By 1585 Bardi had joined the Accademia della Crusca and seems to have withdrawn from the activities of the Alterati.

Bardi's last effort in musical pageantry on behalf of the grand-ducal court was the conceptualization (most of the poetry, and some of the music) for the *intermedi* performed with Girolamo Bargagli's play *La pellegrina* for the wedding of Ferdinando I and Christine of Lorraine in 1589. The story of the *intermedi*, if not the style of all the music, summarizes, in retrospect, the aspirations of Bardi's Camerata in the form of praise (perhaps wishful praise) of the grand duke's patronage of music. The first five *intermedi* portray, one by one, the best-known ancient myths of music's miraculous powers during the Golden Age of the gods, that is, during the period of ancient Greek civilization (*see* figs. 25 and 26). The finale of the last *intermedio*, however, takes place in the present time. In answer to Ferdinando's entreaties, the gods return to earth with the gift of music and dance (presumably the ancient and miraculous types) as a token of the new Golden Age that is seen to commence with the reign of Ferdinando and Christine. Although the music by Bardi, sung by the demons in the underworld, reflects both general and specific aspects of his classically inspired musical revival, much of the rest, by the traditional madrigalists Luca Marenzio (1553 or 1554–99) and Cristofano Malvezzi (1547–99), has nothing to do with the

25. *Third intermedio (Apollo slaying the Python) of the sequence framing Girolamo Bargagli's comedy 'La pellegrina' performed in Florence for the wedding of Ferdinando I de' Medici and Christine of Lorraine, 2 May 1589: engraving by Agostino Carracci after the design by Bernardo Buontalenti (the words were by Rinuccini, and the music by Marenzio)*

Camerata's ideals. The accompanied solo songs by Caccini, Peri, Antonio Archilei (husband of Ferdinando's famous singer Vittoria Archilei) and Emilio de' Cavalieri represent pure virtuosity and little expression of the text.

A close comparison between the customary printed description of the 1589 *intermedi* and the often conflicting content of the extraordinary printed books of its music reveals that Bardi had been engaged in a struggle for control of these spectacles. His rival was Emilio de' Cavalieri, whom Grand Duke Ferdinando had brought from Rome at the start of his reign to serve as general supervisor of all artists, craftsmen and musicians of the court – a position that included the functions previously divided informally between Bardi and several other members of the old Florentine nobility. This appointment was part of Ferdinando's policy of surrounding himself with foreigners and newly created nobility dependent solely on him and of eliminating courtiers, like Bardi and Galilei, who had been close to his older brother, the second grand duke, Francesco, and his hated pro-Spanish politics. Ferdinando's court policies were derived from those of Cosimo, who had installed the Mantuan Alessandro Striggio as highest-paid and *de facto* head musician above the ageing Florentine *maestro di cappella* Francesco Corteccia (1502–71). It was during the

133

26. Jacopo Peri portraying the musician Arion of mythology in the fifth intermedio for 'La pellegrina', 1589

period of Striggio's stay in Florence that Bardi showed his earliest interest in a classically inspired reform of musical style, sponsoring Galilei's studies in Venice about 1563 with Gioseffo Zarlino, to whom Bardi first looked for answers to his questions about Greek music. Striggio, however, left Florence in 1571 when, on the death of Corteccia, he was passed over as *maestro* by Francesco de' Medici, already acting as regent for his father, Cosimo. After the two-year tenure of Giovanni Piero Manenti (*c*1535–97), Francesco appointed as his successor Cristofano Malvezzi, the son of a former court musician and a representative of local musical culture. Bardi received the dedication of Malvezzi's *Ricercari* in 1577; and the earliest meetings of the Camerata, Bardi's first court pageant, the *Mascherata del Piacere e del Pentimento* (1573), and his admission to the Accademia degli Alterati (1574), date from the beginning of Malvezzi's time as grand-ducal *maestro*. But under Ferdinando I, Bardi lost his struggle with Cavalieri and was exiled to a post of protocol chief (*maestro di camera*) to Pope Clement VIII in 1592.

At exactly the time that Corsi assumed leadership of Bardi's former protégés and their successors, he launched an ambitious programme of patronage of musical pageants. In 1586 he paid the costs of a *bufolata* celebrating a Medici wedding. In 1589 he sponsored a mascherata. In 1589 he helped celebrate the wedding of Ferdinando

I with a *sbarra* in the courtyard of the Pitti Palace. Four more mascheratas received funding from him in 1590, 1593, 1595 and 1599.[10] The early seventeenth-century description of Corsi's patronage left by the Florentine poet Carlo Roberto Dati squares in its specifics with documentary evidence:

> The house of Jacopo Corsi, Florentine nobleman, was always open, like a public academy, to everyone who had intelligence or talent in the liberal arts. In it learned noblemen, literati, poets and musicians gathered; and [Torquato] Tasso, [Gabriele] Chiabrera, [Giovanni Battista] Marino, [Claudio] Monteverdi, Muzio Efrem and a thousand others of that group were lodged and entertained there. Entertainments with parade floats (*cocchiate*), celebrations and ballets accompanied by music were arranged and rehearsed there. Recitative style for use on stage was born there through the labour of Ottavio Rinuccini, celebrated poet, and Jacopo Peri, great master of harmony. And their first attempt, *La Dafne*, was staged there. And it is notable that such a beautiful and numerous assemblage always stayed together without the entertainment of games but rather out of true love of accomplishment. Sir Michele Dati, my uncle, who continuously formed part of that noble company, when he was old and nearly all his most intimate friends were dead, used to recount for me from time to time, not without tears, the activities and conversations of that virtuous salon, in which he played an important part.[11]

Dafne, to which Dati refers, was the first full-length opera ever written and was, together with its immediate successor, *Euridice*, the pinnacle of Corsi's patronage and the fruition of decades of musical speculation and experimentation in Florence. Its libretto was written by Rinuccini, while Corsi himself wrote the first pieces of music for it in 1594. Caccini claimed (in 1614) to have written music for this opera too. Eventually, however, Peri completed the work, and Caccini was dropped, in 1595, from Corsi's patronage. *Dafne* was first performed in Corsi's palace in February 1598 and repeated for the grand-ducal court in 1599 and 1600.

Although developed and tried out in private, *Dafne* was meant to ingratiate Corsi with Grand Duke Ferdinando de' Medici, as is evident from the libretto. It is divided into six tableaux based on Ovid's *Metamorphoses*: (1) Apollo liberates the nymphs and shepherds of Arcadia by slaying the menacing dragon Pitone; (2) Apollo humiliates Cupid, who vows revenge; (3) Apollo encounters Daphne, who flees him; (4) Cupid boasts to Venus of his triumph; (5) Apollo pursues Daphne, who turns into a laurel tree; (6) Apollo sublimates his grief by consecrating the laurel tree to triumph and ovation. In the end, through immortalizing his achievements in the arts, Apollo confirms and restores the triumph of order over chaos that he first achieved through arms. Since the laurel was the Medici family tree from the time of Lorenzo *magnifico* and was a particular symbol of the family's regeneration under Cosimo I, and since the personage of Apollo was used as a symbol for Cosimo himself, it is easy to see that *Dafne* is an allegorical capsule history of the Tuscan grand duchy.[12] The musical style evident in the few fragments of *Dafne* that survive is essentially the same as is found in the printed score of *Euridice*, produced by the same poet, composer and patron two years later.

Jacopo Peri, in the preface to *Euridice* (1600), rehearses the theory of Greek music as it had been developed in Bardi's Camerata, including the distinction between the diastematic and continuous voices as presented by Vincenzo Galilei and the conception of a style of singing falling midway between speech and song, which, he says, is the best one for singing plays on the modern stage. Peri describes his advance in theory, which corresponds to his important innovation in style, in these words:

> I knew, likewise, that in our speaking some words are intoned in such a way as can form the foundation of harmony [i.e., they are intoned with a distinct pitch], and in the course of a speech many other [words] are passed over that cannot be intoned, until one returns to other [words] worthy of the progression to a new consonance. And having regard for those manners [of speaking] and inflections that serve us in sorrow, in happiness and in similar things, I made the bass move at the tempo of those [emotions], now more, now less [rapidly], according to the passions. And I held [the bass] still through false and through good intervals [formed by the vocal line against the bass], until, running over various notes, the voice of the speaker arrived at that [syllable] which, in ordinary speech, would be intoned. This opened the way to a new consonance. And this [was done] not only so that the course of the speech would not offend the ear (as if stumbling too often over the repeated notes of the harmonies), or so that [the vocal line] would not seem, in a certain way, to dance to the movement of the bass, especially in either sorrowful or weighty things, since the other more cheerful things require, by their nature, more frequent movement [of the bass], but even more because the use of false [intervals] either diminished or covered over the advantage that was gained from the necessity of intoning every note: it was perhaps for that reason that ancient music had no need of doing that [i.e., of intoning every note with a new harmony]. Nevertheless (although I would not be eager to affirm this to be the singing used in Greek and Roman plays), I therefore believed that this [style] is the only one given us by our [modern] music that would be suited to our speech.[13]

To gain an idea of this *stile recitativo* (dramatic style), as it came to be called, it helps to examine a segment of dialogue from *Euridice* in the following manner. The text is laid out verse by verse. Each syllable that Peri coordinates with the beginning of a new note in the bass (i.e., a new chord) is underlined. Other syllables are accented by higher pitch or prolongation without coordinating with a bass note, and these syllables are shown here with accent marks.

> E tú, mentr'al ciel piacque
> lúce di questi lumi
> fatti al túo dipartir fontane, e fiumi,
> che fai per éntro i tenebrósi orrori?
> Forse t'affliggi, e piagni
> l'acerbo fato e gl'infelici amori.

> And yóu, who, while it pleased heaven,
> were the líght of these eyes,
> which poured out fountains and rivers at yóur departure,
> what are you doing amóng these dárk horrors?
> Perhaps you grieve and weep
> for your bitter fate and your unhappy love.

In fact, there are innumerable levels and additional types of accentuation in Peri's recitative, as well as interpretative inflections, acceleration and deceleration in delivery, and dramatic pauses that impart expression and characterization to his musical declamation. In spite of the competing claims of Emilio de' Cavalieri on behalf of his *Rappresentatione di anima, et di corpo* (Rome, 1600) or of Caccini for his solo madrigals, nothing quite like this had been done before, nor is Caccini's competing setting of *Euridice* as subtle or as dramatic in its declamation. It has often been remarked that Claudio Monteverdi's *Orfeo* was directly modelled on Peri's less well-known pioneering work, both in its libretto and the details of its musical style.[14] Within a decade of Peri's composition of *Euridice, stile recitativo* had become a universally accepted symbol of Florentine cultural achievements, which is everything the grand duke could have wished for it.

The occasion that brought forth Peri's *Euridice* was no less important for Florentines of that time than the opera is for the history of music. It celebrated the event that was the keystone of Ferdinando de' Medici's political opening towards France, which was intended to liberate Florence from Spanish hegemony: the wedding between Ferdinando's daughter Maria de' Medici and Henri IV of France. The negotiations for this union were especially difficult, since it was opposed by both Pope Clement VIII and the Spanish on political grounds and because Henri several times increased his demands for the dowry. It was therefore of enormous importance that Jacopo

Corsi headed both the delegation that eventually secured the agreement with the French and the group of Florentine noblemen who collected the lion's share of the 350,000 golden *scudi* in cash that there was left to pay after Ferdinando was permitted to deduct 250,000 *scudi* of French royal debt from the total dowry of 600,000 *scudi* claimed by Henri. As his reward, Corsi was allowed to present the performance of *Euridice* as a wedding gift. Although political allegory and Medici mythology are not as evident in *Euridice* as in the rival spectacles produced for the same wedding – particularly the *intermedi* for Caccini's opera *Il rapimento di Cefalo* and the banquet mascherata in the form of a dialogue between Juno and Minerva set to music by Cavalieri – its underlying theme is very similar to *Dafne*'s: the lost Golden Age of pastoral bliss is regained through cultivation of the arts (now specifically music). *Euridice* succeeded better than its principal rival because the scenery and costumes for *Il rapimento di Cefalo* were not completely ready for the performance. This led to Cavalieri's immediate return to Rome and to the eventual elevation of Corsi's family to the first rank of Florentine nobility through the purchase of an enormous palace at the head of via Tornabuoni and the town and countryside of Caiazzo in the kingdom of Naples with the title of marquis – purchases that required the permission and protection of the grand duke. Corsi compensated Peri for his role in this triumph of patronage by joining him in a lucrative partnership in the cloth trade, which led to Peri's election to the very prestigious post of Camarlingo dell'Arte della Lana.

After the deaths of Caccini (in 1618), Peri (in 1633) and their immediate successor, Marco da Gagliano (1582–1643), a steady, if small, stream of Florentine operas were presented for the grand-ducal court at the Pitti Palace, Uffizi theatre (fig. 27) and Casino Mediceo (home of the Accademia dei Concordi on the Piazza S Marco) until the construction of the first public opera theatres in Florence by the Accademia degli Infuocati (1650) and the more aristocratic Accademia degli Immobili (1652), which still operates its original theatre today.

The advent of opera in Florence did not signal the end of the older genres of court musical spectacle. Indeed, all of them continued alongside opera for the next century or more, but with the addition of dialogue in *stile recitativo*. The economic declines that more or less coincided with the death of Ferdinando's eldest son, Cosimo II, in 1621 and with the plague of 1630–33 did, however, have a detrimental effect on court patronage.

Those two solemn dates mark off the regency of Cosimo II's widow, Archduchess Maria Maddalena, and his mother, Grand Duchess Christine, who ruled on behalf of Ferdinando II until his 21st birthday in 1631. Faced with the threat of a coup and other less

PRIMO INTERMEDIO DELLA VEGLIA DELLA LIBERATIONE DI TIRRENO, FATTA NELLA SALA DELLE CO
DE DEL SER.^{mo} GRAN DVCA DI TOSCANA IL CARNOVALE DEL 1616. DOVE SI RAP.^{ta} IL MONTE D'ISCHIA CON IL GIGANTE
TIFEO SOTTO.

27. *Stage and auditorium of Bernardo Buontalenti's Uffizi Theatre, with the setting designed by Giulio Parigi for the first intermezzo of 'La liberazione di Tirreno e d'Arnea', performed in Florence for the wedding of Ferdinando Gonzaga, Duke of Mantua, and Caterina de' Medici, 6 February 1617: etching by Jacques Callot (the royal couple took part in the ballet depicted)*

139

28. Scene from Act 3 (St Michael puts Lucifer and the devils to flight) from Marco da Gagliano's 'La regina Sant'Orsola': engraving by Alfonso Parigi after the design by Giulio Parigi

direct challenges to the legitimacy of their reign, these Medici widows used musical pageantry for the same purposes as did their husbands, if with different content. Themes of the heroism, dignity and political rights of women, which began to appear in academic discourse during their reign, are reflected in the court pageantry that they patronized. For the visit of Prince Władisław of Poland in 1625, for instance, they offered a *commedia sacra* concerning a religious heroine, *La regina Sant'Orsola* (*see* fig. 28), with music by the master of their *cappella*, Marco da Gagliano, the tournament *La precedenza delle dame*, on the theme of deference to women, with music by Peri, and the first opera by a female composer, *La liberazione di Ruggiero dall'isola d'Alcina*, by Giulio's daughter Francesca Caccini (1587–1640), to a libretto that reworks an episode from *Orlando furioso* by incorporating Alcina's point of view (ignored by Ariosto), as suggested by the grand duchess herself. The music of this latter work dramatizes the conflict between the male perception of Alcina as ugly witch with the female view of her human qualities. It does this by juxtaposing two clashing keys, F major and A minor (more properly, two hexachords: soft and hard), in the dialogues and even some monologues in which the two viewpoints compete.[15]

Florence: Musical Spectacle and Drama, 1570–1650

In keeping with their status as widows, Maria Maddalena and Grand Duchess Christine made it part of their political policy to project an image of their piety (which may, of course, have also reflected their sincere beliefs). The effect this had on their patronage of musical spectacle was already noticed by the librettist Andrea Salvadori (*d* 1635): 'Nor is it, perhaps, little glory to the name of Tuscany that just as, under the auspices of the Most Serene Grand Dukes, in this [court] theatre, the practice of ancient Greek musical drama was first revived, today, in this same [theatre], a new field [of musical drama] has been opened, which treats true and sacred Christian tales, leaving aside the vain stories of the Gentiles'.[16] Salvadori's analogy is particularly apt because in Florence the history of musical spectacle in the religious sphere is remarkably parallel to that in secular life.

Just as the first secular music dramas presented at the grand-ducal court emanated from private experiments inspired by the humanistic discourse of Florentine academies, official and unofficial, so the development of dramatic religious music, eventually heard by the Medici, emerged from the institutional context of the religious lay confraternities where most Florentine humanists had received their practical training in eloquent oration, by sermonizing there as boys.[17] The confraternities were extremely numerous and well established in Florence. The most important of them, the four companies of the Christian doctrine, were founded in the early fifteenth century as privately endowed, self-governing societies for the religious training of boys not destined for the clergy. By the late sixteenth century, these groups and their numerous imitators included as members adult men as well as children. The wealthier and more prestigious of the confraternities owned their own oratory, where they met every evening for sermons and the singing of nonliturgical religious songs in the vernacular (*laude*), which often used the melodies of well-known popular songs or folksongs with religious words in place of the original secular text.

To celebrate All Souls' Eve, Christmas, Easter and the feast of their particular patron saint, the leading confraternities had, in the fifteenth and early sixteenth centuries, performed rhymed plays (always in *ottava rima*) on religious subjects (*sacre rappresentazioni*), which often incorporated appropriate *laude*. Some may have been sung throughout to formulaic recitational *arie*; as they grew in length, though, this mode of performance would have become tedious. During the sixteenth century, these *sacre rappresentazioni* were replaced in the confraternities' celebrations by modern-style prose dramas on religious subjects (*commedie sacre*). Like their secular counterparts, these plays were performed with entirely sung, dramatic *intermedi* between their acts. A series of ten such *intermedi sacri* that Giovanni

141

Maria Cecchi (1518–87) wrote for his plays between 1549 and 1585 – for the Florentine confraternities of S Giovanni Evangelista, S Sebastiano and La Purificazione – forms an exact parallel to the secular *intermedi* produced for the Medici court. The last of Cecchi's *intermedi sacri*, in fact, was performed in honour of the wedding of 1589, with music by Luca Bati. In parallel to the secular themes of ancient Greek mythology, Cecchi's *intermedi sacri* treat Old Testament subjects with extreme attention to details of Hebrew philology.[18]

Related to these *intermedi sacri* are the brief musical scenes, independent of performances of plays, that began to be presented in the Compagnia dell'Arcangelo Raffaello detta della Scala in 1582 or a little earlier. In outline they are similar to the court mascherata. They begin with an entrance into the sanctuary – of a saint, of shepherds in search of the holy manger, of voices from Purgatory – and continue with monologues or dialogues sung by the personages in costume and with scenery or at least the seasonal decoration of the oratory as a backdrop. The members of this confraternity and the participants in these *mascherate sacre* included the same Florentines who brought forth secular dramatic music: Giovanni de' Bardi, Vincenzo Galilei, Girolamo Mei, Giulio Caccini, Piero Strozzi, Jacopo Peri, Ottavio Rinuccini and Marco da Gagliano and his brother Giovanni Battista (1594–1651). Surviving music from these productions by Caccini, Peri and G. B. da Gagliano incorporates the same styles of expressive and dramatic declamation used in their secular songs and operas. Surviving texts for these religious musical dramatizations from as early as 1622 already reveal the length and outline typical of the sacred dialogues and early oratorios that later emanated from Rome. By the middle of the seventeenth century, these musical sacred dialogues were performed without costumes and scenery, as were oratorios at that time and afterwards.[19]

The Medici court nurtured an important school of polyphonic madrigalists, many of whom were noblemen.[20] The Medici chapel of S Lorenzo, the cathedral and several other churches in Florence gave sustenance to a skilful group of composers who produced colossal multi-choir celebration pieces, very few of which survive today.[21] The Medici court chapel included an excellent band of instrumentalists called the *franciosini* to whose repertory the young Florentine Giovanni Battista Lulli (J.-B. Lully) owed his style of French overture. And Girolamo Frescobaldi (1583–1643) sowed the seeds of a Florentine school of keyboard composers during his service (1628–34) to Ferdinando II. But these features of musical life did not distinguish Florence from its sister cities of Italy as did the development of musical spectacle and drama, for which she will be best remembered.

Florence: Musical Spectacle and Drama, 1570–1650

NOTES

[1] R. Strong, *Art and Power: Renaissance Festivals, 1450–1650* (Woodbridge, 1984), 136.

[2] Found in a contemporaneous manuscript copy and printed in A. F. Cori, *Lyra Barberina amphichordos* (Florence, 1763), iii, 233–48; original language with English translation in C. V. Palisca, *The Florentine Camerata: Documentary Studies and Translations* (New Haven and London, 1989), 90–131.

[3] In its goals, Bardi's Camerata was strikingly similar to Antoine de Baïf's Académie de Poésie et de Musique in Paris, whose principal period of activity (1567–73) occurred immediately before.

[4] From the first sentence of Caccini's preface to *Le nuove musiche*, translated in the edition by H. W. Hitchcock, Recent Researches in the Music of the Baroque Era, ix (Madison, 1970), 43. More on *sprezzatura di canto* is found in the preface to the 1614 collection, also edited and translated by Hitchcock, ibid, xxviii (Madison, 1978).

[5] See N. Pirrotta and E. Povoledo, *Music and Theatre from Poliziano to Monteverdi*, trans. K. Eales (Cambridge, 1982), 197–200. Pirrotta (p. 202) points out that similar language was used to describe singing that was part of a play performance at Reggio Emilia in 1568.

[6] 'Lo esprimere interamente et con efficacia tutto quello che voleva fare intendere col suo significato il parlare per il mezzo et ajuto de la acutezza et gravità de la voce, detta da loro à differenza de la continua con la quale altri continuamente ragiona nel idioma loro diastematica, quasi per dir cosi intervallativa, accompagnata con la regolata temperatura del presto et adagio, pronunziare le parti de suoi termini, secondo che l'una a l'altra qualità, ciascuna da per se per propria natura è accomodata à qualche determinato affetto', as transcribed in C. V. Palisca, 'The "Camerata Fiorentina": a Reappraisal', *Studi musicali*, i (1972), 222.

[7] 'Il cantare nel ricercare delle voci ha da essere solo differente dal parlare quanto basta a distinguere quello da questo', loc. cit.

[8] T. Carter, 'Music and Patronage in Late Sixteenth-Century Florence: the Case of Jacopo Corsi (1561–1602)', *I Tatti Studies: Essays in the Renaissance*, i (1985), 57–104. Carter's study corrects the often repeated idea that Corsi's group was distinct from and partly at odds with Bardi's, as first postulated in N. Pirrotta, 'Temperaments and Tendencies in the Florentine Camerata', *MQ*, xl (1954), 169–89.

[9] Concerning Giacomini's discourse and its context, see C. V. Palisca, 'The Alterati of Florence, Pioneers in the Theory of Dramatic Music', *New Looks at Italian Opera: Essays in Honor of Donald J. Grout* (Ithaca, 1968), 9–38.

[10] Carter, 'Music and Patronage', 75–6. Tim Carter elaborates on the social, political and cultural significance and context of Corsi's Patronage in '*Non occorre nominare tanti musici*: Private Patronage and Public Ceremony in Late Sixteenth-Century Florence', *I Tatti Studies*, iv (1991), 89–104.

[11] My translation from the transcription in A. Solerti, *Gli albori del melodramma* (Milan, 1904), i, 48.

[12] The symbolism of the laurel and of Apollo in this opera was first identified in B. R. Hanning, 'Glorious Apollo: Poetic and Political Themes in the First Opera', *Renaissance Quarterly*, xxxii (1979), 485–513.

[13] My translations. The entire original text is reprinted in A. Solerti, *Le origini del melodramma* (Turin, 1903), 43–9. A complete English translation is in O. Strunk, *Source Readings in Music History* (New York, 1950), 373–6. A more careful translation of the crucial part, with extensive glossing and illustrative examples from Peri's opera, is found in C. V. Palisca, *Humanism in Italian Renaissance Musical Thought* (New Haven, 1985), 427–33. A more thorough analysis of the style described is given in idem, 'Peri and the Theory of Recitative', *Studies in Music*, xv (1981), 51–61.

[14] A. M. Monterosso Vacchelli, 'Elementi stilistici nell'*Euridice* di Jacopo Peri in rapporto dell'*Orfeo* di Monteverdi', *Claudio Monteverdi e il suo tempo*, ed. R. Monterosso (Verona, 1969), 117–27; N. Pirrotta, 'Monteverdi e i problemi dell'opera', *Studi sul teatro veneto fra rinascimento ed età barocca*, ed. M. T. Muraro (Florence, 1971), 321–43; B. R. Hanning, *Of Poetry and Music's Power: Humanism and the Creation of Opera* (Ann Arbor, 1980); G. Tomlinson, *Monteverdi and the End of the Renaissance* (Oxford, 1987), 131–41.

[15] In *Orfeo* Monteverdi had used the same opposition of F major and A minor to represent the different perceptions of Silvia, the messenger bearing news of Eurydice's death, and the first Shepherd, who at first cannot understand the import of her words. This analysis of Francesca Caccini's opera in the context of regency patronage was first presented in S. G. Cusick,

The Early Baroque Era

'Francesca Caccini's *La liberazione di Ruggiero dall'isola d'Alcina* (1625): a Feminist Misreading of *Orlando furioso*?', a paper presented at the annual meeting of the American Musicological Society, Baltimore, 3 November 1988.

[16] 'Nè forse è poca gloria del nome Toscano, che si come sotto gl'auspici de' Sereniss. Gran Duchi prima in questo Teatro fù rinovato l'uso de' gl'antichi Drammi di Grecia in musica, così oggi in questo medesimo, sia stato aperto un nuovo campo, di trattare con più utile, e diletto, lasciate le vane favole de Gentili, le vere, e sacre azzioni Cristiane', as transcribed from a manuscript source in T. Carter, *Jacopo Peri (1561–1633): his Life and Works* (New York and London, 1989), 84.

[17] Concerning the close relationship between humanistic rhetoric and sermonizing by boys in the confraternities, see P. O. Kristeller, 'Lay Religious Traditions and Florentine Platonism', *Studies in Renaissance Thought and Letters* (Rome, 1956), 99–122; idem, 'The Rôle of Religion in Renaissance Humanism and Platonism', *The Pursuit of Holiness in Late Medieval and Renaissance Religion: Papers from the University of Michigan Conference*, ed. C. Trinkaus and H. A. Oberman, Studies in Medieval and Reformation Thought, x (Leiden, 1974), 367–70; and C. Trinkaus, 'The Religious Thought of the Italian Humanists, and the Reformers: Anticipation or Autonomy?', *The Pursuit of Holiness*, ed. idem and H. A. Oberman, 339–66.

[18] See J. W. Hill, 'Florentine *Intermedi Sacri e Morali*, 1549–1622', *IMSCR*, xiii, *Strasbourg 1982*, ii, 265–301.

[19] Concerning the Compagnia dell'Arcangelo Raffaello, see J. W. Hill, 'Oratory Music in Florence, I: *Recitar Cantando*, 1583–1655', *AcM*, li (1979), 108–36. Parallel and later events in other lay confraternities are described in idem, 'Oratory Music in Florence, III: The Confraternities from 1655 to 1785', ibid, lviii (1986), 127–77.

[20] See D. S. Butchart, *The Madrigal in Florence, 1560–1630* (diss., U. of Oxford, 1980).

[21] See Carter, *Jacopo Peri (1561–1633): his Life and Works*.

BIBLIOGRAPHICAL NOTE

Historical-political background

The only thorough history of the Medici grand duchy is R. Galluzzi, *Istoria del granducato di Toscana sotto il governo della casa Medici* (Cambiagi, 1781, 2/Livorno, 1820–21). E. Cochrane, *Florence in the Forgotten Centuries, 1527–1800: a History of Florence and the Florentines in the Age of the Grand Dukes* (Chicago, 1973), includes an extensive and valuable bibliographical note, which admirably summarizes modern scholarship up to the date of publication, but the historical narrative, while rich in ideas and interpretation, tends towards the polemical. A more balanced overview, but without citation of sources, can be had from J. R. Hale, *Florence and the Medici: the Pattern of Control* (London, 1977). For the most interesting treatment of early grand-ducal politics, in the context of social, economic, and cultural history, see S. Berner, 'Florentine Political Thought in the Late Cinquecento', *Il pensiero politico*, ii (1970), 177–99; and idem, 'Florentine Society in the Late Sixteenth and Early Seventeenth Centuries', *Studies in the Renaissance*, xviii (1971), 203–46.

Medici pageantry and spectacle in relation to statecraft

The idea that the Medici grand dukes had a distinct plan for the use of pageantry and spectacle as an instrument of politics originated with Galluzzi (see *Istoria del granducato* above) in the eighteenth century. Modern and detailed analysis of grand-ducal pageantry from this point of view is offered in E. Borsook, 'Art and Politics at the Medici Court', *Mitteilungen des Kunsthistorischen Institutes in Florenz*, xii (1965), xiii (1967), xiv (1969); G. G. Bertelà and A. Petrioli Tofani, *Feste e apparati medicei da Cosimo I a Cosimo II* (Florence, 1969); L. Zorzi, introduction, *Il luogo teatrale a Firenze*, ed. M. Fabbri, E. Garbero Zorzi and A. Petrioli Tofani, Spettacolo e musica nella

Florence: Musical Spectacle and Drama, 1570–1650

Firenze medicea: documenti e restituzioni, i (Milan, 1975), 9–51; L. Zorzi, *Il teatro e la città* (Turin, 1977); idem, *Il potere e lo spazio: la scena del principe* (Florence, 1980); R. Strong, *Art and Power: Renaissance Festivals, 1450–1650* (Woodbridge, 1984); and S. Mamone, *Il teatro nella Firenze medicea*, Problemi di storia dello spettacolo, ix (Milan, 1981). A more descriptive approach to the same material can be found in N. Pirrotta and E. Povoledo, *Music and Theatre from Poliziano to Monteverdi*, trans. K. Eales (Cambridge, 1982); A. M. Nagler, *Theatre Festivals of the Medici, 1539–1637* (New Haven, 1964); W. Osthoff, *Theatergesang und darstellende Musik in der italienischen Renaissance (15. und 16. Jahrhundert)* (Tutzing, 1969); and C. Molinari, *Le nozze degli dèi: un saggio sul grande spettacolo italiano nel Seicento* (Rome, 1968). An excellent and highly relevant social theory of patronage is put forward in R. Weissman, 'Taking Patronage Seriously: Mediterranean Values and Renaissance Society', *Patronage, Art, and Society in Renaissance Italy*, ed. F. W. Kent and P. Simons (Oxford, 1987), 25–45.

The emergence of opera

There are two competing explanations for the emergence of opera. The one that emphasizes the importance of Florence and the late humanistic enquiry that took place in Giovanni de' Bardi's Camerata, the circle around Jacopo Corsi and several formal academies, principally the Accademia degli Alterati, is best summarized in B. R. Hanning, *Of Poetry and Music's Power: Humanism and the Creation of Opera* (Ann Arbor, 1980). More detailed treatment of particular groups can be found in C. V. Palisca, 'The "Camerata Fiorentina": a Reappraisal', *Studi musicali*, i (1972), 203–35; and idem, 'The Alterati of Florence, Pioneers in the Theory of Dramatic Music', *New Looks at Italian Opera: Essays in Honor of Donald J. Grout* (Ithaca, 1968), 9–38. N. Pirrotta, in 'Temperaments and Tendencies in the Florentine Camerata', *MQ*, xl (1954), 169–89, opposed that explanation on grounds of insufficiency. In *Music and Theatre from Poliziano to Monteverdi* (see above), he offered in its place developments in musical theatre and solo singing all over Italy during the sixteenth century. In my review of Pirrotta's book (in *JAMS*, xxxvi (1983), 519–26) I suggest that Pirrotta really offers necessary causes, while Palisca (and his former student Hanning) describe sufficient causes. A full explanation is likely to take both into account. A summary easily accessible to the non-musician that adequately describes the novelty of *stile recitativo* is H. M. Brown, 'How Opera Began: an Introduction to Jacopo Peri's *Euridice* (1600)', *The Late Italian Renaissance, 1525–1630*, ed. E. Cochrane (New York, 1970), 401–43.

145

Chapter VII

Vienna, 1580–1705

THEOPHIL ANTONICEK

In Vienna and throughout the Habsburg Empire the court was constantly the brilliant focal point of all artistic activity, which reached its height, especially in the visual arts and music, in the later years of the reign of the last Habsburg emperor Charles VI (1711–40).[1] But during the preceding centuries as well, the imperial court exerted tremendous influence on the arts. Like everything else, the position of music at court was determined by the domestic and political hierarchy of ceremonial. Music was firmly built into the structure of court life, a position it held in Austria until the time of Maria Theresa. Ceremonial determined not just the place at which music was played but the character of what was performed. With such limitations, it was a challenge to find new variations within the pre-ordained framework. However, it would be incorrect to suppose that the court was hostile to progress: the Habsburgs, particularly in the Baroque period, were generally ready to accept innovation, giving the new its place beside the old. For both ceremonial and music observed the protocol of the court, which was orientated by timeless criteria – beginning with the figure of the emperor – so that, strictly speaking, all activities remained in the present. Ancient music was therefore still in use alongside contemporary works. The older works acted as a yardstick of quality, but they too were liable to be replaced by works considered to be of equal or better quality.

The imperial Hofmusik, like similar institutions at other courts, was not an autonomous organization but part of a larger institution, the Hofkapelle or imperial chapel.[2] Headed by an ecclesiastic, the court preacher, who was normally required to be a doctor of theology and who was assisted by the elemosinarius and the court chaplains, the Hofkapelle conducted the divine service at the imperial court. As music was essential to the service, musicians also belonged to the Hofkapelle (the use of the word to denote the Hofmusikkapelle or court orchestra is thus a misleading simplification). They were under the direction of a Kapellmeister and Vice-Kapellmeister. Some musical ability was also required of the ecclesiastical staff of the chapel, and it was the task of the elemosinarius, assisted by the

Kapellmeister, to audition singers for the choir; the chaplains were also supposed to be good musicians, to ensure the proper conduct of divine service.

Representatives of the Netherlands school of composition, in its prime in the late sixteenth century, held the office of Hofkapellmeister at various times. When the Kapellmeister Jacobus Vaet died in 1567, the court began negotiations with Palestrina (among others) in an attempt to find a successor. But these came to nothing: Palestrina required too high a salary, and there were fears that he might have trouble with the resident Netherlands singers because he was Italian.[3] Other Italian musicians did in fact enter the imperial service, including trumpeters, who for some years had been recruited almost exclusively from Italy, particularly Brescia.[4] Two Italians, Camillo Zannotti and Alessandro Orologio, even rose to the post of Vice-Kapellmeister,[5] but they were there too early to have introduced any Italian Baroque-style innovations to Vienna; nor did Annibale Padovano and Marc'Antonio Ingegneri's dedications to the emperor of work in the *seconda prattica* style have any special significance or influence.[6] Polyphony and cantus firmus-based compositions remained the prevailing style at the imperial court.

It may have been otherwise in the imperial chamber, where Italian names among the instrumentalists have been held to indicate that independent instrumental music, then coming into vogue, was being practised. There is also mention of Franciscus Godefridus Troilus à Lessoth, a humanist aristocrat from Rovereto serving at the court at Prague, who began collecting monodies in 1612, and of a treble who 'sang in Italian' in 1613 at a festive event in Vienna held by the emperor specially for Archduke Ferdinand, whose liking for modern Italian music was well known.[7] And that there was no objection to new music, at any rate in principle, is shown by the presence of the lutenist and courtier Pietro Paolo Melli, who made what was obviously a late addition to his second book of lute tablatures (1614), dedicated to the emperor, and called it *La Claudiana Gagliarda* in honour of Monteverdi.[8] It is significant that Melli was one of the few musicians taken over by Ferdinand II from his predecessor's household when he became emperor in 1619.[9] Obviously Melli suited the tastes of the new ruler (to whom he dedicated his fourth and fifth books of lute music in 1616 and 1620).[10]

Ferdinand's accession to the throne, entailing the removal of his court from Graz to Vienna, which now became the capital city and the emperor's residence, immediately changed the musical situation at the imperial court. Ferdinand brought his own court musicians with him, Italians prominent among them. The court of Ferdinand's father Karl II had itself been the 'modern' opposite pole to the emperor's residence.[11] Because of the division of the inheritance between the sons of Ferdinand I, Karl had ruled the inner Austrian provinces from Graz after his father's death. He had paid particular attention to music from the outset when organizing his household. The basis of his musical staff was taken over from his late father's household; these were Austrian and Netherlands musicians, and Karl's first Kapellmeister, Johannes de Cleve (1529–82, musical director 1564–70), was a Netherlander. However, the picture was already changing. Cleve's successors were all Italians, and a large and growing number of their countrymen were active at the archduke's court, among them the Kapellmeisters Simone Gatto (1540/50–94/5, Kapellmeister from 1581), Pietro Antonio Bianco (c1540–1611, Kapellmeister from 1595), Giovanni Priuli (1575/80-before 1629, Kapellmeister from 1614/15) and Mattia Ferrabosco (1550–1616, Kapellmeister in Graz from 1581 and imperial Vice-Kapellmeister from 1603), the organists Francesco Rovigo (1530/31–97, organist from 1582 to 1590 and also tutor to the archducal couple's children), Annibale Perini (c1560–96, organist 1579–90 and from 1594), Francesco Stivori (d 1605, organist from 1602), Alessandro Tadei (c1585–1667, organist from 1606), and Giovanni Valentini (1582/3–1649, organist from c1614), and also Lodovico Zacconi, engaged as a singer (1555–1627, in Graz 1585–90).

One must not, of course, simplistically equate the Netherlands school only with conservatism and the Italians with progress: Italians such as Padovano composed very much in the style of Netherlands polyphony, particularly in their church music, and conversely the Netherlander Lambert de Sayve could be described as a precursor of the Venetian style.[12] The emphasis, however, was now on the new Italian music, preferred by the ruling families and particularly Ferdinand II, and Netherlands musicians eventually disappeared from the Hofmusik at Graz.

A certain shift can be seen in various organizational features too. Karl II may indeed have modelled his court on his father's, musical activity at court thus being incorporated into the major ecclesiastical institution, the Hofkapelle, with its elemosinarius and court chaplains. But the fact that when the latter were appointed, particular attention was paid in Graz to their suitability as musicians – many court chaplains were composers and practising musicians – shows that music had risen in estimation; even more significant is the merging of the offices of elemosinarius and Kapellmeister in the person of Pietro Antonio Bianco. And although the old order, whereby only singers and organists belonged to the Hofkapelle while instrumentalists came under the department of the royal stables, was preserved, Padovano, Gatto and Priuli all rose from the ranks of instrumentalists to become Kapellmeister, an indication that instrumental music was making its way into church music, after the

Venetian model. The status of instrumentalists was rising all the time.

Venice, which was after all a neighbour, was the principal point of reference in musical matters. Kapellmeisters were often sent to Venice to engage musicians and to buy instruments and material for performance. Good contact was also maintained with leading Venetian musicians such as Andrea and Giovanni Gabrieli (to whom Tadei, for instance, was sent as a pupil). It may well have been the Venetian splendours of combined vocal and instrumental music that particularly took the fancy of the Habsburgs; the monodic style was introduced only later, under Ferdinand, but was then intensively cultivated, for instance by Bartolomeo Mutis, Count of Cesana, *d* 1623/4, known as the first monodist on the Austrian side of the Alps, who was court chaplain and sang tenor in Graz from 1604 onwards.[13]

On journeys to Italy, both archdukes had had the opportunity to gain first-hand experience of the many new forms of the arts that flourished there. In 1565, when his sister Johanna was married to Francesco de' Medici in Florence, Karl saw a magnificently staged performance of courtly *intermedi* with music (now lost) by Alessandro Striggio.[14] On a grand tour that took Ferdinand through Italy in 1598, his hosts introduced him to a number of outstanding musicians and the works they composed and directed: he met Giovanni Gabrieli and Giovanni Croce in Venice, he heard the choir of S Antonio, Padua, under Costanzo Porta, music from the Papal Chapel in Ferrara and of the Collegium Germanicum in Rome; in Florence, Vittoria Archilei, among others, sang before him, and he attended a performance of the *Giuoco della Cieca* by Laura Guidiccioni and Emilio de' Cavalieri.[15]

After the accession of Ferdinand II to the imperial throne, Vienna suddenly became a major European musical centre again, and indeed was one of the advance posts of the modern music of its time outside Italy. In the decades preceding 1619, however, it had been overshadowed by other imperial residences. While the imperial court under Maximilian II had divided its time between Prague and Vienna, Prague became virtually the sole imperial residence during the reign of Rudolf II. Of the archdukes, Karl II seems to have spent some time in Vienna at the beginning of his reign, before his final move to Graz in 1571.[16] Archduke Matthias, who had Alard du Gaucquier and Lambert de Sayve as Kapellmeisters, may well have spent some time in Vienna too before taking up residence there as emperor.[17] For all of them, however, Vienna was only one among many seats, and so it was not a stimulating centre of artistic life, as it was both before and afterwards. Music in Vienna cannot indeed have flourished in the second half of the sixteenth century, as is

29. Procession from St Stephen's Cathedral, Vienna, with medallions of Emperor Matthias and his wife Anna (top left and right): engraving (1614) by Heinrich Ulrich

suggested by accounts of the two most important musical centres there after the court: St Stephen's Cathedral and the Schottenstift, the abbey church Unsere Liebe Frau zu den Schotten.

A directive issued on 15 December 1571 for the choir of St Stephen's[18] was probably intended to settle certain grievances. It lays down that there should be a choirmaster and assistant choirmaster, choristers and choirboys, with two tutors to instruct the latter, one in letters and one in music. Detailed provision is also made for the physical well-being of the musicians: food, clothing and accommodation. However, accounts from the turn of the century show that these proposals remained where they had always been: on paper. Accommodation was very poor, food insufficient, discipline abysmally low. These conditions may have been why, in spite of good remuneration, no outstanding figures held the office of choirmaster. This state of affairs was to continue until the imperial court came to Vienna and, although St Stephen's came within the jurisdiction of the city, exercised its influence on the choice of those appointed to musical posts. Thus, from 1619 to 1631 music was in the hands of Emperor Matthias's former Hofkapellmeister, Christoph Strauss;

subsequent musical directors at St Stephen's included Wolfgang Ebner (1663–5; he had already been organist in 1634–7), Augustin Kärzinger, a Benedictine from Melk (1666–78) and Michael Zacher or Zächer (1679–1712), who was succeeded by Johann Joseph Fux.

At the Schottenstift, the composer and historian Johann Rasch (*c*1540–1612) had been organist since 1570.[19] In his chronicle of the Schottenstift, he provides interesting information about the state of music there. Abbot Johann Krembnitzer, who held office from 1500 to 1518, had, says Rasch, brought music into a flourishing condition by the introduction of a choir, which continued after his time 'until it is now in decline and very bad, slapdash and even knavish' – a remarkable statement coming from an organist who must himself have been involved in the music of the abbey. It can be taken only as a reproach to the house (the *regens chori*, if there was one, must have been an inmate of the abbey himself, according to custom) for wilfully allowing what had once been a flourishing musical institution to fall into decline (this is probably the interpretation of the adjective 'knavish'). Such an explanation lends weight to the conjecture that Rasch, unhappy in his post, devoted himself chiefly to his literary labours.

When Ferdinand II moved into his new capital city, he had long enjoyed the reputation of being a well-informed patron of music. Prominent musical figures, representatives of both old and new styles, such as Orazio Vecchi, Tomás Luis de Victoria, Lodovico Viadana and Giovanni Battista Grillo, had, like his own musicians, dedicated works to him, and the line continued to Monteverdi, whose intended dedication of his eighth book of madrigals, which appeared in 1638, devolved on Ferdinand III as a result of Ferdinand II's death. In 1615 a work dedicated to him appeared in Venice, *Parnassus Musicus Ferdinandeus*, edited by the Graz court singer Giovanni Battista Bonometti, with contributions from 32 composers, nine of them from the Hofmusik in Graz.

It is not known whether Ferdinand II was musically active himself. Francesco Rovigo was described as music master to the children of Archduke Karl II and so could have taught Ferdinand. At least Ferdinand had educated musical tastes, sustained by distinctive ideas of his own, which helped determine the choice of the musicians he engaged as well as the nature of the music they provided. Ferdinand II's musicians also enjoyed high esteem among their colleagues. In the preface to his *Salmi concertati* of 1626, Giovanni Rovetta, describing his progress from instrumentalist to composer, says: 'And let no one be surprised that I first practised the skills of instrumental playing, and then turned to composition, because the masters Striggio, Priuli and Valentini and almost the whole school of composers took that path before me.'[20] Giovanni Priuli and Giovanni

Valentini were the first Italians to hold the office of imperial Hofkapellmeister. Valentini in particular was not just a musician widely recognized outside his own circle; he also enjoyed the confidence and intimate friendship of the imperial house. He instructed the children of Emperor Ferdinand II in music, and in addition seems to have been an authoritative figure in the field of the arts at the imperial court, as is frequently obvious from correspondence of the Habsburgs among themselves. For instance, Ferdinand III prides himself on having written the text of a madrigal of which 'Valentin corrected only one word', and believes that a *Miserere* he has recently composed 'can hold its own with all the Misereres composed by Valentin'. Valentini's opinion carried weight in practical areas too: Ferdinand comments, referring to the Vice-Kapellmeister, taken prisoner by the Swedes, that 'Valentin does not think it good for the musicians to go to war'.[21]

The close relationship of the ruling family to its musicians, the Habsburgs' own obvious musical gifts and the interest they took in music naturally left their mark on musical activity at the Viennese court. Even in medieval times, the arts had been a well-established element in court life. To the Habsburgs, however, music was a genuine essential, and it was cultivated intensively and with great pleasure. Ferdinand II's two passions in life were said to be music and hunting. His children – Ferdinand III, Leopold Wilhelm, Maria Anna and Cäcilia Renata – exchanged letters about their experiences in both fields, as well as in others such as poetry, drama, mathematics, 'chymica' and playing at dice. This fact in itself, and even more so the detail and the obvious committed interest with which the accounts are written, shows the high value placed upon these disciplines, music and poetry especially. The regard in which the arts were held continued unabated until the end of the Baroque period. The fact that the rulers were themselves musically active was reflected in dedications, which frequently alluded to the ruler's dual position in the political and the musical realms; for instance, two works dedicated to Leopold I in 1673, by Giovanni Legrenzi and Carlo Grossi, used the title 'La cetra' with the double meaning of 'sceptre' and 'lyre', as Vivaldi was later to do in his op.9 concertos.

Well-educated and with considerable musical gifts, the Habsburgs naturally had clear ideas about the sort of musicians they wished to appoint, and could judge whether a particular candidate was suitable for their purposes. This fact too was obviously known and acknowledged: Giovanni Antonio Bertoli, for instance, says of the imperial musicians Giovanni Sansoni and Antonio Bertali, when citing them as authorities, that it was evidence enough of their standing to say that they were in the service of Ferdinand III.[22] The Habsburgs' correspondence, referred to above, includes well-informed opinions on musical performance; Ferdinand III, for instance, remarks of a certain 'Giuseppino Castrato Romano' that he does not quite come up to expectations: 'I do not like his disposition, he will have to alter it'.[23]

From the time of Ferdinand II onwards, the Baroque style, not surprisingly, gained the upper hand at the imperial court and thus in Vienna itself, though not at the expense of the old style, the *prima prattica*. Mastery of the traditional techniques of the musician's calling was an absolute necessity for Viennese composers. Palestrina for long remained an ideal, and not only in terms of theory and teaching: works in the so-called Palestrina style, some by earlier masters, some newly composed by contemporary musicians, remained in the repertory, although in the main they were restricted to church music. There was a demand for *a cappella* compositions for those occasions and seasons in the church year when the use of instruments was not allowed, for instance during Lent or Advent. But there were now many concertante masses, sometimes with lavish vocal and instrumental writing involving several choirs, in the Venetian style.

However, the new style reigned almost wholly supreme in instrumental music, vocal chamber music and of course the dramatic genres. Opera[24] came to the imperial court in the 1620s, probably with the performance of the pastoral *Calisto e Arcade* after Ovid, on 27 November 1627. The text was by Cesare Gonzaga, Prince of Guastalla; a relative of the empress, he was very active at the Viennese court at this time. The name of the composer is unknown, and the performers were not yet a special company but a travelling troupe, the Fedeli, who had considerable success with their performances at the imperial court at this time. The first works produced in Vienna that can be described with any accuracy as operas were an 'operetta in musica' on 18 February 1629 and the pastoral *La caccia felice* on 9 March 1631. The texts – and another text for a ballet performed at the wedding of Ferdinand III – were probably again by Cesare Gonzaga, and again it is not known who composed the music.

The first known composer of an opera performed in Vienna is Lodovico Bartolaia (who also sang the title role) with *Il Sidonio* in 1633; it is possible that *Gl'inganni di Polinesso*, performed earlier that year, and two other works performed in 1635 were by Bartolaia too. Nothing has been preserved from this early period except some librettos; musical records do not begin until 1660, with Filippo Vismarri's *Orontea* (it is not certain that it was actually performed) and Antonio Bertali's *La magia delusa*. Bertali (1608–69) was a leading composer. His first known work for the imperial court, *L'inganno d'amore*, with a text by Benedetto Ferrari, was performed at the imperial diet at Regensburg in 1653. Other prominent composers were Giuseppe Tricarico (1623–97) and Pietro Andrea Ziani (1616–

30. Auditorium of the Theater auf der Cortina, Vienna, during the performance of Cesti's opera 'Il pomo d'oro' that marked the birthday of Empress Margarita, 20 July 1668: engraving by F. Geffels after Ludovico Burnacini

31. *Final ballet (involving the Spirits of the Air, Knights of the Earth, and Sirens and Tritons of the Sea) in Act 5 scene xi of Cesti's opera 'Il pomo d'oro' performed in the Theater auf der Cortina, Vienna, 20 July 1668, to mark the birthday of Empress Margarita: engraving by M. Küsel after the design by Ludovico Burnacini*

84). After the Tirolean branch of the Habsburgs died out, with the consequent dissolution of the court at Innsbruck, the services of Antonio Cesti (1623–69), who had been been working there, were acquired for Vienna. No position was vacant, and until the post of Vice-Kapellmeister became available he was appointed 'capellano d'onore' (honorary chaplain), plainly in order to retain his services whatever happened, since this position was certainly not directly linked with any official duties. In addition, he was made director of dramatic performances at court. It was obviously the first such appointment, and was a matter of particular urgency because of the preparations then being made for the wedding of Emperor Leopold to his niece Margarita Teresia of Spain, which was celebrated with the utmost pomp. On 12 July 1666 the birthday of the bride, who had not even arrived yet, was marked by a performance of *Nettuno e Flora festeggianti* by Cesti and the librettist Francesco Sbarra. At the time Cesti was already busy composing the opera for the wedding festivities themselves, *Il pomo d'oro*, also to a text by Sbarra; its performance, however, was delayed until long after the wedding – indeed until the young empress's birthday in July 1668. This production, which opened a newly built theatre, was certainly the biggest and most lavish artistic event of the century in Austria (*see* figs. 30 and 31).

During the reign of Leopold I (1658–1705), texts by successful Italian writers were used at first: in 1659 works with texts by Sbarra, Giacinto Andrea Cicognini, Aurelio Amalteo and Aurelio Aureli, among others, appeared. In 1661 Antonio Draghi (1634/5–1700) began his career in the Vienna court theatre as a writer of texts (with *Almonte*, for Tricarico); he did not figure as composer of an opera until 1666, when he set his own libretto *La mascherata* (the interludes were composed by Emperor Leopold I). *Atalanta* (1669) finally brought together the team which was to dominate the Viennese operatic stage until the end of the century: Draghi as composer, Johann Heinrich Schmelzer as composer of the ballet music (his son Andreas Anton succeeded him in that capacity after his death in 1680), Nicolò Minato as librettist, Santo Ventura as ballet master and Giovanni Burnacini as stage designer. Towards the end of the century their dominance gradually declined, partly no doubt because of the advancing age of the members of the team. From 1694 Donato Cupeda was active alongside Minato, who now confined himself to minor genres. Draghi, whose principal collaborator as a composer had initially been the emperor himself and who was assisted from 1697 onwards by his son Carlo Domenico, remained active until his death. But new composers were increasingly appearing too; there were Carlo Agostino Badia from 1697 (he had been appointed court composer the previous year), Giovanni Bononcini from 1699, Johann

32. Emperor Leopold I in theatrical costume (possibly as Acis in 'La Galatea'): portrait (c1667) by Jan Thomas

Joseph Fux and Marc'Antonio Ziani from 1700. The engagement of Bononcini and M. A. Ziani in particular, both of them among the most successful operatic composers of their day, shows that even in old age the emperor had an eye to musical developments and was far from hostile to innovation. The bypassing of official procedures in the appointment of Fux shows Leopold's continuing direct interest in his Hofmusikkapelle; it should perhaps also be seen in connection with an increasing, politically determined tendency to foster native talent, something to which Fux's later rise to Hofkapellmeister was probably largely due.

From the time of Leopold I, opera on the whole had a fixed annual time-table. Performances were regularly given during Carnival, on the birthdays and name days of members of the royal house, and to mark particular events such as weddings or christenings. The status of these occasions also determined the extent and character of the works performed. The emperor's birthday was celebrated with the lavish production of a large-scale opera, while birthdays and name days of less exalted members of the imperial family were marked by smaller works in more modest productions. Wedding operas were particularly splendid, reflecting the special significance of marriages for Habsburg policies. Theatrical performances, like all other entertainments given publicly or in a large social circle, had to be cancelled if a death in the extensive imperial family demanded court mourning; in such cases the court often resorted to various smaller-scale entertainments given in private (unless it was decided instead to postpone announcement of a death until after a planned performance). As far as the content and form of the works was concerned, the language had to maintain a certain tone, the images of certain roles (e.g., the characters of rulers) had to be preserved, and in general there was a definite, fairly rigid set of rules. A work offered as a tribute to the emperor, for instance, precluded any burlesque tone, whereas the burlesque touch was actually essential on other occasions, as in Carnival operas, which could be surprisingly exuberant. On certain occasions, the court allowed a critical mirror to be held up to it, a pre-ordained component (like the Lenten sermons of the Capuchins) of the whole structure of the artistic and ceremonial process.

Besides the court theatre, which in principle would allow no competition (efforts to establish and run a citizens' theatre were to suffer severely from this attitude during the eighteenth century), there was, however, another kind of drama, although it too was largely connected with the court or indeed dependent on it: this was the drama of the Jesuits,[25] who had controlled the University of Vienna since 1623. As well as the usual prize-giving and end-of-year plays, there was the genre of the festive *Ludi Caesarei*, performed at court on special occasions and with all due splendour. Remarks such as those made in 1627 by Archduchess Cäcilia Renata, who when writing of the prospect that 'the Jesuits are going to give a play' says, with little enthusiasm, 'I shall find it very tedious',[26] lead one to suspect that the court promoted and attended these plays more for reasons of outward convention than because of their artistic attractions. They came to an end under Karl VI. We have no music from the Jesuits' plays until Johann Kaspar Kerll's for *Pia et fortis mulier* in 1677. None is preserved for the plays of the most important Viennese Jesuit dramatist, Nicolaus Avancinus. Most of what we do have is by Johann Bernhardt Staudt (1654–1712), *regens chori* of the university church, mostly to plays by Johann Baptist Adolph. Over time, the role of music in these dramas increased, so that they came more and more to resemble operas.

In Lent, when for religious and liturgical reasons worldly amusements, including dramatic performances, were forbidden, oratorio was performed instead of opera.[27] In the same way as opera had a kind of minor parallel genre in the serenata, oratorio, apparently introduced to Vienna by Empress Eleonora Gonzaga, Ferdinand II's wife, had a similar parallel genre in the *sepolcro*, performed in Holy Week at the Holy Sepulchre. The first of these works, *Santi risorti*, with text and music by Giovanni Valentini, was performed in 1643.[28] Later, the composition of a *sepolcro* for performance on Good Friday in the imperial chapel was usually the duty of the Hofkapellmeister. In oratorio, there was a marked preference for works from outside Vienna (by Legrenzi and Alessandro Scarlatti among others), since obviously the composer's presence was not necessary for performances without stage action. The *sepolcri* were probably performed in front of a stationary backdrop (fig. 33), with the singers making stylized gestures.

The third main sphere of activity, along with church music and theatre music, was chamber music. These fields could overlap to a

33. Design by Ludovico Burnacini for the backdrop for Antonio Draghi's sepolcro 'Il sagrificio non impedito', performed in the imperial chapel, Vienna, 4 April 1692 (the scene shows Abraham preparing to sacrifice Isaac)

great extent. For instance, the dividing line between dramatic works and vocal chamber music was sometimes blurred; in extended chamber compositions some element of dramatic action might be included, so that they came to approach minor dramatic genres. Much the same thing happened in works written for the meetings of the Italian academies at the imperial court, music being a part of the opening and closing ceremonies.[29] A contribution was required to be appropriate to the subject of the verbal debate at the meeting in question. Very little vocal chamber music survives, though records show that it was actively practised.

Very little instrumental music has come down to us either.[30] We have works by Valentini, and Giovanni Battista Buonamente published two volumes (1626, 1629) while he was working at the imperial court. For the period of Emperor Leopold, a representative sample is offered by the musical archives at Kroměříž of Prince-Bishop Karl Liechtenstein-Kastelcorn of Olomouc; it includes printed works. This repertory came into being largely through the good offices of Johann Heinrich Schmelzer, who was in touch with the prince-bishop and was also the most important representative of this school of instrumental music. A keyboard school started with Johann Jakob Froberger, who was in the service of the court (which allowed him a good deal of freedom) from 1637 to 1657; the brothers Wolfgang and Markus Ebner, Johann Kasper Kerll, Alessandro Poglietti, Georg Matthias Techelmann, Ferdinand Tobias Richter and George Reutter the elder belonged to it in the seventeenth century. Lute and theorbo music also flourished. Benedetto Ferrari was engaged as theorbo player in 1651, and George Reutter the elder and Francesco Conti began their careers playing the theorbo for the Viennese court orchestra. Emperor Joseph I in particular seems to have had a preference for lute music, since during the time he was King of Rome (from 1690 until his accession in 1705) Ferdinand Ignaz Hinterleithner (1699), Baron Wenzel Ludwig von Radolt (1701) and Johann Theodor Herold (1702) dedicated collections of lute pieces to him.

The essential, prominent part played by music in court and political life and the lavish resources expended on it (in particular the Habsburgs' passion and talent for the art) produced, in seventeenth-century Vienna, musical activity of a quality and breadth exceeded only under Emperor Charles VI a few decades later. It is only natural that such an intensive cultivation of music should extend its influence to other strata of society, where it was a dominant model for musical activities. Although, as mentioned above, we must remember that much music from outside the court has not survived (and there are some gaps in court music too), the apparent dominance of the music of the imperial court reflected in the surviving sources and accounts of it corresponds to its dominance in historical fact.

NOTES

[1] F. W. Riedel, *Kirchenmusik am Hofe Karls VI. (1711–1740): Untersuchungen zum Verhältnis von Zeremoniell und musikalischem Stil im Barockzeitalter* (Munich and Salzburg, 1977), 9–13; H. Sedlmayr, 'Die politische Bedeutung des deutschen Barock: der "Reichsstil"', *Epochen und Werke: Gesammelte Schriften zur Kunstgeschichte*, ii (Vienna and Munich, 1960), 140–56.

[2] O. Wessely, *Arnold von Bruck: Leben und Umwelt. Mit Beiträgen zur Musikgeschichte des Hofes Ferdinands I. von 1527 bis 1545* (diss., U. of Vienna, 1958), 76–81.

[3] A. Smijers, *Karl Luython als Motetten-Komponist* (Amsterdam, 1923), 9; R. Lindell, 'Die Neubesetzung der Hofkapellmeisterstelle am Kaiserhof in den Jahren 1567–1568: Palestrina oder Monte?', *Studien zur Musikwissenschaft*, xxxvi (1985), 35–42, esp. 44.

[4] Wessely, op cit, 239–52; W. Pass, *Musik und Musiker am Hof Maximilians II* (Tutzing, 1980), 168–214.

[5] For information on the court musicians, see L. von Köchel, *Die kaiserliche Hof-Musikkapelle in Wien von 1543 bis 1867* (Vienna, 1869).

[6] Pass, op cit, 293, 407.

[7] E. Schenk, 'Zur Lebens- und Familiengeschichte von Lambert de Sayve', *Festschrift Hellmuth Osthoff zum 65. Geburtstage* (Tutzing, 1961), 107f.

[8] P. P. Melli, *Intavolatura di liuto attiorbato, libro secondo* (Venice, 1614); new edn, Archivum musicum, xix (Florence, 1979), 67f.

[9] H. Federhofer, *Musikpflege und Musiker am Grazer Habsburgerhof der Erzherzöge Karl und Ferdinand von Innerösterreich (1564–1619)* (Mainz, 1967), 52; Köchel, op cit, 57.

[10] P. P. Melli, *Intavolatura di liuto attiorbato, libro quarto* (Venice, 1616) and *Intavolatura di liuto attiorbato e di tiorba, libro quinto* (Venice, 1620); new edns, Archivum musicum, xix (Florence, 1979).

[11] For information about the musicians of Karl II and Ferdinand II, see Federhofer, op cit, and also idem and R. Flotzinger, 'Musik in der Steiermark: historischer Überblick', *Musik in der Steiermark* [exhibition catalogue], ed. Flotzinger (Graz, 1980), 15–93.

[12] Federhofer, op cit, 27.

[13] Ibid, 26, 40, 185–7; O. Wessely, introduction, *Frühmeister des stile nuovo in Österreich*, ed. idem and E. Kanduth, Denkmäler der Tonkunst in Österreich, cxxv (1973), p. vi.

[14] See pp. 133–4 above.

[15] T. Antonicek, 'Italienische Musikerlebnisse Ferdinands II. 1598,' *Anzeiger der Österreichischen Akademie der Wissenschaften: philosophisch-historische Klasse*, civ (1967), 91–111.

[16] Federhofer, op cit, 25.

[17] See Schenk, 'Zur Lebens und Familiengeschichte von Lambert de Sayve'.

[18] H. Brunner, *Die Kantorei bei St. Stephan in Wien: Beiträge zur Geschichte der Dommusik* (Vienna, 1948), 14–19.

[19] J. Seemüller, 'Über den Schottenorganisten Johann Rasch', *Festgabe zum 100 jährigen Jubiläum des Schottengymnasiums* (Vienna, 1907); C. R. Rapf, *Das Schottenstift* (Vienna and Hamburg, 1974), 39.

[20] C. Sartori, *Bibliografia della musica strumentale italiana stampata in Italia fino al 1700* (Florence, 1952), 305; Federhofer, op cit, 39.

[21] Vienna, Habsburg-Lothringen family archives, family correspondence A, box 11/ii, f.153v: Ferdinand III to Archduke Leopold Wilhelm, Vienna, 24 August 1642; f.20v: Ferdinand III to Archduke Leopold Wilhelm, Vienna, 9 April 1640 (the *Miserere* is probably that found in *Musikalische Werke der Kaiser Ferdinand III., Leopold I. und Joseph I*, ed. G. Adler (Vienna, 1896), 1–16; and Ferdinand III to Archduke Leopold Wilhem, Vienna, 11 November 1642.

[22] A. Bertoli, *Compositioni musicali* (Venice, 1645); Sartori, op cit, 394.

[23] Vienna, Habsburg-Lothringen family archives, family correspondence A, box 11/ii f.116v: Ferdinand III to Archduke Leopold Wilhelm, Vienna, 14 December 1641.

[24] For comments on the opera and subsidiary genres, see H. Seifert, *Die Oper am Wiener Kaiserhof im 17. Jahrhundert* (Tutzing, 1985); idem, *Der Sig-prangende Hochzeit-Gott: Hochzeitsfeste am Wiener Hof der Habsburger und ihre Allegorik 1622–1699* (Vienna, 1988).

The Early Baroque Era

[25] W. Kramer, *Die Musik im Wiener Jesuitendrama von 1677–1711* (diss., U. of Vienna, 1965); K. Adel, *Das Wiener Jesuitentheater und die europäische Barockdramatik* (Vienna, 1960).

[26] Vienna, Habsburg-Lothringen family archives, family correspondence A, box 48, f.25r: Archduchess Cäcilia Renata to Archduke Leopold Wilhelm, Prague, 6 December 1627.

[27] See H. Seifert, 'Die Entfaltung des Barock', *Musikgeschichte Österreichs*, i (Graz, 1977), 232–79 (with detailed bibliography).

[28] G. Gruber, *Das Wiener Sepolcro und Johann Jospeh Fux*, i (Graz, 1972).

[29] U. Hofmann, *Die Serenata am Hofe Kaiser Leopold I. 1658–1705* (diss., U. of Vienna, 1975).

[30] See Seifert, 'Die Entfaltung des Barock'; Högler, *Die Kirchensonaten in Kremsier: ein Beitrag zur Geschichte der Kirchensonate* (diss., U. of Vienna, 1926).

BIBLIOGRAPHICAL NOTE

Primary sources

Copious source material relating to musical life at the Habsburg courts is held by the Haus-, Hof- und Staatsarchiv and the Hofkammerarchiv in Vienna; the records of musical activities of the city of Vienna itself are less rich and have also been less investigated. Important collections of music are to be found in the Österreichische Nationalbibliothek and in the archive of the Gesellschaft der Musikfreunde in Vienna, also the music archive of the bishops of Olmütz in the palace of Kroměříž, Moravia.

The fundamental work concerning the history of music at court is still L. von Köchel, *Die kaiserliche Hof-Musikkapelle in Wien von 1543 bis 1867* (Vienna, 1869), an overview based on archive holdings. Following on from this, and complementing it, there are publications of archive materials or registers, among which the following are specially important: A. Koczirz, 'Exzerpte aus den Hofmusikakten des Wiener Hofkammerarchivs', *Studien zur Musikwissenschaft*, i (1913), 278–303; A. Smijers, 'Die kaiserliche Hofmusik-Kapelle von 1543–1619', ibid, vi (1919), 139–86, vii (1920), 102–42, viii (1921), 176–206, ix (1922), 43–81 and P. Nettl, 'Zur Geschichte der kaiserlichen Hofmusikkapelle von 1636–1680', ibid, xvi (1929), 70–85, xvii (1930), 95–104, xviii (1931), 23–35, xix (1932), 33–40. There is also the edition in three volumes by H. Knaus, *Die Musiker im Archivbestand des kaiserlichen Obersthofmeisteramtes (1637–1705)* (Vienna, 1967–9).

Secondary sources

The best summary of the period under review is found in the relevant chapters in *Musikgeschichte Österreichs*, ed. R. Flotzinger and G. Gruber (Graz, 1977–9); further reading lists can be found there. The overall position of music within the structure of court life and the role of the imperial court in the musical life of the times is described in F. W. Riedel, *Kirchenmusik am Hofe Karls VI (1711–1740): Untersuchungen zum Verhältnis von Zeremoniell und musikalischem Stil im Barockzeitalter* (Munich and Salzburg, 1977), whose findings are in general valid for the entire Baroque period and beyond.

The Hofmusikkapelle of Ferdinand II, which transferred from Graz to Vienna in 1619, is described in detail in H. Federhofer, *Musikpflege und Musiker am Grazer Habsburgerhof der Erzherzöge Karl und Ferdinand von Innerösterreich (1564–1619)* (Mainz, 1967). A comprehensive description of the Kapelle in the rest of the period has still to be written. Among the various aspects of musical life, theatre music has fared best in the literature. The pioneering effort by F. Hadamowsky, *Barocktheater am Wiener Kaiserhof* (Vienna, 1955), 7–117, has been succeeded by H. Seifert, *Die Oper am Wiener Kaiserhof in 17. Jahrhundert* (Tutzing, 1985), an excellent history underpinned by thorough documentation. Among Seifert's other contributions is *Der Sig-prangende Hochzeit-Gott: Hochzeitsfeste am Wiener Hof der Habsburger und ihre Allegorik 1622–1699* (Vienna, 1988). A further chapter of operatic life in Vienna is dealt with in C. Böhm, *Theatralia anlässlich der Krönungen in der österreichischen Linie der casa d'Austria (1627–1764)* (diss., U. of Vienna, 1986; edn in preparation). Other aspects of musical theatre are treated only in unpublished dissertations: W. Kramer, *Die Musik im Wiener Jesuitendrama von 1677–1711* (diss., U. of Vienna, 1965), and U. Hofmann, *Die Serenata am Hofe Kaiser Leopold I 1658–1705* (diss., U. of Vienna, 1975; excerpt in *Musicologica austriaca*, ii (1979), 76–84). An older publication also deserves mention: E. Wellesz, 'Die Opern und Oratorien in Wien von 1660–1708', *Studien zur Musikwissenschaft*, vi (1919), 5–138. Finally, there is G. Gruber, *Das Wiener Sepolcro und Johann Joseph Fux* (Graz, 1972), which offers much cultural history.

Though there are individual studies of composers, there are no modern overviews of chamber music and church music. For information about the musical activities of those emperors who were themselves composers, we still have generally to rely on G. Adler's edition *Musikalische Werke der Kaiser Ferdinand III, Leopold I und Joseph I* (Vienna, 1892–3). Editions of musical works of the time are available in numerous volumes of Denkmäler der Tonkunst in Österreich.

Chapter VIII

Dresden at the Time of Heinrich Schütz

GINA SPAGNOLI

The Lutheran court at the Saxon capital Dresden possessed a musical life as rich as any court in seventeenth-century Europe. The wide
variety of music performed at court in services, in stage works, on
special state occasions, and even at the royal table is known today
largely because of the preservation of an abundance of archival
material pertaining to Heinrich Schütz (1585–1672), the central figure of the city's musical life. Many of Schütz's own letters as well as
a wealth of other documents relating to court life at Dresden – court
correspondence, Hofkapelle lists, musicians' contracts, court account
books and receipts, music and instrument catalogues, *Kantorei-
ordnungen* (chapel orders) and court diaries – provide vivid details of
the role of Dresden's court musicians. These records also form an
illuminating portrait of Schütz and the factors that influenced his
productivity.

In a memorandum of 14 January 1651 to his patron, Elector
Johann Georg I, Schütz provided special insight into his role as
Kapellmeister. He regularly played an important role

> at many diverse festivities in the past, which occurred during this
> time at imperial, royal, electoral, and princely gatherings, in this
> country and abroad, but particularly at each and every one of your
> own royal children's weddings, and no less at the receiving of their
> sacred christenings as well. . .[1]

During his more than 40 years of service, Schütz's principal duties
as Kapellmeister included the composition of theatrical and festive
music for court occasions and the direction of the ensemble on high
feast days in the palace church, particularly, as he wrote in a letter of
May 1645, 'in the presence of foreign rulers or emissaries', such as
Emperor Matthias's visit to Dresden in 1617, for which Schütz was
instructed to ensure 'that His Electoral Grace's ensemble . . . acquit
itself with honor and glory before the visitors'. Schütz himself wrote

in a letter of July 1646 that the 'principal and best performance of my office consists not so much in my perpetual presence and attendance but rather in the composition and arrangement of all sorts of good musical works, as well as in the supervision of the entire operation'. His absences from Dresden, in fact, always fell during periods when no festivities were planned, which seems to indicate that his chief concern was the music for special festivals rather than that for ordinary Sundays.[2]

Just such a special occasion had first brought Schütz to Dresden as a young man of nearly 29. The Elector of Saxony, Johann Georg I, proposed that he come to Dresden to assist with the music at the christening of the elector's son Prince August on 18 September 1614. Johann Georg I has been characterized as a ruler of honest intentions whose efforts on behalf of Germany during the Thirty Years War were sincere, if lacking in political perspective.[3] Upon his accession in 1611, he began immediately to enhance the musical forces at his court. During these early years, the court Kapellmeister was still officially Rogier Michael, who was in semi-retirement from 1613, with Michael Praetorius, Kapellmeister of the court at Wolfenbüttel, serving as Kapellmeister *in absentia*. The elector was therefore in need of musicians, and Schütz, a promising young organist in the employ of Landgrave Moritz of Kassel, had come to his attention. There ensued a long struggle between the two rulers to secure Schütz's services; the elector, as the more powerful political figure, prevailed.

At Schütz's arrival in Dresden, the Hofkapelle had 27 members: four altos, four tenors, three basses, five discantists and eleven instrumentalists; by 1632, membership had increased to 39.[4] By 1634, however, the severe effects of the Thirty Years War were manifest in a drop to 30,[5] which continued precipitously until, by 1639, only ten members remained.[6] In fact, the hardships of war had reached Dresden as early as 1623. In a petition to Johann Georg I dated June 1625, the entire ensemble, including Kapellmeister Schütz, complained that they had not been paid for nearly two years.[7]

During this period, as indeed throughout his lifetime, Schütz was plagued by economic conditions that prevented him from publishing many of his works scored for large forces. In his preface to the first volume of *Kleine geistliche Concerte*, which appeared in 1636 as the forces of the Hofkapelle were rapidly approaching their nadir, he wrote almost apologetically:

> Everyone can see how, as the result of the still continuing, dangerous vicissitudes of war in our dear fatherland of German nationality, the laudable art of music, among the other liberal arts, has not only greatly declined but at some places has even been completely abandoned, succumbing to the general ruination and disorder which unhappy war is wont to bring in its train. I myself am

experiencing this situation with regard to a number of my musical compositions. Publication has had to be abandoned until such time as perhaps the Almighty may graciously grant better days. Meanwhile, however, in order that the talent which God has granted me in such a noble art may not remain completely in desuetude but may create and present something, even though, on a small scale, I have composed and published to the honor of God as heralds of my larger musical works some small *concerti* . . .[8]

Even after the signing of the Peace of Westphalia on 24 October 1648, conditions in Dresden were slow to recover owing to the heavy war debt, and the court continued to withhold the musicians' pay. Schütz's letters illustrate the extraordinary hardships under which many of the musicians struggled to survive. In a letter of August 1651, he wrote

that so far as I am concerned (disregarding the fact that even at my advanced age I might still choose a distant imperial or Hanseatic city for my last lodging place in this world), God knows that I would prefer with all my heart to be a cantor or an organist in a small town to remaining longer amid conditions in which my dear profession disgusts me and I am deprived of sustenance and of courage.

He described further the plight of one of the singers, who

lives like a sow in a pigsty, has no bedding, lies on straw, has pawned his coat and his jacket. His wife came to me yesterday and begged me for God's sake to render fatherly aid and help them get away . . . I find it neither praiseworthy nor Christian that in a land so highly esteemed less than twenty musicians can or will not be supported . . .[9]

Johann Georg I's ensemble continued to decline for the remainder of his reign. Johann Georg II (1613–80), the elector apparent, in a letter to his father of September 1653, wrote that he found his father's Hofkapelle 'down to the heeltap and has dwindled to nothing', and suggested drastic improvements in personnel and pay. Johann Georg II was a man of some musical ability who may have studied with Schütz himself. A catalogue compiled in 1681 for his successor, Johann Georg III, including prints and manuscripts of both sacred and secular works, lists the following sacred work: 'Psalm: Laudate Dominum omnes gentes in four vocal parts with instruments including six trumpets and timpani. Composition by the most serene late Elector of Saxony, Duke Johann Georg the Second.'

While still elector apparent, Johann Georg II began assembling

34. *Title-page of 'Missae' (Dresden: C. Bergen, 1663) by Andreas Hammerschmidt, Kantor of Zittau in the Dresden region*

his own cadre of musicians in anticipation of his succession. A household list from September 1639 includes seven trumpeters, a drummer, three musicians and a choirboy.[10] The elector apparent's ensemble grew until it rivalled the elector's own. In a list dated *c*1651 the Hofkapelle of Johann Georg I, under the leadership of Schütz, included seventeen musicians and four choirboys, while Johann Georg II's ensemble comprised thirteen musicians and five choirboys under the direction of Giovanni Andrea Bontempi, the court ensemble's first Italian castrato.

The Early Baroque Era

Italian musicians were employed in Dresden throughout Schütz's tenure; he himself had travelled twice to Venice, first from 1609 to 1613 as a pupil of Giovanni Gabrieli (who died in 1612) and again in 1628–9. As Kapellmeister, Schütz brought Italian music, instruments and musicians to Dresden, including the violinist Carlo Farina, who had been counted among the members of the Hofkapelle as early as 1616.[11] In his efforts to rebuild the ensemble following the depredations of the Thirty Years War, Schütz proposed to Johann Georg I in September 1645 that the musicians be divided into three groups to be developed successively: the choirboys or discantists, the instrumentalists and the other singers. Schütz believed that the latter group would be the most challenging because they would have to be recruited abroad, primarily in Italy. His efforts at reorganization proved effective, for by 1647 the membership in the ensemble had increased to 21.[12]

As the number of Italians in the Hofkapelle increased, so did internal controversy. In August 1653 Schütz objected to an order made by Johann Georg II as elector apparent that he and the Italian Bontempi alternate in conducting the music on ordinary Sundays, a duty that had become the responsibility of the vice-Kapellmeister:

> As for the command . . . regarding the alternation of the music in the palace church on Sundays, I cannot disguise from my most honorable lords the extent to which it would be demeaning and painful to me, as an old and, I hope, not undeserving man, on those Sundays (on which previously . . . the direction was not my responsibility but that of the vice-Kapellmeister) to alternate regularly and continuously with my lord the elector apparent's director [Bontempi], a man three times younger than I and castrated to boot, and to compete with him for favor . . . before biased and, for the most part, injudicious audiences and judges.

That same year Schütz was personally blamed for the engagement of so many Italian musicians. In an appeal to the elector apparent in August 1653, he lamented

> how more and more each day that (regarding Your Highness's Italian musicians and those installed in the electoral court ensemble) not only repeatedly unpleasant judgment is passed against me by various ecclesiastics and lay persons but, furthermore, to my particular astonishment, I have learned that I am considered, and slandered as, the cause and instigator of the change . . . Because . . . I have never received or obtained the slightest knowledge [regarding the hiring] of any person among the Italians now present here, [and] the perpetrators who . . . have fetched the aforementioned musicians from Italy do so openly, I therefore direct this my most humble and fervent request . . . that you graciously avert this mistrust from me . . .

Schütz was referring to Johann Georg II's practice, common among other German princes, of maintaining agents in European cities to recruit musicians for the court. In fact, the Electress of Bavaria grew so annoyed with his efforts to lure away her Italian musicians in 1652 that she demanded an explanation from Johann Georg I.[13] Schütz further asserted that 'I swear to God that I for my part do not oppose Your Serene Highness's newly installed Italian Director of Music [Bontempi] (even though for me and other Germans here it serves more to the detriment of our abilities than the advancement of them)'.

In a letter of June 1654, Schütz mentioned 'divisiveness and mis-understanding . . . within the company' and requested that the unnamed court official to whom the letter was addressed 'intervene so that equity be maintained', probably with regard to salaries. For example, in that year the Italian tenor Stefano Boni earned 840 talers, while the German Philipp Stolle, also a tenor, earned a mere 300.[14] Payment schedules of the Hofkapelle from later years, how-ever, show that the Italians continued to earn far bigger salaries than the Germans.

During the final years of Johann Georg I's reign, the performance of music by German composers in church services was also increas-ingly eclipsed by the works of their Italian rivals. In a letter of 1654 to the elector, Jacob Weller, the senior court chaplain, wrote in support of a desperate plea from two musicians for some of their outstanding wages:

> May it please you graciously to consider the miserable condition of the good people and [to be mindful] that if they are not looked upon with gracious eyes, these five will leave, who until now have been carrying out the worship service virtually alone and by them-selves, and so there would be almost no one who could simply sing hymns and a German 'Our Father' in church.

Schütz personally directed his *Historia der . . . Aufferstehung* (SWV50), probably for the last time, on 6 April 1656,[15] and in June and July, during the final weeks of Johann Georg I's rule, he conducted services in the electoral front chamber. A court diarist, reporting on a service on 20 July 1656, wrote that Schütz conducted the ensemble and further commented that 'the music . . . was sung in German', as though that were unusual.[16] The last known occasion on which Schütz conducted the Hofkapelle was Christmas 1656, some ten weeks after Johann Georg I's death on 8 October.[17]

Upon assuming power, the new elector, Johann Georg II, set about reorganizing the institutions of his court, beginning with his Hofkapelle. He first united the two Dresden ensembles under three

169

35. Heinrich Schütz aged 65: portrait by Christoph Spetner (1617–99)

Kapellmeisters (Schütz, who at the age of 71 was allowed to go into semi-retirement, Bontempi and Vincenzo Albrici) and two vice-Kapellmeisters (Christoph Bernhard and Marco Gioseppe Peranda). This new unified ensemble of 47 members included ten Italians, many of whom were especially favoured by the elector. For example, he stood as godfather on 24 February 1662 to Albrici's son – who was named Johann Georg – in Albrici's Dresden home.[18] Several of the Italians attained higher position at court, and one, the castrato Bartolomeo Sorlisi, after being made a nobleman in 1666, married the daughter of a burgher of Dresden in 1666, provoking outrage among the citizens of Dresden and decades of legal and theological debate.[19]

Preventing the Catholic foreigners from celebrating Mass in the homes of the Austrian and French envoys, however, became a concern of the elector, who, on 27 March 1661 and on 27 February 1673, issued orders forbidding the practice of the Catholic faith in

Lutheran Dresden. Accordingly, on 6 April 1673 authorities interrupted a Mass at the home of the French envoy; among the 106
worshippers were several Italian members of the Hofkapelle.[20] What
punishment, if any, was meted out is unknown.

In addition to reorganizing his court ensemble, Johann Georg II
renovated the chapel in the Dresden palace. According to reports in
the court diaries of the consecration service on 28 September 1662,
all the music was composed specially for the occasion by Albrici, who
also conducted. Schütz's setting of Psalm 100 (SWV493) was, however, sung as an introit. Contemporary descriptions of the newly
renovated chapel make clear that sacred music and the space in
which it was performed were intended to make manifest the wealth
and significance of the ruler and his court. The chronicler Anton
Weck, in his extensive description of the 'lovely, bright, though not
too large' chapel in the Dresden palace in which most of Schütz's
sacred works were first performed, wrote of a masterpiece of
Renaissance architecture that was

> a completely stone building and its vaulted ceiling so beautiful that
> many of those who understand architecture acknowledge that they
> have seldom seen such a beautiful vaulted ceiling because upon it
> are distinct large dragons or long snakes carved from white sand-
> stone [and] next to each an angel who is holding one of the instru-
> ments of the Passion of Christ as if they had fought successfully
> against the dragon. These the architect of the church constructed so
> artistically that they appear to float in mid-air and yet are somehow
> joined to the vaulted ceiling and responds that such heavy weights
> have remained stable for so many years now without a single
> problem.

In describing the interior of the chapel and its opulent appointments,
Weck referred both to the renovation ordered by Johann Georg II
and to one that took place some 60 years earlier, illustrating the
inseparable nature of church and state.

> In 1602 the entire chapel was renovated, and accordingly at that
> time the costly tapestries, which are interwoven with gold (in which
> the stories of Christ's birth, passion and death are artistically rep-
> resented and afterwards hung only for princely christenings or
> otherwise as church ornaments on the highest feast days) which
> ordinarily were in the chapel at all times, were taken down . . .
> Duke Johann Georg the Second, His Serene Highness, the present
> reigning elector, had this oftmentioned chapel renovated at great
> cost, especially the present aforementioned altar as well as two
> costly galleries found above it which rest upon four red marble
> pillars which were cut from a whole slab 4¼ ells or 8½ feet high
> (such pillars in one piece are not to be found [even] in Rome).

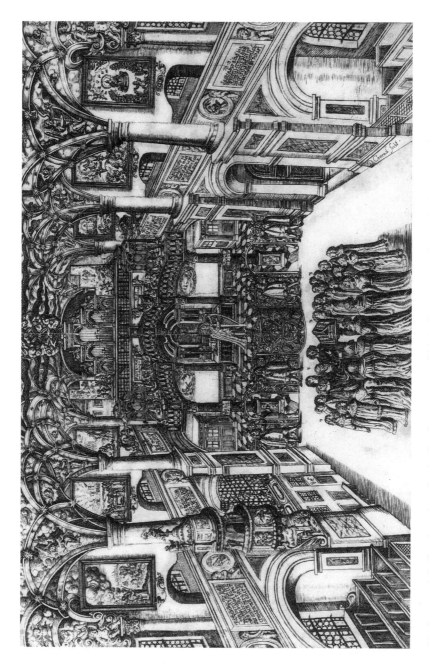

36. *Interior of the Dresden palace church after the renovations of 1662: frontispiece to 'Geistreiche Gesangbuch' (Dresden, 1676), a collection of sacred music published by Christoph Bernhard*

Furthermore the confessionals and so forth, along with the structural work, were improved and decorated, during which, in the passing three-quarters of a year's time and in the midst of which, the sermons were held both in the Sophienkirche and in the chapel of the bequeathed residence of Her Ladyship, the electoral Saxon widow, Lady Magdalena Sibylle. This same [chapel], however, was consecrated on the eighteenth Sunday after Trinity, the day of Michaelmas [28 September] 1662, with Christian devotion and a true [and] excellent service . . .

Weck also describes new instruments that Johann Georg II had added to the chapel:

Also to be seen previously in this church was an organ, which was installed in 1563. The present one, however, was installed in 1612 and has 40 registers; and, with the aforementioned recent renovation, two additional lovely positivs were added to the two front music galleries near the altar.[21]

Weck's description matches David Conrad's visual representation, an engraved frontispiece to the *Geistreiche Gesangbuch* published by Christoph Bernhard, who was, next to Matthias Weckmann, the most important of Schütz's pupils and vice-Kapellmeister and tutor to the prince (fig. 36). At the most fundamental level, the engraving accurately depicts the Dresden palace church as it was in 1662, with the altar, pulpit, two organ positivs in the divided choir galleries over the altar, the main organ, the altar screen, the side galleries (which, according to Johann Georg I's 1637 chapel order, were occupied by the congregation) and the singers of the Hofkapelle with Schütz in their midst.

The engraving's allegorical meaning is also readily apparent from the imposing figure of King David, who stands in front of the altar holding a harp, from the eight doorkeepers at the two gates of the altar screen, and from the performing instrumentalists in the gallery directly over the altar, who play the triangle, tambourine, little drums and other instruments not generally used in sacred music. These figures allude to the three-strophe poem based on Psalm 150 printed on the reverse side of the engraving: Asaph and the Levites, the temple singers of King David from 1 Chronicles, Chapter 25, who are represented as Schütz and the Hofkapelle, perform before King David, a symbol for the musical Johann Georg II and his renewal of the church, structurally and liturgically. The representation of the interior of the church, with stars, clouds and angels upon a groined ceiling, symbolizes 'heavenly music' ('musica coelestis'), with the worldly choir below in the nave.[22]

In spite of Schütz's figurative importance at court, his works became increasingly overshadowed by those of the Italian Kapellmeisters and vice-Kapellmeisters. As the court diaries illustrate, even the sacred music performed in the elector's own chapel was composed primarily by these Italians, who were responsible for setting appropriate texts for important feast days. Although Schütz's contributions to the Dresden *historia* tradition – his *Historia der . . . Aufferstehung* (SWV50), traditionally performed at Easter, *Historia der . . . Geburth . . . Jesu Christi* (SWV435) for Christmas Day, and his settings of the passions of St Matthew, St Luke and St John (SWV479, 480 and 481) for the weeks preceding Easter – continued to be performed in the palace church until the death of Johann Georg II in 1680, his *Historia der . . . Geburth . . . Jesu Christi* was rivalled by Peranda's work of the same name after 1668 and completely supplanted by it after Schütz's death.[23]

In a letter of October 1666 to Johann Georg II, Constantin Christian Dedekind, a bass in the Hofkapelle, went so far as to propose a formal separation of the Italian and German musicians. The court ensemble was then split into three groups: the first choir, or the Italian singers; the second, or the 'kleine deutsche Musik' (the Little German Ensemble), consisting of the German singers; and the third choir of instrumentalists, a mixed ensemble serving both groups of singers. The Italians provided the more important music for special celebrations and Sunday services, while the 'kleine deutsche Musik', under the direction of Dedekind (who held the title of Konzertmeister, indicating that he was to direct performances of concertos), was relegated to the performance of church music during the week or during the frequent periods when the Italian musicians travelled with the elector. It is telling that the native musicians were deemed unworthy of such display.

The shift in musical taste from the German to the Italianate style during the reign of Johann Georg II is reflected in a music catalogue of 1681, which contains almost exclusively Italian music. In addition, the court diaries mention performances of more than 50 Masses by Peranda, Albrici and Carlo Pallavicino between 1650 and 1673, in each case under the direction of the composer himself. The Kapellmeisters were clearly expected to provide original works for performance at court, a requirement specified in Albrici's contract.[24] Although the contract states that he was free to arrange for the vice-Kapellmeister to conduct in church in his place as often as he wished, the court diaries show that the Italian Kapellmeisters were not about to have their vice-Kapellmeisters deputize for them on important and prestigious feast days. The contract also contains an indication of Schütz's responsibilities at court after his semi-retirement following Johann Georg I's death in 1656:

> He [Albrici] shall be particularly responsible for music (except when we specifically command this of our meritorious old Kapellmeister, Heinrich Schütz, or of our Kapellmeister Giovanni Andrea Bontempi) in church as well as at table, likewise to perform most diligently in theatrical compositions, however and wherever we decree. For this he is free to use either his own compositions or others according to his own discretion. . .

Furthermore, a travel pass issued by Johann Georg II in April 1658 showed that Schütz was required to travel to Dresden from his home in Weissenfels, where he had retired, three or four times a year.

During his years of active service, Schütz conducted his own compositions at religious celebrations in the palace church; he also participated in more than 30 special court festivities beginning with the christening of Prince August on 18 September 1614 up to the celebration of a recently concluded peace treaty on 22 July 1668, to which he contributed his own compositions. As we have seen, the duties of office did not require his participation in weekly church services but rather on those special occasions at which ceremonial display was imperative. These events also provided him with his greatest opportunities to produce works of extravagant scoring such as polychoral compositions, concertos for colourful combinations of voices and instruments and theatre pieces.

Unfortunately, a great many of these compositions have not survived, perhaps because works for special occasions were seldom printed and were therefore particularly susceptible to damage and loss. It is only through prints of texts and performance reports that we know of such works at all. Generally only works that were usable in contexts other than special festivities found their way into print.[25] For example, Schütz's theatre music, which evolved from a tradition that is linked inextricably with the court festivities of the late sixteenth century, is entirely lost. Theatrical presentations were an integral part of these great festivals, which included fireworks, balls, banquets and lavish singing and playing by various ensembles as decorative elements. A key feature was the festive procession, elaborate and whimsical productions featuring familiar themes: the planets, mythological and sea creatures, characters from exotic lands and the muses.

The great processions of the sixteenth century were held out of doors; during the seventeenth century, however, they were moved indoors, where they became connected with the development of the ballet. References to these events use inexact terms such as *Aufzug, Tantz, Ritterspiel* or *Mummerei*, and later *Singend Ballett, Singballett, Tanzspiel* or *Sing-Comoedie*. The German court ballet of Schütz's time was an occasion on which the feast table, dramatic presentation and court ceremony were combined and in which the royal family and the court nobility performed spoken texts with interpolated songs and dance scenes alongside professional actors, singers and dancers. A later German variant of the French *ballet de cour*, these ballets were performed at every German court and were at their most popular between 1650 and 1680, by which time the *ballet de cour* in France was declining.[26]

Since the nineteenth century, scholars have studied the texts of these works and speculated on their musical character. Schütz's *Dafne*, for example, often called 'the first German opera', has continued to be the subject of intense debate for the last decade. Several writers have asserted that *Dafne* was a German opera written in recitative style and not a continuation of the procession tradition of the German courts.[27] It has recently been demonstrated that *Dafne* was probably not an opera in the sense that it was set to music throughout with a unified dramatic treatment but was, rather, a work of spoken theatre containing interpolated songs and dances. The court diary entry for 13 April 1627 – 'the musicians enacted with music a pastoral tragi-comedy about Daphne' – seems too casual a reference to the birth of German opera, suggesting that the work was nothing but an ordinary *Sing-Comoedie*. Furthermore, Schütz did not experience the new Italian recitative style until his second visit to Italy in 1628–9, which he mentions in a letter of February 1633:

> during my recent journey to Italy I engaged myself in a singular manner of composition, namely how a comedy of diverse voices can be translated into declamatory style and be brought to the stage and enacted in song – things that to the best of my knowledge . . . are still completely unknown in Germany.

He again refers to his use of 'stylo recitativo' in the preface to his *Historia . . . der Geburth . . . Jesu Christi* published in 1664 (SWV435), stating that the style is 'new and has hitherto, so far as he knows, not appeared in print in Germany'; the court diary references to this work all comment upon its unusual nature.[28]

Venetian opera did not gain a foothold in Germany until after the middle of the century. In Dresden, the popularity of this new style was not triggered by Schütz but by the Italian Kapellmeisters of the Hofkapelle. Bontempi's five-act opera *Il Paride*, which has been called 'the decisive step towards the introduction of Italian opera in northern Germany',[29] was performed during the celebrations for the wedding of Johann Georg II's daughter Erdmuth Sophia to Margrave Ernst Christian of Brandenburg-Bayreuth in 1662.

Another significant event in the development of opera in Dresden took place during the festivities celebrating the return of Johann Georg III, the elector apparent, from Copenhagen with his new

37. *Act 2 scene iii (Battle between Romans and Turks) of the 'Opernballet von der Wirckung der sieben Planeten', performed in the celebrations on the state visit in February 1678 of the three brothers of Johann Georg II, Duke August of Saxe-Magdeburg, Duke Christian of Saxe-Merseburg and Duke Moritz of Saxe-Zeitz: watercolour by Johann Oswald Harms (showing the 1679 repeat performance)*

bride, Princess Anna Sophia of Denmark, the eldest daughter of King Frederick III. The occasion included the opening of the new opera house on 27 January 1667. The work performed was *Il Teseo* with Giovanni Andrea Moniglia's libretto probably set by Pietro Andrea Ziani.[30] In 1671 Bontempi and Peranda collaborated on *Apollo und Daphne*, the first German opera for which both libretto and score survive, providing the earliest complete evidence of a full opera in German.[31] The following year Bontempi and Peranda collaborated again, on *Jupiter und Jo*, another lost work.

A visit by Johann Georg II's three brothers, Duke August of Saxe-Magdeburg, Duke Christian of Saxe-Merseburg and Duke Moritz of Saxe-Zeitz, provided the occasion for the last major theatrical event of his reign. The performance of the *Opernballett von der Wirckung der sieben Planeten* (fig. 37), an anonymous work which scholars have attributed to Christoph Bernhard or to one of the French dancing-masters in Dresden, Charles du Mesniel or François de la Marche, took place on 3 February 1678.[32]

Banquets for special visitors also required the service of the instrumentalists, singers and even the choirboys of the Hofkapelle. Such so-called Tafelmusik had even been specified in the charter *Kantoreiordnung* of 1548, in which Elector Moritz had directed his musicians to serve 'in church and at our table'.[33] It is clear from the Dresden court diaries, musicians' contracts, catalogues of the period and Schütz's letters that Tafelmusik continued to be one of the most frequent responsibilities of the court musician. Music performed at table was both sacred and secular, using a great variety of instrumental and vocal combinations.

Perhaps the most vivid descriptions of Tafelmusik at Dresden are provided by Philipp Hainhofer, an acquaintance of Schütz and an Augsburg patrician who visited Dresden in both 1617 and 1629. Describing a meal in the upper hall of the royal garden house that contained a great many life-sized portraits, he wrote,

> The space behind every picture is hollow and set up in such a way that one can perform a certain kind of music. When one dines in this upper hall, the musicians are also positioned in the lower hall with the doors closed so that the resonance ascends delightfully through the ventilators. Above, under the ceiling, there is also an arrangement for hidden music, so that one can hear such music from thirty-two different locations, each separated.[34]

Hainhofer describes another meal during which several soloists alternated, including the English musician John Price, who played the viola da gamba and, at the same time, a little English pipe held in his right hand.[35]

The existing documents make little mention of the specific repertory performed at table. A rare exception is the 1681 catalogue, which includes an inventory of Tafelmusik in use during the reign of Johann Georg II. The list includes madrigals (many with instruments) and symphonias by Peranda and an introit by Bernhard. Of perhaps greater interest are the third, fourth and seventh books of Marenzio's madrigals for five voices, and the fourth, fifth, sixth and seventh books of Monteverdi's madrigals. These and Schütz's request of April 1632 to Hainhofer for the eighth book of madrigals by Gesualdo show an abiding interest in the late Italian virtuoso madrigal at the Dresden court.

The court diaries also provide detailed information about Tafelmusik, particularly at important royal gatherings. A diary entry of 2 March 1680, describing the festivities at the wedding in Merseburg of Duke Johann Ernst of Saxe-Gotha and Princess Sophia Hedwig of Saxe-Merseburg, contains a banquet seating arrangement that shows the placement of the musicians. The guests are shown seated to the right of the table while the musicians are placed directly in the centre before them. The performers included the French violinists, the chamber harpsichordist, royal and military shawm players, mountain singers, Wallachian bagpipers and the *Stadtpfeifer*, or municipal musicians.[36]

This seating arrangement displays some of the more colourful and exotic resident ensembles at the Dresden court, whose existence and popularity is confirmed by numerous other references in the court diaries. They included a quartet of shawm players; the little Turkish drum with the little shawms; bagpipers known as the six Wallachians or Haiduks with bagpipes; the dulcimer players; and the mountain singers, who performed national songs in traditional costumes with or without instrumental accompaniment. The French violinists, not mentioned until the last quarter of the century, were probably an imitation of the *petits violons* of Louis XIV. These ensembles occasionally played at court meals, dances and pageants.[37]

One of the largest and most active groups was the court and field trumpeters and kettledrummer, who were used in both musical and military settings. The Dresden Kapellmeisters, including Schütz, composed music for the court trumpeters as the 1681 catalogue bears witness. During the seventeenth century there were twelve court trumpeters; for special occasions, their numbers were increased by players from the various regiments of field trumpeters. In 1658 Johann Georg II had no fewer than 31 trumpeters and one kettledrummer in his employ. A list from 1680 shows nineteen 'court and field trumpeters' and five 'musical trumpeters'. These last must have been required to play the more complicated parts and polyphonic music while the court and field trumpeters played signals, cavalry calls and flourishes and sounded the call to table.

Court trumpeters in Germany belonged to guilds and, beginning in the seventeenth century, all German court and military trumpeters were subject to the statutes of the Dresden *Oberkameradschaft* ratified by the 1623 Regensburg Diet, which restricted the performance of trumpet music to members of the guild. Johann Georg II himself was the *Reichserzmarschall*, making him the most powerful representative of the guild in the empire. In fact, frequent disputes arose between the court trumpeters and Dresden's *Stadtpfeifer*, who provided music at various city proceedings, compelling Johann Georg II to issue a mandate in March 1661 forbidding the *Stadtpfeifer* to play trumpets at most civic functions. These musicians, who were originally *Türmer*, or waits, frequently had both civic and musical duties: they sounded the alarm in times of fire and war, acted as timekeepers and performed polyphonic music on special occasions, frequently with the musicians from the Kreuzkirche, one of Dresden's five seventeenth-century churches. The *Stadtpfeifer*, who during this period consisted of crumhorns, recorders, flutes, dulcians, trumpets and cornetts, took

38. *Herald, preceded by the court kettledrummer and trumpeters, in procession to announce events (such as the chariot- and ring-races) held during the festivities for the state visit to Dresden of the three brothers of Johann George II in February 1678: engraving from George Tzschimmer, 'Die Durchläuchtigste Zusammenkunfft' (Nuremberg, 1680)*

part in the performances for the emperor's visit in 1617 along with 24 trumpeters.

A court diary entry of 6 January 1658 provides details of a state occasion at which the court trumpeters served chiefly as a ceremonial manifestation of royal power.

> Your Serene Highness's entire trumpet choir sounded in the New Year, which was conducted in the following manner:
>
> Finally in the afternoon you took your places in the Great Hall near the window, and when Your Serene Highness went to the table as soon as the Oberhofmarschall entered the Great Hall, the trumpets played 'Nun Last uns Gott den Herren', which they continued until Your Serene Highness and all your high officers and servants were in the dining room. Afterwards, when Her Serene Highness and the princess came to the table, the afore-mentioned song was played again until they were in the dining room. However, when the emissaries, barons of the King of Hungary and the Archduke of Austria, were led to table, only a trumpet flourish was played.
>
> But as the royal company [came] to the table, the trumpeters arranged themselves on one side of the giant chamber in the ante-chamber near the middle entrance and there played 'Joseph, lieber Joseph mein', after which the drummers and pipers also did their part in the entrance between the Great Chamber and Great Hall, and thus it ended.[38]

A vast number of other contemporary sources could be cited in support of the conclusion that musicians were integral members of the Dresden court. Whether they were performing at table, in the elector's chapel or in a dramatic work, these musicians, from the most exalted such as Schütz himself to the more modest who worked under him, played a central part in displaying the power and gran-deur of the elector and his court.

NOTES

[1] The letters of Schütz quoted in this chapter may be found in *Heinrich Schütz: Gesammelte Briefe und Schriften*, ed. E. H. Müller von Asow (Regensburg, 1931). G. Spagnoli, *Letters and Documents of Heinrich Schütz, 1656–1672: an Annotated Translation* (Rochester, New York, 2/1992), contains English translations of many of Schütz's letters as well as many other relevant documents presented together with the original German texts. Translations in this chapter are from this volume unless otherwise indicated.

[2] E. Schmidt, *Der Gottesdienst am kurfürstlichen Hofe zu Dresden* (Göttingen, 1961), 169.

[3] C. V. Wedgwood, *The Thirty Years War* (London, 2/1981), 59–60.

[4] Schmidt, op. cit., 163.

[5] J. Rifkin, 'Schütz – Weckmann – Kopenhagen: zur Frage der zweiten Dänemarkreisen', *Von Isaac bis Bach – Studien zur älteren deutschen Musikgeschichte: Festschrift Martin Just zum 60. Geburtstag* (Kassel, 1991), 181–5.

[6] W. Steude et al., 'Dresden', *Grove 6*, v, 616.

[7] A. Kobuch, 'Neue Aspekte zur Biographie von Heinrich Schütz und zur Geschichte der Dresdner Hofkapelle', *Heinrich Schütz im Spannungsfeld seines und unseres Jahrhunderts. Bericht über die Internationale wissenschaftliche Konferenz am 8. und 9. Oktober 1985 in Dresden im Rahmen der Bach-Händel-Schütz-Ehrung der Deutschen Demokratischen Republik 1985*, ed. W. Steude, *Jahrbuch Peters*, viii (1985), 61, and idem, 'Neue Sagittariana im Staatsarchiv Dresden,' ibid, ix-x (1986–7), 130.

[8] Trans. in H. J. Moser, *Heinrich Schütz: his Life and Work*, trans. C. F. Pfatteicher (St Louis, 1959), 160.

[9] Trans. ibid., 196–7.

[10] Kobuch, 'Neue Aspekte', 63.

[11] ibid., 62–3.

[12] Steude et al., loc. cit.

[13] M. Fürstenau, *Zur Geschichte der Musik und des Theaters am Hofe zu Dresden* (Dresden, 1861), i 10, 169–70.

[14] *D-Dla* Loc. 32751, *Kammerkollegium*, Rep. LII. Gen., no.849, f.146r.

[15] Schmidt, *Der Gottesdienst*, 169.

[16] ibid., 200, n. 92.

[17] *D-Dla* Loc. 4384, *Churfürst Georg des Ersten zu Sachsen, Absterben und Begräbnis, Ander Theil*, i.

[18] ibid., Loc. 8681, no.6, 1662–7.

[19] H. Schnoor, *Dresden: 400 Jahre Musikkultur. Zum Jubiläum der Staatskapelle und zur Geschichte der Dresdener Oper* (Dresden, [1948]), 63.

[20] Fürstenau, *Zur Geschichte*, i, 14, n., and M. B. Lindau, *Geschichte der Haupt- und Residenzstadt Dresden* (Dresden, 1859–63), i, 144–7.

[21] A. Weck, *Der Fürstl. Sächs. weitberuffenen Residentz- und Haupt-Vestung Dresden Beschreibung und Vorstellung* (Nuremberg, 1680), 199–202.

[22] After Elector Friedrich August I converted to Catholicism in 1697, the newly built Catholic church superseded the old palace church as the place of worship for the elector. When the Protestant Sophienkirche was built in 1737, the palace church also became obsolete as a place of worship for Protestants and shortly afterwards was made into living quarters. Fires and renovations continued to alter its appearance until its final destruction in the bombing of Dresden in 1945. See W. Blankenburg, 'Der Conradsche Stich von der Dresdner Hofkapelle (1676)', *Heinrich Schütz in seiner Zeit*, ed. idem (Darmstadt, 1985), 317–28 and W. Steude, 'Sächsische Musik- und Theologietraditionen bei Heinrich Schütz', *Jahrbuch Peters*, viii (1985), 47–54.

[23] W. Steude, 'Die Markuspassion in der Leipziger Passionen-Handschrift des Johann Zacharias Grundig', *Deutsches Jahrbuch der Musikwissenschaft*, xiv (1969), 96–116, and foreword to *Heinrich Schütz, Marco Gioseppe Peranda; Passionsmusiken nach den Evangelisten Matthäus, Lukas, Johannes und Markus*, facsimile edn (Leipzig, 1981), 5–8.

[24] This contract appears to have been lost after it was first published; see Fürstenau, *Zur Geschichte*, i, 160–62.

[25] W. Breig, 'Höfische Festmusik im Werk von Heinrich Schütz', *Heinrich Schütz in seiner Zeit*, ed. W. Blankenburg, 378; see 399–404 for a list of court festivities for which Schütz composed music.

[26] W. Braun, 'Zur Gattungsproblematik des Singballetts', *Gattung und Werk in der Musikgeschichete Norddeutschlands und Skandinaviens*, ed. F. Krummacher and H. W. Schwab (Kassel, 1982), 41–50.

[27] idem, 'Schütz und der "scharffsinnige Herr Claudius Monteverde"', *Heinrich Schütz im Spannungsfeld seines und unseres Jahrhunderts*, ed. Steude, 19; H. Grüss, 'Zwischen madrigalischem und liturgischem Usus – Hypothesen zur Vertonung von Opernlibretti durch Heinrich Schütz', *Musik und Gesellschaft*, xxxv (1985), 539–43; and J.-U. Fechner, 'Zur literatur-geschichtlichen Situation in Dresden 1627 – Überlegungen im Hinblick auf die "Dafne"-Oper von Schütz und Opitz', *Schütz-Jahrbuch*, x (1988), 5–29.

[28] W. Steude, 'Heinrich Schütz und die erste deutsche Oper', *Von Isaac bis Bach*, 169–79.

[29] R. Engländer, 'Zur Frage der *Dafne* (1671), von G. A. Bontempi und M. G. Peranda', *AcM*, xiii (1941), 60.

[30] W. Steude, 'Heinrich Schütz und die musikgeschichtliche Rolle der italienischen Musiker am Dresdner Hofe', *Dresdner Operntraditionen*, ed. G. Stephan and H. John (Dresden, 1986), 115.

[31] Engländer, 'Zur Frage der *Dafne*', 60.

[32] G. Bittrich, *Ein deutsches Opernballett des 17. Jahrhunderts: ein Beitrag zur Frühgeschichte der deutschen Oper* (Leipzig, 1931), and Steude, 'Heinrich Schütz und die erste deutsche Oper', 175.

[33] M. Fürstenau, 'Churfürstliche sechsische Cantoreiordnung', *Monatshefte für Musikgeschichte*, ix (1877), 236.

[34] O. Doering, *Des Augsburger Patriciers Philipp Hainhofer Reisen nach Innsbruck und Dresden* (Vienna, 1901), 217.

[35] Moser, *Heinrich Schütz*, 139.

[36] *D-Dla* Loc. 8682, no.13; *Hofdiaria*, 1679–80, f.286r.

[37] Fürstenau, *Zur Geschichte*, i, 200–10.

[38] *D-Dla* Oberhofmarschallamt N.I. no.8, *Ordnung wie es an hohen Fest- und Residenz Dresden, gehalten sollte*, 1657–1721.

BIBLIOGRAPHICAL NOTE

Historical and cultural background

For an excellent survey of the political, religious, and cultural aspects of the period, see T. Munck, *Seventeenth Century Europe: State, Conflict and the Social Order in Europe 1598–1700* (London, 1990). There are currently a number of thorough studies of the Thirty Years War in English, but perhaps the most engaging is still C. V. Wedgwood's *The Thirty Years War* (London, 2/1981). G. Benecke has translated primary source material pertaining to the war in *Germany in the Thirty Years War* (London, 1978). Another important study is J. V. Polisensky, *The Thirty Years War*, trans. R. Evans (London, 1971). Economic and social conditions during and after the war are covered in R. Vierhaus, *Germany in the Age of Absolutism*, trans. J. B. Knudsen (Cambridge, 1988). G. Grass has created a thoroughly enjoyable account of a fictional meeting in 1647 of musical and literary luminaries, including Schütz, in *The Meeting at Telgte*, trans. R. Manheim (New York and London, 1981). A useful overview of seventeenth-century lyric poetry precedes G. Schoolfield's translations of the work of important poets in *The German Lyric of the Baroque in English Translation* (Chapel Hill, 1961). Several important essays may be found in B. L. Spahr, *Problems and Perspectives: a Collection of Essays on German Baroque Literature* (Frankfurt, 1981), and *German Baroque Literature: the European Perspective*, ed. G. Hoffmeister (New York, 1983). For descriptions of the art collection of the Saxon rulers housed in Dresden, see J. Menzhausen, *The Green Vaults*, trans. M. Herzfeld, rev. D. T. Rice (Leipzig, 1968), and the Metropolitan Museum of Art's exhibition catalogue *The Splendor of Dresden: Five Centuries of Art Collecting. An Exhibition from the State Art Collections of Dresden, German Democratic Republic* (New York, 1978).

Music

Schütz's music has been edited in *Heinrich Schütz: Sämtliche Werke*, ed. P. Spitta and others (Leipzig, 1885–1927), which is being superseded by *Heinrich Schütz: Neue Ausgabe sämtlicher Werke*, ed. on behalf of the Internationale Schütz-Gesellschaft (Kassel, 1955–) and *Heinrich Schütz: Sämtliche Werke*, ed. G. Graulich and others (Stuttgart, 1971–). For prefaces of several of Schütz's works in English translation, see G. J. Buelow, *A Schütz Reader: Documents of Performance Practice*, Journal of the American Choral Foundation, Inc., xxvii/4 (Oct 1985); and for translations of the dedications and forewords to Schütz's three collections of *Symphoniae sacrae*, see O. Struck, *Source Readings in Music History* (New York, 1950), 432–41. H. J. Moser, *Heinrich Schütz: his Life and Work*, trans. C. F. Pfatteicher (St Louis, 1959), remains the standard biography of the composer; for a condensed version of it, see *Heinrich Schütz: a Short Account of his Life and Work*, trans. and ed. D. McCulloch (London, 1967). Important new work has been done by J. Rifkin in 'Heinrich Schütz' (with C. Timms), *The 'New Grove' North European Baroque Masters* (London, 1985), 1–50;

183

The Early Baroque Era

'Towards a New Image of Henrich Schütz', *MT*, cxxvi (1985), 651–8, 716–20; and 'Whatever Happened to Heinrich Schütz?', *Opus*, vi (Oct 1985), 10–14, 49. R. Petzoldt has assembled a fine collection of pictures and facsimile reproductions presented with German and English commentary in *Heinrich Schütz und seine Zeit in Bildern* (Kassel, 1972). R. A. Leaver has translated one of the most important primary sources for Schütz's biography in *Music in the Service of the Church: the Funeral Sermon for Heinrich Schütz* (St Louis, 1984). Other relevant documents may be found in G. Spagnoli, *Letters and Documents of Heinrich Schütz: an Annotated Translation* (Rochester, New York, 2/1992). Current research on Schütz and seventeenth-century music in general appears in the *Schütz-Jahrbuch*, ed. W. Breig under the auspices of the Internationale Heinrich-Schütz-Gesellschaft.

Chapter IX

Protestant North Germany

GEORGE J. BUELOW

For most of Europe, the first three-quarters of the seventeenth century was a period of almost continuous war. Even though much of the Thirty Years War (1618–48) took place in central Europe, its death, misery and destruction spread to the northernmost regions, even the lands bordering on the North and Baltic seas. In addition, the continuing rivalry between Sweden and Denmark added constantly to the unrest in this region until the last decades of the century. In the second decade of the Thirty Years War, the Habsburg army of Wallerstein invaded Denmark and went on to overwhelm much of the Baltic coast of eastern Pomerania. Sweden, under the leadership of King Gustavus Adolphus, entered the war in 1630 by invading Pomerania, and quickly swept into the heartland of Germany as far south as the Rhineland. The Peace of Westphalia (1648) formulated solutions, albeit often temporary, to the various international conflicts, but peace did not endure. France and Spain continued their war, and soon England and the United Dutch Provinces initiated their own hostilities. After Sweden invaded Poland in 1655, Denmark again attacked Sweden, but the Danes were defeated by the superior forces of Sweden's Charles X. The Treaty of Roskilde (1658) established the territorial integrity of the Swedish mainland. However, five months later the Swedes invaded the Danish mainland, beginning yet another war that achieved little but an impasse between these two northern powers. Their armies would meet again in battle in 1676, and at Lund the Danes suffered another defeat, and for the last time were forced to withdraw from the Swedish homeland.

This sketch of some of the continuing hostilities inflaming the northern part of Europe gives only a small part of the political picture of seventeenth-century Europe. However, it conveys the fact that peace was not endemic to the region, and the general populace, the poor as well as the wealthy burghers and the nobility, all experienced the constant uncertainties that war brought into their lives. These wars placed enormous financial burdens on cities and courts alike, and inevitably music as well as other forms of culture suffered.

While the Danish and Swedish courts managed to maintain a semblance of cultural display, many lesser aristocratic enclaves in northern Germany were often left destitute and unable to support much in the way of a musical establishment.

There were, however, exceptions to these conditions primarily in the imperial free cities of Hamburg and Lübeck. They had belonged to the Hanseatic League, which came into existence in the Middle Ages as a means of protecting the trading interests of a widespread network of European towns and cities. More than 50 trading centres on major sea and land routes belonged to the league in the fifteenth century, with cities as far north as Reval and Riga, as far east as Kraków, as far south as Cologne, Erfurt and Naumburg and as far north-west as Staveren and Groningen. The greatest strength and influence was centred in port cities on the North or Baltic seas, such as Hamburg, Lübeck, Danzig and Königsberg. For the most part, these cities had a culture based on the tastes and wealth of the merchant class, and while individual cities had individual characters, there was an overall similarity related to the structure and purpose of the Hanseatic League. This chapter focusses on Hamburg and Lübeck, the two most important ones for us.

HAMBURG: INTRODUCTION

Among the north German cities that had been integrated into the Hanseatic League, Hamburg is not only typical but stands out as the one that grew most impressively as a metropolis and cultural centre, with an especially rich musical environment. Like that of Lübeck to the east, Hamburg's musical life in the seventeenth century focussed primarily on two predominant social forces: the Protestant church, with its educational organization; and the political structure of city-state government, with its many ritualistic and ceremonial responsibilities.

Because of its impregnable system of defensive battlements and also because it successfully maintained political neutrality, Hamburg remained untouched by the series of wars that raged in central and northern Europe in the seventeenth century. Its population expanded significantly from around 38 000 in the first decades of the century to about 70 000 in 1680. Wars and internal political unrest, often sparked by religious persecution, brought a large foreign population to the city. Not the least important aspect of Hamburg's attraction to migrating populations was its commercial vitality and the availability of jobs. The wars between Spain and the Netherlands swelled the population of Hamburg to the point that about a quarter of the total were former Dutch citizens. Also, a significant part of the population became Jewish, as Jews from Portugal and other regions of Europe came to the city, giving Hamburg one of the largest Jewish populations of any city in Europe.

Located on the Elbe river, Hamburg was connected by ship and barge not only to the ports on the North and Baltic seas but also to points beyond reach from the Atlantic ocean. It also drew river traffic by means of the Elbe and its tributaries – as well as a waterway of rivers and a canal connecting it to the Oder – from a vast central and east European region. In the seventeenth century, therefore, the city became one of the great centres for trade and mercantile exchange, a crossroads of the business world of Europe. Free of a ruling aristocracy, with no political connections to any German principality or lesser oligarchy, the city was liberal in its politics and one of the most progressive in placing much governmental authority in the hands of its citizens, albeit the wealthiest ones. Equally important, in a century of almost continuous political unrest elsewhere, Hamburg used its neutrality to advantage in financial, manufacturing and political dealings with all the warring powers of Europe. By 1678 it had become the richest and largest city in northern Europe and claimed the title of the 'Venice of the North', because of its network of canals connecting the Elbe river with the Alster lake on which the city was built. Prosperous, with a mixed citizenry of various nationalities, a solid and conservative Protestant ethic unifying its middle- and upper-class burgher population, Hamburg had the luxury of devoting a good part of its financial resources to its cultural growth, and as a consequence music flourished.

During the seventeenth century, music came to play a very important role in the four main parish churches of the city: the Petrikirche, Nikolaikirche, Catharinenkirche and Jakobikirche. By the end of the sixteenth century, each of them paid a regular salary to an organist. One of Hamburg's musical distinctions in the seventeenth century as well as in the eighteenth was the particular genius of the organists working in these churches. Among them were several pupils of the famous Dutch organist, composer and teacher Jan Pieterszoon Sweelinck (1562–1621), which led the eighteenth-century Hamburg composer and theorist Johann Mattheson to describe Sweelinck as the 'creator of Hamburg's organists'. These organists were Jacob Praetorius at the Petrikirche (1603–51), Heinrich Scheidemann at the Catharinenkirche (1625–63) and Ulrich Cernitz at the Jakobikirche (1632–54). In addition Matthias Weckmann studied with Praetorius and became organist at the Jakobikirche in 1655, and Johann Adam Reincken, a pupil of Scheidemann, became Scheidemann's successor at the Catharinenkirche in 1663.

In both the Netherlands and north Germany this period witnessed an age of major organ construction and reconstruction. The building

39. Organ built by Arp Schnitger (1688–93) in the Jakobikirche, Hamburg

of many new organs in Hamburg as well as the presence of so many distinguished organists who composed for the organ emphasized the growing significance of the instrument both within and outside the church service. In the sixteenth century the organ still had no integrated role in Protestant services, since it served largely to give support to choral singing but not to the congregational singing of chorales. This became but one of the organist's new responsibilities in the Hamburg churches in the seventeenth century. At this time his role was expanded to include playing music in place of a vocal work that would be appropriate within the service. Often he would intabulate a motet, that is, arrange it as a keyboard transcription. During the singing of appropriate Gregorian chants within the service the organist would alternate with the chorus, and as the century progressed, the organist was required more often to accompany (from a basso continuo) one or more instrumentalists and singers in sacred vocal works. The organist was also called upon to perform various free keyboard forms such as preludes and postludes and to improvise on chorale and other sacred melodies as required by the service. The new and central importance of chorale melodies to the Protestant religion led to an extensive organ literature based on chorales, including preludes, variations and various large-scale compositions such as chorale fantasies.

HAMBURG: THE ORGANISTS AND THEIR MUSIC

Jacob Praetorius (1586–1651), son of the famous Hamburg organist Hieronymus (1560–1629), was the first to establish Sweelinck's influence in Hamburg. Unfortunately, little of his music remains beyond organ preludes based on the chorales *Christum wir sollen loben schon* and *Herr Gott dich loben wir* and an impressive though fragmentary setting of *Durch Adams Fall ist ganz verderbt.*[1]

Of far greater significance is the organ music of Heinrich Scheidemann (*c*1595–1663), the most influential of Sweelinck's pupils in establishing a north German style of organ music. Scheidemann enlarged the excellent organ at the Catharinenkirche in the 1630s to 56 stops with four manuals and pedals. His influence was spread not only by the popularity of his organ music, more of which survives than of any other Hamburg organ composer of the period, but also as the teacher of, among others, Johann Adam Reincken (1623–1722), who succeeded him at the Catharinenkirche. Reincken undoubtedly influenced many organists of the next generation, including Buxtehude, who was a friend from at least the 1670s.[2] Even as late as 1720 Johann Sebastian Bach paid a visit to Hamburg to play for the 97-year-old Reincken.

Scheidemann's compositions fall into two main categories: elaborate, multi-sectional settings of chorales and other church melodies, and free, improvisatory explorations of various forms of keyboard technique, principally in his Praeambula. The key to Scheidemann's importance lies in the more than 50 settings of sacred melodies, including an especially remarkable collection of pieces on the eight tones of the *Magnificat*. In the latter work, as in the organ chorales, Scheidemann created an idiomatic organ style using the keyboard technique established by Sweelinck but also employing to great advantage the technical and sonorous resources of the north German Baroque organ. In his works, which essentially are variations on church melodies, the melody is usually placed in long-held notes in the pedals or sometimes in the top voice. On this cantus firmus various kinds of keyboard variations take place: contrapuntal imitations often based on the opening motif of the chorale, fanciful echo effects between contrasting sections of the organ (*Rückpositiv* versus the keyboard manuals) of motifs taken from the chorale, elaborate keyboard figurations such as cascading scales, arpeggios and other motifs that develop from under the fingers of an organist trained in improvisation. In some works the chorale itself is ornamented in various florid and contrapuntal designs. It is both the variety of

Scheidemann's ideas and the vitality and frequent textural and sonorous contrasts that make his organ music so important historically and so rewarding musically.[3]

Among other organists giving Hamburg a special place in the history of the instrument was Matthias Weckmann (*c*1619–74). A pupil of Heinrich Schütz, he came on the latter's advice to Hamburg to study with Jacob Praetorius. After service as organist in Dresden from 1637, as well as in Nyköping, Denmark (at the court of Crown Prince Christian), in the 1640s, Weckmann became organist at the Jakobikirche in 1655, thus carrying into the second half of the century the traditions of organ playing and composition generated by Praetorius and Scheidemann. He composed much sacred vocal music as well as organ music and also founded the first collegium musicum in Hamburg (see below). According to Mattheson,[4] Weckmann faced the great keyboard virtuoso and composer Johann Jacob Froberger in a contest of performance skills at the Dresden court, which led to a lifelong friendship between the two. Little of Weckmann's keyboard music remains: a few chorale-based compositions, fugal pieces, toccatas and keyboard suites. Much of the music is conservative in style, looking back to Sweelinck and Samuel Scheidt, and imitation and canon are common features. His keyboard figuration is less individual than Scheidemann's. But as a pupil of Schütz and Praetorius he was a significant figure in Hamburg music.

HAMBURG: MUSIC IN THE CHURCHES [5]

In 1529 the old Johanniskloster was taken over to become the Johanneum, a Latin school for boys with a humanistic orientation. Later, in 1613, the Akademisches Gymnasium was established as the preparatory educational institution for students intending to enter a university. In both schools, music had equal importance with other academic subjects. Music in the Johanneum was directed by the Kantor, who was employed by the city and who had the responsibility of organizing and directing the music in the services of the four parish churches. Together with the teachers (preceptors) and students of the Johanneum, he provided daily music for the liturgy by dividing the singers among the four churches, where they sang in unison Latin chants and hymns. In Hamburg, throughout the seventeenth century, church services continued the practice of singing introits, antiphons, responses and hymns in Latin. It is probable that students from the Johanneum also performed periodically at the smaller churches and chapels in the city as well as at the Dom, the former cathedral, which retained its administrative independence from the city throughout the century. The Kantor not only organized the teaching of music in the Johanneum through the eight grades but also taught students in the advanced classes the rudiments of music theory as well as the singing of works in contrapuntal style. After 1600, the city required that contrapuntal music be performed six times a year in each of the four main churches, that is, a total of 24 performances of polyphonic music by the students of the school.

The first of three outstanding Kantors working in Hamburg in the seventeenth century was Erasmus Sartorius (1577–1637), who was appointed in 1605. During his Kantorship he greatly increased the amount of polyphonic music heard in the churches, and he required regular support of this music by the *Ratsmusikanten* – the city's instrumentalists (see below). In 1609 he initiated the practice of performing the Passions, from 1612 with instrumental accompaniment. From one of his treatises, *Institutionum musicarum tractatio nova et brevis* (Hamburg, 1635), one gains some insight into the probable composers and polyphonic repertory the Kantor taught to his students. In his discussions about the modes Sartorius mentions music by Lassus, Hieronymus Praetorius and Clemens non Papa, as well as by Giaches de Wert, Claudio Merulo, Philippe de Monte, Ludwig Senfl, Alfonso Ferrabosco (i) and Alessandro Striggio. Evidence of the growing frequency of performing polyphonic music with instrumentalists is seen in the fact that during the first three decades of the century most of the churches in Hamburg needed to enlarge or construct new choir space and to add galleries from which musicians could perform.

The most splendid developments in church music during the seventeenth century came during the Kantorship of Thomas Selle (1599–1663), who held the position from 1641 until his death. A prolific composer of vocal music, he preserved his compositions in a manuscript compendium comprising sixteen partbooks and three volumes of tablature, which contained music on 89 Latin and 193 German texts.[6] He was a student in Leipzig, perhaps with Sethus Calvisius (1556–1615), Kantor at the Thomasschule. Selle's music shows influences of a former Kantor there, Johann Hermann Schein (1568–1630). A strong element of stylistic continuity evolves from the works of Michael Praetorius (c1571–1621), through the concerted style of using instrumental music for articulating the vocal forms and for providing instrumental sonorities in sinfonias, interludes and ritornellos in the sacred concertos.

Selle composed a St Matthew (1636) and a St John Passion (1643), the latter with a rich body of instruments, especially in the interludes. The St John Passion[7] is an example of the so-called oratorio Passion, in which the biblical story is not recited continuously but is broken up by the insertion of contemplative passages based on sacred texts from the Gospels, other books of the Bible, and various non-biblical sacred lyrics. In Selle's St John Passion there are three interludes for five-part chorus and three solo voices supported by a five-part orchestra, solo violin and basso continuo. The Evangelist sings in recitation style, as was true of earlier German passions, but he is accompanied by two bassoons. The variety of instrumental and vocal forces is described in Selle's title: *Passio secundum Johannem cum Intermediis Thomae Sellii mit 6 Vocalstimmen und 6 Instrumentalstimmen sampt einer Vocal capella à 5 pro Choro remoto und dem Choro pro Organo à 4 gesetzt einfältigst in Stylo recitativo* (St John's Passion, with interludes for six vocal parts and six instrumental parts, together with a five-part vocal ensemble for a 'remote' [i.e., placed at a distance from the organ] chorus, and a four-part chorus at the organ, composed with insertions in recitative style by Thomas Selle). The colourful richness of Selle's Passion is evident also in his instructions for adding instruments to the parts for soloists:

1. Evangelist. Add as is possible – 2 bassoons or viola da gambas and 2 bandoras. Tenor I.
2. Jesus. 2 violins and 2 lutes. Bass.
3. Handmaiden. 2 violins and violas. Cantus.
4. Peter. 2 recorders and trombone. Tenor II.
5. Pilate. 2 cornetts and trombone I. Alto.
6. Servant. 2 recorders and trombone. Alto II.

For major church feast days as well as for more routine additions of music to Sunday services, Selle persuaded the Hamburg City council to increase the number of performing groups responsible to him. He enlisted singers from the Gymnasium and the orphanages, as well as teachers who could sing. He also convinced the council that they should pay a salary for a group of eight excellent singers as well as to give them room and board. This Kantorei gave the Kantor support in ways other than singing, such as helping with the copying of scores and parts. Similarly, Selle laid down greatly strengthened principles for the participation of the instrumentalists. He requested in 1642 that at least eight instrumentalists be made available at each church every Sunday; failing this number, five was to be the absolutely acceptable minimum. Each of the five performers, as was typical for the period, needed to be proficient on more than one instrument. Selle required two cornettists who would bring with them two violins and two recorders; an alto trombonist who could play violin and recorder; a tenor trombonist capable of playing bass trombone, but who would bring also a tenor violin and a recorder; and a string bass player who could also play bassoon, dulcian and bass trombone.

Hamburg churches found that they had to add considerably to their instrument collections, and together with the Hamburg city council fully supported Selle's energetic programme of making church music an outstanding feature of the city's cultural and religious life. At the beginning of the century, as we have seen, only 24 performances of polyphonic music were heard during the year in the four parish churches. During Selle's Kantorate, each Saturday Vesper service as well as two services every Sunday presented a rich array of concerted vocal and instrumental music to the congregations. Selle extended similar musical performances to other churches in the city, and the singing of the Passions became one of the main features of the year. Selle's Kantorei often participated in funeral services as well as in various festive church occasions, for example the dedication of the new church of St Michael on 14 March 1661.

The third in the distinguished line of Hamburg Kantors was Christoph Bernhard (1628–92). He came to Hamburg from Dresden after the death of Selle, obtaining the position in competition with six other applicants. He had sung in the court chapel choir under Schütz, whose pupil he became. Schütz so admired Bernhard as a composer that he requested from him a motet for his own funeral. Only one collection of Bernhard's sacred music was published, the *Geistlicher Harmonien, I. Teil* (Dresden, 1665).[8] This is written along the formal lines of Schütz's *Kleine geistliche Konzerte*; most of the texts are biblical and are set for from one to four solo voices with continuo. Some of the pieces have parts for two solo violins. Among Bernhard's compositions in manuscript are several funeral compositions written for distinguished citizens of Hamburg. One such work was performed on 12 September 1667 at the funeral service for Johann Rist, a well-known theologian, poet and composer, whose poetry was set by many composers from north Germany, including Jacob Praetorius, Scheidemann, Selle and the outstanding Hamburg violinist Johann Schop. In 1674 Bernhard was called back to the Dresden court to become the teacher of the elector's children. Shortly before he left Hamburg, his friend and colleague Weckmann died, and thus Hamburg lost two of its most influential musical leaders in the same year. The city would soon experience a decline in the sphere of sacred music, but a new focus would develop in the city's cultural life when the Hamburg opera began in 1678.

Weckmann's activities in Hamburg had also included the founding in 1660 of a collegium musicum, which performed on Thursdays in the refectory of the cathedral.[9] The purpose of the Collegium, according to Mattheson, was to present concerts of the best music being composed in such cities as Venice, Rome, Vienna, Munich and Dresden. Mattheson comments that the collegium attained such fame that the greatest composers wished to be associated with it. The concerts drew singers from the churches, and instrumentalists from the city *Ratsmusikanten*, and also from talented merchants and other citizens. While collegia of this type that gave concerts of new music had existed much earlier in other German cities, this was Hamburg's first experiment with public concerts. The collegium did not, however, survive Weckmann's death, and would be revived only in the eighteenth century.

HAMBURG: INSTRUMENTAL MUSICIANS

With some 25 officially recognized instrumentalists, Hamburg had a larger official organization of instrumental musicians than any other German city. This was true even without taking into account the many musicians among the students of the Johanneum and the Gymnasium. Since medieval times German cities had employed one or more Stadtpfeifer, wind players who performed at various civic ceremonies. In the seventeenth century the Hamburg city council paid salaries to eight *Ratsmusikanten* (or *Ratsinstrumentalisten*) and also to two *Expectanten* (substitutes prepared to take the place of a council instrumentalist who died or became incapacitated). In addition, the city organized a brotherhood of fifteen instrumentalists, the *Rollbrüder*, a union of musicians ranking second to the *Ratsmusikanten*; they participated in many social activities when the latter were unavailable. Strict rules, enforced by the city police chief, were established by the city council to regulate the duties of the city's instrumentalists. These included how many instrumentalists might perform at weddings, the number being determined by the social ranking of the families involved. If no music were desired at a wedding reception and banquet, the participants had to pay the council an *Entschädigungssume* (indemnity fee). Other secular festivities were also a major source of income for the instrumentalists. In addition to these secular duties, council musicians and also the *Rollbrüder* were frequently required to participate in various church services as the Kantor required. The leader of the *Ratsmusikanten* was always the first violinist, the most famous of whom in the seventeenth century was Johann Schop (*d* 1667).

Schop had come to Hamburg after leading the musical establishment of King Christian IV at Copenhagen. His appointment by the Hamburg city council in 1621 gave him the freedom to undertake what might be described as concert tours in Germany as well as back to Copenhagen. In 1634 he travelled in the company of Heinrich Schütz and Heinrich Albert to Copenhagen for the wedding of Crown Prince Christian. During the celebrations a contest was held between Schop and the French violinist Jacques Foucart which Schop won. He published two sets of instrumental dances in Hamburg in 1633 and 1635 and was also (like Thomas Selle) an important composer of sacred songs to texts by Johann Rist.

40. Frontispiece to 'Frommer und Gottseliger Christen Alltägliche Haussmusik' (Lüneburg, 1654), a collection of settings by Johann Schop (and others) of sacred poems by Johann Rist, intended for domestic performance

While in the service of the Danish court, Schop became acquainted with William Brade, a distinguished English violinist, who may have been his teacher. Brade (1560–1630) was one of several English instrumentalists who lived most of their lives in Germany. He was widely known as a virtuoso, being employed at various German courts. He stands out as an important figure in Hamburg as a city musician between 1608 and 1610, then again in 1613 as the leader of the city musicians. He left again in 1615 but retired to the city in 1625. His several published collections of pavans, galliards, canzonas, allemandes, courantes and other dance forms present important evidence of the kinds of instrumental music that the *Ratsmusikanten* played at various social entertainments.

Hamburg became a significant centre for the publication of secular dance music. In the earlier part of the century these dances were usually in four, five or six parts, but later in the century the characteristic Baroque combination of two violins, bass and basso continuo prevailed. Among outstanding collections of this type published in the city was Samuel Scheidt's *Paduana, galliarda, courante, alemande, intrada, canzonetto* . . . (Part I, 1621; II–IV, 1622, 1624, 1627).

As was true of most cities from as early as medieval times, Hamburg employed a brass player for the towers of the Catharinenkirche, Nikolaikirche, Jakobikirche and the cathedral. This trumpeter, according to a sheet of instructions for the position at the Jakobikirche, had the following duties:

1. Every night, after the church clock has struck nine, midnight and, in the morning, three and ten, he will honour God by playing a sacred psalm.
2. In the event of misfortune in the city, or danger of fire, he will sound his trumpet.
3. He will join the other trumpeters at weddings.
4. When needed, he will play in the music for church services.

Today it is hard to imagine, in Hamburg or any other large German city, the impression given by a lonely trumpeter high in one of the church towers sounding forth into the night or morning stillness.

HAMBURG: OPERA

In 1678 Hamburg became the first city to emulate the Venetian achievement of establishing a public opera house. Although operas had been performed sporadically at the numerous German aristocratic courts, nowhere outside Venice (since 1637) had opera flourished as a commercial enterprise dependent to a considerable extent upon public enthusiasm for the new art form.

This notable event in Hamburg's musical history evolved from the efforts of a city councillor, Gerhard Schott (1641–1702), a member of a Hamburg patrician family and a well-known lawyer educated at the universities of Helmstedt, Heidelberg and Basle, who had travelled extensively on the Continent and in England. While documentary evidence is lacking, it seems probable that he acquired his love and knowledge of opera, both as a business and as an artistic institution, during these travels, especially in Venice, a city that had long-established commercial relationships with Hamburg, which it resembled in more than one way. Both cities were centres of trade and commerce, seaports with characteristically transient populations of sailors, merchants, diplomats and all manner of travellers from many other places; in both, the population was heterogeneous, and there was a great deal of wealth for investment in new cultural as well as social undertakings.

Schott, who became director and frequently also artistic impresario for half the theatre's 61-year history, initiated Hamburg's opera by entering into a business partnership with another lawyer, Peter Lütjen, as well as with the distinguished organist of St Catherinen,

Johann Adam Reincken. Probably he also received encouragement, if not financial support, from the opera-loving Duke Christian Albrecht of Schleswig-Gottorf, who lived in exile in Hamburg from 1675 to 1679, as did the Duke's court composer, Johann Theile (1646–1724), who became the first Hamburg opera composer.

Schott engaged the Italian architect Girolamo Sartorio (designer also of opera houses at Amsterdam and Leipzig), who built the theatre on rented land on the Gänsemarkt, adjacent to the location of the present Hamburg State Opera. A contemporary account[10] describes the building as unusually large (seating approximately 2000 persons), with a stage area about 79 feet deep and an auditorium 80 feet deep and 65 feet wide. The theatre consisted of a parterre, four levels of boxes, each holding between nine and twelve seats, and a gallery. The stage was praised for its superb machines and for the large number of sliding side-scenes – fifteen. The opera season began in January and continued through the year; normally it was closed for Lent, on all other major church feast days and during the summer months. Performances took place two or three times a week on Monday, Wednesday or Thursday afternoons and lasted between four and six hours.[11] During the year an average of between 90 and 100 performances usually took place.

The Hamburg opera opened on 2 January 1678 with a performance of Theile's *Der erschaffene, und gefallene und auffgerichtete Mensch [Adam und Eva]*. The biblical subject matter of this opera, as well as of many others performed during the earliest years, reflects an attempt, albeit unsuccessful, to silence the vociferous attacks against opera from the pulpits of the city's churches. The ministers of the Pietist movement in particular condemned all stage entertainments. For at least a decade church congregations heard inflamed rhetoric against the opera, and a copious stream of pamphlets and other documents either attacked opera as against the Protestant religion and as the evil work of 'dark forces', or praised it as meeting the approval of biblical philosophy. After a while the controversy slowly faded, and myth and history largely furnished the subjects of librettos, many of which were adaptations and translations of texts originally used by Italian composers.

Composers represented during the first decade of the Gänsemarkt theatre, in addition to Theile, included Nicolaus Adam Strungk (1640–1700) and Johann Philipp Förtsch (1652–1732). However, the most frequently performed composer during this period was Johann Wolfgang Franck (1644–?c1710), who wrote at least a dozen scores for Hamburg audiences between 1679 and 1685. None of the operas by these composers has been preserved, but fortunately several collections of arias from Franck's operas still exist: from *Aeneas* (1680), *Vespasianus* (1681), *Diocletianus* (1682) and *Der glückliche Gross-Verzier*

41. Scene from J. W. Franck's opera 'Charitine, oder Goettlich-Geliebte', first performed in Hamburg, 1681: engraving from the libretto

Cara Mustapha (1686). The arias in these collections underline the overriding influence of Venetian opera.[12] But there are other strong stylistic elements as well, especially German secular and sacred song, including chorales. As in Venetian operas of the same period, strophic arias dominate. Franck, like Venetian composers, often ends his arias with an instrumental ritornello based on the final phrase or phrases of the vocal material. He seems to be the first Hamburg composer to accompany some of the arias with orchestral instruments (usually strings), using short, often concerted interjections to highlight a vocal motif of particular expressiveness, and suggesting the probable influence of Venetian composers such as Sartorio, Legrenzi and Pietro Andrea Ziani.

It is important to note that unlike most performances of operas at various German courts, operas in Hamburg were always sung in German and in the main were by German composers. It was in the final years of the seventeenth century and the opening decades of the eighteenth that Hamburg's opera became famous, especially during the period when most of the works to be performed were written and directed by Reinhard Keiser.[13]

LÜBECK: INTRODUCTION

The exceedingly varied musical life of Hamburg came about in part through the spirited cooperation of church and city institutions in supporting the various activities. This achievement served as a model for other north German cities especially Lübeck, a major Baltic port, today the most important city in Schleswig-Holstein. In the seventeenth century Lübeck, formerly the leading administrative centre for the Hanseatic League, began to decline both economically and politically. But except for Hamburg it remained the most important free imperial city in northern Europe. Histories of music in Lübeck invariably emphasize the period of the late Baroque era during which the great organist and composer Dietrich Buxtehude was organist of the Marienkirche. However, as might be expected of a great commercial centre and former Hanseatic city which, again like Hamburg, escaped the ravages of the Thirty Years War, Lübeck developed a rich musical culture in the first three-quarters of the seventeenth century.

Lübeck, too, has a skyline dominated by church towers. In the seventeenth century its parish churches were the Jakobikirche, Marienkirche, Petrikirche, Ägidienkirche and Catharinenkirche; there was also the former cathedral. Of these, the Marienkirche, the official church of the town council, was the most important. It stands above all the others on the highest ground, dominating both city and harbour. As in Hamburg, it was in these parish churches that music held a place of central importance.[14]

Organ music likewise became a central feature of the musical life of Lübeck, and the organs in the major churches were repaired, enlarged or newly built during the seventeenth century. Organists had duties in the Lübeck churches similar to those described above for Hamburg organists. In Lübeck, however, the organist apparently did not accompany the congregational singing of chorales. The choristers for the churches were trained at the St Catharinen school. Each student was expected to join the choir of the church in the district in which he lived. This edict seems to have been difficult to enforce, since numerous complaints arose concerning the failure of students to participate in the choirs on Sundays. This was less a problem for Saturday Vesper services, when the teachers would lead their students in procession from school to the appropriate church.

The general supervision of church music in Lübeck was the res-

42. Group portrait (c1674) by Johannes Voorhout: Dietrich Buxtehude has been identified as the musician on the right (head on hand), with Johann Adam Reinken at the keyboard and Johann Theile playing the bass viol (the figure behind Theile is thought to be the artist, and the lutenist the artist's wife)

ponsibility of the Kantor, who was employed by the city and belonged to the faculty of the St Catharinen school. A course plan for the school from 1622 indicates the importance of music instruction: music was taught from 12 noon to 1 p.m. on Monday, Tuesday, Thursday and Friday; chorus rehearsals were held on Saturday from noon to 1 p.m., and private lessons were given on Wednesday afternoons. The fifth and fourth classes received instruction in the elements of music, the third, second and first classes in part-singing. On Saturdays between noon to 1 p.m. the seventh and sixth classes rehearsed appropriate music for funerals, while the third, second and first classes practised various choral music. The Kantor was responsible only for training the upper three classes (the third, second and first). The hour of music instruction generally was divided between lessons in music theory and in practising singing. The Kantor was the director of music for the Marienkirche, while teachers from the St Catherinen school were assigned duties as chorus masters at the Petrikirche, Jakobikirche and Ägidienkirche.

LÜBECK: CHURCH MUSIC

Although organists apparently did not accompany congregational singing, and even though for parts of the year no organ music was permitted in the churches (during Lent and days of penitence and prayer), the organist's position was central to Lübeck's sacred music. Much of the liturgy required the organist to alternate his performance with the singing of chants and chorales by the Kantor and the choir. In addition, some of the music would be introduced by organ preludes, and the service normally ended with a solo organ postlude. The organist at the Marienkirche often played ensemble music together with two *Ratsmusikanten*, a violinist and lutenist, most often during the Communion part of the service. For this purpose the organist often purchased trio sonatas, for example those by Johann Heinrich Schmeltzer.

There are records of many talented organists who were employed by the Lübeck churches during the seventeenth century. Most of them are now little more than names, but before the appointment of Buxtehude to the Marienkirche in 1668, one name does stand out, that of Franz Tunder (1614–67), Buxtehude's predecessor and father-in-law, who took up this position in 1641. He had been employed at Gottorp, the court of the dukes of Gottdorf-Holstein. Only seventeen vocal works, fourteen organ works and a sinfonia by him remain. The Latin sacred works show a strong influence from mid-century Italian composers, for example Monteverdi and Giovanni Rovetta. They are for solo voice and concerted violin duet or five-part string ensemble, or for larger vocal ensembles in from two to five parts. Tunder here exhibits a gift for beautiful and intensely expressive vocal writing. Of his German sacred compositions, some are in the style of Schütz's vocal concertos, while others are dominated by the chorale. The latter consist of variations on chorales, with diverse forces and textures from one verse to another. The formal concept gives some insight into the origins of the German cantata, especially the chorale cantata still employed much later by J. S. Bach, for example *Christ lag in Todesbanden*, BWV4. Tunder's organ music, continuing the north German keyboard style, is equally striking. The preludes are toccata-like works in which free, improvisatory opening and concluding sections frame a middle section in imitative style. The chorale-based works are extremely impressive. The chorale is treated in a fantasy-like manner in which each phrase usually functions in two different ways: it is developed in some way – by ornamentation, motivic development, echo effects or other keyboard elaborations – while it is also stated a second time in the lowest voice, usually in the pedals. These pieces are richly varied, with striking harmonies, and lively textures built on a remarkable command of the contrapuntal interaction of motifs generated by Tunder's impressive keyboard technique.[15]

Not only was Tunder the most gifted organist and composer at the Marienkirche before Buxtehude; he was also important for establishing weekly organ recitals in the Marienkirche. Caspar Ruetz, a Kantor at the Marienkirche about a century later, states in his book *Widerlegte Vorurteile von der Beschaffenheit der heutigen Kirchenmusik* (Refutation of Prejudices Concerning the Nature of Contemporary Church Music) (Lübeck, 1752) that it was Tunder who began the custom of giving concerts on Thursdays for the town's citizens to pass the time until they went on to the stock-market. The programmes were so successful, according to Ruetz, that several rich burghers who loved music encouraged Tunder to add a few violins and then singers to the concerts. Later, these concerts were moved to the last two Sundays in Trinity and the second, third and fourth Sundays in Advent. It was this tradition of Abendmusiken that Buxtehude would develop into events of far-reaching significance and popularity, known far beyond Lübeck and attracting many musicians to the city during his career at the Marienkirche.

LÜBECK: INSTRUMENTAL MUSIC

Lübeck, like Hamburg, paid a yearly salary to a small group of instrumentalists, the *Ratsmusikanten*. Others were part of the highly structured system of employing instrumentalists who, while not on the city council's payroll, nevertheless had to conform to the rules determining how many of them could perform at which public and private events. Lübeck, too, from the Middle Ages paid trumpeters to serve as watchmen from the church towers of the city, both to warn of fire and other dangers and to sound specific hours of the day and night. On important church holidays they might also be joined by students or other instrumentalists to play appropriate four-part settings of chorales.

The council employed seven instrumentalists together with two *Feldtrompeter* (military trumpeters), one *Ratspfeifer* (council piper), and a *Ratstrommelschläger* (council drummer). In addition, many of the instrumentalists were organized into groups whose purposes were to play in church services and at various private festivities, especially weddings. Again as in Hamburg, there were laws decreeing how many instrumentalists might be allowed to perform at wedding celebrations, a major source of income for musicians. The instrumentalists were not free to participate on their own initiative at these affairs but were assigned by the town council, which used a strict division into social classes to decide the make-up of the instrumental ensemble. The citizens of Lübeck were divided into a number of classes:

1. Members of the council, distinguished doctors and their families.
2. Young doctors, scholars, pensioners living on their own financial

resources, distinguished citizens, burghers of the merchant company (*Kaufleutekompanie*), as well as others who, though not belonging to patrician families, had good connections and resources.

3. Other wealthy merchants and other companies.
4. Less wealthy merchants, shopkeepers, brewers etc.
5. Sailing-masters, members of the four major professions – bakers, blacksmiths, tailors, shoemakers – and other important professions
6. Remaining small businessmen, sailors and others of less important social standing.

Weddings were classified according to whether they took place during the day or in the evening and according to the type of food and drink consumed. The three social orders of weddings were:

1. *Pastetenhochzeit*, for the uppermost social class only.
2. *Weinhochzeit*, for the next two social classes.
3. *Kuchenhochzeit*, weddings without wine, for social class 4 (see above).

A city official (the *Spielgreve*) carried out the council's orders, ensuring that the instrumentalists received their appropriate fees according to the law. The wedding could involve a procession to and from the church by the groom or the bridal pair with their guests, accompanied by trombones decorated with banners, as well as elaborate banquets and dancing. Council instrumentalists were allowed to perform only at weddings of the upper social divisions; the lower divisions were allowed to employ musicians from the other organizations of instrumentalists (the *Chor-* and *Köstenbrüderschaft*). City ordinances permitted all the *Ratsmusikanten* to perform at a *Pastetenhochzeit* (the so-called *Grosses Spiel*). *Weinhochzeiten* could hire *Das grosse Spiel*, but without the council trumpet and drum players. For weddings classified as 'without wine', four council musicians with a *Positiv* or regal were specified. Similar laws affected weddings in Hamburg, but there, as at Lübeck, these rules were observed less and less towards the end of the seventeenth century.[16]

NOTES

[1] Published in *Jacob Praetorius: Choralbearbeitungen für Orgel*, ed. W. Breig (Kassel, 1974).

[2] Conjecture regarding the friendship of Reincken and Buxtehude can be substantiated by a previously unknown portrait (now the Museum für hamburgische Geschichte) that shows Buxtehude and Reincken seated in the company of other performing musicians. See C. Wolff, 'Das Hamburger Buxtehude-Bild', *800 Jahre Musik in Lübeck* (Lübeck, 1982), 64–79.

[3] Scheidemann's organ works are discussed in detail in W. Breig, *Die Orgelwerke von Heinrich Scheidemann*, Beihefte zum Archiv für Musikwissenschaft, iii (1967). A high proportion of the

organ music is available in *Heinrich Scheidemann: Magnificat-Bearbeitungen*, ed. G. Fock (Kassel, 1970), and *Heinrich Scheidemann: Choralbearbeitungen*, ed. idem (Kassel, 1967).

[4] J. Mattheson, *Grundlage einer Ehrenpforte* (Hamburg, 1740), 396.

[5] Unless otherwise noted, information for this section and the next is taken from L. Krüger, *Die hamburgische Musikorganisation im XVII Jahrhundert* (Strasbourg, 1933).

[6] In *D-Hs*.

[7] Ed. in *Das Chorwerk*, xxvi (1934).

[8] Ed. O. Drechsler and M. Geck, *Das Erbe deutscher Musik*, lxv (Kassel, 1972). Further regarding Bernhard's vocal music see F. Fiebig, *Christoph Bernhard und der stile moderno* (Hamburg, 1980).

[9] See M. Seiffert, 'Matthias Weckmann und das Collegium Musicum in Hamburg', *SIMG*, ii (1900–01), 76–132.

[10] A document by Nicodemus Tessin, an architect employed in Sweden, who visited Hamburg in 1687. See H. C. Wolff, *Die Barockoper in Hamburg* (Wolfenbüttel, 1957), 352.

[11] Concerning these and other details about the earliest history of the Hamburg opera, see H. J. Marx, 'Geschichte der Hamburg Barockoper: ein Forschungsbericht', *Hamburger Jahrbuch für Musikwissenschaft*, iii: *Studien zur Barockoper* (1978), 7–34.

[12] They are discussed in greater detail in G. J. Buelow, 'Hamburg Opera during Buxtehude's Lifetime: the Works of Johann Wolfgang Franck', *Church, Stage, and Studio: Music in its Contexts in Seventeenth-Century Germany*, ed. P. Walker (Ann Arbor, 1989), 127–61.

[13] See G. J. Buelow, 'Hamburg and Lübeck', *The Late Baroque Era*, Man & Music (London, 1993), 190–215.

[14] Information for this section is drawn from W. Stahl, *Musikgeschichte Lübecks*, ii: *Geistliche Musik* (Kassel, 1952).

[15] The cantatas are ed. M. Seiffert, *Denkmäler deutscher Tonkunst*, iii (1900), and the organ chorale preludes are in *Dietrich Buxtehude: Sämtliche Choralbearbeitungen*, ed. R. Walter (Mainz, 1959).

[16] Further on instrumental music in Lübeck, see J. Hennings, *Musikgeschichte Lübecks*, i: *Weltliche Musik* (Kassel, 1951), and, especially for details regarding *Hochzeitsfeierlichkeiten*, E. Spies-Hankammer, 'Die Lübecker Luxusordnungen als musikgeschichtliche Quelle', *800 Jahre Musik in Lübeck*, 32–46.

BIBLIOGRAPHICAL NOTE

The Hanseatic League

The history of the Hanseatic League is largely peripheral to the content of this chapter, since as an organization of cities and towns it had ceased to exist by the later seventeenth century. Cities such as Hamburg and Lübeck, however, were shaped politically as well as culturally by the league, and as sources of background information three books can be recommended. The best one in English is J. Schildhauer, *The Hansa: History and Culture*, trans. K. Vanovitch (Leipzig, 1985). It is beautifully illustrated with colour plates and numerous photographs and drawings, which convey a vibrant impression of the League's cultural achievements. Another book, a basic source, is P. Dollinger, *The German Hansa*, trans. D. S. Ault and S. H. Steinberg (London and Stanford, 1970). Also important is K. Pagel, *Die Hansa* (Brunswick, 2/1952), which has many photographs of the art and architectural monuments generated by the Hanseatic League. Many of the architectural remnants of the Middle Ages and the Renaissance, especially in eastern Europe, were destroyed in World War II.

Hamburg: instrumental and sacred music

The best work on instrumental music in seventeenth-century Hamburg remains L. Krüger, *Die hamburgische Musikorganisation im XVII. Jahrhundert* (Strasbourg, 1933).

There are brief though informative discussions of the organ music of Jacob Praetorius, Scheidemann, Weckmann and Reincken in W. Apel, *The History of Keyboard Music to 1700*, trans. and rev. by H. Tischler (Bloomington, 1972). These composers mostly lack studies in English, except for articles in *Grove 6*. Useful works in German include: W. Breig l, *Die Orgelwerke von Heinrich Scheidemann*, Beihefte zum Archiv für Musikwissenschaft, iii (1967); M. Seiffert, 'Matthias Weckmann und das Collegium Musicum in Hamburg', *SIMG*, ii (1900–01), 76–132; G. Ilgner, *Matthias Weckmann: sein Leben und seine Werke* (Wolfenbüttel and Berlin, 1939); and F. Fiebig, *Christoph Bernhard und der stile moderno* (Hamburg, 1980). Concerning the Johanneum, see E. Kelter, *Hamburg und sein Johanneum im Wandel der Jahrhunderte 1529–1929* (Hamburg, 1928).

Hamburg: opera

Most of the literature concerning Hamburg opera focusses on the period from the last decade of the seventeenth century up to the closure of the theatre in 1738 (see *The Late Baroque Era*, Man & Music (London, 1993). Regarding the earliest history of the opera the following are important: H. C. Wolff, *Die Barockoper in Hamburg* (Wolfenbüttel, 1957); H. J. Marx, 'Geschichte der Hamburger Barockoper: ein Forschungsbericht', *Hamburger Jahrbuch für Musikwissenschaft*, iii: *Studien zur Barockoper* (1978); and idem, 'Politische und wirtschaftliche Voraussetzungen der Hamburger Oper', ibid., v: *Opernsymposium 1978 in Hamburg* (1981). A valuable list of the sources for music and librettos of Hamburg operas is W. Schulze, *Die Quellen der Hamburger Oper (1678–1738)* (Hamburg and Oldenburg, 1938).

Lübeck

The standard work on the history of music is the two-volume study: J. Hennings, *Musikgeschichte Lübecks*, i: *Weltliche Musik* (Kassel, 1951); and W. Stahl, ibid, ii; *Geistliche Musik* (Kassel, 1952). Further concerning the Abendmusik concerts held in the Marienkirche during the seventeenth and eighteenth centuries, see W. Stahl, *Die Lübecker Abendmusiken im 17. und 18. Jahrhundert* (Lübeck, 1937), and O. Söhngen, 'Die Lübecker Abendmusiken als kirchengeschichtliches und theologisches Problem', *Musik und Kirche*, xxvii (1957), 181. In addition to the discussion of Tunder's organ music in Apel, *The History of Keyboard Music to 1700* (see above), see K. Gudewill, *Franz Tunder und die nordelbingische Musikkultur seiner Zeit* (Lübeck, 1967).

Chapter X

The Low Countries

MARTIN MEDFORTH

The decades around the end of the sixteenth century do not immediately strike us as a period in which the Low Countries initiated fresh developments in music. Nor do the Low Countries even appear as an important area in the musical life of Europe. In fact they were becoming more and more isolated from the rest of Europe. This isolation emerged, on the one hand, through the continuing war which was to leave the North and South Netherlands permanently severed and, on the other, by the waning of the Renaissance, whose musical forms and styles had been adopted and developed to their highest level by a seemingly unending succession of musicians born and bred within the Low Countries.

It is, of course, the long roll-call of distinguished composers who dominated western European musical life from the second half of the fifteenth century through to the later sixteenth century of whom we think first in connection with music and the Low Countries. Yet they should not be seen as a foil against which to write off the achievements of the seventeenth century.[1] In terms of musical forms the future lay in the main not with the motet, mass or madrigal but with the new music developing in Italy and with instrumental forms emerging in England. Moreover, music was to become more widespread in its appeal. In the Low Countries, and in particular the young Dutch Republic, so-called serious music was to be transformed from an activity existing only within the confines of Church and State to one that flourished in the everyday lives of the common people.

At the threshold of the new age stands the considerable figure of Jan Pieterszoon Sweelinck (1562–1621). Regarded by many as the last in a line of illustrious composers, he might well have provided the means through which the musical traditions of the Low Countries could be 'modernized' in accordance with developments abroad. Although he never travelled outside the Low Countries, he was able to gain early acquaintance with the theoretical teachings of Zarlino and the music of Giovanni Gabrieli. From this knowledge he developed a mastery not only of the traditional form of the motet but also of the instrumental forms of canzona, fantasia, fugue and variation. Enriched by the experience of English music, and in particular by his friendship with both John Bull and Peter Philips, he developed a style, seen most strikingly in his keyboard works, that was a true synthesis of the best that Europe had to offer. He was a notable teacher, but only his students from outside the Low Countries made a name for themselves as composers, most of them in north Germany. By this time the Low Countries had developed the ideal of the musician as craftsman, and only a few succeeded in being 'personalities' as well. Sweelinck, the 'Orpheus of Amsterdam', was one, Jacob van Eyck, the 'flute man of Utrecht', was another. Apart from these two, though, there was no continuation of the long tradition of Low Countries composers whose names were known and highly regarded throughout Europe.[2] Sweelinck's main achievement was that through his example he helped to establish a position for practising musicians within the Northern Netherlands which was to enable town councils to maintain a level of musical activity far beyond what we might expect in a country dominated by a Calvinist church.

Traditionally, the situation which existed in the early years of the seventeenth century has been viewed negatively. Writers have readily concluded that the death of Sweelinck in 1621 marks the closing of a chapter in the history of music. A sorry state of affairs is seen not just in the lack of a natural successor to him but also in the dying out of patronage from both court and Church throughout the Southern or Spanish Netherlands. The lowest point was reached when, following the death of Archduchess Isabella in 1633, the court chapel in Brussels was forced to close. Political and religious pressures did not alleviate the problem; indeed the division into North and South which became formalized in 1609 with the consent of Spain to a twelve years' truce, separated the region, although simplistically, into Protestant North and Catholic South. This polarization has been thought to contribute to the demise of the region's great musical inheritance. Indeed one minor poet of the time, Jan Hermonszoon Krul, complained, through the voice of the muse of music that 'Once I was glorified by great men of the nation,/ Now am I trodden by a blunt new generation'.[3]

The Low Countries, however, continued to distinguish themselves throughout the seventeenth century. Although they no longer produced leading musicians, they still served as a focal point. While much of Europe was seen to be enduring some kind of crisis, the Low Countries had no reason to suffer similarly. For long enough, even with regard to music, the area had been better known for its ability to develop rather than to invent. It is as if the Netherlanders possess an ability to observe and to remain detached.

The most striking way in which the Low Countries differed from

43. Interior of the Oude Kerk, Amsterdam, looking towards the west end, with the organ (1539–45, by H. Niehoff, with H. van Keulen and J. Janszen) played by Sweelinck during his employment there as organist from c1580 until his death in 1621

the rest of Europe was in their attitude to the common people. Particularly in the North, it was recognized that the success of the country as an independent nation, after the truce of 1609, lay with the people at large. If the Low Countries failed to maintain standards at the grass-roots level, then it was likely that they would fail to command respect among nations whose right to exist was far more firmly established than theirs. While the clearest examples of such developments can be drawn from the North, many of the forms in which the republic sought to better itself had their roots firmly in the shared experience of the Northern and Southern Netherlands.

One of the reasons advanced for the diminished number of proficient professional musicians is that education was of a lower standard than it had been. But while it is difficult to decide on the validity of such a claim, it does appear that the wide spread of common education much impressed those travellers in the area whose reports survive. The importance of this availability of common education, which included music in the curriculum, cannot be overstated. The general level of awareness of the theory and practice of formal music among the common folk of the Low Countries was far higher than anywhere else in Europe at the time.[4] The Quadrivium had long persisted here, and music thus remained an important part of the curriculum of *gemeente schoolen* (common or community schools) in both North and South. Even after the formal establishment of the republic in the North, the schools and their Quadrivium-based education continued. Many travellers in the early seventeenth century were impressed by how seriously schools were regarded, in even the smallest communities: in many villages the post of schoolmaster was second only to that of priest. Interestingly, it is not possible to correlate the existence of such schools with areas in which we would expect to find a predilection towards book learning. Though such an attitude may well have contributed to a general furthering of education in Protestant areas, the most striking evidence of the strength of music education in village schools is found in the predominantly Catholic areas of the North Eastern Provinces. From here there are many extant treatises of music theory written for use in particular schools.[5]

In general terms the music education offered in schools was based on the practice of singing, and more formally on the study of the classical authorities whose theories were explained, along with the writings of authorities in the related disciplines of geometry, arithmetic and astronomy. Much would have been learnt by rote, but inadequate as such a method may now seem to be, it cannot be disputed that the general level of awareness of the theoretical disciplines of mathematics (in which music was included) was far higher in the Low Countries than elsewhere in Europe. Few were untouched by the force of this discipline, particularly in the more rural areas. As a result, a farmer, for example, was able to make music for his own enjoyment far more readily than we might expect. At first this ability was strongly influenced by the largely oral tradition of folk memory, but it was only a matter of time before people who aspired to better themselves, in order to gain respect within their communities, began to read and demand written music.

This aspiration to self-betterment is a curious by-product of the unique manner in which the inhabitants of the Low Countries handled the problem of inheritance. If a man had three sons, on his death his property was normally distributed equally among the three of them.[6] There appears however to have been an exception to this, illustrated by the will of one sixteenth-century Friesian farmer who stipulated that 'of the three brothers, he who turns out the most learned will have the major part of the property'.[7] This transparent encouragement of learning became enshrined in the North through the republican encouragement of 'beschaving'. This peculiar Dutch word, meaning 'civilization' or 'culture', has overtones connected with the use of the verb 'beschaven', meaning 'to plane' or 'to polish', and came into its own during this period as the Dutch discovered more and more about the 'savages' of the world and how, with perseverance, it was possible to mould them to conform with contemporary ideals of civilization.

The ideal of 'beschaving' was applied just as much to the emerging society of the young Dutch Republic as it was to the Dutch-influenced areas of the East and West Indies. It must be acknowledged that moves directed towards improving the cultural well-being of the common people were largely limited to the North, but such a distinction is blurred by the way in which institutions which had their roots in the Southern Netherlands were developed in the North, a trend helped by the growing number of political and religious refugees welcomed into the Dutch Republic. At a purely amateur level, collegia musica (private musical societies) were formed in many towns, both north and south of the border.[8] These societies, many of them taking the form of what we would now think of as small choral societies, served as regular meeting-places for 'upwardly mobile' members, such as lawyers, town councillors and merchants, who doubtless enjoyed the act of meeting as much as the making of music. Indeed, it was the town council that often not only positively encouraged the formation of a collegium but also instituted regular public concerts. These latter took the form of recitals given by town musicians, in particular the town organist, who was employed not by the church but by the council. Many, indeed, were placed under contractual obligation to provide such regular performances. In Leiden, for instance, a penalty was exacted if the organist failed in this duty. The demand that the organist perform so regularly lay, according to the Leiden records, in the belief that time was better spent in the morally edifying activity of listening to music than in the all too common pastime of drinking. The town council clearly regarded culture, and music in particular, as a means of controlling the citizens of the town. If music helped to reduce the incidence of alcohol-induced disobedience then it had to be seen as desirable, whatever the Church's view of music may have been.

Sweelinck's appointment to the Oude Kerk, Amsterdam (*see* fig. 43), included a demand that he perform for an hour each day, before or after the daily service. In addition he apparently gave several 'unofficial' recitals, often at the behest of the town councillors, who wished to impress visiting dignitaries. Reports have even come down to us that one church official encouraged Sweelinck to apply his talents to the elaboration of secular tunes, several of them associated

44. The Dancing Couple: painting by Jan Steen (c1626–79)

with disreputable songs. Despite the often stiff rules of the church, the exceptions made the situation far livelier than one would suppose. Besides, the nature of a musician's calling included the demand that he offer his talents to God, and the technique of extemporising variations on an often banal subject was regarded as being the ultimate challenge to musical talent. Sweelinck's activities provided an important precedent. Once he had established the manner in which an organist could interact with the demands of his church, the way remained open, despite continuing debates concerning the 'use and abuse of the organ' which persisted throughout the seventeenth century.[9]

The general attitude of the Protestants towards music is of little significance except in matters relating to the musician's calling. This is reflected by the way in which music was a central part of the common experience and traditions of the Low Countries. If in France, Italy, Germany and England there was something of a formalized separation between serious and common music, between the musics enjoyed by the various social classes, such a distinction is far harder to pinpoint within the Low Countries. It is the lack of such a distinction that has led several writers to overemphasize the forms of musical activity documented in the works of contemporary artists such as Pieter Breughel and Jan Steen. Musical activity has been placed firmly within the field of folk music, while the activities of groups meeting for the purpose of making music of a serious nature have been largely ignored. In fact the degree to which folk and art music merged has never been properly explored. It is witnessed, though, in the well-documented practice of organists and other musicians improvising on popular tunes, many associated with the *Geuzenliederboek*, the so-called Beggar's or Revolutionary Songbook, whose popularity continued well into the seventeenth century.

In the phenomenon of the *klokkenspel* or carillon we likewise find that few boundaries existed in the choice of repertory. When it came to programming the carillon to a fixed tune played on every half-hour of every day it appears that tunes were chosen simply on the grounds of current popularity. Late seventeenth-century records from Alkmaar demonstrate that the tune was just as likely to be a sonata movement by Corelli or Vitali as a popular song of more local origin. In many respects the carillon was as important a part of a town's musical life as the existence of, say, a collegium musicum. The chimes of the bells, and the associated tunes, marked off the day for every inhabitant. Many towns prided themselves on the size and quality of their carillon. In a similar manner to that prescribed for organists, carillonists would give regular recitals, often on Sunday afternoons or market days, such recitals often being stipulated as part of their duties by the town council which employed them. In smaller towns the organist's contract included a clause stating that he was responsible for the carillon. In larger towns, however, the two posts were separate, as in Utrecht, where the carillonist was Jacob van Eyck, perhaps better known now as a flautist who used to entertain the passing crowds on market days and holidays.[10]

There has been a tendency to overlook the fact that musicians working in the Low Countries were generally regarded as craftsmen and also to write them off as mere imitators of foreign styles – this last is at best an unfortunate prejudice and at worst a total misjudgment of the situation. As the products of a craft which was developing a more cosmopolitan musical language, the works of Matthias Mercker, Nicolas Vallet, Hendrick Anders, Dirk Scholl, Carol Hacquart, Constantijn Huygens and Jacob van Eyck undoubtedly imitate the works of Italian and French composers, but this was no slavish imitation. Indeed, strong indications, strikingly apparent in, for example, Huygens's *Pathodia sacra et profana* (1647), lead one to conclude that the influence was exploited deliberately, and was not simply compensation for a lack of skill among these composers. For many years the leading composers of the Low Countries tradition had figured on a European stage, and during the seventeenth century an attempt was made to set up a stable tradition within the more limited sphere of the Dutch Republic in particular. As the confidence of the political and economic state grew through its dealings with its neighbours following independence in 1609, there was a concerted attempt to enhance and harmonize its intellectual and social life. The production of works of art was nurtured from the models of countries whose artistic primacy was well established.

A key factor in the drawing of sustenance from outside was the relationship between the republic of Venice and both the Northern and Southern Netherlands. It was largely on the basis of this relationship that Italian music came to form the foundations of the musical experience of many inhabitants of the North. In particular, printers and publishers, first in Antwerp and later in Amsterdam, drew on music previously published in Venice in order to meet the increasing demand in the domestic market for both instrumental and vocal music. The young Dutch Republic saw itself as being in alliance with the Venetian republic and believed that a system of government based on the Venetian model would lead to greater security and stability. The geographical separation of the two republics, however, led to much confusion in the minds of the Dutch. In particular, Venice was perceived as the chief of all the Italian states, and 'Venetian' and 'Italian' grew to be synonymous among the Dutch, a view no doubt inherited from the tradesmen of Antwerp, who, because it was convenient to do so, had for a long time dealt almost exclusively with Venice rather than with other Italian states.

This situation ensured that until comparatively late in the seventeenth century nearly all the Italian music republished in the Low Countries was based on Venetian prints. Even when music from, say, Rome was available from a printer in Antwerp it is likely that it had filtered through only because it had been reprinted or sold in Venice. This is as true of the early editions of Corelli's trio sonatas as it had been of, say, the lesser-known anthology of Roman motets published by Jan Van Geertsom at Rotterdam in 1656. Thus a single trading link, supported by a political alliance, can be seen as crucial to the development of musical experience in the Low Countries. It also goes some way towards explaining why the Dutch, who outwardly had so little to do with Italy in general in respect of politics, religion or culture, should respond so differently in their choice of popular music: Venice was simply a ready source of popular music.

The growing number of amateur musicians and performing groups did not, however, rely entirely on what was available from local sources. The activities of the collegium musicum at Utrecht, which have been well documented, reveal that while most of their music was bought from local agents, a good deal was obtained from abroad, some from Paris, some from London, and some from Venice. Clearly such music may have passed through local booksellers, but not as stock items. By the mid seventeenth century, the possession of a quantity of Italian music was almost as prized by the Utrecht

45. Family Music-Making: painting by Pieter de Hooch (1629–83); the instruments are (left to right) bass viol, recorder, cittern and violin

collegium as their Ruckers harpsichord, which though technically the property of the town council was on permanent loan to the group.[11] Again, publishers were quick to recognize a potentially lucrative market, and significant collections of instrumental music intended mainly for private performance often contained no more than a few works by Dutch composers. Most of their contents stem from foreign sources, especially Italian ones. It would be wrong to claim that foreign music had totally obliterated the Netherlands musical tradition. The legacy of Sweelinck and his predecessors remained, primarily in the well-developed traditions of improvisation which, like folk and popular music, was rarely documented. But by the end of the century the Italian style as represented by the works of such men as Corelli, Torelli and Vitali did 'through its novelty grasp hold of our inquisitiveness and lead us, by a different key, by modulation, from major to minor, and then leap[ing] from one tempo to another'.[12]

Once a general audience had emerged at home it was not long before the publishing trade in Amsterdam began to recognize the potential that lay in the market abroad. By 1702 the publishing house of Etienne Roger had established agencies not only in several other Dutch towns but also in London, Berlin, Halle, Cologne, Brussels and Hamburg.[13] The setting up of such a network was much encouraged by the interests of the Huguenot refugees who had become scattered around the Protestant lands of Europe. Their need to keep in touch was paramount, and as a result the dissemination of music, not only from Italian but also from French, German and English sources, benefited directly. Gradually, during the early years of the eighteenth century the musical expectations of the greater part of Europe were transformed, just as during the seventeenth century those of the inhabitants of the Low Countries had been.

At the time of his death, Sweelinck had for some time been described as the 'Orpheus of Amsterdam'. The town council had rightly been proud of him, even if their outlook was highly parochial. Yet like Sweelinck himself, his fellow countrymen were beginning to be aware of developments elsewhere, and by the end of the century the figure of Orpheus was no longer so localized. Music had become a more cosmopolitan medium, largely through the attitudes of the Dutch and the trade they engendered. However important published music was, and however significant the attempts of the Dutch to mould foreign forms and styles to their own needs (as with the abortive attempts to form a Dutch opera company in the late seventeenth century), it was still music in performance that had the greatest impact. In the words of a late seventeenth-century commentator, this impact was clear. Italian instrumental music had captured the imagination of the inhabitants of the Low Countries at large, not just in court and intellectual circles but also in the countryside and among the craftsmen and tradesmen of the towns:

> Torelli! You grace our land with your art, / and win favour from our hearts. / For the greatest and the least, the charm of your playing / lovingly caresses the stoniest of hearts. / Orpheus Torelli tames the court and the country folk, / while courteous town chatter tells of his great art.[14]

NOTES

[1] See, for example, G. J. Renier, *The Dutch Nation* (London, 1944), 96: 'Generally speaking it was all the seventeenth century could do to keep alive its musical inheritance'.

[2] Sweelinck was the last 'Netherlands musician [to make] a significant contribution to the history of music': 'Low Countries', *Grove 6*, xi, 267.

[3] Quoted in D. Regin, *Traders, Artists, Burghers: a Cultural History of Amsterdam in the 17th Century* (Assen and Amsterdam, 1976), 48.

[4] The ratio of schools and schoolmasters to populations in both the Southern and Northern Netherlands is remarkably high for the period. For figures relating to the South at the turn of the century, see G. Parker, *The Dutch Revolts* (Harmondsworth, 1981).

[5] Examples include Jacques Vredeman's *Isagoge musicae* (Leeuwarden, 1618), G. de Haes's *Musicae rudimenta* (Hardervijk) and Joan Albert Ban's *Dissertatio epistolica de musicae natura, origine, progressu* (Leiden, 1637).

[6] As a result, property and wealth were less important in determining suitability for govern-

ment. Idealists held that culture, erudition, honesty and virtue were indispensable in preserving the future health of a truly free government within a republic such as was held to exist in the Northern Netherlands.

[7] Quoted in Parker, *The Dutch Revolts*, 21.

[8] We know that collegia musica existed in Alkmaar, Amsterdam, Arnhem, Deventer, Groningen, The Hague, Leeuwarden, Leiden, Middelburg, Nijmegen, Rotterdam, Utrecht and Zierikzee.

[9] The phrase comes from the titles of two seminal publications: Constantijn Huygens, *Gebruik of ongebruyck van't orgel* (Leiden, 1641), and Jan Jacob Calckmann, *Antidotum, tegen-gift vant gebruyck of on-gebruyck vant orgel* (The Hague, 1641).

[10] Van Eyck was in fact paid an extra twenty guilders, over and above his salary as Utrecht's *klokkenspeler*, on the condition that he entertain the citizens by playing on his pipes. In general this entertainment would take the form of improvisations on secular tunes similar to the examples in his *Der fluyten lust-hof* (Amsterdam, 1644–9); see R. van Baak Griftsen, *Jacob van Eyck's 'Der fluyten lust-hof' (1644–c1655)* (Utrecht, 1991).

[11] See J. C. M. Riemsdijk, *Het Stads-Muziekcollegie te Utrecht (Collegium Musicum Ultrajectinum)* (Utrecht, 1881).

[12] C. Sweerts, *Inleidung tot de zang en speelkunst* (Amsterdam, 1698).

[13] See I. H. van Eeghen, *De Amsterdam boekhandel (1680–1725)* (Amsterdam, 1960–78).

[14] 'Torelli, die ons Land vereert door uwe kunst, / En die de herten weet te winnen en de gunst. / Van Groote en kleenen, als gy door aantreklyk speelen, / Het aldersteenigst hert weet liefelijk te streelen.' / Orpheus Torelli temt het volk in 't hof en 't veld, / Terwyl de heusheids steeds zyn groote kunst vertelt.' 'In thanks for Giuseppe Torelli (who gave me the greatest of privileges by allowing me to hear him play)', cited in Sweerts, *Inleidung*, appx.

BIBLIOGRAPHICAL NOTE

General

For the English reader the best introduction to the cultural history of the Low Countries during the seventeenth century is K. H. D. Haley, *The Dutch in the Seventeenth Century* (London, 1972), the first major study of Dutch society in English and probably still the best. Useful consolidation of the subject is given in J. L. Price, *Culture and Society in the Dutch Republic during the 17th Century* (London, 1974), which picks up from Haley's work and provides a useful perspective. Both books are indispensable in provoking questions for further investigation. Somewhat more specialized is D. Regin, *Traders, Artists, Burghers: a Cultural History of Amsterdam in the 17th Century* (Assen and Amsterdam, 1976); and G. J. Renier, *The Dutch Nation* (London, 1944), is still an important work, though now somewhat dated. P. Geyl, *The Dutch in the Seventeenth Century* (London, 1936) presents a unified approach to the general historico-political scene throughout the period and is recognized as a classic. A more recent book, G. Parker, *The Dutch Revolts* (Harmondsworth, 1981), is not only an easy read but perhaps the best of all works to date on the prelude to the seventeenth century. Parker's approach recognizes that history is made by ordinary people, not just leaders, and his book is required reading for anyone wishing to obtain a feel for the seventeenth century. More relevant to the subject of the Dutch example to Europe, and particularly to England, is C. Wilson, *The Dutch Republic and the Civilisation of the Seventeenth Century* (London, 1968), while P. Geyl, *History of the Low Countries: Episodes and Problems* (London, 1964), tackles various issues and assumptions through the eyes of experience.

Art, literature and cultural interaction

In art, a good starting-point is provided by J. Rosenburg, S. Slive and E. H. ter Kuile, *Dutch Art and Architecture, 1600–1800* (Harmondsworth, 1966). A similar work, but biased towards the Southern Netherlands, is H. Gersen and E. H. ter Kuile, *Art and Architecture in Belgium 1600–1800* (Harmondsworth, 1960). Those with an interest in the literature of the time should consult T. Weevers, *Poetry of the Netherlands in its European Context 1170–1930* (London, 1930), and J. A. van Dorsten, *Poets, Patrons and Professors: Sir Philip Sidney, Daniel Regius and the Leiden Humanists* (Leiden, 1962). Printing and the sale of printed matter ensured that the Dutch nation was a principal agent in the ever-growing market for the exchange of cultural ideas. D. W. Davies, *The World of the Elseviers* (The Hague, 1954), provides a good overview. I. H. van Eeghen, *De Amsterdamse boekhandel (1680–1725)* (Amsterdam, 1960–78), is indispensable for any study which delves below the surface.

The affinity between the Dutch and Venetian republics is explored in an excellent study, P. Burke, *Venice and Amsterdam: a Study of 17th Century Elites* (London, 1974). In the field of the visual arts the connections are emphasized and explored in K. Clarke, *Rembrandt and the Italian Renaissance* (London, 1966). The two books seem to occupy different worlds, indeed they treat totally different concepts of 'Italy'; a reading of both would most certainly raise a number of topics for further investigation. The influence of a single man on the study of sciences is provided in A. E. Bell, *Christian Huygens and the Development of Science in the Seventeenth Century* (Leiden, 1947). Huygens was a noted polymath, famous for his scientific work, but he was also a musician with a truly European talent.

Music

For the general background we still have to refer to C. van den Borren, *Geschiedenis van de Muziek in de Nederlanden* (Antwerp, 1948), though the article 'Low Countries' in *Grove 6* (xi, 261–83) provides a useful recent view. Although excellent when originally published, D. J. Balfoort, *Het muziekleven in Nederlande in de zeventiende en achttiende eeuw* (Amsterdam, 1938) is now somewhat dated but remains unchallenged as the standard work on music as culture. Among more specialized studies mention must be made of J. C. M. Riemsdijk, *Het Stads-Muziekcollegie te Utrecht (Collegium Musicum Ultrajectinum)* (Utrecht, 1881), and three excellent recent ones: F. Noske, *Music Bridging Divided Religions: the Motet in the Seventeenth-Century Dutch Republic* (Wilhelmshaven, 1989), G. O'Brien, *Ruckers: a Harpsichord and Virginal Building Tradition* (Cambridge, 1990), and R. van Baak Griftsen, *Jacob van Eyck's 'Der fluyten lust-hof' (1644–c1655)* (Utrecht, 1991).

Chapter XI

Paris, 1600–61

CATHERINE MASSIP

THE GEOGRAPHY OF PARIS

At the beginning of the seventeenth century France, with over twenty million inhabitants, was the most densely populated country in Europe; Paris was its largest urban centre and had about 250 000 inhabitants. These numerical statements, however, call for some elaboration.

France itself was not a single unit but consisted of provinces with their own distinctive characteristics: climate, landscape, language, economic activity, common law, wealth, agricultural resources, trade and commerce, religious practices and political status – there were State-held lands, free cities and great noblemen's fiefs – all varied considerably. The religious wars emphasized these differences, and a modest amount of control began to be exercised by royal power only when Cardinal Richelieu sent out the first provincial administrators. Division into the areas known as *généralités* was not to come until the eighteenth century.

From the viewpoint of royal power alone, there were marked contrasts between the various stages of the seventeenth century; the periodization adopted by historians applies reasonably well to the history of art in general and of music in particular, a situation owing much to the strong influence of Paris and the cultural environment created by the presence of the court. The early seventeenth century was like a continuation of the late sixteenth: the assassination of Henri IV in 1610 represented only an artificial break, far less significant than the death of Louis XIII in 1643, just after the death of Richelieu, or the assumption of personal authority by Louis XIV in 1661. The turning-point of the first part of the seventeenth century is to be found, rather, in the years 1627–30, which saw, in home affairs, the first wars against the Protestants (with the siege of La Rochelle in 1628) and the installation of Cardinal Richelieu as chief minister; influential foreign affairs included the beginning of the Thirty Years War and Richelieu's struggle against the ambitions of the house of Austria.

The period 1643–61 was marked by political troubles of which Paris was the epicentre. The court's flight to St Germain-en-Laye on a January night in 1649 was only the prelude to a more permanent removal of the apparatus of monarchy from the capital. It was to mean the progressive move of the adult Louis XIV and his court from Paris to Versailles between 1670 and 1683. The Frondes, a series of first parliamentary and then feudal insurrections, had a serious effect on the economy of the region surrounding Paris, the Ile de France: the calamitous balance sheet has been drawn up by historians. The Fronde movement was xenophobic in character and directed against the Italian-born Cardinal Mazarin, but it affected the fortunes of himself and his art collections rather than his policy of patronage in the musical sphere.

The broad framework within which artistic life in Paris evolved had not changed much between the Middle Ages and the reign of Henri IV; Henri himself perceptibly reshaped it, though not all his great schemes bore fruit. Paris owed its pre-eminence as a centre of commerce to its excellent geographical situation. On the edge of the valley of the Seine, not far from the valleys of the Oise and the Marne (which served as a link with northern France), and situated in the middle of a very rich agricultural area, the city had also benefited over the centuries from the presence of the royal court and the consequent flow of money.

Before Henri IV, the heart of Paris was still to be found in the Ile de la Cité: the massive elegance of the cathedral of Notre Dame dominated a network of alleys containing some twenty further churches and as many parishes. Opposite rose the Palais, the seat of the basic juridical institutions of France: Parlement, the Chambre des Comptes and the Cour des Monnaies. The slender spire of the Sainte-Chapelle, built by St Louis in the thirteenth century to house the Crown of Thorns, towered above these buildings. The choir of the Sainte-Chapelle was one of the finest musical institutions in France. On the Left Bank, within the precincts of Philippe-Auguste, which ran in a great loop from Notre Dame to the end of the Ile de la Cité, stood France's institutions of learning: the Sorbonne university, the Collège de France founded by François I and the Collège de Clermont, a fief of the Jesuits, as well as the abbey of Ste-Geneviève. Another powerful abbey, but situated 'without the walls', the abbey of St Germain-des-Prés, housed one of the finest libraries in France (now in the Bibliothèque Nationale, the Fonds St-Germain). From 1482 onwards, an annual fair was held over about three weeks, beginning two weeks after Easter. The fair of St Germain, a high spot of Parisian life, played a significant part in musical and theatrical activities; even before the rise of the fair theatres in the eighteenth century there were numerous puppet plays and other shows which

46. *Carousel (7 April 1612) in the Place Royale (now Place des Vosges), built for Henri IV (1605–12) in the 'Marais' quarter*

offered employment to the many instrumental players who had set up in the Faubourg St-Germain.

On the Right Bank stood the commercial centre of Paris, Les Halles. In its streets, lined with narrow houses, merchants and artisans were grouped according to their trades. The master instrument makers were to be found in the rue des Arcis, their workshops backing on to the church of St Jacques-de-la-Boucherie, and the instrumental players chose to live around the parish of St Julien-des-Ménétriers, the seat of their professional fraternity. To the east of the Hôtel de Ville stretched the aristocratic quarter of the Marais, the centre of the 'Précieux' movement. Noblemen's houses here, such as the Hôtel de Rambouillet, were to see the flowering of those literary salons where poetry of an elevated nature and intellectual pastimes held sway, and poets, musicians, singers and lutenists shared the same ideals.

Paris as a whole was still a loose urban structure where densely populated sectors (the oldest ones) alternated with large districts which had not been built over, representing the possessions of religious establishments. As a builder, Henri IV left his mark on the capital. He built great galleries between the Louvre and the Tuileries, installing artists in studios at street level. He conceived and financed the Place Dauphine and the Place Royale (the Parc Royal des Tournelles, now the Place des Vosges; *see* fig. 46). He built the hospital of St Louis for contagious illnesses. As a result of his initiative, new quarters appeared throughout the seventeenth century: the Ile St-Louis (formerly the Ile aux Vaches), developed by the architect Christophe Marie; the part of the Faubourg St-Germain reaching to the present-day Place de la Concorde on the Left Bank, and on the Right Bank the area around the Palais Cardinal (the precincts of the Fossés Jaunes) built by Richelieu and then bequeathed to the Crown, when it became the Palais Royal. These developments – notably that of the hill of Les Moulins (the rue des Petits-Champs) – attracted some of the king's musicians, such as Claude Balifre, in the 1620s. Later, Lully was to invest the money he had earned in the king's service in the same quarter, not far from the Hôtel Mazarin and the Hôtel de Nevers built by Colbert.

Some aspects of the musical geography of Paris deserve a closer look. One definite centre of attraction for the lodgings of the king's musicians – similar to the centres which would come into being later at St Germain-en-Laye and Versailles – was the Palais du Louvre and the quarter around it, with the rue Travercine and the rue St Thomas-du-Louvre. Lully set up house in the rue St-Anne in this quarter. Another centre of attraction was the Faubourg St-Germain. Musicians were drawn there by the presence of the fair and of the Palais du Luxembourg, the residence of the Orléans family. Gaston d'Orléans, Louis XIII's brother, maintained the largest royal musical establishment after that of the king himself. His adventurous political life did not prevent him from passing on his taste for music and dancing to his daughter, La Grande Mademoiselle. Around the Palais du Luxembourg, too, a literary and Bohemian Paris existed, with taverns where music and poetry went side by side with wine; the Cabaret du Bel-Air, in the rue de Vaugirard, famous in the years 1640–50 for its customers - Michel Lambert, the women singers of the Dupuis family, Isaac de Benserade, Sainctot – was only one among many.

THE CHURCHES

The churches were among the main contributors to the musical life of Paris. The cathedral church of Notre Dame, the collegiate churches and the 43 parishes of Paris regularly, if to a restricted extent, united music with worship. Martin Sonnet's *Directorium chori* (1656) and the *Ceremoniale parisiensis* (1662) carefully enumerated the rules to be followed for the proper conduct of divine service. Plainsong took pride of place; there were few opportunities for any other kinds of music except during Holy Week, when it was permissible for the Lamentations of Jeremiah (the Tenebrae) to be sung by performers from outside. The music of the royal household led the way, performing the Tenebrae services in the church of the Feuillants (strict Bernardines); the instrumentalists of the Chambre shone in these performances, and in the years 1650–60 one might even hear the female voices usually employed for the parts of heroines in *ballets de cour*. Florid counterpart was acceptable only during Advent. There was no question of allowing instruments into church, although certain priests were known to have viols in their private houses. This rigidity probably explains why sacred music in the concertante style developed in the only place that favoured it, the Chapelle Royale. Its influence was to benefit the other great choirs of Paris, those of the Sainte-Chapelle, Notre Dame and St Germain-l'Auxerrois.

The parochial and chapter registers, even when incomplete, provide information about the numbers of singers (including choirboys), the conditions under which they were engaged or dismissed, and the appointment of choirmasters and organists. In most parishes there were only two to four singers, and they remained in their posts to an advanced age, their main function being to provide plainsong for services, including the many masses for which people left money in their wills. In the three great choirs mentioned above, there were enough singers for a true chorus (sixteen at Notre Dame, 24 at the Sainte-Chapelle, six to twelve at St Germain-l'Auxerrois). Most parishes employed two to four choirboys. They were of humble origin, chosen for their good voices and good conduct, and subject to rigorous discipline; they learnt grammar and liturgical chant as well as the Catechism. The most gifted of the boys from the great choir schools could make a professional career in the music of the royal household, but the great majority would leave their churches and use their modest savings to set themselves up in the small world of Parisian artisans.

INSTRUMENT MAKERS AND MUSIC PUBLISHING

Corresponding to these different musical locations, there were different audiences, which are now hard to define. Among the clues to the musical practice of the time are brief mentions in inventories of the possessions of the dead which go into great detail when describing a person's background. Extensive investigations of material in the central records office of the notaries of Paris show that one inventory in fifteen contains some indication of the presence of a musical instrument. It must be remembered, however, that these documents were not drawn up systematically. Musical instruments were still expensive, lutes and harpsichords in particular; the value of violins, full-size or miniature, was much less. The lute was usually still the dominant instrument throughout the first half of the seventeenth century. Instrument makers' workshops show that there was a good deal of custom from professional and amateur musicians. The former comprised instrumentalists and dancing-masters as well as musicians employed by the king and the princes, and some church musicians. They all wanted good instruments either made in Paris, where the manufacture of violins and viols was fast developing, or imported from Italy. A great maker of lutes and guitars such as Jean Desmoulins founded his prosperity more on international trade than on actual manufacturing. Men in a smaller way of business confined themselves to making instruments and above all to repairs. But all had one thing in common: the considerable quantity of instruments present in their workshops, whether completed or not, which can be counted in hundreds and sometimes in thousands. This at least indicates the existence of a large potential clientele.

Music publishing reveals other aspects of the taste of this Parisian public, and displays features peculiar to the seventeenth century. The relative richness and diversity of publishing in the sixteenth century was followed by a period of concentration, if not actual stagnation, with music publishing becoming largely a monopoly of the Ballard family. The Ballards included some prominent persons and fine musicians who contributed to the fame of the house and the quality of the music it published. Their speciality, during the first half of the seventeenth century, was the publication of collections of

airs for voice and lute tablature or for several voices. They set their
seal on the relative abandonment of polyphony for accompanied
monody. The abundance of printed material (several thousand
pieces) and the length of this tradition – these collections of *airs*
would continue in existence with a few adaptations until the early
eighteenth century – show that the public, which liked lyric poetry,
was much attached to such collections. A first collection of *Airs de
différents autheurs mis en tablature de luth* appeared in 1608. The first six
volumes, up to 1615, were prepared by Gabriel Bataille, who featured in them his own works and those of his contemporaries such as
Pierre Guédron. Volumes 9–16 were compiled by Antoine Boësset,
the leading composer of the time, who offered *airs* of his own, some
for several voices, some for solo voice with lute accompaniment.
Many solos from court ballets also figured in these little quarto
volumes, which were printed in elegant type. Robert Ballard also
published books by the official court musicians, Etienne Moulinié
and Boësset. Each book contained about twenty *airs*, published as
separate parts or presenting the music with lute tablature. This last
habit disappeared entirely around the 1640s. These years saw the
appearance of the first manuscripts for voice and continuo, but the
Ballards remained faithful to their custom of publishing in separate
parts until the end of the century. This custom, though it was
convenient for amateurs, contributes to our lack of knowledge about
the music of the period, since many of the sets are now incomplete;
such is the case with books of *airs* by Charles Coypeau d'Assoucy,
Moulinié and Jean de Cambefort.

The year 1643 saw the temporary interruption of these extensive
series, which were to be revived from 1658; they then became series
of *airs de cour*. Other publications offered a more popular kind of
music: dance-songs, drinking songs in which Bacchus and Apollo,
the vine and the lyre, went hand in hand. Their melodies are simpler,
and the picquant rhythms, often derived from dance music, more
regular. The Ballards remained faithful to their old fount, easily
recognizable with its lozenge-shaped notes and fragmented staves.
There was no place in music publishing for religious music, apart
from a few masses, and little for instrumental music. For such music,
therefore, we must turn to manuscript sources. A few other publishers tried to exist on the fringes of the Ballard monopoly, Gabriel
Senlecque for example. The event which was at last to transform the
rather uniform appearance of music publishing in Paris came in
1660–61, when the singer, composer and teacher Michel Lambert
was granted a licence for the engraving of his *airs*. In the course of
the next decade instrumental music and then vocal music began to
be independently distributed. Only the late association of the
Ballards with Lully and the Académie Royale de Musique was to

47. 'Le concert': painting by Nicolas Tournier (1590–1639); the instruments depicted are bass viol, virginals, violin and lute

save their house temporarily from the competition which was beginning to threaten it.

MUSIC OF THE ROYAL HOUSEHOLD

The court remained the centre of musical life in Paris. The reign of Louis XIII opened a period of splendour in which ballets and masquerades made use of all the resources of the Musique Royale, the musical side of the royal household which made it possible quickly to produce a sumptous spectacle. Since the sixteenth century it had been organized into three bodies: the Chapelle, the Chambre and the Ecurie, the last-named including performers of open-air and military music as well as oboists, players of the Poitevin bagpipes, and trumpeters.

Louis XIII's personal interest in the Chapelle should be emphasized. He is known to have composed *Le ballet de la Merlaison*; his contemporaries had already been struck by his feeling for music:

As the King was very fond of Music, he had made up his own band from a very great number of Musicians, all exquisite and very skilled; it was said that for the beauty of the voices, the great number of instruments, the sweetness of the symphony, his Music infinitely surpassed that of all his predecessors and all the Princes of Europe . . . His Majesty took pleasure in mingling his voice with theirs, sometimes bringing them back to the notes . . .[1]

Louis XIV, a true son of his father, received an excellent musical education and is known to have taken a consistent and well-informed interest in his musicians.

The three institutions were administrative as much as musical subdivisions, often being associated with each other on those occasions when the music of the royal household was on display. The custom known as 'the venality of offices' applied to posts or offices within them, and the sales and reversions of such appointments were completed before a notary. The musicians' remuneration was in the form of fixed wages corresponding to their various offices, and variable indemnities which assured a musician of the highest and most regular salaries to which he could aspire in France. The *Etats de la Maison du Roi* give official lists which can be complemented by or compared with documents from private sources, deeds authenticated by a notary, and registry office certificates.

Between the reigns of Henri III and Henri IV there was a marked decrease in the numbers on the staff of the Chapelle: from 72 to 51.[2] In 1595, the music of the Chapelle was in the charge of three *sous-maîtres*, Eustache Du Caurroy, Etienne Le Roy and Nicolas Morel, who held office for four months each, and also had six choirboys in their charge. The musicians – to the number of fourteen: an alto, four countertenors, four tenors, four basses and a cornettist – served for a six-month period. After the replacement of Du Caurroy by Nicholas Formé, and the subsequent arrival on the scene of Eustache Picot, the music of the Chapelle was in the charge of two *sous-maîtres* during the reign of Louis XIII. The personnel were augmented by the addition of a second alto, two choirboys and a teacher of the lute for the latter; an organist appears at an indeterminate date after 1638.

The Chapelle, like the court as a whole, was an itinerant organization which had to move according to circumstances between royal residences such as St Germain-en-Laye and Fontainebleau. It followed the king and his army during military campaigns, which generally took place in the spring and went on into the summer; in Paris itself, it officiated at whatever church it pleased the king or queen to honour with their attendance and worship. This intrusion sometimes entailed conflict with the Parisian choirs. Although the conduct of the Offices – hourly and self-contained – was laid down with great precision, the role of polyphonic music in them remained imprecise. We know that the two fixed times of royal worship were a daily Mass at 9 a.m. and Vespers on Sunday at 4 p.m. The testimony of Pierre Perrin in 1661 indicates that one or two motets might be sung at the Elevation of the Host. If, however, we look for records of the performance of the double-choir motets of Formé and Veillot, we find them not within the Chapelle itself but in the admittedly vague accounts of the budding press, which report regular performances of them, sung together with the musicians of the Chambre or another choir such as that of Notre Dame. Two platforms would be erected, and the two choirs sang antiphonally, as at the funeral of Louis XIII in the basilica of St Denis in 1643.

The presence of musical instruments is also a matter for conjecture; we cannot expect to find instrumentalists on the official staff, but, at very solemn ceremonies, lutes and viols might be played before the Office itself. Few clues as to the repertory of the Chapelle remain, but we do know of works in traditional style by composers such as Du Caurroy, still highly contrapuntal and of a certain grandeur, as well as the works by Formé and Veillot, mentioned above, for double choir and in the concertante style.

The musicians of the Chambre included some of the best of their time – Paul Augé, Antoine Boësset and Henry de Bailly. Under the direction of two *surintendants*, who served alternate six-monthly terms, it comprised five instrumentalists: two lutenists, a spinet player, a flautist (replaced by a theorbist in 1656) and a viol player. There were also five singers: a countertenor, a bass, and three others the compass of whose voices is not specified. Two *maîtres* were in charge of the three children or pages of the Chambre. A composer completed this body, which would normally have numbered nineteen, a total reduced, however, by pluralism. In the time of Cardinal Mazarin, for instance, Jean-Baptiste de Boësset was both *surintendant* and *maître des enfants*, and François Richard was both lutenist and 'composer of music'.

Women's voices as yet had no official place in the royal household: their introduction, as a consequence of the prestige of Italian singers such as Anne of Austria's favourite, Anna Bergerotti, was to come belatedly, in the time of Mazarin. The first royal warrant, granted to Hilaire Dupuis on 21 June 1659, merely ratified an existing situation, since women singers had been performing in *ballets de cour* all through the 1650s. The warrant granted to Anne de La Barre specifically mentioned that 'the King, being retired into his cabinet' wished 'to hear French or Italian *airs*'.

Under the term 'cabinet', originally meaning a small private room, are mentioned those Italian and French musicians for whom no place could be found within the context of the main body of the Musique Royale. The Cabinet du Roi accommodated at various periods violinists such as Jacques Cordier, also known as Bocan, and Guillaume Dumanoir, *roi des violons*; composers such as Carlo Caproli (in 1654); and, in 1656, twelve violinists independent of the main band of the 24 Violons du Roi: they were known as the *petits violons du roi*, made their first appearance in *Le ballet de la Galanterie du temps* and then performed regularly in *ballets de cour* under the direction of Lully.

The 24 Violons du Roi performed 'when the king commands them: as when a ballet, etc., is given; and at certain ceremonies, such as the coronation, entries into cities, marriages and other solemnities and rejoicings, the other band of violins of the Grande Escurie plays with them, and the oboes, fifes, etc. . . .' They had existed since the sixteenth century, but were not formed into an official association until the beginning of the seventeenth; the association was renewed in 1643, and the violinists were members by virtue of their office. The 24 made up a five-part orchestra: six violins, four each of three inner instruments all of the viola type, and six bass instruments. Their repertory is known only from certain anthologies: *Terpsichore musarum* by Michael Praetorius and Pierre-Francisque Caroubel (1612), the first volume of the Philidor collection (in the Bibliothèque Nationale, Paris), the suites from a Kassel manuscript published by Jules Ecorcheville in 1906, the *Pièces pour violon à quatre parties* produced by Ballard in 1665, and a manuscript of Gustav Düben at Uppsala. These were dance suites adapted for balls and ballets. The most usual dances were the courante, sarabande, allemande and branle. Some of these pieces have lost their dance associations: their harmony is very full, but differences between the sources show that invention of the inner parts was now being left to the instrumentalists themselves.

INSTRUMENTALISTS

The 24 violinists all came from the large pool of talent represented by the community of Parisian instrumentalists, which can be estimated at 500. Dynastic factors came into play, helping an instrumentalist to attain the ultimate objective of his professional and social rise: the purchase of a post as violinist in the music of the royal household. Marriages, professional associations and sponsorships allow us to identify the intricate network of relationships linking musical families. We know of the Mazuels, violinists to the king, a family connected through the female line with the Poquelins: Molière (Jean-Baptiste Poquelin) was well acquainted with the world of dancing- and singing-masters through his grandmother. Other families – the Bruslards, Duprons and Faviers – were co-opted within the group. To be skilful in dancing as well as playing an instrument was another

48. A branle being danced at the Palais du Louvre: drawing (1662) by Israël Silvestre

way of rising higher in the social scale. Letters patent for dancing-masters (who were indispensable to the education of a young noble-man), taken out in March 1661 at the time of the formation of the Académie de Danse, express the internal tensions of a community which was still ruled, early in the seventeenth century, by the sta-tutes of 1407. These statutes had been extended in 1540 to include the appointment of a 'king' (*roi*) of instrumentalists. This position was held in the seventeenth century by violinists in the royal household: Louis Constantin from 1624 to 1657, followed by Guillaume Dumanoir.

The career of Dumanoir (1615–97) is particularly instructive in showing the links that existed between musicians in the royal household and those in the city. He was the eldest son of an instrumentalist. In 1639 he paid 1700 *livres* for a post as violinist in the Chambre, and he married the sister of two other violinists of the Chambre, the Dupron brothers. In 1645 he purchased another appointment, as dancing-master, on payment of 2200 *livres*. Widowed in 1644, he married again in 1646. His second wife died in 1650, probably in childbirth. In 1655 he thought of resigning his position as one of the 24 Violons, but the king thought that his departure 'could do harm to this Band if he should be excluded from the Society he had with it, in that because of his ability, his good nature and his diligence he is thought necessary to maintain this Band in its perfection'; the king therefore granted him a warrant as 'conductor and chorus master of the ballets'. On 20 November 1657 he received letters of appointment as '*roi* and *maître* of the violinists and of all the players of instruments both high and low in the Realm'. An intelligent man and well respected at court, Dumanoir was able in 1658 to bring about a thorough reform of the statutes of the community, confirming the monopolistic situation that existed in France. This unequivocal view of his profession, however, had within it the germs of both an imminent conflict with the dancing-masters, in which Dumanoir proved himself a clever pamphleteer, and a later disagreement with those 'players of instruments' who were not violinists. Theoretically, they were placed in a subordinate position by the statutes of the community; they included lutenists, organists and harpsichordists.

The importance and quality of the lute music of Robert Ballard, the Pinels, the Dubuts, Dufaut, the Gaultiers, the Gallots and, later, Charles Mouton is evident;[2] and we can certainly speak of a distinctive French school of lute music, whose influence extended well beyond France: the music of these composer-players has been found in Germany, Austria, Sweden and England. Foreign gentlemen visiting Paris sought out well-known lutenists. Many of these lutenists also played the guitar, the favourite instrument of the young Louis XIV and easier to play than the lute; it became fashionable even in *ballets de cour*. The lute often found in middle-class households must have been used for solo playing as well as for accompanying singing.

Organists occupied a place of their own, since they were essential to the proper conduct of religious services, and the most famous among them, like the Richards and, later, Michel-Richard de Lalande and François Couperin, were to win recognition and financial reward for the quality of their performances. They could play all keyboard instruments with equal facility, and wrote for the harpsichord and organ: Louis Couperin (François's uncle) was one who did so, and he also played the viol in the royal household.

The idea of the concert may have originated with the activities of these instrumentalists. The seventeenth century saw a number of such departures. During its first decades the lutenist Fleurent Indret (from 1617), and perhaps Charles Fleury, Sieur de Blancrocher, regularly invited distinguished gatherings to their houses. In 1650 the concerts of sacred music, or 'second Vespers', given by Pierre de La Barre, organist of the Chapelle Royale, attracted 'persons of great standing', thanks to the high quality of the performers, who came from the royal household. A particular kind of repertory, ambiguous to say the least, was prompted by these occasions: paraphrases of the psalms in French, which were very popular, since they brought together divine worship and fashionable *airs*. Even bolder was Jacques Champion de Chambonnières, another of the king's musicians and an eminent composer: in 1641, before a notary, he set up an Assemblée des Honnêtes Curieux ('Assembly of the Honourable and Interested'), a rather high-flown title for what was in fact a series of regular concerts for which audiences paid. The ten musicians engaged – they were well paid – included two women singers and a viol player, and they performed twice a week, on Wednesdays and Saturdays, at midday in the Salle de Mandosse in the parish of St Eustache.

The cult of the interpreter originated in these years, though it was still on a modest scale. We can see signs of it not in the official press, the *Mercure françois* or the *Gazette*, but in those letters in verse which recorded the social events of Paris. The letters of Loret bear witness to the admiration felt in the years 1650–65 for the beautiful voices of Anne de La Barre, Anna Bergerotti, Hilaire Dupuis and Anne Fonteaux de Cercamanan. He includes in his praises the castrato Blaise Berthod, although the French were lukewarm about the castrato voice.

THEATRICAL WORKS: BALLET, ITALIAN OPERA, PASTORAL

Through the medium of the *ballet de cour*, the theatre dominated the musical life of Paris in the seventeenth century. It gave the king and the young nobles of his court the opportunity to perform as dancers and to relax from political tensions. The *ballet de cour* is one of those rare genres to which an actual date of birth can be assigned. On 15 October 1581 there was a performance of *Circé, ou Le balet comique de la Royne*, devised by Balthasar de Beaujoyeulx. Unlike previous masquerades and festivities, the various authors of this work aimed to provide 'a unified and continuous dramatic action', the union of

49. Design by Daniel Rabel for the Entrée of the Great Khan in the 'Ballet de la Douairière de Billebahaut' (music by Antoine Boësset) in the Grande Salle du Louvre, 1626 (M de Liancourt, as the Great Khan of Asia, arrives on a dromedary; the Tartars in his retinue invite him to jump down and join in their leaping dance)

poetry and music being supposed to lead to a mystical accord, according to the ideals of the Académie de Poésie et de Musique founded in 1570 by Jean-Antoine Baïf.

The *ballet de cour*, a synthesis of all the arts – poetry, music and painting – preserved an almost unchanging pattern during the seventeenth century: a division into *entrées*, devoted to very different subjects even though the general pretext for them might be the same, the absolute primacy of dance and instrumental music, and a limited amount of vocal music in the form of a solo setting out the subject at the beginning of each *entrée*. Some of the ballets have left permanent traces in the works of historians such as Claude-François Menestrier. *La délivrance de Renaud* (1617) and the *Ballet de Tancrède* (1619) reveal the influence of Tasso. We have a record of the stage sets for *Le ballet de la Prospérité des armes de France* (1641), intended to show the reconciliation between Louis XIII and his brother Gaston d'Orléans, himself a dancer and a great lover of ballets. A renaissance of the *ballet de cour* was to come after the Fronde, when it came into contact with Italian productions, thanks in particular to the imagination and poetic sense of Isaac de Benserade, librettist by appointment from 1651. The young Jean-Baptiste Lully was soon to make his mark as a composer of ballets. The insertion of Italian scenes, the importance of scenes that were both sung and acted and were often comic, the coherence of the subject, the magnificence of the danced divertissements: these are the characteristic features of the works that the young Louis XIV, an excellent dancer, honoured with his presence.

What impact did these spectacles have on the Parisian public? According to the lists of participants preserved in the librettos, which were regularly published, and judging by accounts in the *Gazette*, professional dancers and singers mingled with young nobles and talented commoners. Loret, always enthusiastic and inclined to exaggerate, speaks of thousands of people. No figure can really be suggested, since the halls where the performances took place, the Petit Bourbon and the Palais Royal, have been destroyed, but there is reason to believe that the *ballet de cour*, while not a 'popular' spectacle, was not the preserve of a small élite. If it had been, it would have lost part of its *raison d'être*, the glorification of the royal person. Louis XIV first appeared as Apollo in *Le ballet de la Nuit* in 1653 (*see* fig. 50), and many ballets exalted a hero, for instance Alexander, who could also be a model for a king. When the libretto of a ballet offers a collection

50. Louis XIV as Apollo in 'Le ballet de la Nuit', 1653

of 'realistic' situations and characters, we can see a social microcosm confined to the usual entourage of the nobility: an opposition between the worlds of town and country (the latter always seen in hierarchical terms and organized around the lord of the manor or the schoolmaster); satire exclusively aimed at the middle class, the legal profession and the judiciary; an absence of criticism of the nobility (except of a moral nature); all these show that the *ballet de cour* could admit everyday matters, if in a distorted form.

These features may have contributed to the difficulty Italian opera had in taking root in Paris. It arrived very late, and thanks only to the influence of Cardinal Mazarin: his opinions on the choice of troupes, singers, composers and the works to be presented were of fundamental importance. The whole enterprise followed the changes in his own political fortunes, the Fronde imposing a break between 1649 and 1653. The vicissitudes of this musical adventure have been reconstructed in detail by Henry Prunières,[3] but a score of *La finta pazza*, the first Italian opera known to have been given in Paris, on 14 December 1645 in the hall of the Petit Bourbon (*see* fig. 51), was not rediscovered until the 1980s. How much of the music by Francesco Sacrati, composed for the original production in 1641, survives in the extant version is uncertain.[4] As the spectators were fascinated by Giacomo Torelli's sets and stage machinery, it had long been supposed that music played only an episodic part in the work. However, it turns out to have had a good deal of music, with recitatives and arias of a gripping dramatic character. It must all have seemed confusing to an audience used to brief courtly *airs* in which the text took precedence over emotion.

La finta pazza was followed by *Egisto* by Francesco Cavalli (1646) and *Orfeo* by Luigi Rossi (1647). Rossi, unlike his compatriots, spent several years in Paris, including the period of the Fronde. He seems to have liked the French style of singing, and the French appreciated his attitude. The success of his opera, produced at the Palais Royal with Torelli's machines, extended beyond court circles since, at the fair of St Germain, the king's puppeteer joined forces with a Venetian engineer to create a show modelled on the plot and stage sets of *Orfeo*. In 1653, Mazarin realized just how xenophobic the Fronde movement was: *Le nozze di Peleo et di Theti* by Carlo Caproli, produced with French musicians in 1654, was a compromise between the two styles of music. The last productions of Italian operas took place on the occasion of the marriage of Louis XIV to the Infanta Maria Theresa: Cavalli's *Xerse* (1660) and *Ercole amante* (1662) ended fifteen years of efforts to establish Italian opera which were finally interrupted by the death of Mazarin on 9 March 1661.

It cannot, however, be said that the break was complete, for performances of Italian operas in Paris would contribute to the slow

51. Set design for a square in Skiros by Giacomo Torelli for Sacrati's 'La finta pazza', the first Italian opera known to have been performed in Paris, in the hall of the Petit Bourbon, 14 December 1645: engraving by N. Cochin

gestation of native French opera. Unfortunately, no music survives to allow us to evaluate such early attempts as the pastorale of Charles de Beys and the organist Michel de La Guerre (1655) or the pastorale by Pierre Perrin and Robert Cambert performed in 1659 at Issy, a village near Paris, with great success, according to the librettist. The idea of setting a long text to music, developing the characters through words and music and expressing contrasting emotions, was still wholly foreign to French vocal art. As can be seen in the next chapter, Lully gradually forged the necessary language in the ballets and *comédies-ballets* of the years 1660–70, though the short French type of *air* never disappeared from his theatrical work. He also skilfully nourished his *tragédies en musique* on that essential element of the *ballet de cour*, the dance.

Despite having its own well-defined musical character, the Paris of the seventeenth century was open to influences from outside, and itself exerted an influence elsewhere in Europe. In 1633 the king's *valet de chambre* and singer Pierre de Nyert went to Rome to find material with which to revive 'the method of singing well', which he was then to pass on to a generation of virtuoso pupils such as Michel Lambert and Hilaire Dupuis. Paris was also able to attract a leading German composer such as Johann Jacob Froberger in 1656, or an important Fleming such as Henry Du Mont, who had a brilliant career as organist and composer in the Chapelle Royale. Queen Christina of Sweden's visit to France in 1657 was marked by festivities which reflected her interest in French music. There were significant links between Paris and London: Chambonnières's works show the influence of Byrd as well as of Frescobaldi; the work of certain lutenists and guitarists was known on both sides of the Channel; and the 24 Violons du Roy served as a model for the court of Charles II as well as in Germany.

The brilliant flowering of French music from Lully to Rameau should not lead us to overlook the remarkable activity in the period leading up to it.

NOTES

[1] L. Archon, *Histoire de la chapelle des rois de France* (Paris, 1704–11), ii.

[2] See *Corpus des luthistes français*, a series produced by the Centre National de la Recherche Scientifique (1957–).

[3] H. Prunières, *L'opéra italien en France avant Lulli* (Paris, 1913).

[4] L. Bianconi and T. Walker, 'Dalla *Finta pazza* alla *Veramonda*: storie di Febiarmonici', *RIM*, x (1975), 379–454. *La finta pazza* was given in 1986 at the Fenice Theatre, Venice.

BIBLIOGRAPHICAL NOTE

General

An excellent survey of political history during Louis XIII's reign is provided in V. L. Tapié, *La France de Louis XIII et de Richelieu* (Paris, 1952; Eng. trans. by D. M. Lockie as *France in the Age of Louis XIII and Richelieu*, 1974). Social life in the French capital is expertly reviewed in O. Ranum, *Paris in the Age of Absolutism* (New York, 1968), and *Les Parisiens du XVIIe siècle* (Paris, 1973). Also of interest to the English reader will be J. Lough, *An Introduction to Seventeenth Century France* (London, 1954); idem, *France Observed in the Seventeenth Century by British Travellers* (Stocksfield, 1984); and D. Maland, *Culture and Society in Seventeenth Century France* (London, 1970). Two books by A. Adam, *Histoire de la littérature française au XVIIe siècle* (Paris, 1948–51) and *Grandeur and Illusion: French Literature and Society 1600–1715* (trans. H. Tirt, London, 1972), explore the relationship between social and literary history. A valuable reference work is F. Bluche, *Dictionnaire du grand siècle* (Paris, 1990).

Music

The most comprehensive and informative book on the music and musicians of the period is J. R. Anthony, *French Baroque Music from Beaujoyeulx to Rameau* (London,

1973, 2/1978; Fr. trans. as *La musique en France à l'époque baroque*, Paris, 1981, 2/1992). R. M. Isherwood, *Music in the Service of the King* (Ithaca, 1973), links music to general historical developments, focussing on productions at the French court. M. Benoit's *Dictionnaire de la musique en France, aux XVIIe et XVIIIe siècles* (Paris, 1992) is a valuable reference work for the period.

Contemporary descriptions of ballets are found in M. de Pure, *Idée des spectacles anciens et nouveaux* (Paris, 1668), and C.-F. Ménestrier, *Des ballets anciens et modernes selon les règles du théâtre* (Paris, 1682). Other court festivities and the beginnings of opera are discussed in idem, *Des représentations en musique anciennes et modernes* (Paris, 1681). M. M. McGowan, *L'art du ballet de cour en France 1581–1643* (Paris, 1963), provides a detailed history of the *ballet de cour* and M.-F. Christout, *Le ballet de cour au XVIIe siècle* (Geneva, 1984), offers numerous illustrations of décor and costumes with expert commentary. H. Prunières, *Le ballet de cour en France avant Benserade et Lully* (Paris, 1914), provides more comment on the music; idem, *L'opéra italien en France avant Lulli* (Paris, 1913), remains the fullest account of French productions of operas by Sacrati, Rossi, Cavalli and Caproli.

M. Jurgens, *Documents du Minutier central concernant l'histoire de la musique 1600–1650* (Paris, 1967), provides a treasure trove of archival documentation on professional and amateur musicians, instrument makers and printers, and the working conditions of musicians in Paris during the minority of Louis XIV (1643–61) are effectively outlined in C. Massip, *La vie des musiciens de Paris au temps de Mazarin* (Paris, 1976). More fleeting archival information is presented in Y. de Brossard, *Musiciens de Paris 1535–1792: Actes d'état-civil d'après le fichier Laborde de la Bibliothèque nationale* (Paris, 1965). Musical life observed by the court chronicler Jean Loret and his successors is reviewed in idem, 'La vie musicale en France d'après Loret et ses continuateurs (1650–1688)', *RMFC*, x (1970), 117–93, and other contemporary reports are selected in N. Dufourcq, 'En parcourant le *Mercure françois* 1605–1644', ibid, xviii (1978), 5–28, and idem, 'En parcourant la *Gazette* 1645–1654', ibid, xxiii (1985), 176–202.

The musical organization of the Sainte-Chapelle is described in M. Brenet, *Les musiciens de la Sainte-Chapelle de Palais* (Paris, 1910), and that of the royal chapel in M. le Moël, 'La Chapelle de musique sous Henri IV et Louis XIII', *RMFC*, vi (1966), 5–26. Vernacular psalms are discussed in D. Launay, 'A propos du chant des psaumes en français au XVIIe siècle: la paraphrase des psaumes de Godeau et ses musiciens', *Revue de musicologie*, l (1964), 30–75, and Latin church music in idem, 'Les motets à double choeur en France dans la première moitié du XVIIe siècle', ibid, xl (1957), 173–95. There is a more general account in idem, 'Church Music in France (*a*) 1630–60, *New Oxford History of Music*, v, ed. A Lewis and N. Fortune (London, 1975), rev.2/ 1986), 414–37.

On the *air de cour*, see G. Durosoir, *L'air de cour en France 1571–1655* (Liège, 1991), and on the composers of lute music L. de la Laurencie, *Les luthistes* (Paris, 1928). The composers of harpsichord music are surveyed in A. Pirro, *Les clavecinistes* (Paris, 1925), and their music in B. Gustafson, *French Harpsichord Music in the XVIIth century* (Ann Arbor, 1978). M. Brenet, *Les concerts en France sous l'ancien régime* (Paris, 1900), includes details on concert life in the period.

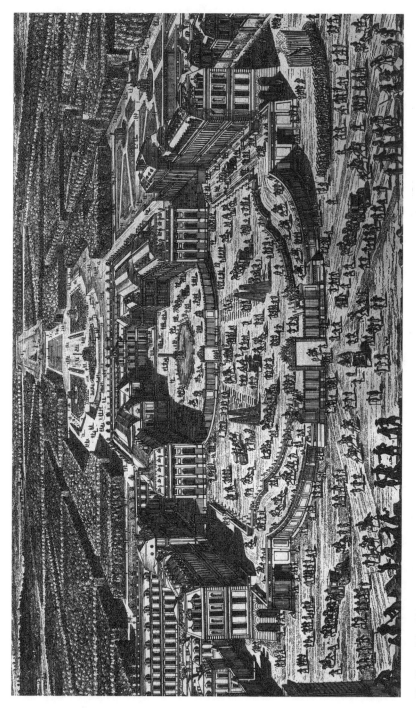

52. *View of the Château de Versailles, enlarged from 1678 by J. H. Mansart from a core of 1623 (Louis XIII's hunting lodge, retained as the Cour de Marbre), enlarged by Le Vau, 1661–5, with gardens laid out by Le Nôtre, 1661–8: engraving (late 17th century) by Perelle*

Chapter XII

Paris, 1661–87: the Age of Lully

MARCELLE BENOIT

THE COURT: INTRODUCTION

Though the Treaty of Westphalia (1648) brought the Thirty Years War to an end, another ten years were to pass before the new map of Europe could be seen. Louis XIV's coming of age, declared in 1651, when he was thirteen, concluded the regency of his mother Anne of Austria, but Mazarin's ministry continued in power, giving rise to the insurrections of the Fronde (1652–3), which would force the young king to flee from the capital and his minister to go into exile in Cologne. Louis XIV never forgot these events, which caused ideas about authority and order to germinate in his mind. The Peace of the Pyrenees (1659), followed by the king's marriage to the Spanish princess María Teresa (Marie-Thérèse), meant that the possibility of a period of calm on the European scene could be glimpsed. However, the opportunity for such a change came only with the death of Cardinal Mazarin in 1661.

Meanwhile, a young Italian-born player of the guitar and violin, who was six years older than the king, happened to find himself in the opposite camp, employed to entertain Mlle de Montpensier, the daughter of Gaston d'Orléans and a cousin of Louis XIV. She had just turned the cannon on the royal troops, and Jean-Baptiste Lully (1632–87) had followed her to her refuge in the château of St Fargeau, where he soon became bored and felt that he should aim higher and look for more permanent employment. In 1653 he took up a post as a dancer and composer of instrumental music in the king's service. Thus did fate bring these two ambitious men together, and for the next 34 years Lully was to live, one might almost say, in the protective shade of the Sun King. Louis XIV had chosen as his motto 'Nec pluribus impar' (Superior to all); did not Lully perhaps, in his heart of hearts, opt for the imprudent motto of Fouquet, 'Quo non ascendet?' (To what may I not rise?)? Louis assumed the throne in 1661, the year in which Lully also began his reign as *surintendant de la musique* at court.

The Early Baroque Era

'LES PLAISIRS ET LES FÊTES'[1]

Music flourished throughout the period 1661–87. The itinerant court followed a route that may be traced thus. First came Vincennes and Paris (the Louvre, the Tuileries, the Palais Royal). Outside the capital, priority went to St German-en-Laye (the Château Vieux and Château Neuf), Fontainebleau for hunting in the autumn, and sometimes Chambord. One might sometimes get away from court to visit the Superintendent of Finance, Fouquet, at Vaux-le-Vicomte and the Condés at Chantilly, the Orléans at Villers-Cotterets and St Cloud, and other eminent personages at their various seats. Periods of residence at Versailles and Trianon became more and more frequent, even while work was still in progress, until the court was finally installed there in 1682. The move did not put an end to its visits to Fontainebleau, but the king lost his taste for St Germain, of which he would finally grow tired, while he became increasingly fond of Marly in the summer.

Music could be heard in every royal residence. The years 1661–72 mark the end of the age of the *ballet de cour*. Such spectacles were still collaborative works, generally with verses by Isaac de Benserade, music by Lully, Michel Lambert or Jean-Baptiste Boësset, choreography by Pierre Beauchamp, scenery and stage machinery by Carlo Vigarani and costumes by Henry de Gissey. The king himself took part in the dancing, and certain aristocrats with a gift for it followed his example, foremost among them the Duke of Saint-Aignan, chief organizer of the royal *fêtes*, the Duke of Armagnac, the Comte de St-Germain and the Comte de Brionne. The most famous of these spectacles were the *Ballet de l'impatience* and *Ballet des saisons* (performed at Fontainebleau, 1661), the *Ballet des arts* (Palais Royal, 1663), the *Ballet de la naissance de Vénus* (Palais Royal, 1665), the *Ballet des muses* (St Germain-en-Laye, 1666), the *Ballet de Flore* (Tuileries, 1669), the *tragédie-ballet Psyché* (Palais Royal, 1671) and the *Ballet des ballets* (St Germain-en-Laye, 1671).

At the same time the court was enjoying *comédies-ballets* and divertissements in which the text played a more important part, alternating with the songs and dances. This was the great epoch of the collaboration between Molière and Lully: of *Le mariage forcé* (performed at the Louvre, 1664), *L'Amour médecin* (Versailles, 1665), *Monsieur de Pourceaugnac* (Chambord, 1669), *Les amants magnifiques* (St Germain-en-Laye, 1670) and *Le bourgeois gentilhomme* (1670).

Let us look more closely at some of the *fêtes* which bear witness to the luxury of Louis XIV's reign.

1662. The carousel given in this year was a sumptuous spectacle, part aristocratic and part popular, the like of which had never been seen in Paris. A parade went down the rues de Richelieu, St-Honoré and

53. Trumpeter and kettledrummer of the Fourth Quadrille (representing India) of the carousel held at the Tuileries in honour of Louis XIV's bride, 5–6 June 1662: engraving from C. Perrault, 'Courses de testes et de bague' (Paris, 1670)

St-Nicaise and ended at the Tuileries. Seats for 15 000 spectators had been erected in the château courtyard, which was closed for the occasion. The king, in the costume of a Roman emperor, led a long procession of horsemen decked with plumes, grouped into five troops and each bearing his own emblem and motto. Trumpets and kettledrums announced their entries and manoeuvres (fig. 53). The tournament lasted three days, and the victors received, from the hands of the queen, a diamond worth 25 000 crowns and a portrait of Louis XIV.

1664.

> The King, wishing to give the Queens and all his Court the pleasure of some unusual festivities, in a place adorned with all the amenities that may make a country house admired, chose Versailles, four leagues from Paris. This château might well be called an enchanted palace, so well have the ornaments of art complemented the care taken by Nature to perfect it. It was at this beautiful place, to which the whole court resorted on the fifth of May, that the King entertained over six hundred people until the fourteenth, besides a great number of persons necessary for the dancing and the plays, and craftsmen of all kinds come from Paris: so many that they seemed like a little army . . .[2]

This *fête*, held with little pretence of secrecy in honour of the king's

54. *Conclusion of the third day of the 1664 grand divertissement at Versailles (the eruption of the palace of the enchantress Alcina): engraving by Israël Silvestre*

mistress Mlle de La Vallière, and freely based on Ariosto's *Orlando furioso*, told the tale of the visit by Ruggiero (Louis XIV) to the enchantress Alcina's island and palace, and featured the following:

> The Pleasures of the Enchanted Isle. Tilting at the Ring. A Collation attended by Stage Effects. A Comedy by Molière, with Dancing and Music. Ballet of Alcina's Palace. Fireworks. And other elegant and magnificent entertainments given by the king at Versailles on the seventh of May 1664. And continued for several more days.[3]

During these days, trumpets and kettledrums and other players were to be heard everywhere – during the procession of the king and his knights, the *Ballet des quatre saisons*, and the banquets served to guests in arbours erected in the park facing a great expanse of water. *La Princesse d'Elide*, a *comédie-ballet* written and performed by Molière, included *airs* and dances composed by Lully. Mlle Hilaire sang in the play, wearing a costume designed by Gissey. Vigarani had devised all the stage effects. All was enchantment, right up to the final firework show, in which Alcina's palace went up in flames (fig. 54).

1668. Versailles made such an impression on the court that the king thought it desirable to present further divertissements there four years later. He made use of this *fête*, given in honour of Mme de Montespan, unacknowledged queen of the occasion, to show his courtiers the park of Versailles. Much progress had been made in laying it out over the last few years. It was now adorned by alleys in perspective, rocky grottos, fountains, a maze and an open-air theatre, and in this realm of the ephemeral Louis le Vau, Molière and Lully, Vigarani and Gissey collaborated to present the comedy of *Georges Dandin* and the *ballet-pastorale Les fêtes de l'Amour et de Bacchus*.

> It may be said that in this work, the Sieur de Lully has discovered the secret of satisfying and charming everyone, for never was there anything so fine or so well devised. If one takes the dances, there is no step that does not speak of the action the Dancers are to perform, or whose accompanying gestures are not as good as words that may be understood. If one takes the Music, there is nothing which does not perfectly express all the passions, delighting the spirit of the Hearers. But what was never before seen is that pleasing harmony of voices, that symphony of instruments, that delightful union of different choruses, those sweet songs, those tender and amorous dialogues, those echoes, in short, that admirable conduct in every part, in which it might always be seen from the first words that the Music was increasing, and having begun with a single voice, it concluded with a concert of over one hundred persons, seen all at once upon the same Stage, uniting their instruments, their voices and their steps in a harmony and cadence that brings the Play to an end, leaving everyone in a state of admiration that canot be adequately expressed.[4]

Collations, illuminations, a ball and fireworks enhanced the natural background to this memorable event, to which the best of the king's musicians made their contribution.

1674. At Versailles again, six days of *fêtes* were held on the occasion of the king's return from the (temporary) conquest of Franche-Comté. Molière had died in 1673, but Philippe Quinault had just joined with Lully and Vigarani to inaugurate successfully the new art of French opera, the *tragédie en musique* (discussed below). Montespan had been 'reigning' at court as the king's mistress for several years. The *fêtes* were as follows.[5]

First day, 4 July, a performance of *Alceste, ou Le triomphe d'Alcide*, 'a play with music, accompanied by stage effects', in the marble courtyard of the château, given by the artists of the Académie Royale de Musique.

Second day, 11 July, a performance of the *Eglogue de Versailles* in the 'porcelain' Trianon, the domain of the king's mistress, built in a pseudo-Oriental style ('in the Chinese manner'). This divertissement united the musicians of the Académie with those of the royal household. During the supper that followed, violins and oboes played.

Third day, 19 July, an expedition to the Ménagerie, a visit that aroused great interest.

55. *Concert preceding the 'Eglogue de Versailles', in the enclosed garden of the Trianon on the second day of the 1674 fêtes at Versailles celebrating the king's return from his second conquest of the Franche-Comté (note the musicians in four alcoves of the octagon): engraving by F. Chauveau*

> After the collation, which was very magnificent, His Majesty, being out on the Canal in superbly decorated gondolas, was followed by the Music of Violins and Oboes, which were in a great Vessel. He remained there about an hour to enjoy the cool of the evening and hear the pleasing concerts of voices and instruments which alone broke the silence of the night that was beginning to fall.

There followed a performance of Molière's *Le malade imaginaire*, with music by Marc-Antoine Charpentier.

Fourth day, 28 July, Their Majesties 'went to the end of the alley of the Dragon, beside the water tower, where They found a Stage set for the Opera of the *Festes de l'Amour et de Bacchus* . . . the music for which was the work of the Sieur de Lully'. After a collation in the marble courtyard, sumptuously decorated by Vigarani, the guests took supper 'to the sound of the waters of the fountain, while on their other side the violins and oboes filled the place with pleasing harmony'.

Fifth day, 18 August, in a grove between the Allée Royale and the Allée de Bacchus, a lavish collation 'to the sound of violins and oboes' preceded the performance of Racine's *Iphigénie*, on a stage set up at the end of the alley leading to the Orangery. For the evening, Charles Le Brun, the king's chief painter, had devised a dazzling firework display in the middle of an expanse of water, where the designs traced by the 5000 rockets took symbolic forms.

Sixth day, 31 August, on the great canal, the nocturnal illuminations designed by Vigarani set off the shapes of the pools and the long stretch of water to good effect. Gondolas carried violinists and oboists, who struck up dance tunes or military songs addressed to the victorious monarch.

1681. The first performance of *Le triomphe de l'Amour* was given at St Germain-en-Laye; it had been intended for Versailles in 1680, but was deferred until January 1681 because of the illness of the Dauphin. This royal ballet in a prologue and twenty *entrées*, with text by Quinault, epigrams by Benserade and music by Lully, is a final example of the *ballet de cour* with *entrées*, while at the same time prefiguring the *opéra-ballet*. Created by and for the court, it called for an aristocratic cast. Graces, Naiads and Nymphs appeared alternately with Pleasures, Loves and Sea Gods. Mars and his warriors preceded Dreams, Indians, Shepherds and Fauns.

Monseigneur took the part of Zephyr, Mlle de Nantes played Youth and the Princess of Conti Ariadne. However, the masters of the Académie de Danse, Beauchamp, Pécourt, Favier, Lestang and Magny, went back and forth not far away, close to the actors and guiding their steps. The king's musicians (Gaye, Guillegaut, Puvigné and Mlles Ferdinand and Rebel) sang. Professional women dancers, notably Mlle La Fontaine, attracted attention – this was perhaps the first time they had been seen.

1686. The famous royal carousel of 1662 at the beginning of Louis XIV's reign was paralleled, at the end of Lully's career, by the one given in honour of the Grand Dauphin. *Les airs de trompettes, timbales et hautbois faits par Mr de Lully par l'ordre du Roy pour le Carousel de Monseigneur, l'an 1686* was his last instrumental score. André Danican Philidor had the parts of the fanfares, performed by the musicians of the Grande Écurie and the Army, copied out.

> Du Mont, major-general of the troops . . . was followed by the drummer and the two trumpeters of M. le Duc de Saint-Aignan . . . After this came the drummers of Monseigneur, his trumpeters and his oboists . . . Next marched the drummers, trumpeters and oboists of M. le Duc de Bourbon . . . The two troops went around the barriers to the sound of instruments accompanying them and a great number of others lining the barrier, playing tunes composed especially for this festival by the famous J. B. Lulli . . . The troops moved in such a way that the ladies . . . found themselves beside His Majesty, and when this was done, the drummers, trumpeters and oboists who had played during the march . . . placed themselves at the four corners of the barriers.[6]

But the heart had gone out of it all. The time of the great *fêtes* of love and war was past. The city of Paris took over, with the Académie de Musique, and the court turned to its devotions. Now came the reign of Mme de Maintenon: the age of Michel-Richard de Lalande and the *grand motet*.

MUSIC OF THE ROYAL HOUSEHOLD

The royal household comprised three departments into which musicians were grouped: the Chapelle, the Chambre and the Ecurie.[7]

The Chapelle. Besides the Chapelle Oratoire, comprising the celebrants, and under the same authority – that of the *maître*, a high ecclesiastical dignitary – there was the Chapelle-Musique, whose task it was to embellish the liturgy in an artistic manner. At its head, the *sous-maître*, whose title indicated that he was under the orders of the *maître*, was in fact the real choirmaster and director of the entire musical side of the ceremonies. (In the eighteenth century, he came to be called *maître*.) It was he who chose works suitable for the liturgy of the day, often composing them himself, who supervised rehearsals of these works and always conducted the performances of them. Since the court attended the chapel once or twice a day, the *sous-maître*'s was an arduous position; it also entailed supervising the moral and musical education of the children who sang in the choirs.

At the beginning of Louis XIV's reign these duties had been carried out by two *sous-maîtres*, Jean Veillot and Thomas Gobert. But by the 1660s religious music had become more important at court, and after the competitive examination for the post in 1663 the duties were carried out alternately, in six-monthly periods, by Thomas Gobert (*d* 1672), Pierre Robert, Gabriel Expilly (who resigned in 1668) and Henry Du Mont. The court's move to Versailles in 1682, the consecration of the new chancel,[8] and the advanced age of Robert and Du Mont prompted another competitive examination in 1683, when the duties were re-divided into three-monthly periods. Thirty-five candidates from Paris and the provinces offered themselves. Charpentier fell ill. Fifteen competitors were still in the running for the second part of the examination, the composition of a *Beati quorum*. Four were appointed: Nicolas Goupillet, a priest, for the January quarter; Pascal Colasse, recommended by Lully, for the April quarter; Guillaume Minoret, a tonsured clerk, for the July quarter, and Lalande, who was now entering upon a brilliant career at court, for the October quarter.[9] The jury thus chose one ecclesiastic and one layman for each six-month period, and the former, besides fulfilling the musical duties of his own quarter, was to be in charge of liturgical and educational duties for the whole six months.

Secularization of the chapel administration would come only by degrees.

The *sous-maître* was in authority over the choir, whose members came from Parisian or provincial parishes. Priests, clerics and celibate laymen were preferred so as to ensure the maximum religious commitment to the posts and the maximum availability of those who stood near the altar. However, like the *sous-maîtres* themselves, during the second part of Louis XIV's reign the singers were recruited more and more frequently from the ranks of professional singers in the secular world. The men comprised countertenors and high tenors, low tenors or baritones, basses and 'basses able to play the serpent'. The higher voices were sopranos or trebles and altos – boys whose voices had not yet broken and Italian castratos. During the 1670s the choir, which might be used as a whole or in part according to circumstances, was probably about 60 strong. From the time when opera began to develop, women, too, occasionally sang in the chapel as soloists, though they were never entered in the records of the royal household, and they never supplanted the boys and castratos during the Ancien Régime.

The organ remained, *par excellence*, the instrument for sacred music. The size of the organs varied from chapel to chapel: they might be simple choir organs, portable ones set up in a chapel, or larger ones with two or three keyboards and pedals. The Clicquots, a family of organ builders, saw to their maintenance. The organist – the most respected of His Majesty's musicians – usually came from a famous organ loft in the capital or from a provincial cathedral. His importance in the life of the court was emphasized by the competitive examination for the post in 1678. Hitherto, one holder of the position had sufficed: Joseph de La Barre, who had held it since 1656 and who died in 1678. After that date, four were required: Jacques Thomelin (*d* 1693) for the January quarter; Jean-Baptiste Buterne (*d* 1727) for the April quarter; Guillaume Gabriel Nivers (*d* 1714) for the July quarter; and Nicolas Lebègue (*d* 1702), the most famous of them, for the October quarter. Their task was to accompany the voices; support the singing of plainsong; alternate with the officiating priests; play or improvise verses inspired by the texts of the Mass, the services proper to the day or the *Magnificat*; and support the choir, whether large or small, in motets.

Soon, too, he was required to reinforce a larger ensemble of voices and instruments, for orchestral players gradually came to take part in divine service, integrating their music with the Office. Besides the cornett to complement high voices, there were the bassoon, sackbut and serpent to accompany the lowest voices, all of them instruments mentioned by the theorist Marin Mersenne. This predilection for wind instruments, well adapted to the acoustics of church architecture, was to evolve in parallel with developments in musical taste and composition.

The rise of the concerted style, which came from Italy; the opposition of choral and instrumental forces; the simplification of polyphonic textures; the birth of the orchestra, with its varied colours: all these were to favour a type of musical discourse in which instruments had a significant role. They imitated vocal themes, and played preludes and ritornellos, and some of the lower instruments played the basso continuo. The *grand motet*, with its double choir and orchestral writing, came into existence, and with it there entered the Chapel Royal not only lutes, theorbos, viols and flutes but also violins and oboes, which were associated with dance music and thus held in low esteem. In this respect the Chapelle Royale seems to have been ahead of the parish churches, which is perhaps not surprising, for who, apart from the king, could have maintained an orchestra to play in his church?

The Chambre. This department was under the authority of the Great Chamberlain. The musicians belonging to it performed an exclusively secular repertory at court and provided music when the king commanded it. Their services, which were not required at such regular intervals as those of the Chapelle choir and organists (and had less prestige), did, however, expand to a remarkable degree during the 1670s when any occasion was an excuse for *fêtes* and divertissements. Balls, ballets, *comédies-ballets*, *tragédies en musique*, *symphonies* and chamber music followed one another as circumstances or the king's pleasure decreed.

The Musique de la Chambre was in the charge of two *surintendants*, who alternated every six months. They commanded a world of singers and instrumentalists, dancers and makers of stage machinery, scene painters and costume designers, who all drew their salaries from the funds of the 'king's revels', the *menus plaisirs*. 'The *Surintendant* must understand voices and instruments, in order to make the King good music. Everything sung by the Musique de la Chambre is his business; and he may have, close to his person, a Page whose voice has broken.'[10]

It may seem surprising that this key post, or at least half of it, was held by a man of mediocre talent, who was also attached to the Musique de la Reine: Jean-Baptiste Boësset (1614–85). However, he was the son of Antoine Boësset and had inherited his father's position. His *airs* and his contribution to *ballets de cour* marginalized him at a time which saw the development of opera, and his dynasty came to a lacklustre end when he handed the reins of power to his son, Claude Jean-Baptiste, whose talents were even slighter.[11]

The star of the other *surintendant*, another Jean-Baptiste, was rising

56. Jean-Baptiste Lully: engraving by J.-L. Roullet after Paul Mignard

at the same period, and the Boëssets' star paled beside it. Lully, a brilliant dancer and a great organizer of spectacles, whose authority was recognized and sometimes bitterly resented, could compose to order and as circumstances required. He surrounded himself with a gifted team, and nothing escaped his criticism and his control. The king took a great fancy to him. Between 1661 and 1672, Lully was able to make him laugh and dance and to present him with *comédies-ballets* and divertissements worthy of a young, dynamic monarch. Then, as the king grew older and the seriousness of the national situation made itself felt, the tone changed. From 1673 to 1687, thanks to the operatic privileges that Louis XIV granted his *surintendant*, Lully produced in the city of Paris works of quality, skill and lofty tone which the courtiers were the first to see.

Alongside the *surintendant* there was the *maître*, who was in charge of the education and musical training of the children attached to the Musique de la Chambre, three or four of them, who learnt grammar, had a teacher of the lute and the theorbo and above all studied singing. Ecclesiastical status was not required for this position, which could not have been better filled than it was by Michel Lambert, a highly gifted teacher of voice training and composer of *airs*, of which he left many collections.

Lambert and Lully: there was never a more effective collaboration. The two colleagues had first met in the service of La Grande Mademoiselle, which they left to enter the king's service. Lully married Lambert's daughter, and Lambert became a kind of musical duplicate of his son-in-law. The family all lived together in the Hôtel de la rue Ste-Anne, and helped to lend incomparable brilliance to secular music during the 1670s. The musical personnel Lully had at his disposal comprised firstly singers, performing as soloists or, in an ensemble, as choirs of men's and women's voices. There were about 40 of them, although they could equally well perform in smaller groups if that is what the music required. They comprised sopranos (male or female), countertenors, tenors, baritones and basses.

The *airs de cour* of earlier in the century were to give way to serious songs, *brunettes* or little *airs tendres*, devotional *airs*, dance-songs, and *récits* for one or more voices, and all these elements became integrated into a more expansive structure, paving the way for the arias of the emerging opera. On a smaller scale, too, they also soon led to the cantata.

Women became prominent in these vocal groups. At the beginning of Louis XIV's reign, the fashion was for all things Italian, which explains the success of Anna Bergerotti, summoned to court thanks to Mazarin; she returned to Rome in 1669. Several Frenchwomen were popular at the time when Lully took up the post of *surintendant*. One was accepted into the Musique de la Chambre amid high praise:

> The Fine qualities with which Damoiselle Anne de la Barre is endowed, the excellence of her voice, her way of managing it and the grace which accompanies all her actions, and have often won her admiration, in the narratives of the Ballets danced before his Majesty as well as in his other private pastimes, have made him consider that for such entertainments, and when, having withdrawn privately into his Closet, he wishes to hear French or Italian *airs*, no one else can please him more agreeably than this lady.[12]

Another woman singer, the gifted Hilaire Dupuis, linked by family and professional ties to Lambert and Lully, in whose home she lived, retired from the king's service in 1677. Her colleague Anne Fonteaux de Sercamanen followed a similar career, singing *airs de ballet*, and was to receive a pension from the king's privy purse to the end of her

57. 'Le concert', with a
lute and viol (Versailles
can be seen in the
background): engraving
by N. Bonnart

Concert

Sur les accords de ces deux jnstrumens   Et le ciel n'a point d'armonie
Rien n'est si doux que la voix d'Vranie   Dont les concerts paroissent plus charmans

Chez JBonnart au Coq avec privillege.

life. Marthe le Rochois left the Opéra, which she joined in 1678, and
also sang at court; so did Mlles Saint-Christophle and Anne Rebel.

Men's voices were appreciated in the Chambre too. In the 1670s
certain names recur frequently, for example those of Louis Donc (or
Dun), Pierre Bony, Guillaume d'Estival, Philippe le Roy de
Beaumont, Laurent Hébert, Antoine Maurel, the Gayes, the
Tiphaines, the Fernons and Clédière. Several of them sang in the
Chapelle.

The singers were accompanied on the lute and theorbo by players
such as the Molliers, the Ithiers or the Pinels, on the guitar by, for
instance, Bernard Jourdan de La Salle or on the viol by men such as
Nicolas Hotman, Sébastien Le Camus, Gabriel Caignet or Marin
Marais. These players also appeared in the orchestra which played
for ballets, and they had an important role in supporting the recitatives in operatic performances at court.

The Early Baroque Era

Most important of them all, keyboard instruments were entering upon the finest period of their history to date. Jacques Champion de Chambonnières (1601/2–72) left his mark on the court by dint of his personality, the distinguished qualities of his compositions and the excellence of his teaching. However, his social pretensions led to his downfall and disgrace, and he relinquished his post to his pupil Jean-Henri d'Anglebert, who held it for a dozen years before passing it on to his son in 1674. In 1689 d'Anglebert published a book of 60 pieces, either original or transcribed from the work of others, which are of great interest. Lebègue, Nivers and François Couperin continued the tradition. Engaged at court as harpsichordists, these men also played the organ, either in the Chapelle Royale or in one of the parishes of Paris. Women had a contribution to make here too – Elisabeth Jacquet de La Guerre, born into a family of organists and destined to marry one, 'from her earlier youth gave evidence of extraordinary talents and aptitude for Music, and for the Art of playing the Harpsichord. She was scarcely fifteen years old when she appeared at Court. The King took much pleasure in hearing her play the Harpsichord, which caused Madame de Montespan to keep her with her for three or four years, so that she might be pleasantly entertained, and also those persons of the Court who visited her, in doing which the young Lady succeeded very well . . .' (Titon de Tillet).

The most numerous instruments, naturally, were those of the violin family. They were divided into two groups: the 21 Petits Violins or Petite Bande and the 24 Violons du Roi or Grande Bande (six violins, four each of three inner instruments of the viola type, and six bass instruments). From 1655 onwards, a 25th received a warrant to 'cause the Band to play in concert'; this was the 'conductor'. String players did not play at court regularly, only when the king commanded them. Their traditional functions linked them to the dance: they demonstrated steps, accompanied balls, played at certain of the king's dinners and suppers, and performed at dawn on such occasions as New Year or the Feast of St Louis. The bands could be divided up at will and sometimes played together with wind instruments, particularly oboes, recruited from the Ecurie or the two companies of musketeers. Finally, of course, the strings became the basis of the orchestras required for divertissements and *tragédies en musique*.

String players saw their social position improve between 1660 and 1690, thanks to the example of Lully himself. And the dissemination of Corelli's works in France soon reinforced the high status of the instrumentalists responsible for the creation and diffusion of such prestigious forms as the concerto and sonata.

The Ecurie. This department, which came under the Master of the

Horse, comprised the Petite Ecurie, containing riding and carriage horses for the king's use, and the Grande Ecurie, comprising war-horses, riding-school horses and the staff who looked after them. It was to the latter that the musical body called the Musique de l'Ecurie administratively belonged. The institution went back at least to the time of François I in the early sixteenth century. Faithful to tradition, it retained titles from the sixteenth century that did not always correspond to the services it rendered. The musicians were divided into five categories: twelve trumpeters; twelve players of violins, oboes, sackbuts and cornetts; six oboists and players of the Poitevin bagpipes; eight players of the fife and drum; and six players of crumhorns and trumpets marine. In practice, the group consisted of some 40 instrumentalists mostly playing wind instruments. Some played 'loud' instruments: trumpeters accompanied by kettledrums, mounted on horseback; and players of oboes and bassoons and of crumhorns, which soon were abandoned. Others played 'soft' instruments such as recorders. Finally there were those playing bowed instruments: trumpets marine, also becoming obsolete, and no doubt violins too. Fifes and drums might also be used, but these were more appropriate to the army.

This show or parade body performed on official occasions, most frequently out of doors: at proclamations of peace, colour parades, the reception of foreign legations, processions for royal baptisms, weddings and funerals, tournaments and carousels (*see* fig. 53 above), *fêtes* on the water, for a visit to the town hall in Paris, or as the hunt set out. The livery of the Ecurie was made from rich fabrics, laced with gold and silver, enhanced by large hats and buff leather belts and by trumpet slings.

The musicians of the royal household just described did not stay strictly within their own departments: there were no fixed boundaries. Some of the singers from the Chapelle performed in secular divertissements; the harpsichordist of the Chambre sometimes played the organ during divine service; the trumpeter of the Ecurie might join the orchestra of a musical *tragédie en musique*; players from the 24 Violins might play in a concerted motet, as might an oboist from the Ecurie, and so forth. What mattered to the administrators was whether a musician was the official holder of an office or not. If he was, he owned his office, which he had bought in the presence of a notary, in accordance with the Ancien Régime custom known as 'the venality of offices'. Three conditions were required: the king's consent, ability on the part of the person seeking office, and possession of the sum of money necessary for the purchase and for all the other expenses entailed (this sum might be borrowed).

A musician was sometimes engaged on the recommendation of a

high-ranking person, sometimes after competition but most often when he had already given proof of his skill at court: assumption of the office confirmed his merits. There was not always an exact correspondence between the title and its function within each department (one might, for example, buy the office of a tenor which was vacant when one happened to be a bass): what mattered was to become an office holder in order to derive from the office the revenues called 'gages'. The office could be passed on to a relative or friend by reversion, or it could be sold or exchanged; all such operations were conducted only with the king's consent.

Most musicians were not office holders and might be of either 'ordinary' or 'extraordinary' status. The former, as the term indicates, served the royal music in one or other of its departments, or in more than one, in an 'ordinary', that is, a regular, manner. They had a daily maintenance allowance, to which were added bonuses, gratuities, pensions and, if they were ecclesiastics, prebends. The second category, the 'extraordinary' musicians, performed their functions on an irregular basis. Some acted as additional singers or instrumentalists for special performances. Others – visiting artists – were invited to court, where the applause they received is recorded in the chronicles of the time: an Italian singer, an infant prodigy, an ingenious instrument maker, in fact anyone who was unusual or fashionable. In 1682, for instance, Johann Paul von Westhoff, a violinist in the employ of the Elector of Saxony, performed some of his own music before Louis XIV. The *Mercure galant* not only reported the event but even printed a sonata and a suite by him within its pages.

THE CITY: INTRODUCTION

At first sight it might seem that the court was the whole life of the nation during the reign of Louis XIV. And it is true that it is the court which we read about most: the hired chroniclers report its slightest words and deeds. But in fact the city of Paris, which now had about 400 000 inhabitants and was divided into sixteen quarters, was in a flourishing state; thanks to Gomboust's plan (1647–52)[13] we can see its layout and its social groupings.[14]

The Ile de la Cité, with Notre Dame and the Sainte-Chapelle, constituted the religious centre of the capital. Some musicians lived around the Palais de Justice. On the Right Bank, to the east, were the protective bastions of royalty: the Bastille, the Arsenal, the Temple. In the centre, the working people of Paris followed their trades or crafts along the river and in the markets. The bankers were concentrated around St Eustache.

To the west, near the Louvre and the Tuileries, a new, residential quarter was about to arise. The nobility settled in spacious houses in the parishes of St Thomas and St Roch. Painters, sculptors and architects came to live in and around the Louvre as the academies were being set up. This development went even beyond the Faubourg St Honoré, to the Ville-l'Evêque (now the Madeleine), where Lully was to spend his last years.

On the Left Bank stood the university, the colleges, the religious houses (the Franciscans, the Dominicans, the seminary of St Sulpice, Ste Geneviève, Port Royal, the Carthusians, the Carmelites, Val-de-Grâce), the printing presses and booksellers, and privileged places of study and contemplation where few musicians lived. Around the abbey of St Germain-des-Prés the suburb reached to the Plaine de Grenelle.

Strictly speaking, there was no quarter reserved for musicians, who were distinguished less by their social origin than by the services they performed for a nobleman, church, corporation, theatre or academy. They might thus live in the precincts of a church, in a great lord's house or near the Opéra. The most favoured needed a *pied-à-terre* at St Germain-en-Laye or Fontainebleau when they were on duty at court, and from 1682 they sometimes even had to stay at Versailles itself or have an apartment built there.

THE CHURCHES

It was in the churches that a degree of continuity in musical thought was transmitted. They acted as schools for the boys who joined the choir schools of their own parishes, or those of a church further afield if their parents felt it had a higher reputation. These children, aged from seven or eight to thirteen or fourteen (the age at which their voices broke) were taught Latin, grammar, some of the elements of mathematics, and singing, by an ecclesiastic whose duty it also was to supervise their morals. The altar boys, who would be serving during the Offices, received a more intensive training in the liturgy and plainsong and also learnt sight-reading. They all studied an accompanimental instrument: viol, lute, harpsichord or organ. If a boy wished to specialize in playing the organ and composition, the capital had plenty of excellent organists to teach him in the years 1660–90: the La Guerres at the Sainte-Chapelle, Lebègue at St Merry, the Couperins at St Gervais, D'Anglebert at the Dominican convent in the rue St-Honoré, Nivers at St Sulpice, Lalande at St Jean-en-Grève, and so on.

Religious music differed according to the nature of the place in which it was performed. We may distinguish between the privileged churches, the parish churches and the religious houses. At the head of the first category was the Sainte-Chapelle du Palais, where the finest church services in the capital were held. For instance, in 1665 the Masses, Vespers and processions founded by a religious fraternity required three sopranos, two altos, three countertenors, three tenors, a baritone, four basses, two choirboys and an organist. These forces could bear comparison with the Musique du Roi, which indeed often recruited singers from the choir of the Sainte-Chapelle; important musicians such as the La Guerres, Louis Chein, Thomas Gobert, René Ouvrard, Etienne Loulié and François Chaperon worked there.

At Notre Dame the *Te Deum* was sung with many extra singers and instrumentalists, musicians in the king's service joining those of the cathedral itself. The musical director of Notre Dame from 1664 to 1694 was Jean Mignon, who composed a number of masses. At St Denys, where the kings and queens of France were buried, the funeral of Queen Marie-Thérèse in 1683 called for a large number of musicians.

The parish churches of Paris played a more modest part than these great churches (and were rather conservative compared with the Chapelle Royale). This was primarily because of financial restrictions: two to six choirboys, some other singers, an organist and a player of the cornett or serpent were the usual musical personnel of such churches. There were reinforcements from outside on feast days for High Mass, Vespers and so on. The repertory had not anticipated the use of orchestral instruments in masses, where plainsong alternated with organ verses improvised on liturgical themes. One or two singers for each part, with continuo, were enough for polyphonic choruses. Dialogues and *petits motets* for one or two voices were adequately accompanied by the organ alone. In any case, it might not seem fitting to introduce into divine service violins and oboes, which were the instruments of dance music, or flutes and trumpets, which were heard at the opera. Several parish priests complained to the archbishop about the so-called novelties introduced into church music which made the Office resemble a play and brought 'indecencies' into the liturgy.

Modern taste was preferred in religious houses and colleges (particularly by the Jesuits), where favourable financial conditions and a high intellectual and artistic level justified experimentation and created new fashions. The Théatins were in the vanguard:

> It was complained to the King that the Théatins, on the pretext of making a devotion to the souls in Purgatory, had a veritable Opera sung in their Church, where people went on purpose to hear the music, that the door was guarded by two Swiss, that seats were sold there for ten sols, that with all the alterations, and everything it was found possible to add to this devotion, it was billed as if it were a new play . . .[15]

The height of snobbery was to attend the service of Tenebrae at the Assumption or the Abbaye-aux-Bois, especially if 'what one heard was by M. Charpentier'.[16]

These complaints were to be reiterated by both humble ecclesiastics and eminent men of letters such as La Bruyère and Le Cerf de la Viéville:

> Very many people no longer go to High Mass or Vespers in the Cathedrals unless the Bishop is officiating there with additional Musical forces; nor to Tenebrae unless the lessons are set by the hand of a famous composer. It is only twenty-five years ago that Drums and Trumpets were added. Finally, I know of Churches, among others one in a Parish of this City, where the Passion is sung to music on Good Friday.[17]

Paris during the 1680s (lagging some decades behind the music of the royal household) was to see religious music transformed under the combined influence of the court, Italian oratorio and the operatic style.

Should it be regretted that the Church was no longer the bulwark of an outworn tradition, which had allowed Gregorian chant to degenerate while the psalms were sung as unconvincing paraphrases, disguising songs as devotional *airs*, and which fabricated Christian stanzas that were a long way from the Catholic liturgy? All in all, Lalande's *grands motets*, with their *symphonies*, more faithfully conveyed the thought of the psalmist.

In the first rank of composers of religious music in the capital, mention must be made of Marc-Antoine Charpentier (1643–1704), Lully's unfortunate rival in the opera house but a composer loaded with commissions by Mlle de Guise, the Dauphin, Port Royal, the academies and colleges. An admirer of Carissimi and a frequenter of the pro-Italian circles of St André-des-Arts and its parish priest the Abbé Mathieu, he was soon to be appointed *maître de musique* to the Jesuits at St Paul and St Louis and *maître de musique* to the Duke of Chartres (the future regent of France) before ending his career at the Sainte-Chapelle in 1698. His massses, motets, litanies, hymns, psalms, lessons for Tenebrae, canticles and *tragédies sacrées* combined skill with sensitivity, treated sacred texts with equal success on both a grand and an intimate scale, and respected tradition while favouring innovation.

THE STREET

Once the political unrest of the mid-century abated, the ordinary citizen could enjoy some peace and quiet again. The revolts had had their day. However, the famous were never immune from criticism.

58. Some of the street cries of Paris: engraving

Great lords, tamed by the centralization of power, became courtiers; but perhaps the people preferred them as political rebels than as the pale reflections of a blazing sun. Song-writers continued lampooning them and making fun of their amorous adventures. They also took as their target the strong men of the regime, chosen by Louis XIV to help him in his task, and the industrious bourgeoisie, whose new riches, however well deserved, did not escape mockery.

The street songs of the time mercilessly show us the reverse of the coin: the trial of Fouquet, the king's mistresses, the taxes imposed by Colbert, and his death ('Caron étant sur le rivage / Voyant Colbert dit aussitôt: / Ne vient-il pas mettre un impôt / Sur mon pauvre passage?' – 'Charon, on the bank, seeing Colbert said at once: is he not going to put a tax on my poor ferry?'), the king's quarrels with the papacy, and so on. The Pont Neuf with its twelve arches, dominated by the statue of Henri IV, was the scene of festivals in which merchants and sellers of trinkets rubbed shoulders with tumblers, dancers and mountebanks, water-sellers and instrumentalists. It was a place where contesting versifiers would give their couplets to humble anonymous musicians who arranged familiar tunes. The musical stock-in-trade on which these song-writers drew came from popular songs, carols and, from 1673 on, parodies of operatic arias. Other festivities also brought the people out into the streets: the fireworks on St Louis's Day, the pre-Lenten carnivals, aquatic sports on the Seine. There was musical accompaniment on these occasions, but simply as a background.

At the fairs, on the other hand, theatre and music combined to amuse any passer-by who stopped to watch. Two fairs were held in Paris: the Foire St Laurent and the better-known Foire St Germain, which went back to the Middle Ages. In the later seventeenth century it brought together in the area around the abbey of St Germain, in February, merchants who set up shop, trading freely, and entertainers of every kind: tumblers, tightrope walkers, puppeteers, keepers of performing animals. Gambling booths and wine-shops attracted the riff-raff, servants and soldiers, and society gentlemen, licentious when they pleased, made their way there too. Increasingly, amusement supplanted trade. Entertainers found themselves in such demand at the fairs that the Académie Royale de Musique, newly granted its privilege, was upset, fearing competition from an attractive form of theatre which made people laugh, and worried by the satirical wit of the plays performed on these boards which mocked the *tragédie en musique*. Lully had restrictive rules passed regulating the use of singers and instrumentalists in these farces. All they did was stimulate public taste for opera – comic opera, which was to develop in the eighteenth century.

However, the common people were not wholly lacking in respect. Occasions of royal pageantry entailed festivities with lavish musical accompaniment provided by trumpets, kettledrums, oboes, bassoons and violins. The first of these was the triumphal entry of Louis XIV after his marriage to the Infanta Maria Theresa in 1660, and mention has already been made of the people's readiness to applaud the parade in the carousel of the Tuileries in 1662. Or the king might fall seriously ill; to celebrate his return to health, the Hôtel de Ville held a banquet for him on 30 January 1687. The provost of the merchants and the aldermen fussed around him, while an orchestra played during the meal.

THE CORPORATIONS

On the streets the people might be bustling about and amusing themselves; indoors, in the shops and workshops, they were at work. Dancers, instrumentalists and instrument makers, who taught their trade or sold their wares, lived in rather circumscribed areas: the Ile de la Cité (in the parishes of St Barthélemy and the Madeleine), around the Hôtel de Ville (in the parishes of St Gervais and St Jean-en-Grève), along the rue St-Martin (in the parishes of St Jacques-de-la-Boucherie, St Merry and St Josse), near the chapel of

St Julien-des-Ménétriers, their patron saint (in the parishes of St Leu and St Gilles and St Nicolas-des-Champs), or in rather less central areas such as the parishes of St Eustache and St Etienne-du-Mont.

Dancing-masters and instrumentalists depended on an outworn corporate system and were subject to the King of the Minstrels, Guillaume Dumanoir, one of the 24 Violons du Roi.[18] At his request, Louis XIV renewed the statutes of the corporation in 1658. The period of apprenticeship was set at four years. However, the dancing-masters tried to break away from Dumanoir's moral and financial authority. Conflict soon ensued between musicians and dancers (we hear an echo of it in Molière), the latter claiming superiority, thanks to the king's support. Questions of honour, power and money were at stake. In 1682 there was a break between the dancing-masters and the master instrumentalists, to the disadvantage of the latter, who lost their status for a while. The violin, freed from its association with the dance, to which it had been tied for too long, could now express itself in works that imposed fewer constraints and were more personal in nature, and it at last found its true identity. It was in the years 1660–90 that the fate of the violin family was decided, to the benefit of a national school of violin playing.

The corporation of instrument makers still operated in accordance with its statutes of 1599; they were to remain in force until 1776. Apprentices engaged to serve six years with a master who would give them board and lodging and teach them the trade. An apprentice must not work for another master or absent himself without leave. The sworn members of the corporation ratified the contract. A young man emerged from his apprenticeship furnished with a certificate of proficiency when he had made his 'masterpiece'. Private teachers flourished in the capital. Du Pradel[19] gives their names and addresses: masters who taught organ and harpsichord, singing-masters, lute, theorbo, viol and violin masters, teachers of wind instruments, dancing-masters. At the end of the century, about 130 were listed in this little book. The most famous were already in the king's service or about to join his household, among them Marais, Lalande and François Couperin. The addresses of several good makers of instruments, tuners and music sellers complete the picture; for example, 'Roman strings for Instruments are sold wholesale in the rue Saint Denis, at the Trois Maillets', or 'At the Reigle d'Or, in the Place aux Chats, near Saint Innocent, may be found a large assortment of Ruled Paper for Music'.

CONCERTS

As a result of private enterprise, concerts were often held in the houses of celebrated musicians, who thus established a reputation as performers, got a hearing for their compositions and ensured them-selves a supply of pupils.

Pierre Chabanceau de La Barre, His Majesty's organist, gave *concerts spirituels* in his house in Paris, attended by 'very important' persons. Professionals performed there, for instance the violinists Louis Constantin and Lazzaro or Lazzarini Salami, called Lazarin, the viol player Nicolas Hotman, the organist Michel de La Guerre, Jean Granouilhet Sablières, the Duke of Orléans's *intendant* of music, singers from the Chambre du Roi, the singer Anne de La Barre. For a time the lutenist Dessansonières invited his friends every Thursday to 'a kind of little opera' written by Louis de Mollier, with Elisabeth Jacquet de La Guerre at the harpsichord. The harpsichord also featured 'at the house of the illustrious Certain'. Rémy Médard asked the *Mercure galant* to announce his guitar concerts, which took place once a fortnight. Sainte-Colombe and his two daughters performed viol trios at his house, while the lutenist Jacques Gallot opened his house to his music-loving friends every Saturday and even invited the ambassadors of Siam when they were visiting Paris.

There was no shortage of musical soirées at the houses of the aristocracy either. The chronicler Loret, the *Mercure galant* and the letters of Mme de Sévigné mention some of them. Mme de La Fayette had Mlle Hilaire singing in her apartment; the Countess du Lude invited the singer Mlle Raymond, who herself held soirées. Ninon de Lenclos seemed to go to them all. Mlle de Guise enter-tained a very select musical group at her house, where Loulié and Charpentier shone. M. de Marsillac promised his guests 'celestial music'. At the Hôtel de Condé, the Princess of Conti presented singing, dancing and fine spectacles.[20]

THE ACADEMIES AND THEATRES

Private persons were not alone in promoting the arts in Paris. The State played its part. The current fashion was for academies more or less on the Italian model. Did the chronology of their foundation reflect the prior claims of one over another? First came the Académie de Peinture et Sculpture (1648), then the Académie des Sciences (1658) and the Académie de Danse (1661), the Académie des Inscriptions et Belles Lettres (1663) and the Académie d'Architec-ture (1670), not forgetting the Académie de France in Rome (1668). Music might seem to have been of minor importance, since the Académie Royale de Musique was not founded until 1669 and did not actually come into being until 1672. A century earlier, however, Jean-Antoine de Baïf had associated it with his work in his Académie de Poésie et de Musique (1570), an institution in which, however, men of letters predominated.

The steps now taken were quite different. Louis XIV wished to endow the capital with a large musical theatre, a theatre open to the paying public, although he reserved for himself and his court the first hearing of works written for it. In the 1650s the influence of Cardinal Mazarin, who had invited Italian theatrical troupes, singers and composers such as Cavalli to France, had introduced an operatic mode new to the Parisians, who did not always take to it.[21] But might it not be possible to take this new genre and adapt it to the French language and French taste? Pierre Perrin, a poet in the circle of Gaston d'Orléans, made the project reality, working together with the composer and organist Robert Cambert: in 1669 he requested and obtained from the king the privilege for the setting up of musical theatres in France on the Italian model, but exclusively for works in the French language. The performances would be charged for, to reimburse the director for the expense incurred in the course of this onerous enterprise: the salaries of the singers, dancers and instrumentalists, machines, scenery and costumes, the hiring of halls and the maintenance of order.

The first attempts at opera, which derived from the *ballet de cour* and the *pastorale*, do not seem to have been very successful. Moreover, the administration of the Académie, which had been imprudently entrusted to unscrupulous men, involved Perrin in debts that he could not meet. He found himself in prison, while Cambert went into exile in London, where he was to come to a sad end in 1677. It was thus necessary to reconsider the project, since the public, intrigued by the novelty of the spectacle, wanted more. Lully, fortified by the trust of Louis XIV, attracted by the spirit of enterprise, and sure of having a solid financial basis (amassed since he took up the post of *surintendant*), suggested to Perrin with the king's consent that he might buy his privilege, thus liberating him from prison and his creditors. After several quarrels and legal actions involving the collaborators of the dispossessed poet, Lully finally, and thanks to Colbert, obtained registration of the letters patent in March 1672.

The new privilege was different in some respects from that laid down in the original text. It envisaged 'musical pieces which will be composed in French verse as well as in other, foreign languages'. This was a pointless clause, since the *surintendant* was not going to have any pieces but his own performed. 'Private schools of music' were to train performers for the new style. Lully set up temporarily near the Jardins du Luxembourg, gathered together the performers who made up the first troupe, and improvised a spectacle consisting of fragments from previously produced ballets (*Les fêtes de l'Amour et de Bacchus*, with words by Molière, Isaac de Benserade and Philippe Quinault, 1672). It was a year of transition, which allowed him to perfect his first *tragédie en musique*, *Cadmus et Hermione* (1673), to appoint his collaborators, the poet Quinault and the stage designer Carlo Vigarani, to form his orchestra and train his singers. He was granted the use of the hall of the Palais Royal, and undertook alterations to extend it and make it suitable for the requirements of stage settings with machinery.

Now began the long sequence of Lully's dramatic works performed at the Académie Royale de Musique, one a year between 1673 and 1687. The *tragédie en musique* was based on a mythological and/or pastoral libretto. The genre became fixed – rigidly so, some said – in a structure comprising an overture in the French style (a slow movement dominated by dotted rhythms, followed by a fugal allegro), which all Europe would take as a model for many years to come; an allegorical prologue that was a kind of compliment to the king, depicting some current event; and five acts divided into scenes of varying length and importance. The music alternated between recitative responding to the accentuation of the text (Lully's contemporaries said that he took his inspiration from the declamation of the actress Marie Champmeslé, famous for her performance in the works of Racine), *airs* with varying amounts of ornamentation but close to the spoken word, dialogues, duets and trios, choruses which were usually for five voices and often homophonic, ballets integral to the action or danced divertissements, instrumental ritornellos and interludes, and descriptive *symphonies* depicting storms, battles, hunts or the appearances of deities.

The composer himself excelled in several important areas: overtures, chaconnes and passacaglias, *airs* evoking sleep, scenes in the underworld. Some of his music is still widely remembered: the *airs* of Charon in *Alceste* and Venus in *Thésée*, the trio of the Fates and the trembling chorus in *Isis*, the duet of Proserpine and Pluto in *Proserpine*, Amadis's *air* 'Bois épais' in *Amadis* and, in *Armide*, the sleep scene of Renaud and the great dramatic recitative of Armide, 'Enfin, il est en puissance', which is a pinnacle of French declamation. Lully was supported by a company of extremely talented artists, who could do full justice to his music.

We may deplore the fact that the draconian application of the system of privilege stifled other efforts, delayed the development of other composers, and lent uniformity to a theatrical language which would have benefited from greater diversity. But despite a certain stiffness, Lully, the Racine of music, established a model that was to last for nearly a hundred years, by way of Rameau, up to the time of Gluck.

For those who preferred a less grandiloquent and more entertaining kind of theatre there were comic operas. The Comédie-Italienne offered laughter, singing and dancing; its influence increased during

59. Lully's opera
'Thésée' (Act 5 scene iv:
King Aegeus recognizes
his son Theseus by his
sword), first performed
at St Germain-en-Laye
in 1675: drawing
(school of Berain) for
the frontispiece of the
libretto

the Mazarin epoch, although there was opposition to it later. At once entertainment and satire, French comedy grew out of the Italian farce of the *commedia dell'arte* to raise itself to a genre of a nobler kind, even if it was not acceptable to the moralists. In Paris, people attended spectacles where music and dance mingled: *comédies en musique*, *comédies-ballets*, *pastorales comiques*, masquerades. Molière's troupe met with general approval, first at the Petit Bourbon and then at the Palais Royal. He himself was applauded in *Le mariage forcé*, *La comtesse d'Escarbagnas* and his last play, *Le malade imaginaire* (1673), from the time when he had just quarrelled with Lully. La Grange, the faithful secretary of the troupe, speaks in his records of the great expense incurred in this last play for the music alone: twelve string players, three other instrumentalists, seven singers, fees to Beauchamp for the ballets, Charpentier for the music and Baraillon for the costumes. Lully could not stand the competition; he got the king to order a reduction in the musical content of comedies on the grounds of the privilege granted to the Académie de Musique. Molière died, the troupe broke up and took refuge in the rue Mazarine, and from then on the Opéra occupied the hall of the Palais Royal. But France could not do without its comedians. Relief would come, and from 1680 the troupe was known as the Comédie-Française.

*

The functions of the court musician and the city musician differed, but sometimes the same person fulfilled both roles. It is difficult to establish an exact hierarchy of the status of the various types of musician. Roughly speaking, we may place on the bottom rung of the ladder – occupied by the *petits bourgeois* who manufactured things and thus belonged to the manual trades – the makers of instruments and also the shopkeepers who sold instruments, strings, musical equipment and music paper. (M. Jourdain, according to Molière, never got over having a father who was a cloth merchant.)

The reputation of violinists and oboists was not much more enviable. Classed with the hurdy-gurdy players and fiddlers of former times, vagabonds and bear-leaders who played music for dancing at weddings and banquets, they suffered from the low esteem in which their corporation was held (years after Lully's death, Couperin would spell it out in *Les fastes de la grande et ancienne Ménestrandise* in his eleventh *ordre* for harpsichord).

We may pass over the army musicians – players of trumpets and kettledrums, fifes and drums, with fine uniforms but poor manners: rough, given to bad language and frequenters of taverns. Lutenists, theorbists, viol players and harpsichordists, on the other hand, were better regarded because of the respectable tradition to which they belonged and the more polished and sophisticated music they played.

Dancers were less esteemed than singers. Among singers, however, we must distinguish between those who performed in the salons and were treated attentively and with courtesy and those who performed on the stage for the Académie de Musique and belonged, more or less, to the world of actors. The greatest prestige was enjoyed by the singers of the parish churches and the Chapelle Royale, who were often churchmen respected for their morality, though the facts might sometimes give the lie to such *a priori* reasoning. The palm went to the organist because of the musical dialogue he held with the priest at the altar, and his skill in composition.

On each rung of the ladder, success was variable, and it was always possible for a lutenist, violinist or opera singer to gain fortune and even fame. The composer towered above them all. But his creativity was subject to many constraints. He wrote only on commission, whether for the churches, the colleges, the middle class, the aristocrats or the king. From the motet to the opera, from the dance suite to the divertissement, everything was designed for a particular occasion. Music reflected the society in which it was conceived. Sometimes the servile status of music even obliged composers to write easy pieces when amateurs wanted to perform in an ensemble.

The composer had to take account of the cliques which divided music and sometimes had to belong to them. What place should he give in his works to Italian influence, secretly admired but officially deplored? Did the Lullist supremacy succeed in scrambling the messages that came from Rome, Florence and Venice? Did not the *surintendant* himself, whether consciously or not, respond to the call from his native country in certain areas of his work?

The composer thus saw himself confronting aesthetic problems which forced him to follow fashions dictated by men of letters. He obeyed watchwords such as 'the natural': less an injunction to imitate nature than a pastoral sentiment, and one not free from affectation either – rejecting artifice and encumbrances and favouring the humanization of characters and situations. He took as his basic tenets reason, equilibrium and, in vocal music, the comprehensibility of the words, avoiding pedantry. He left the last word to good taste, a fitting compromise between heart and mind. And if composers could not be 'men of quality' some could justifiably consider themselves 'gentlemen'.

NOTES

[1] 'Pleasures and festivals'; I quote the title of Emile Magne's classic study: see Bibliographical Note below.

[2] *Les Plaisirs de l'isle enchantée ou les festes et divertissemens du Roy à Versailles, Divisez en trois journées et commencez le septième jour de may de l'année 1664* (Paris, 1673).

[3] ibid.

[4] A. Félibien, *Relation de la feste de Versailles du 18e juillet 1668* (Paris, 1668).

[5] A. Félibien, *Les Divertissemens de Versailles donnez par le Roy à toute sa Cour, au retour de la conqueste de la Franche-Comté, en l'année 1674* (Paris, 1676).

[6] Mémoirs du marquis de Sourches, 28 May 1686, quoted in *La Musique à la cour de Louis XIV et de Louis XV d'après les Mémoirs de Sourches et Luynes (1681–1758*, excerpts collected by Norbert Dufourcq (Paris, 1970), 13.

[7] This organization had been set up earlier; for discussion of it earlier in the seventeenth century, see Chapter XI above.

[8] This was on the site of the vestibule of the present chapel, raised above the present Salon d'Hercule. Du Mont and Lully would have seen only the foundations of the great chapel of today; building of it was constantly deferred for lack of money, and it was not consecrated until June 1710.

[9] Goupillet was obliged to leave his post in 1693, accused of claiming authorship of motets composed by Henry Desmartes; Colasse (d 1709) made his career in secular rather than sacred music; and Minoret left his post in 1714. Lalande (1657–1726), on the other hand, gradually took over all four quarters himself.

[10] *L'Etat de la France*, 1684.

[11] He was to give up the post in 1686 in favour of one of Lully's sons, Jean-Louis, who himself was succeeded after his early death by the much more talented Lalande in 1689.

[12] Secretariat of the royal household, 1661.

[13] *Plan monumental de Paris au XVIIe siècle . . . dédié à Sa Majesté le Roy Louis XIV en l'An de grâce 1653, par Jacques Gomboust, Ingénieur de la Couronne*.

[14] For a fuller description of the geography of Paris, see pp. 218–22 above.

[15] Actes du Secrétariat de la Maison de Roi, 6 November 1685.

[16] *Le Mercure galant*, April 1680.

[17] J. L. le Cerf de la Viéville, *Comparaison de la musique italienne et de la musique françoise*, 98.

[18] Further on Dumanoir, see p. 230 above.

[19] N. de Blégny (called A. Du Pradel), *Le livre commode des adresses de Paris* (Paris, 2/1692).

[20] The real *grand concert* did not appear until 1725, at the time of the founding of the Concert Spirituel at the Tuileries.

[21] See p. 234 above

BIBLIOGRAPHICAL NOTE

General history

Out of the great abundance and diversity of books on Louis XIV himself, pride of place goes to P. Gaxotte, *Louis XIV* (Paris, 1974). Also important are P. Goubert, *Louis XIV et vingt millions de français* (Paris, 1966); D. Ogg, *Louis XIV* (Oxford, 1967); and F. Bluche, *Louis XIV* (Paris, 1986). To these may be added J. -P. Néraudau, *L'Olympe du Roi-Soleil* (Paris, 1986), associating mythology with the royal ideology, a point of central importance in the arts of the period. *Destins et enjeux du XVIIe siècle* (Paris, 1985), ed. J. Mesnard, throws light on the heritage, continuing traditions and innovations of a century with many different facets. F. Bluche, *Dictionnaire du grand siècle* (Paris, 1990) is invaluable.

In the musical sphere, an introduction to French music of the *ancien régime* is provided by two small complementary syntheses: J.-F. Paillard, *La musique française classique* (Paris, 1960), and M. Benoit, *Les musiciens du roi de France, 1661–1733* (Paris, 1982), both in the 'Que sais-je?' series. However, the standard reference work, on a larger scale, is J. R. Anthony, *French Baroque Music from Beaujoyeulx to Rameau* (London, 1973, 2/1978; Fr. trans., as *La musique en France à l'époque baroque*, Paris, 1981, 2/1992). There is also M. Benoit, *Dictionnaire de la musique en France, aux XVIIe et XVIIIe siècles* (Paris, 1992).

The court

An understanding of the music of the time requires some knowledge of the places where that music was made. P. de Nolhac's important two-volume study is our main source of information about Versailles: *Versailles et la cour de France* (Paris, 1925). There is also a remarkable and more recent synthesis by P. Verlet: *Versailles* (Paris, 1961). For St Germain-en-Laye, the king's favourite residence during the first part of his reign, G. Lacour-Gayet, *Le château de Saint-Germain-en-Laye* (Paris, 1935), is of interest. The arts were practised so intensively there, both at the Château-Vieux and the Château-Neuf, that some musicians went to live within its precincts; here C. Massip, 'Musique et musiciens à Saint-Germain-en-Laye, 1651–1683', *RMFC*, xvi (1976), 117–52, is useful. M. Benoit has used contemporary documents to demonstrate the importance of the various royal residences to the composition of music: see *Versailles et les musiciens du Roi, 1661–1733* and *Musiques de cour: chapelle, chambre, écurie, 1661–1733* (both Paris, 1970).

A great many musical *fêtes* and other musical entertainments were given at these residences. Contemporary documents provide us with a number of written accounts of these events, some of them official, such as the reports of the *Mercure galant*, an inexhaustible source of information which we have only just begun to tap. More precise information comes from recognized historians: A. Félibien, *Relation de la feste de Versailles du 18e juillet 1668* (Paris, 1668); idem, *Les divertissements de Versailles donnez par le roy à toute sa cour au retour de la conqueste de la Franche-Comté en l'année 1674* (Paris, 1676); and the Abbé Bourdelot, *Relations des assemblées faites à Versailles dans le grand appartement du roy pendant le carnaval de l'an 1683* (Paris, 1683). Their accounts served as the basis for later works such as C. Racinet, *Les plaisirs de l'isle enchantée [1664], La*

The Early Baroque Era

feste de Versailles du 18e juillet 1668 et les divertissements de Versailles donnés par le roy en 1674: Notice historique, bibliographique et judiciaire (Paris, 1859).

More realistic and less respectful writers of the age include G. Tallemant des Réaux in his *Historiettes*, ed. L. J. N. Monmerqué and P. Paulin (Paris, 3/1854–60), and J. Loret in *La muze historique ou Recueil des lettres en vers contenant les nouvelles du temps* (Paris, 1650–65): see Y. de Brossard, 'La vie musicale en France d'après Loret et ses continuateurs, 1650–1688', *RMFC*, x (1970), 117–93. Private correspondence sometimes gives a more personal view of events, either superficial, as with the Marquise de Sévigné – see M. Vilcosqui, 'Une mélomane au XVIIe siècle: Madame de Sévigné, 1626–1696', ibid, xvii (1977), 31–93 – or knowledgeable, as in the exchange of letters between René Ouvrard and Claude Nicaise: see A. Cohen, 'The Ouvrard-Nicaise Correspondence (1663–93)', *ML*, lvi, (1975), 356–63. E. Magne provides a superb account of the court festivities in his standard work *Les plaisirs et les fêtes: les fêtes en Europe au XVIIe siècle* (Paris, 1930). More recent studies include R. M. Isherwood, *Music in the Service of the King* (Ithaca, 1973), and M.-C. Moine, *Les fêtes à la cour du Roi-Soleil, 1653–1715* (Paris, 1984).

The city

The Church, still a dominant force, employed a great many musicians, who had to be familiar with the ceremonial then in force: see M. Sonnet, *Cérémonial de Paris* (Paris, 1662). Two places of worship were especially prominent. On the Sainte-Chapelle du Palais, see M. Brenet, *Les musiciens de la Sainte-Chapelle de Paris* (Paris, 1910); and on the cathedral of Notre Dame, see A.-M. Yvon, *La vie musicale à Notre-Dame de Paris aux XVIIe et XVIIIe siècles* (Paris, 1966), and D. Taitz-Desouches, 'Jean Mignon (1640–1710), maître de chapelle de Notre-Dame de Paris: Contribution à une histoire de la messe polyphonique au XVIIe siècle', *RMFC*, xiv (1974), 82–153. On other places of worship in the city, see B. Gérard, 'La musique dans les églises de la Cité, aux XVIIe et XVIIIe siècles, d'après les registres paroissiaux, 1611–1773', *RMFC*, xvi (1976), 153–86.

On the organ, see the relevant parts of the magisterial five-volume study by N. Dufourcq, *Le livre de l'orgue français, 1589–1789* (Paris, 1969–85). On secular music in private establishments see M. Brenet, *Les concerts en France sous l'Ancien Régime* (Paris, 1900), and T. Gérold, *L'art du chant en France au XVIIe siècle* (Paris and Strasbourg, 1921).

Early writings on the stage music of the period include M. de Pure, *Idées des spectacles anciens et nouveaux* (Paris, 1667); P. C.-F. Menestrier, *Des représentations en musique, anciennes et modernes* (Paris, 3/1685); and idem, *Des ballets anciens et modernes, selon les règles du théâtre* (Paris, 4/1686). More recent important studies include C. Nuitter and E. Thoinan, *Les origines de l'opéra français d'après les minutes des notaires, les registres de la conciergerie et les documents originaux conservés aux Archives nationales* (Paris, 1886); L. de La Laurencie, *Les créateurs de l'opéra français* (Paris, 1921); P. Mélèse, *Le théâtre et le public à Paris sous Louis XIV: 1659–1715* (Paris, 1934); idem, *Répertoire analytique des documents contemporains d'information et de critique concernant le théâtre à Paris sous Louis XIV* (Paris, 1934); M.-F. Christout, *Le ballet de cour de Louis XIV, 1643–1672: mises en scène* (Paris, 1967); J. de La Gorce, *Bérain: dessinateur du Roi-Soleil* (Paris, 1986); idem, *L'Opéra à Paris au temps de Louis XIV: Histoire d'un théâtre* (Paris, 1992).

On the great many obscure musicians, instrument makers, music teachers and music sellers in Paris, see N. de Blégny (called A. Du Pradel), *Le livre commode des adresses de Paris* (Paris, 1692), F. Gaussen, 'Actes d'état civil de musiciens français, 1651–1681', *RMFC*, i (1960), 153–203; and Y. de Brossard, *Musiciens de Paris, d'après le fichier Laborde, 1535–1792*, (Paris, 1965). The irreverent and satirical street songs popular with these people have been collected: see P. Barbier and F. Vernillat, *Histoire de France par les chansons*, ii (Paris, 1956). The craftsmen working in shops formed themselves into corporations but often quarrelled: see G. Dumanoir, *Le mariage de la musique avec la dance* (Paris, 1664); B. Bernhard, *Recherches sur l'histoire de la corporation des ménestriers ou joueurs d'instruments de la ville de Paris*, Bibliothèque de l'Ecole des Chartes, iii–v (Paris, 1841–4); C. Pierre, *Les facteurs d'instruments de musique* (Paris, 1893); P. Loubet de Sceaury, *Musiciens et facteurs d'instruments de musique sous l'ancien régime* (Paris, 1949); and M. Benoit, 'L'apprentissage chez les facteurs d'instruments de musique à Paris', *RMFC*, xxiv (1986), 5–106.

There are numerous studies of individual Parisian composers who spent part of the year at least at court. Among them are: N. Dufourcq, *Jean-Baptiste de Boësset: un musicien officier du roi et gentilhomme campagnard, 1614–1685* (Paris, 1962); H. Quittard, *Un musicien en France au XVIIe siècle: Henry Du Mont* (Paris, 1906); N. Dufourcq, *Un officier de la maison du roi: Nicolas Lebègue, organiste de la Chapelle royale et de Saint-Merry, 1630–1702* (Paris, 1954); C. Massip, *Michel Lambert, 1610–1696: contribution à l'histoire de la monodie en France. L'homme et l'oeuvre. Catalogue* (diss., Sorbonne, Paris, 1985). There are three works by H. W. Hitchcock on Charpentier: *Marc-Antoine Charpentier: catalogue raisonné* (Paris, 1982); 'Marc-Antoine Charpentier: Mémoire and Index', *RMFC*, xxiii (1985), 5–44; and *Marc-Antoine Charpentier* (Oxford, 1990), as well as C. Cessac, *Marc-Antoine Charpentier* (Paris, 1988).

There have been numerous books and a great many articles about Lully and his works. They include L. de La Laurencie, *Lully* (Paris, 1911); H. Prunières, *La vie illustre et libertine de J.-B. Lully* (Paris, 1929); idem, *Lully* (Paris, 2/1927); *J.-B. Lully: the Founder of French Opera* (London, 1973); J. E. W. Newman, *Jean-Baptiste de Lully and his tragédies lyriques* (Ann Arbor, 1979); J. Hajdu Heyer, ed., *Jean-Baptiste Lully and the Music of the French Baroque* (Cambridge, 1989); J. de La Gorce and H. Schneider eds, *Jean-Baptiste Lully: Actes du Colloque tenu à Saint-Germain-en-Laye et Heidelberg en 1987* (Laaber, 1990); P. Beaussant, *Lully ou le Musicien du Soleil* (Paris, 1992); and M. M. Couvreur, *Jean-Baptiste Lully: musique et dramaturgie au service du prince* (Brussels, 1992). There is also a monumental catalogue of his works: H. Schneider, *Chronologisch-thematisches Verzeichnis sämtlicher Werke von Jean-Baptiste Lully* (Tutzing, 1981).

Chapter XIII

London, 1603–49

PETER WALLS

The years between the accession of James I and the execution of his son saw unparalleled political and religious turmoil. Musically, though very rich, these years were less revolutionary than in some other parts of Europe. English music in this era might almost be described as 'reluctantly Baroque'. A real divide in the history of English musical taste is marked by the period of the Commonwealth: London after the Restoration was more obviously cosmopolitan than before. In the first half of the century, awareness of continental developments seems to have been haphazard and their adoption rather idiosyncratic. But this was not entirely negative; so often the real eloquence and interest of music in this period (and this has been seen as a characteristic of English music in other ages as well) comes from a peculiar blend of avant-garde expression with more conservative styles and techniques.

Needless to say, this division between pre- and post-Commonwealth is not totally clear cut. Despite the obvious administrative continuity between the establishments of the first two Stuarts, it happens that the end of James I's reign coincides with the deaths of so many remarkable composers that it might well be considered something of a turning-point. William Byrd died in Essex in 1623. In the same year, Thomas Weelkes died in London (though alcoholism had effectively put an end to his career as organist at Chichester Cathedral some years earlier). Orlando Gibbons died in 1625 at Canterbury, where he had gone as a member of the Chapel Royal to welcome Henrietta Maria from France. (His sudden death caused a smallpox scare among the royal entourage.) Giovanni Coprario lived long enough to be appointed the first 'composer in ordinary' by Charles I, but died within a few months. John Dowland died in 1626 and Alfonso Ferrabosco (ii) in 1628. (Even Thomas Tomkins, who lived until 1656, retreated from the London musical scene in the 1630s, living in Worcester and concentrating on his position as cathedral organist there.) The reign of Charles I was dominated by composers whose interests seem more clearly Baroque: Nicholas Lanier, William and Henry Lawes, John Jenkins, John Wilson.

270

Moreover, with the exception of William Lawes, all of these Caroline musicians lived on to re-establish some sense of continuity in the early years of the Restoration.

LONDON: INTRODUCTION

London was growing at an extraordinary rate. In the course of the sixteenth century its population had expanded from 40 000 to an estimated 250 000; by 1640, at 400 000, it had almost doubled again, making it much the biggest city in Europe. Historians attribute the growth partly to changing economic patterns – London became the major port for the export of cloth – and partly to the fact that the Stuart court was much more London-centred than the Tudor court had been. The major legal courts were based in London. James I did not continue Elizabeth's practice of staying for extended periods in the country houses of the nobility (her shrewd way of limiting household expenses). Instead, Whitehall became the permanent base for the court's activities. Those who worked within the orbit of the court numbered about 2000, and their impact on the life of London was considerable. At any one time there would have been about 20 000 apprentices in the city area, and a huge number of citizens were really poor. It has been estimated that towards the end of this period 33% of the male population in England (and 10% of women) could read. Literacy was higher in towns than in the country and better in London than anywhere else. All but 18% of apprentices and 31% of servants could at least sign their names.[1]

People seeking access to the court had to come to the city, and the wealthy began acquiring London houses simply for the enriched social and cultural life of the metropolis. In 1616 James I complained to the Star Chamber that 'one of the greatest causes of all gentlemen's desire, that have no calling or errand to dwel in London, is apparently the pride of women . . . because the new fashion is to be had no where but in London.'[2] Successive royal proclamations attempted (unavailingly) to discourage gentry and peerage from remaining in London during those periods when the legal courts were not in session. A census carried out in 1632 found that a quarter of the peerage lived in London without any particular reason, and it has been estimated that by then three-quarters of the aristocracy kept houses there.[3] This, together with the recruitment of musicians from the provinces for the court musical establishment, means that music in London cannot be considered entirely separately from music in other regions. John Wilbye (1574–1638), for example, was very much a provincial musician. He spent his life in the service of the Kytson family in Cambridgeshire and Essex, but he must have spent some time in London with the family; the Augustine Friars, the

60. *A Fête at Bermondsey: painting (c1570) by Joris Hoefnagel (note the two fiddle players accompanying dancers on the right)*

Kytsons' London house, is the address he uses in the dedication to his *First Set of English Madrigals* (1598).[4]

We get some sense of the music of the less privileged from play texts such as Beaumont and Fletcher's *The Knight of the Burning Pestle*. Musicians frequented taverns. Morris dancing and the singing of catches and rounds were popular. Broadside ballads – 'broadside' because they were printed on a single folio sheet – catered to unsophisticated tastes. These commented on topical events, and normally the sheet indicated what well-known tune would fit their words. (Some of these tunes – 'Sellenger's Round' for example – ended up in more complex musical arrangements.) The consort-song settings of the Cries of London by Gibbons, Weelkes, Dering and others, together with some of Thomas Ravenscroft's rounds, allow us a satirical glimpse of the street music of tinkers, fish merchants, beggars and their kind.[5] Citterns hung in barber shops for the amusement of waiting customers.

THE THEATRES

The public theatres, located of necessity outside the jurisdiction of the city on the south bank of the Thames, were at the peak of their popularity in the early seventeenth century. The most famous of all, the Globe (in which so many of Shakespeare's plays were performed), was erected in 1599. When it burnt down in 1612, it was replaced immediately. This second Globe Theatre, able to hold an audience of 3000, was demolished in 1644 after the theatres had been suppressed. It seems likely that musicians were accommodated in different parts of the structure according to the demands of a particular production. A great deal of music was heard in the playhouses and their environs. Indeed, in the eyes of the extreme Puritan William Prynne one of the things that made theatres unhealthy places for the virtuous was the fact that plays were always accompanied by 'amorous Pastoralls, lascivious ribaldrous Songs and Ditties . . . [and] effeminate lust-provoking Musicke'.[6] Apart from the songs, signals (tuckets, sennets, flourishes etc.) and loud or soft music which formed part of the plays' texture, the theatre provided opportunities for incidental musical entertainment. Until 1614 at the Globe (and longer in other theatres) plays concluded with a jig – a comic song-and-dance routine for which (in the Jacobean period) the actor William Kemp was particularly famous. The Swiss traveller Thomas Platter left a fascinating account of seeing Shakespeare's *Julius Caesar* on an autumn afternoon in 1599:

> . . . after lunch, about two o'clock, I and my party crossed the water, and there in the house with the thatched roof witnessed an excellent performance of the tragedy of the first Emperor Julius Caesar with a cast of about fifteen people. When the play was over they danced marvellously and gracefully together as is their wont, two dressed as men and two as women.[7]

Women did not appear on the public stage; female roles (and consequently songs associated with them) were performed by boys. The one notorious exception was Marion Frith, who caused a scandal at the Fortune Theatre, where she sat on stage 'in the public viewe of all the people there presente [dressed] in man's apparel & played upon her lute and sange a song'.[8]

The public theatres – large, open to the skies and accommodating aristocrat and apprentice alike – declined in the Caroline period. The smaller indoor theatres (often called 'private', though the only barrier to entrance was a considerably higher admission charge) assumed greater importance in the overall picture. Initially the venue for plays performed by children from the choir schools (principally the children of the Chapel Royal and St Paul's), such theatres became the home for established acting companies. In 1608 Shakespeare's company, the King's Men, began using the second Blackfriars Theatre as a winter base. Burbage had actually built his theatre there in 1596, shrewdly utilizing a central city site which, as an ancient monastic 'liberty', lay outside the control of the city

273

61. Interior of the Swan Theatre: sketch by Johannes de Witt, made during a visit to London in 1596

authorities. He was, however, prevented from using it because the wealthy residents of the area succeeded in obtaining an injunction from the Privy Council on the grounds that, among other things, 'the playhouse is so neere the Church that the noyse of the drummers and trumpetts will greatly disturb and hinder both the ministers and parishoners in tyme of devine service and sermons'.[9] Ironically, such musical signals seem to have been less evident in the indoor theatres than in the public playhouses. On the other hand, the more favourable acoustics of the private theatres encouraged the use of music there. In an afterword to *Sophonisba* (1606) John Marston seems even to be a little self-conscious about the amount of musical reference: 'let me entreat my reader not to tax me after the fashion of the entrances and music of this tragedy, for know it is printed only as it was presented by youths and after the fashion of the private stage'. The indoor theatres seem to have had a music room: musicians were normally located in a curtained recess above the stage and flanked on either side by galleries for members of the audience.

THE PROFESSION

The great dramatists of the age were, by and large, professional writers and men of the theatre. The position of the composer is, broadly speaking, analogous. A few (whose situation parallels that of many poets in the period) did not earn their living through music. Michael Cavendish (*c*1565–1628) was a gentleman composer, though he complained that he had been 'humbled with adversities'.[10] Thomas Campion, who was both poet and composer, qualified in medicine at the University of Caen; he lived on the fringes of court life and in serving one of his patrons became (unwittingly it seems) mixed up in the scandal of Sir Thomas Overbury's murder by the Earl and Countess of Somerset. Tobias Hume (identified in court records as a Scot)[11] had served as an army officer in Sweden and Russia; he turned to the arts in his retirement.

These were exceptions, however. Some composers entered the service of wealthy noblemen. Thomas Vautor, for example, was in the household of James I's favourite, the Duke of Buckingham. John Ward rose to the rank of attorney in the Exchequer, but also served as a household musician to the Remembrancer of the Exchequer, Sir Henry Fanshawe. Employment in the service of the nobility could function as a stepping-stone to service at court. Nicholas Lanier, first appointed to the King's Musick as a lutenist and singer in 1616, had been in the service of the Cecil family until April 1614. Others found employment as church organists. Martin Peerson was choirmaster at St Paul's in London from about 1624, and John Hilton was organist and clerk at St Margaret's, Westminster, from 1628 (both retained their posts even after the onset of the Civil War).

Among musicians we find quite a degree of social mobility. Henry Youll was a pauper who ended up as a respectable household musician. Wilbye was the son of a tanner, but prospered to the extent that when he died in 1638 he was able to leave his 'best vyall' to the Prince of Wales. Giles Farnaby was a joiner's son and was himself apprenticed at the age of twenty to the Joiners' Company (though it seems likely that he may have been first and foremost a virginal maker).

Music was for certain families the obvious and expected profession. Ten members of the Lanier family were active as musicians in the reign of James I. William and Henry Lawes were the sons of a bass singer at Salisbury Cathedral (and their two brothers were also employed as cathedral singers). The other two sons followed in their father's footsteps as cathedral singers (Thomas at Salisbury and John at Westminster). Places within the King's Musick tended to pass to other members of the same family. When Alfonso Ferrabosco (ii) died in 1628 the four positions he held in the royal establishment passed to his sons.

The Early Baroque Era

Many musicians tried to earn a living in London, some simply by playing in taverns or in the streets. The need for some form of control on this sort of activity was clearly felt. In 1604 the guild of London musicians (recognized by the City authorities early in the sixteenth century) were granted royal letters patent incorporating them as the Company of Musicians. This body was thus able to take responsibility for the behaviour of musicians and to protect their interests. Two years later the provisions of their charter were reinforced by a set of by-laws.[12] These, for example, protected musicians from sharp practice and from casual employers trying to engage groups of fewer than four. Throughout the period there was an uneasy relationship between the Company and the members of the King's Musick, who insisted on their independence. In 1635 the king's musicians gained a royal charter which gave them exclusive control over the profession and which, by asserting continuity with one given in the reign of Edward IV, effectively ignored the rights over music making in London claimed for the Company of Musicians in 1604. The feuding between the two groups continued; in 1638 London's aldermen gave the Company a new ordinance which recognized them as 'an ancient brotherhood of this city' and insisted on their right to act independently of the royal musicians.

The City maintained its own musical organization, the Waits. By the early seventeenth century they had long since lost their original function as a watch and operated solely as professional performers on call for civic needs. At this time there were on average ten men and up to twice as many apprentices in the group. With a basic annual salary of £20, these musicians were reasonably well paid (though there were instances of several men sharing one post). Their expertise on a range of instruments (including, in the seventeenth century, violin and lute) was considerable. In 1613, a special section of the Waits called 'the city music of voices' was established. The Waits played in public at the Royal Exchange on holidays and Sundays (though in 1642 Puritan objections put paid to the Sunday performances). In addition to their official duties, it is clear that members of the Waits picked up a lot of casual work (notably in the theatres). Westminster (governed separately from London by appointees of the Westminster Abbey chapter) appointed six musicians of its own in 1611 and thereafter sought to prevent outsiders playing in inns and public places within the city's boundaries.

The most prestigious kind of employment for a musician was to be found in the service of the king (or other members of his family). The Chapel Royal was the group of singers and organists (normally 32 gentlemen and twelve boys) retained to perform divine service in the royal presence. When necessary, these musicians would travel: in 1617 and 1633, for example, they accompanied the king to

62. *The Ratification of the Spanish marriage treaty in the Chapel Royal, Whitehall, 20 July 1623 (note the musicians in the left-hand balcony): engraving*

Scotland. Although the children would sing throughout the year, the full group of singing-men was heard only on special occasions – the funeral of James I and the coronation of Charles I are well-documented examples. For most of the time, the chapel worked on a rota system which allowed the gentlemen alternate months off. Thomas Tomkins was able to remain as the organist in charge of music at Worcester Cathedral even after his appointment to the Chapel Royal in 1621. Likewise, in 1623 Orlando Gibbons added the post of organist at Westminster Abbey to his duties as organist of the Chapel Royal (a position he had held since about 1605). This system was clearly open to abuse; in the records of the chapel (kept by the Clerk of the Cheque and hence known as 'the Cheque Book') we find – amid the injunctions not to wear spurs or large boots under surplices – attempts to spell out the limits of permissible absences under the rota system. On the other hand, pluralists in the Chapel Royal were often forced by court duties to neglect their other posts.[13]

Alongside these adult professionals, boys sang the treble and mean lines. They formed a very important section of the Chapel Royal and of all other established collegiate or cathedral choirs. (In London this meant, in addition to the Chapel Royal itself, Westminster Abbey and St Paul's.) In 1604 Nathaniel Giles, as Master of the Children of the Chapel Royal, was commissioned to visit 'cathedralls, Collegiat

Churches, Chappells and Schooles Where publique teaching of Musicke is used' to find boys who could sing well. (Henrietta Maria had boys trained in France for her music.) Once recruited into a choir, boys were given a good music education. Moreover, when their voices broke (much later than in modern times) choristers from the Chapel Royal were entitled to a place at university.[14] The contract which Martin Peerson as Master of the Choristers at St Paul's signed with the Dean (the poet John Donne) conveys a good sense of the kind of care that children attached to such establishments might expect. In addition to looking after their physical welfare, Peerson was enjoined to 'teach the children the grounding of Christian Religion as contained in the short catechism, also in writing and also in the Art and Knowledge of Musicke that they may be able thereby to serve as choristers. They must also be brought up in vertue, civility and gentleness of manners.'[15]

The King's Musick was the secular branch of the royal musical establishment. In James I's reign this accounted for about 40 musicians, and the number rose to an average of 65 under Charles I. They did not normally perform as a single ensemble, although grand occasions such as court masques involved most of the members of the King's Musick in one way or another. For other state occasions – royal baptisms, funerals and the like – groups from the King's Musick would unite with members of the Chapel Royal. Wind players were rostered to play at royal dinners. The biggest sub-group in the King's Musick were the lutes, viols and voices (with 25 members from 1625). Violinists had been listed among those in the service of the court since the mid-sixteenth century; by the early seventeenth they constituted a violin band – a balanced five-part group. (It has been pointed out that this group – a regular part of the King's Musick in Jacobean and Caroline times – makes Louis XIII's '24 Violons du Roi' seem less of a landmark than has often been thought.[16]) Composers were attached to each group. The sense of the various sub-groups operating separately comes through strongly in a memorandum from the Lord Chamberlain's office addressed in 1630 to members of the King's Musick reminding them that Nicholas Lanier, as Master of the King's Musick, had dining rights with each section. The note stresses that this arrangement (which it seems some of the musicians may have resented) was necessary so that Lanier could see that 'the king bee well & duly served wth his severall Musiques according to ye times & order of their wayting'.[17]

Other members of the royal family – notably the queen and the Prince of Wales – retained their own groups of musicians. What is most striking here is the exceptional quality of these musicians (some of whom held positions in the King's Musick concurrently). Prince Henry's establishment included the outstanding keyboard performer and composer John Bull, the lutenist and songwriter Robert Johnson, the lutenist Thomas Cutting, the violinist Thomas Lupo (appointed as the first Composer for the Violins in the King's Musick in 1622) and Thomas Ford. After his death, many of Prince Henry's musicians were taken into Prince Charles's establishment (when that was officially formed in 1616). They were joined by other illustrious figures: Orlando Gibbons, John Danyel and (in 1618) Giovanni Coprario.

The households of the children and wives of the first two Stuarts have a particular interest because of their concentration of highly-favoured foreign musicians who may have played a significant role in familiarizing their English colleagues with continental styles. Among the servants of Queen Anne who were provided with livery for the funeral of Prince Henry, five Dutch and four French musicians were listed. No further mention of these Dutch musicians (who are not individually identified) appears in the court records, but French musicians were a regular part of the queen's establishment (seven took part in her funeral). These were absorbed into the even larger group of French musicians attached to the household of Charles I's queen, Henrietta Maria. Among the French musicians, violinist/dancing-masters were prominent. In 1604 two Frenchmen were appointed to instruct Prince Henry in defence and dancing (though when the dancing-master died he was replaced by the Englishman Thomas Giles). Prince Charles, as Duke of York, also had two French tutors appointed, one to teach writing, the other, Sebastian de La Pierre, as a dancing-master. De La Pierre subsequently became one of Henrietta Maria's musicians and, together with Etienne Nau, was responsible for the composition and choreography of dances in a number of Caroline masques and plays. In 1623 yet another French dancing-master, F. de Lauze, published an *Apologie de la Danse*, dedicated to James I's favourite, the Duke of Buckingham (whose own dancing in court masques had drawn considerable admiration). These Frenchmen left their mark on the elaborate dances so central to masques at court, and they may well have had an influence on violin playing.

The lutenist Jacques Gautier came to England in 1617, on the run after murdering a nobleman. By 1625 he had received a post at court, and he became Henrietta Maria's lute teacher. In 1627 Gautier, in trouble once more, was imprisoned in the Tower and possibly even tortured for scandalous behaviour which, it was rumoured, included the boast that 'by the dulcet tones of the lute he could make his way even into the royal bed'. His disgrace was not permanent, however, and he remained in the royal service. Ennemond Gaultier (1575–1651) also played at the English court in about 1630. Since French lutenists devised the tunings associated with the Baroque rather than the Renaissance lute, the presence of these players may well have acted as a catalyst. New tunings do crop up in English lute manuscripts of the period (such as the Margaret Board Lutebook compiled in the 1620s). English interest in things French, especially after the accession of Charles I, can be seen in George Filmer's *French Court-Aires with their Ditties Englished* (1629) and in the way the court masque adopted structural features from the *ballet de cour* (particularly the succession of 'entries' or character dances).

There had been an influx of Italian musicians in the reign of Elizabeth I and the interest then in the Italian madrigal is well documented. The generation of the *stile rappresentativo* is less well represented, but again the musicians retained by the queen and the Prince of Wales ensured that English musicians had at least some opportunity to hear native exponents of the new style. In 1607 the lutenist John Maria Lugario was appointed by Queen Anne as a groom of her privy chamber at the exceptionally high salary of £100 'in regard of his skill and verie speciall quality in Musicke'. More important, Prince Henry (and then Charles as Prince of Wales and king) employed another Italian lutenist, Angelo Notari, whose *Prime musiche nuove*, published in London in 1613, contained some Italian monody.

Not that Italian musicians necessarily had to bring the new style in person. Robert Dowland's *A Musicall Banquet* (1610) contains two songs by Caccini, one the extraordinarily popular *Amarilli mia bella* (which appears in other English manuscript sources and in an arrangement by Peter Philips in the Fitzwilliam Virginal Book). Some English musicians went to Italy. Dowland was in Florence in 1595 and probably met Caccini. Nicholas Lanier visited Venice acting as a courier for the Privy Council early in 1611. A year earlier he had made a similar trip to Paris. At the beginning of Charles I's reign he made a more extended visit to Italy with a budget of £2000 to buy paintings for the royal collection.

The relative prestige of these modes of employment is reflected in the salary scales they attracted in the reign of James I. Some musicians ostensibly in the service of a member of the nobility seem to have received little more than a badge or livery which acted as some protection against being treated as a vagrant. At the top end of private patronage, those retained by Robert Cecil, first Earl of Salisbury (1563–1612), were paid an annual salary of £20. This was equal to the stipend paid to members of the Waits in London. By and large, employees of the court were more generously rewarded. The most common payment was £30 (usually expressed as 20*d*. per day) plus a livery allowance of just over £16. Foreigners tended to fare better than Englishmen: the violinist Jacques Cordier and the lutenist Adam Vallet both received salaries of £60. The Gentlemen of the Chapel Royal were well paid: in 1604 their salaries were set at £40, roughly three times the national average for ecclesiastical singing positions.

Musicians retained by members of the royal family other than the king seemed, on the whole, to do considerably better. The appointment of Alfonso Ferrabosco (ii) as a music teacher to Prince Henry brought him £50 per annum, and the salaries paid to Queen Anne's five French musicians ranged as high as £155. The position of Master of the King's Musick, created by Charles I in 1626, carried an annual stipend of £200, which Nicholas Lanier received over and above his salary as lutenist. All of these salaries could be supplemented by special payments for engagements like performing in court masques.

Pluralism was common. There were, too, perquisites for some of the more favoured members of the royal establishment. Orlando Gibbons and four others were granted a monopoly on making strings ('called Venice, or Romish minikin, and Catlin strings') for musical instruments. Few monopolies bore such a direct relationship to the holders' professional interests. Alfonso Lanier was authorized to check the weights of hay and straw brought into London and Westminster (and to charge a levy on each load weighed), while his brother Innocent shared with Alfonso Ferrabosco and another man a monopoly for dredging the Thames (which again brought with it a share of fines and levies).

A few other figures might help place these salaries in perspective. Court records suggest that £10 would have bought a reasonable lute or viol in the Jacobean period, though Alfonso Ferrabosco was paid twice that for a lyra viol purchased in 1623. A treble cornett in the late Jacobean era cost less than £2. Violin prices in the period ranged from £2 paid in 1607 to £24 for 'a Cremona violin' bought in 1638. (Two tenor violins acquired for the court at about the same time cost £12 each.) A labourer earned about 10*d.* a day (about £12 a year), while a yeoman working the land would have an income somewhere between £40 and £200 per annum. A pint of beer cost a halfpenny, admission to the yard in the public theatres a penny, a seat in a gallery twopence or (for a cushion and an even better view) threepence. The cheapest place in the indoor theatres cost sixpence. In 1626 Nicholas Farnaby leased a house from the Parish of St Olave's Jewry (where he was parish clerk) for 30*s.* (£1. 10*s.*) per annum; in the 1630s the Countess of Carlisle paid an annual rent of £150 for what has been described as a modest house in the Strand.[18]

63. *The Temple of Speculative Music from Robert Fludd, 'Utriusque Cosmi . . . Historia' (1617); the structure embodies various aspects of the theory of music*

MUSIC EDUCATION AND SOCIETY

Many professional musicians got their training through being apprenticed for seven years to an experienced member of the Musicians' Company or the King's Musick. Such a person could eventually apply for the degree of Bachelor of Music from Oxford or Cambridge by presenting a musical exercise (and this did not require a period of residence as a student). The training of a professional musician is clearly important, but what about their audience? What kind of musical education could be expected among the gentry and aristocracy? The question needs to be tackled in two parts, since a true humanist would, on the one hand, want to know about music and, on the other hand, to have some facility in practical music.

The preamble to Thomas Morley's *Plaine and Easie Introduction to Practical Musicke* (1597) had assumed – despite the book's explicit concentration on practical matters – that an educated person would be able to participate in a discussion about speculative music. *Musica speculativa* sought to explain music's position in the whole scheme of creation by describing the interlocking of *musica mundana* (which informs the well-ordered workings of the macrocosm), and *musica humana* (which informs the human body – the microcosm – and, by analogy, the body politic) with *musica instrumentalis* (the actual music we perform). These ideas, transmitted from Plato to European Renaissance civilization via Boethius, were the basis of the study of music as one of the seven liberal arts. In the early Stuart period the basic tenets of these theories were being called into question as the Ptolemaic cosmology on which they were ultimately founded was displaced by the theories of Copernicus. (These, although formulated in the 1530s, had still not gained total acceptance a century later, as the trials of Galileo so vividly illustrate.) Francis Bacon, whose thinking provided a foundation for empirical science, expressed his impatience with traditional musical understanding, complaining that it was 'reduced into certain mystical subtilties, of no use and not much truth'.[19] The undermining of a world view which had seemed so secure was lamented by John Donne in *The First Anniversary*, where the death of the young girl who is the subject of the poem is made one with a sense of a disintegrating cosmos. Donne's conceit here is, of course, to speak of the loss of a particular kind of perception as a destruction of order itself:

> And new Philosophy calls all in doubt
> The element of fire is quite put out;
> The sun is lost, and th'earth, and no man's wit
> Can well direct him where to look for it . . .
> 'Tis all in pieces, all coherence gone . . .

The new world order directly affects music. Plato, Donne remarks, would have described the young girl *as* harmony:

> She by whose lines proportion should be
> Examin'd, measure of all Symmetry,
> Whom had that Ancient seen, who thought souls made
> Of Harmony, he would at next have said
> That Harmony was she, and thence infer
> That souls were but Resultances from her . . .

Despite – or rather because of – this dismantling of its rationale, the countless allusions to the ideas of speculative music in the early years of the century have a peculiar imaginative force. Martin Peerson still felt neo-Platonic metaphor to be appropriate in the dedication he wrote for *Mottects or Grave Chamber Music* in 1630. There he refers to 'that heaven upon earth, which it found here, in Musicke and Harmonicall proportions, the being whereof is beyond Mortalitie and regulates the whole frame of nature in her being and Motions'.

Shakespeare assumes familiarity with the theories. Lorenzo's explanation to Jessica of the power of music in *The Merchant of Venice* (Act 5, scene i) is a classic assertion of music's ability to influence states of mind. In *Troilus and Cressida* (l.iii) Ulysses analyses the troubles of the Grecian state in terms of discordant music:

> Take but degree away, untune that string,
> And hark what discord follows! Each thing melts
> In mere oppugnancy: the bounded waters
> Should lift their bosoms higher than the shores,
> And make a sop of all this solid globe . . .

When Henry Lawes uses the same metaphor ('these dissonant times') in his preface to *Choice Psalmes*, published in 1648 as a memorial to his brother William, it is hard to be sure whether this is a rather casually used (though personally appropriate) metaphor or the residue of an obsolescent perception of social order. In a sense the problem is still with us, since, for example, we happily allow a working assumption that the sun rises in the east to coexist with a completely different understanding of the workings of the solar system.

What we might now call music's therapeutic powers (its ability to restore *musica humana* through a kind of sympathetic vibration) is used in *King Lear*, *The Winter's Tale* and, most beautifully, in *Pericles*, where the physician Cerimon uses music to revive the apparently dead Thaisa (3.ii):

> The still and woeful music that we have,
> Cause it to sound, beseech you.
> The viol once more. How thou stirr'st, thou block!
> The music there! I pray you give her air.
> Gentlemen,
> This queen will live; nature awakes; a warmth
> Breathes out of her. She hath not been entranc'd
> Above five hours. See how she 'gins to blow
> Into life's flower again.

Attitudes to the place of practical music in the upbringing of a gentleman ranged from suspicion of effeminacy to the view that no person could claim to be truly educated without some accomplishments in music and dancing. An ambivalence comes through when Shakespeare's Troilus gives expression to unfocussed jealousy that some cultivated Greek might seduce his Cressida. He attributes to his rivals the kind of musical and dancing skills that a self-respecting Englishman would wish to possess (4.iv):

> I cannot sing,
> Nor heel the high lavolt, nor sweeten talk,
> Nor play at subtle games – fair virtues all,
> To which the Grecians are most prompt and pregnant . . .

Sir Andrew Aguecheek in *Twelfth Night* is a comic parody of this type. When he is accused of being a fool and a prodigal, his friend Sir Toby Belch launches into a mock defence: 'Fie, that you'll say so! he plays o' th' viol-de-gamboys, and speaks three or four languages word for word without book, and hath all the good gifts of nature' (1.iii). Sir Andrew's gentlemanly aspirations are again underlined by his claims as a dancer. The puns used here assume a familiarity with dancing terms, including seventeenth-century *franglais* for cinq pas, an alternative name for a galliard (1.iii):

> Wherefore are these things hid? Wherefore have these gifts a curtain before 'em . . . Why dost thou not go to church in a galliard, and come home in a coranto? My very walk should be a jig; I would not so much as make water but in a sink-a-pace.

It is not only Shakespeare who shows (and expects from his audience) a familiarity with the technical language of music and dancing. In *The Malcontent* John Marston extracts humour from the intricacy of technical instructions. When one character admits to having forgotten how to dance a brawl (French *branle*), another explains (4.i):

> Why, tis but two singles on the left, two on the right, three doubles forward, a traverse of six round: do this twice, three singles side, galliard trick-of-twenty, coranto-pace: a figure of eight, three singles broken down, come up, meet, two doubles fall back, and then honour.

Clarendon presents William Cavendish, Duke of Newcastle, one of Charles I's most successful military leaders, as the embodiment of an ideal, describing him as 'active and full of courage and most accomplished in those qualities of horsemanship, dancing, and fencing which accompany a good breeding; in which his delight was'. And then he adds, 'Besides that, he was amorous in poetry and music to which he indulged the greater part of his time'.[20] This is exactly what courtesy books from Castiglione on sought to encourage, an image (as Peacham has it) of the complete gentleman.[21]

An equivalent ideal was held up for women, though an anxious concern with modesty meant that the opportunities for them to reveal their accomplishments to others were limited. This modesty was thought of as a feminine attribute (rather than something imposed on women by a patriarchal society) and, as an attribute of the coy mistress, could seem almost teasing. An anonymous Jacobean song plays with what were really clichés about female accomplishments in this way:

> My mistress is in musicke passinge skillful
>   and singes & plaies her part at the first sight
> But in her play she is exceeding wilfull
>   & will not plaie but for her owne delight.
> Nor touche a stringe nor plaie a pleasinge straine
>   unless you catch her in a merie vaine . . .[22]

Sight-singing was valued as a desirable skill. Women were encouraged to play the lute or the virginals, and the titles of various collections of music bear witness to this. The illustration on the 1613 title-page of *Parthenia* (the first virginal book and the first engraved music ever published in England; fig. 64) is a minor addition to a whole genre of works of art depicting ladies playing the virginals (and it is an idea which Shakespeare plays with in his beautiful Sonnet 128). Oliver Cromwell's niece owned a virginal book ('Anne Cromwell's Book', dated 1638).

Sir Andrew Aguecheek's vaunted expertise on the viol was typical of the class to which he aspired. Charles I studied the bass viol with Coprario. Many wealthy families possessed a 'chest' of viols for consort playing – ideally (according to Thomas Mace in 1676), two basses, two tenors and two trebles. In the sixteenth century, Sir Thomas Hoby had recommended that gentlemen should be able 'to play upon the Vyole, and all other instruments with freates', implicitly denigrating the violin as an instrument tainted by its association with dancing-masters and professionals. It was not until the middle of the seventeenth century that educated amateurs began to play the violin rather than the viol.

The Inns of Court were like colleges and provided young men with a legal training for the business of the city and for the developing civil service. There were four – The Middle Temple, the Inner Temple, Gray's Inn and Lincoln's Inn – and they commonly served as a transition to the 'real' world for students who had already had a liberal academic education at Oxford or Cambridge. The curriculum was vocationally orientated and included not just legal training but such social accomplishments as dancing. The poet Francis Quarles sold his gown while at Lincoln's Inn in order to pay for a lute case.[23] In 1633, while a masque was in preparation, Thomas Coke wrote from Gray's Inn to a relative: 'No law studied in the Inns of Court, now all turned to dancing schools'. The diary for 1635 of the young John Greene, a student at Lincoln's Inn, gives a picture of numerous

*64. Title-page of
'Parthenia' (London: G
Lowe, 1612/13), the
earliest collection of
English virginal music*

evenings there being passed in music making and dancing.[24] Standards, though, may have declined over the years. At any rate, one member of the Middle Temple in the Caroline period complained that 'the measures were want to be trulie danced, it being accounted a shame for any inns of court man not to have learned to dance, especially the measures. But nowe their dancing is tourned into bare walking.'[25]

A gentleman's education was often completed by what came to be known in this period as the Grand Tour. A number of accounts make it clear that cultural pursuits, including music, formed part of the agenda, and many young noblemen took their tutors along with them. When William Cecil, Viscount Cranborne, was planning his

European journey in 1610, he had wanted to take Nicholas Lanier with him as companion and viol tutor.

THE REPERTORY OF AMATEURS

Music printing flourished in London in the first decade of the seventeenth century – there were 42 separate publications. This, though, is not a straightforward reflection of demand since it coincides with important changes in trade practice. For the first time, a monopoly on the printing of music and manuscript paper did not have the effect of stifling publication. When James I came to the throne, he suspended all monopolies, although his stand on this was short-lived. When the patent was revived, however, it operated rather differently from in the sixteenth century. In 1606 William Barley was accepted as the legitimate successor to the music printing privilege (originally granted to Tallis and Byrd in 1575 and renewed in favour of Thomas Morley in 1598 after a gap of one year in which music printing had flourished unencumbered by any restrictions). As a printer rather than, like his predecessors, a musician, Barley had a more direct interest in ensuring that the monopoly was commercially profitable. For a time, business seems to have thrived. (When Barley died, the monopoly was taken over for five years or so by three members of the Stationers' Company before it finally lapsed in 1619.[26]) Music publishing tailed off again in the 1630s. The reasons for this decline are not entirely clear, especially since this trend runs against those in the larger book-publishing trade (where the number of books published each year more than doubled between 1600 and 1640).

Songs, consort music, and pieces for lute, virginals or viol circulated in manuscript. To many, the normal and natural way of acquiring new compositions was to copy them (or, if you were wealthy enough, to engage someone else to copy them for you). In 1582 it was observed that the monopoly on publishing actual music was worth less than the exclusive rights on manuscript paper, a claim Morley was to repeat when negotiating for the privilege in 1598. This would still have been true 40 years later. Many manuscripts have the character of commonplace books – personal anthologies which tell a story of informed taste and musical enthusiasms. Thomas Myriell, the rector of St Stephen's Walbrook from 1616 to 1625, painstakingly copied several manuscripts of music for voices and viols.[27] Their contents show that he must have been in touch with court musical circles and that he had a particular interest in Italian music. Francis Tregian, the compiler of the Fitzwilliam Virginal Book, also copied a sizable vocal manuscript while in the Fleet prison. This manuscript reflects the recusant's Italianate taste.

In the early seventeenth century the vogue for madrigal publication was waning; the lute song now predominated in published collections. These songbooks regularly offer different performing possibilities – solo voice with lute (and/or viol), or four-part vocal ensemble – and they were set out so that performers seated around a table could all face their own parts. From the composer's point of view, publication in itself did not guarantee any significant financial returns, although a gift of money from the dedicatee seems often to have followed. Tobias Hume received £5 in 1607 when he dedicated his *Poeticall Musicke* to Queen Anne (who herself played the lyra viol).[28] The vast majority of poetry set in the lute-song volumes is anonymous, and it seems that lyrics may have been given to composers by people whose social status meant that they would have been embarrassed by any publicity their literary efforts might have brought. This is most clearly suggested in Robert Jones's preface to his *First Booke of Songs or Ayres* published in 1600: 'I confesse I was not unwilling to embrace the conceits of such gentlemen as were earnest to have me apparell these ditties for them; which though they intended for their private recreation, never meaning they should come into the light, were yet content upon intreaty to make the incouragements of this my first adventure'. The process of composers' acquiring lyric poems for setting became quite an important way in which these poems were transmitted to a wider public. The first poems by both Sidney and Donne to appear in print did so because they were set to music.

The two most prolific composers of lute-songs, Campion and Dowland, have been seen as representing opposing tendencies in the genre. Campion's professed aim was to provide a musical equivalent of the epigram – short, apparently artless, pithy songs. Dowland's approach was both more complex and technically more conservative. His vocal lines fit into a basically contrapuntal texture. But by 1612, when *A Pilgrimes Solace* appeared, a new style was emerging. Dowland's preface to this volume has a defensive tone: '. . . yet do these fellowes giue their verdict of me behinde my backe, and say, what I doe is after the old manner: but I will speake openly to them, and would haue them know that the proudest Cantor of them, dares not oppose himselfe face to face against me'. As if to prove his point, *A Pilgrimes Solace* contains songs which show an awareness of the avant garde. Apart from the Italian song 'Lasso vita mia', there are a number of ayres in a declamatory style – ones with a relatively static bass line supporting a chordal/harmonic accompaniment which allows the vocal line to retain the flexibility of natural speech. The opening section of 'Welcome blacke night' is a superb example. There is an obvious parallel between this and the *stile nuovo*.

The manuscript collections of the 1630s are dominated by continuo song, with, for the most part, a simple bass line rather than lute tablature. The composer most closely identified with the development of a new declamatory style is Nicholas Lanier. It is with Lanier that the first use in English of the term *stilo recitativo* is associated: according to Ben Jonson, the masque *Lovers Made Men*, performed in 1617, was 'sung (after the Italian manner) *Stylo recitativo*, by Master Nicholas Lanier'. Although the reliability of that reference has been questioned, it is clear that Lanier was an innovator.[29] His song 'Bring away this Sacred Tree' (from Campion's *Somerset Masque* of 1613) is thoroughly declamatory in the way the accentuation and pacing of the vocal line is governed by the inflection and stress patterns of normal speech.

Declamatory writing dominates the song manuscripts of the 1620s and 30s. While the style may have developed as an English response to Italian innovations the results were distinctive. The approach of Alfonso Ferrabosco (ii) to setting Italian words in a declamatory style was very different from his treatment of English. While the declamatory ayre in the Caroline period is not always very interesting, in the hands of composers such as Robert Johnson (*c*1598–1633) or John Wilson (1596–1674) it could be wonderfully eloquent. The literati were quick to see that the style was one which by its very nature respected the rhythmic structure of the verse being set. This is the essence of Milton's appreciative sonnet addressed to Henry Lawes (the master of declamatory writing):

> *Harry* whose tuneful and well-measur'd Song
> First taught our English Musick how to span
> Words with just note and accent, not to scan
> With *Midas* ears, committing short and long . . .

The distinctive character of English declamatory writing has led some to question whether it has very much at all to do with an awareness of the principles of *seconda prattica* composition. There was, in fact, only one vocal writer who explicitly acknowledged a debt to the Italians: Walter Porter (*c*1595–1659), reputedly a pupil of Monteverdi. Porter's *Madrigales and Ayres* (1632) advertises some of its novel Italian features – 'continued Base, with Toccatos, Sinfonias, and Rittornellos' – on the title-page. (Perhaps only George Jeffreys's sacred works – written anyway at the very end of this period – share so explicit an interest in Italian *seconda prattica* devices.[30])

The tension between a respect for tradition and an awareness of new directions is a productive force in the instrumental music of the period. The continuation of Renaissance contrapuntal practices is nowhere more obvious than in the In Nomine repertory – keyboard and consort works using the Benedictus from Taverner's Mass *Gloria tibi Trinitas* as a cantus firmus. This tradition, which goes back to

Taverner himself, is continued in the early Stuart period by, among others, Orlando Gibbons, Thomas Tomkins, John Ward, John Bull, Alfonso Ferrabosco (ii), Thomas Weelkes, William Lawes and John Jenkins. (Purcell was still writing In Nomines in the 1680s.) The fantasia or fancy was by nature contrapuntal; Christopher Simpson described it as a sort of music in which 'the composer, being not limited to words, doth employ all his art and invention solely about the bringing in and carrying on of . . . fugues'.[31] Yet the most striking characteristic of many Jacobean and Carolean fantasias is their emotional force. Some of Coprario's five- and six-part consort pieces appear to be transcriptions of Italian madrigals, a link which perhaps helps explain the mannered harmonic vocabulary in this literature as a whole. The kind of expressiveness found particularly in the works of William Lawes – a pupil of Coprario – is thoroughly Baroque. Lawes's priorities were well summed up later in the century by Anthony Wood, who observed that 'to indulge the ear – he broke sometimes ye rules of mathematicall composition'.[32]

A considerable amount of consort music in the first half of the seventeenth century included violins. There are 23 fantasia-suites by Coprario for one or two violins, bass viol and organ (according to Playford, Charles I preferred these above all other music[33]). Jenkins and William Lawes both wrote a comparable number of such works. They have a special appeal in the way they combine some of the pleasures of contrapuntal consort music with the more extrovert Baroque character of idiomatic violin music. Lawes's 'Royal' and 'Harp' Consorts (comprising approximately 100 separate movements in total) all include violins. They are also notable for their use of theorbo in a basso continuo role (although the parts are never figured).

Music for lyra viol and division viol is distinctively English but was to have a profound influence on the Continent later in the Baroque period. The terms refer primarily, not to specific instruments, but to styles of playing – chordal on the one hand and characterized by rapid passage-work ('divisions') on the other. Nevertheless various writers refer to a lyra viol as an instrument (Queen Anne bought one), and Christopher Simpson advised the division violist to use a smaller instrument than a normal bass viol (in order to make rapid left-hand passage-work more possible).[34] Tobias Hume brought the lyra viol a certain notoriety since he attracted Dowland's wrath by suggesting that it was the equal of the lute. Ferrabosco and Lawes made the most significant contribution to the development of this style. Ferrabosco's playing in particular amazed the French viol player André Maugars, who spent some time in England as one of Henrietta Maria's musicians.[35]

The Early Baroque Era

SACRED MUSIC

Sacred music in this era is surrounded by conflict and debate. The forms of the Anglican liturgy were those of the 1559 revision of the Book of Common Prayer. The Act of Uniformity which legislated for its use is the classic exposition of the Elizabethan *via media* in religious matters. In relation to music this attempts to balance a Protestant insistence on textual clarity ('as yf it were read without syngyng') with provision for anthems at Matins and Evensong 'in the best sort of melodye and musice that may be conveniently devysed'.[36] Looked at from an early Stuart perspective it might be thought that, rather than forging a broadly acceptable compromise, this may simply have postponed the final debate. In practice, the Injunctions must have been interpreted with a wide degree of latitude – services in the Chapel Royal were clearly very different indeed from those in London parish churches. An extensive and beautiful repertory reveals that, at the more 'Catholic' end of the spectrum, sections of the liturgy were sung for which the Prayer Book made no explicit provision. A complete 'Service' provided music for what we might now think of as three distinct liturgies: settings of *Venite*, the *Te Deum* and *Benedictus* for Matins, of the *Magnificat* and *Nunc dimittis* for Evensong, and of the Kyrie (as responses to the Commandments) and Nicene Creed for the 'second service' (actually the first part of the Communion service). The emphasis on non-sacramental liturgies is underlined by the absence of any settings from the first half of the seventeenth century of the Sanctus and the Gloria (both of which occur near the consecration in the Eucharist). Services and anthems (essentially non-liturgical motets) were classified as 'great' (polyphonically elaborate) or 'short' (in a more succinct note-against-note style). The Jacobean era is particularly associated with the development of the 'verse' style, in which full choral sections alternate with 'verses' for solo voices and organ (and sometimes other instruments).

Something of the achievements of the age is indicated by John Barnard's magnificent retrospective collection, *The First Book of Selected Church Musick* (1641). Barnard's intention had been to follow up this volume with others 'till the order of my Collections bring me downe to our newest, and now living Composers'. But this was not to be; and the evidence of surviving copies suggests that even *The First Book* was little known until the Restoration period.

It is hard to be sure quite what James I's personal attitude to the liturgy was. When, in his first year of office, he was presented with the Millenary petition by Puritans hoping that he would be more sympathetic to their point of view than Elizabeth had been, his response was to convene the Hampton Court Conference – a diplomatically non-committal gesture (whose most significant outcome was the initiation of the 1611 Authorized Version.) Peter Smart (writing in 1629) was adamant that the High Church innovations of Bishop Richard Neile in Durham ran counter to the king's own wishes. It is hard to believe that James was quite as insistent as Smart implies, but the passage is worth quoting if only because it portrays Puritan anxieties about the use of an elaborate liturgy in such vivid colours:

> . . . Can such paltry toyes bring to our memory Christ and his blood-shedding? Crosses, Crucifixes, Tapers, Candlesticks, gilded Angels, painted Images, golden Copes, georgious Altars, sumptuous Organs, with Sackbuts and Cornets piping so loud at the Communion table, that they may be heard halfe a mile from the Church? *Bernard* saith, no . . . The consideration of which impediments of devotion, moved our most learned and religious *King Iames*, when he received the holy Communion in this Cathedrall Church, upon Easter-day 1617, to give charge, or at least in his name charge was given (upon my knowledge I spake it, and in my hearing, in mine owne house) that the Communion should be administered in plain māner; it was expressly commanded, that no chanting should be used by the Quire-men, nor playing Organs or other Instruments. . .[37]

Nevertheless, the Jacobean period produced some of the greatest music for the Anglican liturgy. This flowering was aided by the ascendancy towards the end of James's reign of clerics with a High Church outlook. (Interestingly, all the known liturgical sources for music, which provide for performance by a divided cantoris/decani choir, date from after 1617.[38]) In 1619 Lancelot Andrewes, who preached that music was intended by God to be 'the conveyer of men's duties into their minds',[39] was appointed dean of the Chapel Royal – a position which made him directly responsible for its policy and conduct. He was succeeded in 1626 by William Laud, the person most strongly identified with a High Church outlook in the period.[40] As Charles I's Archbishop of Canterbury (from 1633 until his execution in 1645), Laud did his utmost to see that music, along with other aspects of service, conformed to an ideal of sophistication and dignity worthy of a liturgy rooted in an ancient past. In 1634 he carried out a visitation throughout the archdiocese requiring cathedral chapters and parish councils to report on (and, if necessary, to improve) the state of their choirs and organs. In some senses, the results speak for themselves. Within the confines of the Chapel Royal at least there is a strong stylistic sense of a 'great tradition' – Tallis, Byrd, Gibbons, Tomkins – sheltered from the most intense of the debates raging outside.

The atmosphere in which all of this was achieved was not straightforwardly supportive. An anonymous commentator on the state of church music in Jacobean England outlines in tones of regret the way in which inflation and a more general decline in the prosperity of choral foundations had conspired with indifference and antagonism to produce a situation in which the continuing viability of some of the established choirs seemed very much in doubt.[41] The fate of the organ vividly illustrates the contradictions of the Arminian era. Between 1605 and 1641 a good number of new organs were installed in provincial cathedrals and Oxford and Cambridge colleges (principally by Thomas and Robert Dallam).[42] But while this apparent organ revival was taking place, many London churches resisted the idea that they should replace the organs removed in the previous century. In response to a directive in 1637 that they repair their organ, the vestry of St Michael's in Crooked Lane, London, produced a set of 'Reasons against the Organ'. Their objections were, on the face of it, economic ones: the prosperity of the parish had declined.[43] But organs and the singing of choirs were regarded as popish vanities, and the production of tracts denouncing them grew to something of a torrent in the later Carolean period.[44]

In this context, George Herbert's poem 'Church Musick' – indeed *The Temple* (1633) in its entirety – seems less like an expression of innocent piety than part of a Laudian manifesto. In flaunting the language of love poetry to acknowledge that music induces a kind of sensual ecstasy, the poem goes right to the heart of what so worried the Puritans about music in church – they could not be so sure that it led straight to Heaven's door:

> Sweetest of sweets, I thank you: when displeasure
>   Did through my bodie wound my minde,
> You took me thence, and in your house of pleasure
>   A daintie lodging me assign'd
>
> Now I in you without a bodie move,
>   Rising and falling with your wings:
> We both together sweetly live and love,
>   Yet say sometimes, *God help poore Kings*.
>
> Comfort, 'Ile die; for if you poste from me,
>   Sure I shall do so, and much more;
> But if I travell in your companie,
>   You know the way to heavens doore.

The Puritans, for their part, approved of only one kind of music within the service: the singing of metrical psalms. Despite contemptuous references to 'Geneva jigs', psalm paraphrases found favour for both domestic and public devotions within a broad spectrum of the community. (Thomas Mace tells us how moved he was by the besieged royalists' singing of psalms in York Minster in 1644.)[45] The standard title-page of the Sternhold and Hopkins *Whole Booke of Psalms* emphasized their dual public and private applicability: 'Set forth and allowed to be sung in all churches, of all the people together before and after morning and evening prayer, and also before and after sermons: and moreover in private houses, for their godly solace and comfort, laying apart all ungodly songs and ballads, which tend onely to the nourishing of vice, and the corrupting of youth'. Well over a hundred separate editions of Sternhold and Hopkins appeared in the first half of the seventeenth century.[46] Such was the demand that the Stationers' Company were able to use their monopoly for the printing of metrical psalters (acquired from Thomas Day in 1603) to keep printers in business.

Publications of harmonized metrical psalms catered primarily to the domestic side of the market.[47] The first of these, published by Thomas East in 1592, went through a number of editions up to 1611 and provided a model for the metrical psalter that Thomas Ravenscroft produced in 1621 with harmonizations of the common tunes 'composed' by some very distinguished musicians, including Tallis, Dowland, Morley, Farnaby, Tomkins and Peerson. A few other publications, carefully staying outside the boundaries of the Stationers' Company monopoly, complemented the harmonized psalters. George Wither's *Hymns and Songs of the Church* (1623) is notable for the fact that the two-part settings are by Orlando Gibbons, and George Sandys's *Paraphrase upon the Divine Poems* (1638) for both the relative sophistication of the verse and for Henry Lawes's fine solo settings.

Recusant musicians found different ways of responding to the discomfort of official disapproval. John Bull joined Peter Philips in exile in 1613, and although he was to claim that this was for religious reasons it seems possible that his need to avoid prosecution for adultery was actually more pressing. Richard Dering lived abroad for a time but returned to England as a member of Henrietta Maria's household in 1625. William Byrd is not just the greatest composer among the English Catholics; he was also apparently the one prepared to risk most for his beliefs. While retaining nominal membership of the Chapel Royal in this period, Byrd effectively retired to Stondon in Essex, near Ingatestone Hall, which was the seat of the Catholic Petre family. In 1605, 1607 and 1610 he published the three parts of his *Gradualia*, which, together with his mass settings that had appeared in the 1590s, provide all the music needed for Mass according to the Roman rite for a large part of the liturgical calendar. This music was doubtless used in the clandestine celebrations of Mass which took place in the houses of the Catholic nobility, but it is thought that the publication may have had some form of Jesuit sponsorship and that it was intended for a continental audience.

65. *View of Whitehall from St James's Park, showing (left) the Banqueting Hall built by Inigo Jones (1619–22) for the performance of court masques: painting by Henry Danckerts (1630–78)*

What is certain is that a Jesuit named Noiriche was arrested for possessing copies of the first part. The worst harassment Byrd and his family suffered seems to have been their regular listing as recusants (and the consequent levying of fines). Anti-papist feeling ran high, particularly after the Gunpowder Plot of 1605, but it was held in check by the volatile equilibrium created by the episcopal sympathies of James I and the even more 'Catholic' attitudes of Charles I and Laud.

THE DECLINE AND FALL OF THE STUART MYTH

Music played a major part in the projection of the ideology of the Stuart court. The list of music written on the death of Prince Henry in 1612 is extensive and distinguished, a beautiful testimony to the hopes that surrounded the Prince of Wales. Moreover, it seems that the English settings of David's lament for Absalom (thirteen in all) and for Jonathan (nine) were also occasioned by the prince's death. The Absalom text gave composers an opportunity to portray James I's real grief for a son with whom he had had his differences.[48]

The most obvious occasions for the projection of the Stuart myth were masques at court. Although these entertainments had their origins in the sixteenth century, they entered a new phase with the accession of James I. He and his son were prepared to spend increasingly extravagant sums on masques – glamorous events calculated to impress foreign ambassadors with the court's apparent affluence and sophistication. The key persons behind this development were the poet Ben Jonson and the architect Inigo Jones. Both brought humanist ideals to their creations, and even though these entertainments were created for a single night they were determined not to treat them as casual and ephemeral. Instead, they strove to invest them with an artistic and moral integrity. Jonson insisted that his task was to devise a dramatic entertainment which would relate the particular event being celebrated at court to broader issues of state – to make 'present occasions . . . lay hold on more remov'd mysteries'. Jonson and Jones first collaborated on *The Masque of Blackness* in 1605; the way in which its plot related the visual and musical delights of the production to the specific circumstances of the court was to become typical. The masquers, the principal participants in these events, were always members of the court, not professional

66. Design by Inigo Jones for the costume of a Daughter of Niger in Ben Jonson's 'Masque of Blackness' performed at Whitehall, 6 January 1605; the costumes were criticized as indecorous and because the queen and her ladies had painted their arms and faces instead of wearing masks

actors or dancers. In the case of *The Masque of Blackness*, they were twelve ladies, the daughters of Niger (*see* fig. 66), whose quest for a land warmed by a greater light than the sun ends at the court of James I. (Louis XIV was not the only monarch to be depicted as a sun king in court entertainments.) Masquers' set dances and the social dances of the revels were normally introduced by songs and accompanied by large ensembles of lutes and violins. Here, and in the wild dances and grotesque or comic sequences of the anti-masque, professional musicians and actors were involved.

Unlike the writing of the text or the designing of sets and costumes, the composition of music for these masques was not the responsibility of a single person. For one of the masques performed at the infamous Somerset wedding in 1614, Thomas Campion, Giovanni Coprario and Nicholas Lanier all contributed songs. The music for dancing was separate again. Dancing-master musicians devised the tunes, which might then have been arranged by someone else. Records of payments paint an interesting picture of a collaborative effort. For Jonson's *Oberon*, for example, Alfonso Ferrabosco (ii) composed the songs, the lutenist Robert Johnson was paid £20 for 'making' the dances, and Thomas Lupo five pounds for 'setting them to the violins', while the violinist/dancing-master Thomas Giles was also paid 'for three dances'.

The correspondence between the device (or plot) of court masques and the actual events of the day continued into the reign of Charles I. *Britannia Triumphans*, performed in 1638, contains oblique but positive references to Charles I's hated ship money and stresses the wisdom of his government. *Salmacida Spolia* (*see* fig. 1(b) above), the very last court masque, took place at the beginning of 1640 in an atmosphere of political tension. The opening song, a dialogue between the Good Genius of Great Britain and Concord acknowledges the difficulties the king was having in retaining the allegiance of his subjects:

> . . . much I grieve that, though the best
> Of kingly science harbours in his breast,
> Yet'tis his fate to rule in adverse times,
> When wisdom must awhile give place to crimes . . .

Two years later the king and his supporters fled from a hostile London. By the end of 1642 Charles had established his court in Oxford, where those of his musicians still with him appear to have been sustained only by fees paid to them by candidates for ennoblement.[49] In London, the theatres were closed, and acting forbidden. A Parliamentary Ordinance of 9 May 1644 directed that, along with vestments, raised altars, and pictures of religious subjects, 'all organs, and the frames or cases wherein they stand in all Churches and Chappels aforesaid shall be taken away, and utterly defaced, and none hereafter set up in their places'.[50] (Not all the organs ended up being 'utterly defaced': Cromwell appropriated the Hampton Court chapel organ for his own residence.) Two months earlier, Parliament had replaced the Book of Common Prayer with the predictably anti-musical *Directory for the Publique Worship of God*. Its final – and shortest – section recommended the singing of psalms 'publiquely . . . in the congregation, and also privately in the family'. The congregational emphasis was seen as a justification in the long term for trying to improve literacy and in the meantime for the practice of 'lining out':

> That the whole Congregation may joyne herein, every one that can reade is to have a Psalme book, and all others not disabled by age, or otherwise, are to be exhorted to learn to reade. But for the present, where many in the Congregation cannot read, it is con-venient that the Minister, or some fit person appointed by him and the other Ruling Officers, doe read the Psalme, line by line, before the singing thereof.[51]

Years later, John Gardiner was to comment: 'it was only fit for those mens rudeness to abandon Church Musick, who intended to fill all things with the alarums of war, and crys of confusion'.[52]

For many prominent musicians – servants of the crown – the Civil War was a disaster. William Lawes was killed in one of the bloodiest encounters of the war at Rowton Heath, Cheshire, in 1645, despite the fact that he had been made a Commissary in the king's forces to protect him ('such *Officers* being normally shot-free by their place'[53]). Matthew Locke left Exeter with the Prince of Wales in 1646 to join the royal forces in the Netherlands. There he would have met up with the Master of the King's Music, Nicholas Lanier, who described himself as 'old, unhappye in a manner in exile, plundered not only of his fortune, but of all his musicall papers, nay, almost of his witts and vertue'.[54]

At the end of January 1649 Charles I walked from the Banqueting Hall, Whitehall, on to the execution scaffold. Andrew Marvell (in *An Horatian Ode*) saw it as the king's final masque role:

> That thence the Royal Actor borne
> The tragic scaffold might adorn,
>   While round the armed bands
>   Did clap their bloody hands.
> He nothing common did or mean
> Upon the memorable scene;
>   But with his keener eye
>   The axe's edge did try;
> Now called the gods with vulgar spite
> To vindicate his helpless right,
>   But bowed his comely head,
>   Down as upon a bed.

Marvell was not the only writer to be struck by the irony of Charles I's place of execution; one eyewitness wrote that the king came 'out of the Banquetting-house on the scaffold with the same unconcerned-ness and motion that he usually had when he entered it on a Masque-night'. Two weeks after the execution, on 14 February 1649, Thomas Tomkins composed 'A Sad Pavan for these distracted times'.

*

The Commonwealth government seems to have been willing to assume some responsibility for musicians who had been in the service of the king – and not just for those who showed some allegiance to the parliamentary cause. In 1651 a payment of £20 was authorized 'To Thomas Mell, one of the Musicons to the late king . . . hee being att Sea in the Parliament service, in part Arrears of his wages'.[55] The Puritans did approve of music as a domestic activity. Even Prynne conceded that 'no man, no Christian dares denie' that 'Musicke of itselfe is lawfull, and usefull and commendable'.[56] Roger North's description of music-making during the Civil War period suggests that for many people it became a particularly consoling diversion: '. . . when most other good arts languished Musick held up her head, not at Court nor (in the cant of those times) profane Theatres, but in private society, for many chose rather to fidle at home, than to goe out, and be knockt on the head abroad . . .'[57]

Yet the five musicians retained by Cromwell became keenly aware of what had been lost in the dismantling of the musical institutions of court and church. In 1656 they petitioned Cromwell to re-establish a Musicians' Corporation:

> . . . by reason of the late dissolucōn of the Quires in the Cathedralls where the study & practice of the Science of Musick was especially cherished, Many of the skilfull Professors of the said Science have during the laste Warrs and troubles dyed in want and there being now noe p^{r}ferm^t or Encouragemt in the way of Musick Noe man will breed his Child in it, soe that it must needes bee that the Science itselfe must dye in this Nacōn, with those few professors of it now living, or at least it will degenerate much from the perfeccōn it lately attained unto . . .[58]

Their analysis might well be read as an epitaph for the early Stuart era.

NOTES

[1] See D. Hirst, *Authority and Conflict, England 1603–1658* (London, 1986), 20, and A. Gurr, *Playgoing in Shakespeare's London* (Cambridge, 1987), 54.

Quoted in L. Stone, *The Crisis of the Aristocracy 1558–1641* (Oxford, 1965), 391.

[3] ibid, 395; D. C. Price, *Patrons and Musicians of the English Renaissance* (Cambridge, 1981), 10.

[4] See J. Caldwell, *The Oxford History of English Music*, i: *From the Beginnings to c. 1715* (Oxford, 1991), 414.

[5] For street cries, see *Consort Songs*, ed. P. Brett, Musica Britannica, xxii (London, 2/1974). Thomas Ravenscroft's three volumes (all available in modern facsimiles) are *Deuteromelia* (1609), *Pammelia* (1609) and *Melismata* (1611).

[6] *Histriomastix* (London, 1633), 262, 274.

[7] Quoted in Gurr, *Playgoing in Shakespeare's London*, 213.

[8] ibid, 61–3.

[9] ibid, 24.

[10] Dedication to *14 Ayres in Tabletorie* (1598).

[11] *Records of English Court Music*, ed. A. Ashbee, iv (Snodland, Kent, 1991), 197.

[12] For translations of the 1604 charter and the 1606 by-laws, see H. A. F. Crewdson, *The Worshipful Company of Musicians* (London, 1971), 110–37. The 1635 charter is in *Records of English Court Music*, ed. Ashbee, v (Aldershot, 1991), 245–51.

[13] See W. L. Woodfill, *Musicians in English Society from Elizabeth to Charles I* (Princeton, 1953), 152.

[14] *Records of English Court Music*, ed. Ashbee, iv, 8.

[15] M. Wailes, 'Martin Peerson', *PRMA*, lxxx (1953–4), 67.

[16] See P. Holman, *Four and Twenty Fiddlers: the Violin at the English Court 1540–1690* (Oxford, 1993).

[17] *Records of English Court Music*, ed. Ashbee, iii (Snodland, 1988), 53.

[18] Information about court payments from Ashbee, *Records of English Court Music*, iii and iv. Other figures from L. Hulse, 'The Musical Patronage of Robert Cecil, First Earl of Salisbury', *JRMA*, cxvi (1991), 28; M. Ashley, *Life in Stuart England* (London, 1984), 27–40; *Giles and Richard Farnaby: Keyboard Music*, ed. R. Marlow, Musica Britannica, xxiv (London, 1965), 22; and Stone, *The Crisis of the Aristocracy*, 396 (and see pp.424–49 for the operation of monopolies etc.).

[19] *Sylva Sylvarum*; see *Lord Bacon's Works*, ii, ed. J. Spedding and R. L. Ellis (London, 1887), 385.

[20] Woodfill, *Musicians in English Society*, 220f.

[21] H. Peacham, *The Compleat Gentleman* (London, 1623). Peacham has a chapter on music, but it has been shown that in this section he virtually plagiarizes Morley's *Plaine and Easie Introduction to Practicall Musicke* (London, 1597): see S. Hankey, 'The Compleat Gentleman's Music', *ML*, lxii (1981), 146–54.

[22] *GB-Lbl* Add. 29481, f.22.

[23] Price, *Patrons and Musicians of the English Renaissance*, 29.

[24] Woodfill, *Musicians in English Society*, 230.

[25] W. R. Prest, *The Inns of Court under Elizabeth I and the Early Stuarts, 1590–1640* (London, 1972), 113.

[26] A new patent was issued to William Braithwaite in 1635, but it seems to have had little practical effect.

[27] See C. Monson, *Voices and Viols in England, 1600–1650* (Ann Arbor, 1982), and Caldwell, *The Oxford History of English Music*, i, 390n.

[28] *Records of English Court Music*, ed. Ashbee, iv, 198, and p.200 for mention of a bow bought for the queen's lyra viol, and for manuscript paper ruled for lyra (with six-line tablature staves) and for viol (normal five-line staves).

[29] See P. Walls, 'The Origins of English Recitative', *PRMA*, cx (1983–4), 25–40.

[30] See P. Aston, 'Tradition and Experiment in the Music of George Jeffreys', *PRMA*, xcix (1972–3), 105–15.

[31] *A Compendium of Practical Music in Five Parts* (London, 2/1667), ed. P. J. Lord (Oxford, 1970), 75.

[32] M. Lefkowitz, *William Lawes* (London, 1960), 6.

[33] *An Introduction to the Skill of Music* (London, 4/1664), Sig.[A7].

[34] *The Division Violist* (London, 2/1659), 1f.

[35] See C. MacClintock, *Readings in the History of Music in Performance* (Bloomington and London, 1979), 120f.

[36] The full text of this injunction is reproduced in M. C. Boyd, *Elizabethan Music and Musical Criticism* (Philadelphia, 2/1962), 9.

[37] *A Short Treatise of Altars, Altar-Furniture, Altar-Cringing, and Musick of all the Quire, Singing Men and Choristers* (London, 1641), 19.

[38] See J. Morehen, *The Sources of English Cathedral Music c.1617–1644* (diss., U. of Cambridge, 1969), p.viii.

[39] L. Andrewes, *Ninety-Six Sermons*, ii (Oxford, 1841), 1.

[40] Woodfill, *Musicians in English Society*, 162.

[41] *GB-Lbl* Royal 18.B.XIX.

[42] Thomas Dallam provided organs for St George's, Windsor (1610), Worcester Cathedral (1613), Eton College (1614), Holyrood Palace, Edinburgh (1616), St John's College, Oxford (where Laud was Master, 1617), Wells Cathedral (1620), Wakefield Cathedral (1620), Durham Cathedral (1621) and Bristol Cathedral (1629). Robert Dallam built organs at York Minster (1632–4), Magdalen College, Oxford (1630s), Jesus College, Cambridge (1638), St John's College, Cambridge (1638), Lichfield Cathedral (1639) and Gloucester Cathedral (1641). See 'Dallam', *The New Grove Dictionary of Musical Instruments* (London, 1984), i, 537; Woodfill, *Musicians in English Society*, 149.

[43] N. Temperley, *The Music of the English Parish Church* (Cambridge, 1979), 52. Temperley concludes: 'Hundreds of parish church records, from London and other parts of the country, have been examined, and have yielded very few references to choirs or organs at any time during the reigns of James I or Charles I . . . We must conclude that these musical aids were exceptional during the period'.

[44] Some of these are listed in P. Yeats-Edwards, *English Church Music: a Bibliography* (London, 1975), 22ff. The Thomasen tracts, probably the largest collection of this literature, is housed in the British Library (it is also available in a Harvester microfilm series).

[45] David Pinto argues convincingly that William Lawes's 'Psalmes for 1, 2, and 3 partes, to the common tunes' (*GB-Och* Mus 768–70) were written at this time; see 'William Lawes at the Siege of York', *MT*, cxxvii (1986), 579–83.

[46] D. W. Krummel estimates that probably 500 different editions, issues and states of Sternhold and Hopkins appeared between 1560 and 1700; see *English Music Printing 1553–1700* (London, 1975), 35.

[47] Krummel argues on the basis of the octavo format of East's 1592 publication that it may have been intended for use in church: ibid, 20. Nicholas Temperley also suggests that East's book could have been 'used by a choir while the ordinary psalm books were in the hands of the congregation': see 'Psalms, metrical', *Grove 6*, xv, 369.

[48] See I. Godt, 'Prince Henry as Absalom in David's Lamentations', *ML*, lxii (1981), 318–30.

[49] *Records of English Court Music*, ed. Ashbee, iii, p.xiii. On these years, see also the following chapter below.

[50] *Two Ordinances of the Lords and Commons for the Speedy Demolishing of all Organs, Images and Supertitious Monuments in all Cathedralls Parish Churches and Chappels throughout the Kingdom of England and Dominion of Wales* (London, 1644), 3.

[51] *A Directory of Publique Worship* (London, 1644), 84.

[52] *Considerations touching the Liturgy of the Church of England* (London, 1661), 36.

[53] Thomas Fuller, quoted in Lefkowitz, *William Lawes*, 20.

[54] Letter to Constantijn Huygens, quoted in I. Spink, 'Lanier', *Grove 6*, x, 454.

[55] *Records of English Court Music*, ed. Ashbee, v, 24.

[56] *Histriomastix*, 274.

[57] *Roger North on Music*, ed. J. Wilson (London, 1969), 294.

[58] *Records of English Court Music*, ed. Ashbee, v, 251.

BIBLIOGRAPHICAL NOTE

History

The best recent account of England in the reign of the first two Stuarts is D. Hirst, *Authority and Conflict, England 1603–1658* (London, 1986). J. Caldwell, *The Oxford History of English Music*, i: *From the Beginnings to c.1715* is an excellent account which makes generous provision for the period dealt with here: another very useful recent volume is *The Seventeenth Century*, ed. I. Spink, Blackwell History of Music in

Britain, iii (Oxford, 1992). W. L. Woodfill, *Musicians in English Society from Elizabeth to Charles I* (Princeton, 1953), remains the most comprehensive account of the social history of music in London during the reigns of the first two Stuarts. D. C. Price, *Patrons and Musicians of the English Renaissance* (Cambridge, 1981), is more limited in scope but thoroughly interesting. M. C. Boyd, *Elizabethan Music and Musical Criticism* (Philadelphia, 2/1962), is a quirky but useful handbook which, despite its title, extends into the reign of James I. D. W. Krummel, *English Music Printing 1553–1700* (London, 1975), is an interesting account of the technological and trade aspects of music publication in this period. C. M. Simpson, *The British Broadside Ballad and its Music* (New Brunswick, 1966), traces the history of the entire repertory of ballad tunes and texts. A. Ashbee's series *Records of English Court Music* is an invaluable resource; iii (Snodland, Kent, 1988), iv (Snodland, 1991) and, in part, v (Aldershot, 1991) deal with the reigns of James I and Charles I. E. F. Rimbault, *The Old Cheque-Book, or Book of Remembrance of the Chapel Royal* (London, 1872), is a transcription of the manuscript containing records of the Chapel Royal from 1561 to 1744. An important new book is P. Holman, *Four and Twenty Fiddlers: the Violin at the English Court 1540–1690* (Oxford, 1993). The standard study of music and religion in this period is P. le Huray, *Music and the Reformation in England 1549–1660* (London, 1967, repr. with corrections, Cambridge, 1978). N. Temperley, *The Music of the English Parish Church* (Cambridge, 1979), gives a fascinating account of the response at parish level to the doctrinal and liturgical upheavals of the period (the paperback reprint of 1983 excludes the second of the two original volumes containing the music examples). An extended stylistic study of the repertory may be found in P. Phillips, *English Sacred Music 1549–1649* (Oxford, 1991).

Composers

There are a number of studies of individual composers: D. Poulton, *John Dowland* (London, 2/1982), M. Lefkowitz, *William Lawes* (London, 1960), D. Stevens, *Thomas Tomkins* (London, 2/1967), and D. Brown *Thomas Weelkes* (London, 1969), are all important. Two out of three volumes of *The Music of William Byrd* have appeared, both first-rate, i: J. Kerman, *The Masses and Motets of William Byrd* (London, 1981) and iii: O. Neighbour, *The Consort and Keyboard Music of William Byrd* (London, 1978) (ii: P. Brett, *The Songs, Services and Anthems of William Byrd* is in preparation). Another useful study is J. Duffy, *The Songs and Motets of Alfonso Ferrabosco, The Younger* (Ann Arbor, 1980). More books have been written about Thomas Campion than any other composer in the period, but none is particularly satisfactory; the introduction to *The Works of Thomas Campion*, ed. W. Davis (London, 1969), is perhaps more useful.

The poems set by lute-song composers are reproduced in E. H. Fellowes, *English Madrigal Verse 1588–1632* (Oxford, 3/1967, rev. and enlarged by F. W. Sternfeld and D. Greer), and in E. Doughtie, *Lyrics from English Airs 1596–1622* (Cambridge, Mass., 1970). I. Spink, *English Song: Dowland to Purcell* (London, 1974, 2/1986), remains the most comprehensive discussion of seventeenth-century lute-songs and continuo songs. The relationship between poetry and music has been the subject of a number of books, of which the most interesting are E. Doughtie, *English Renaissance Song* (Boston, 1986), and W. Maynard, *Elizabethan Lyric Poetry and its Music* (Oxford, 1986). J. Hollander, *The Untuning of the Sky* (Princeton, 1961), is a stimulating study of the way in which the ideas of speculative music degenerated into easy metaphor by the end of the seventeenth century.

Theatre

A. Gurr, *Playgoing in Shakespeare's London* (Cambridge, 1987), gives a fascinating picture of what went on in and around the theatres. There are a number of major studies of the theatre itself: G. Wickham, *Early English Stages* (London, 1972), G. E. Bentley, *The Jacobean and Caroline Stage*, vi (Oxford, 1968), and J. Orrell, *The Human Stage: English Theatre Design 1567–1640* (Cambridge, 1988). J. Orrell and A. Gurr, *Rebuilding Shakespeare's Globe* (London, 1989), can be regarded as an interim account of the way in which recent archaeological investigations on the sites of the Globe and Rose theatres have clarified questions about these structures. J. Stevens, 'Shakespeare and the Music of the Elizabethan Stage', *Shakespeare in Music*, ed. P. Hartnoll (London, 1964), is a useful introduction (although the idea that the broken consort was a fixed ensemble particularly favoured in the theatres has been discredited since this book was published). There are two detailed studies of music in Shakespeare's plays: F. W. Sternfeld, *Music in Shakespearean Tragedy* (London, 1963), and J. H. Long, *Shakespeare's Use of Music* (Gainsville, Florida, 1957–71). A. Brissenden, *Shakespeare and the Dance* (London, 1981), complements these musical studies. S. Orgel and R. Strong, *Inigo Jones: the Theatre of the Stuart Court* (London, 1973), contains reproductions of all Jones's masque designs together with many of his Italian models. Both Orgel and Strong have produced valuable studies of the relationship between political ideology in this period and the literary and visual arts.

Music

A number of important series cover English music in the period. Various volumes of the national series Musica Britannica (London, 1951–) are devoted to keyboard music: v: Tomkins; xiv, xix: Bull; xx: Gibbons; xxiv: Giles and Richard Farnaby; and xxvii–xxviii: Byrd. Other relevant volumes are: vi: Dowland, *Ayres for Four Voices*; ix: *Jacobean Consort Music*; xxi: William Lawes, *Select Consort Music*; xxii: *Consort Songs*; xxiii: Weelkes, *Collected Anthems*; xxxiii: *English Songs 1625–1660*, and xlvi: Coprario, *Fantasia-Suites*. The published songbooks of the period are covered by two series, originally edited by E. H. Fellowes and revised by T. Dart and others: *The English Madrigalists* (London, 1956–76, formerly known as *The English Madrigal School*) and *The English Lute-Songs* (London, 1956–, formerly *The English School of Lutenist Song Writers*; also available in facsimile reprints as *English Lute Songs 1597–1632*). Two series deal with sacred music. Tudor Church Music (Oxford, 1923–9), despite its title, contains some seventeenth-century material: iv: Gibbons's services and anthems; viii: Tomkins's services; and ix: Byrd's *Gradualia*. All Byrd's sacred music has been newly edited by P. Brett as part of The Bryd Edition (London, 1976–). Early English Church Music has volumes of Gibbons's verse anthems (iii) and Tomkins's *Musica Deo sacra* (v, ix, xiv). The series Le Choeur des Muses (Paris) contains several volumes of music with interesting literary associations: *Poèmes de Donne, Crashaw, Herbert, mis en musique par leurs contemporains*, ed. A. Souris (1961), *Trois masques à la cour de Charles 1er d'Angleterre*, ed. M. Lefkowitz (1970), and *La musique de scène de la troupe de Shakespeare*, ed. J. P. Cutts (1971). The most comprehensive collection of music for the courtly masque is A. Sabol, *Four Hundred Songs and Dances from the Stuart Masque* (Providence, Rhode Island, 1978).

Chapter XIV

London: Commonwealth and Restoration

PETER HOLMAN

The Civil War effectively began on 10 January 1642. On that day Charles I and his French-born queen, Henrietta Maria, left London, she to return to Paris to gather support for her husband, he to prepare for war in the royalist stronghold of York. England at the time was still a personal monarchy. Day-to-day government was conducted in Whitehall by the king and his advisers in the private apartments and in dozens of financial and legal offices in the ramshackle old palace. With the king removed from his seat of power, normal government effectively ceased. And Charles's remedy, which was to order Whitehall to move to York, only made things worse. It was seen, especially by those who worked in offices that had not moved around with the king for generations, as a test of loyalty, and the court broke up in confusion. When Charles raised his standard at Nottingham in August he faced a parliamentary army commanded by none other than the head of his household – the Lord Chamberlain, the Earl of Essex.

1642 was inevitably a year of drastic change for English music, for the court maintained the country's leading musical institutions. In normal times the Lord Chamberlain had controlled over a hundred musicians in the Chamber, the section of the household 'above stairs'. Under the Master of the Music, Nicholas Lanier, were six separate ensembles or groups, each with their own role in the daily round of court life. Two of them, the fifes and drums and the state trumpeters, were more court attendants than musicians, for their task was to provide simple, improvised music for court ceremonial, and they were not part of the literate musical culture of the time. The Chapel Royal, the largest group with a choir of twelve Children and twenty Gentlemen, provided the king with daily choral services in the chapel at Whitehall (or its equivalent in one of the other palaces), and provided a useful pool of singers for special court events, such as the production of masques.

Secular music was provided by three ensembles. Two of them, the wind musicians and the violin band, operated in the public areas of the palace, known collectively as the Presence Chamber, while the members of the third, the Lutes, Viols and Voices, had access to the private apartments of the royal family, the Privy Chamber. The twenty-odd wind musicians had formerly been divided into separate consorts of shawms and sackbuts, flutes and recorders. In the 1630s they were reorganized into a single group working in shifts, and they went over to the more modern combination of cornetts and sackbuts. As well as providing music for secular ceremonies, such as the daily ritual of the sovereign's dinner, they also served in the Chapel Royal. The violin band was mainly used to accompany dancing, though it may also have played at dinner. It had a formal establishment of fifteen, though it was augmented on occasion by extra players, such as the court dancing-masters, who were also violinists. The Lutes, Viols and Voices (also known as the Private Music) was not a single ensemble but a pool of distinguished soloists – singers, lutenists, viol players, violinists, keyboard players and a harpist – who provided the royal family with a range of chamber music.

Things came to a head for the royal musicians at the beginning of April 1642, when they were ordered to attend the king at York along with other members of the Chamber. For them the problem was not a crisis of conscience, for they were royalists virtually to a man, but a simple lack of money. In March, the wind players had petitioned the Treasury for more than two years' arrears of pay, claiming that 'through want whereof they are not only become miserable in their poore families, But unable to travell and fit themselves for a Journey', and a little later two members of the violin band complained that their wages were two and a quarter years in arrears, while those of their colleagues were one and a half years behind.[1] When it became apparent that no more money was forthcoming, the royal musicians began to fend for themselves. The French musicians in Henrietta Maria's household had already left the country with the queen, and they were followed by most of the foreigners in the main royal music, as well as a few of the Englishmen. A letter from Nicholas Lanier to his friend Constantijn Huygens shows that he was in the Netherlands in 1646, 'old, unhappye in a manner in exile, plundered not only of his fortune, but of all his musicall papers, nay, almost of his witts and vertue'. A few, like William Lawes, joined the royalist army. But the rest either slid into retirement and obscurity, or began to eke out a living by teaching. A number of notable court musicians, including Henry Lawes and Charles Coleman, were listed in John Playford's *A Musicall Banquet* (London, 1651) as 'excellent and able Masters' who could take pupils in London.

Royal musicians, of course, were not the only ones to suffer. On 2 September 1642 Parliament ordered 'Publike Stage-Playes' to 'cease and be forborne'. The London theatres were closed, and their companies, including musicians, fell on hard times. 'Our Musike that was held so delectable and precious', wrote the author of *The Actor's Remonstrance or Complaint* (London, 1644), 'now wander with their Instruments under their cloaks, I meane such as that have any, into all houses of good fellowship, saluting every roome where is company with *Will you have any musike Gentlemen?*' He may have had in mind the famous six-man group of the Blackfriars theatre, the home of London's leading company, the King's Men.

Cathedral musicians, too, began to lose their places soon after the beginning of the Civil War. As early as 1641 the two organs at Durham were damaged, and in the next two years most of the cathedral instruments suffered a similar fate or were dismantled for safe keeping. At Exeter, for instance, soldiers

> brake down the organs, and taking two or three hundred pipes with them in a most scorneful and contemptuous manner, went up and downe the streets piping with them; and meeting with some of the Choristers of the Church, whose surplices they had stolne before, and imployed them to base servile offices, scoffingly told them, 'Boyes, we have spoyled your trade, you most goe and sing hot pudding pyes'.[2]

Indeed, the profession of cathedral musician was soon abolished by Parliament. In 1642 it ordered 'in these times of public danger and calamity' that 'such part of the Common Prayer and service as is performed by singing men, choristers, and organs in the Cathedral church be wholly forborne and omitted, and the same be done in a reverent, humble and decent manner without singing or using the organs'; in 1644 church organs were among 'superstitious monuments to be demolished'.

It used to be thought that the establishment of Parliamentary government produced conditions that were universally detrimental to England's musical life. Indeed, the destruction of the country's main musical institutions must have entailed at least a temporary reduction in the level of musical activity, and there were many cases of individual misfortune. William Lawes was killed at the Siege of Chester in 1645; the court musician William Saunders petitioned Charles II in 1661 for a court place, pointing out that he had 'suffered much by the late Usurpers' for his loyalty to the Crown; and in February 1657 a group of prominent musicians, John Hingeston, Davis Mell, William Howes, Richard Hudson and William Gregory, pointed out in a petition to the Commonwealth government that,

> by reason of the late dissolucion of the Quires in the Cathedralls where the study and practice of the Science of Musick was espe-

cially cherished, Many of the skilfull Professors of the said Science
have during the late Warrs and troubles dyed in want, and there
being now noe preferrment or Encouragement in the way of
Musick, noe man will breed his child in it, soe that it must needes
bee, that the Science itselfe, must dye in this Nacion, with those few
Professors of it now living, or at least it will degenerate much from
that perfection lately attained unto. Except some present maintenance and Encouragement bee given for educating of some youth in
the study and practice of the said Science.[3]

But the Puritans, as Percy Scholes pointed out in the 1930s, were
not opposed to music as such, only against elaborate church music
and the public exhibition of plays and dancing. And Parliament did
a certain amount to alleviate the hardship of former court musicians,
paying arrears of salaries over several years. During the
Commonwealth there was even a 'Committee of the Council for
Advancement of Musicke', the body to which the petition just quoted
was addressed; it requested that 'there bee a Corporacion or
Colledge of Musitians erected in London with reasonable powers to
read and practise publiquely all sorts of Musick'. The matter was
considered by the Council several times, but nothing seems to have
come of the project. Cromwell himself, as the antiquarian and bi-
ographer Anthony Wood put it, 'loved a good voice and instrumental
musick well'. He obtained Cambridge music degrees for Charles
Coleman and Benjamin Rogers; he had organs installed at Hampton
Court and Whitehall; and he employed ten musicians during his
period as Lord Protector from 1653 to his death in 1658. This group
was, in effect, a miniature version of the pre-war royal music, for
among them were singers (two boys, reportedly, sang Cromwell's
favourite pieces, the Latin motets of Richard Dering), lutenists, violinists (two of whom also played the cornett), and the 'Master of the
Music', the organist John Hingeston.[4]

The upheaval of the Civil War undoubtedly changed the course of
English music. Exile on the Continent brought some of England's
leading musicians into contact with current styles of French, Italian
and German music. It was the means by which the new musical
styles that had been developed at court were disseminated to the
musical community at large. And it encouraged the cultivation of
domestic music. To take the last point first: 'during the troubles',
wrote the historian Roger North,

> when most other good arts languished Musick held up her head,
> not at Court nor (in the cant of those times) profane Theatres, but
> in private society, for many chose rather to fidle at home, than to
> goe out, and be knockt on the head abroad; and the entertainment
> was very much courted and made use of, not onely in country but
> citty familys, in which many of the Ladys were good consortiers;

and in this state was Musick dayly improving more or less till the time of (in all other respects but Musick) the happy Restauration.[5]

North's own family furnished him with an excellent example. He grew up in the 1650s at Kirtling, Cambridgeshire, the seat of his grandfather, Lord North. Lord North 'play'd on that antiquated instrument called the treble viol' and 'kept an organist in the house, which was seldome without a profes't musick master' – none other than John Jenkins on occasion. With the help of musical servants, the family made up a 'society of musick' three days a week, usually 'all viols to the organ or harpsicord', though on Sundays 'voices to the organ were a constant practice'. After the Restoration some of the Kirtling music collection was sold to the Oxford Music School (and still survives in the Bodleian Library). It shows that, in addition to viol consorts, they also played the more modern repertory of fantasias and fantasia suites for varied combinations of two trebles, two basses and organ by Jenkins, Orlando Gibbons, John Coprario and William Lawes.

'Voices to the organ', that is, devotional vocal chamber music, had particular attractions at the time because it enabled some semblance of formal Anglican observance to be continued in private, and it was a convenient vehicle for royalist sentiments, covert or not so covert. In 1648 Henry Lawes published the collection *Choice Psalmes*, scored for the versatile combination of two sopranos (or tenors), bass and continuo. It is dedicated to Charles I and includes a series of tributes to William Lawes, the royalist musical martyr. The political message is even more explicit in John Wilson's *Psalterium Carolinum, the Devotions of his Sacred Majestie in his Solitudes and Sufferings* (1657), a collection with the same scoring. A third book, Walter Porter's *Mottets of Two Voyces*, appeared in the same year. It contains pieces in verse-anthem style that were presumably used for private services. The music in all three collections is mostly simple and unpretentious, and there are better things in manuscript, particularly in the autographs of George Jeffreys. Jeffreys spent most of his career as steward to Sir Christopher Hatton in rural Northamptonshire, but he was the English composer of his generation most receptive to the new music of Monteverdi and his contemporaries, which he encountered in part through imported prints in his employer's library.

The activities of the music publisher John Playford also illustrate how the troubles encouraged the cultivation of domestic music. The English music publishing business, always relatively undeveloped, more or less came to a halt in the reign of Charles I, apart from the production of psalm books, in part because it had been controlled by a monopoly that was regarded as unprofitable. With the Civil War came the abolition of court monopolies and patents, which left the way open for a businessman of genius, John Playford. He opened a shop in the porch of the Temple Church in the late 1640s, and set out to corner the market in a systematic fashion, beginning with *A Musicall Banquet* (1651), with its sections of theory, lyra viol music, two-part consort music, and rounds and catches. He later developed each of them into a separate volume, and added collections of country dances, continuo songs and dialogues, cittern and gittern music, three-part consort music, Latin motets, violin tunes, psalms, and flageolet music as the business developed.

Playford succeeded where his predecessors failed because he set out to appeal to the amateur musician. He published easy music in simple notation for instruments and ensembles that were readily available in middle-class homes. Elizabethan and Jacobean prints had mostly contained complex ensemble music, some of which, such as Morley's *Consort Lessons* (1599) or Notari's *Le prime musiche nuove* (1613), were clearly of most interest to professionals. But amateurs traditionally learnt music through a solo instrument, and Playford still catered mainly for them. What consort music he published, such as Locke's three-part *Little Consort* of 1656, was relatively simple; complex consorts of the sort played by the Norths would only have been of use to the most accomplished amateurs, and remained in manuscript.

The amateur musician of the period best-known today is, of course, Samuel Pepys, who recorded his multifarious musical activities in minute detail during the ten-year span of his diary, 1660–69. He played several of the current solo instruments, such as the lute, the lyra viol and the fashionable five-course guitar. They were particularly suitable for amateurs because they were played from tablature, the letter system that indicates finger positions, not actual notes. Pepys could also read a single line from staff notation, and used it for his violin and recorder, and to play consort music on the viol. But, try as he might, he was never able to master the more complex aspects of musical notation and theory. He needed a professional to add the bass when he composed a tune, and to realize the accompaniments of his songs. The Pepys Library at Magdalene College, Cambridge, has a number of songbooks written out for him by his Italian servant Cesare Morelli with the continuo realized in guitar tablature.

The problem, Richard Luckett has pointed out, was that musical practice had become divorced from theory. The written theory Pepys had access to, such as Campion's *New Way of Making Fowre Parts in Counterpoint* (reprinted in Playford's *Introduction to the Skill of Musick* between 1655 and 1683) dealt with Renaissance counterpoint and the hexachord system, while his musical experience was mostly of homophonic music of his own time, written in modern major and minor

67. The Music Lesson: painting (1654) by Peter Lely; the girl is playing a five-course guitar

keys.[6] A few amateurs, such as Thomas Salmon and Francis North (Roger's elder brother), tried to remedy the situation by publishing treatises of their own, but they made little headway, and Salmon was even ridiculed in print by Matthew Locke for his pains. But the problem was not confined to amateurs: some quite prominent and prolific composers never really learnt to write with assurance in more than two parts, as the works of Henry Cooke, John Banister or Solomon Eccles show.

The activities of amateurs also stimulated another trade associated with music, the making of instruments. In the sixteenth century most instruments, it seems, were either imported or made by immigrants. The Bassano family of court musicians, for instance, made high-quality wind instruments for themselves and their colleagues, and exported them to courts abroad. The English viol-making tradition effectively started in Elizabeth's reign with the Rose family, and gathered pace in the next century with the work of such makers as Henry Jaye, Richard Meares and the Baker family. The making of domestic keyboard instruments also developed slowly in England, but the Interregnum evidently stimulated the making of rectangular virginals, for about twenty of them survive from between 1641 and 1679. Pepys observed during the Great Fire of London that 'hardly one lighter or boat in three' on the Thames 'that had the goods of a house in, but there was a pair of virginalls in it'.[7] A decade or so later makers went over to the wing-shaped or bentside spinet, a design that was probably invented by Girolamo Zenti, who worked in London in the 1660s. Both old and new types are simple but effective instruments, ideal vehicles for the amateur keyboard repertory of simple teaching pieces, dances, and arrangements of popular songs. Harpsichords were not, it seems, made in great numbers in England until the eighteenth century, and their use was largely confined to professionals.

The best illustration of how the Civil War was an agent for musical change is provided by the violin. The instrument was well established in England by 1600, but it was played almost entirely by professionals, and was used almost exclusively for dance music. During James I's reign it began to be used for contrapuntal chamber music by a coterie of composers, including John Coprario, Thomas Lupo and Orlando Gibbons, who worked in the household of the Prince of Wales, Prince Charles. This new idiom, principally fantasias and fantasia suites for one or two violins, bass viol and organ, was further developed at court in the 1630s by William Lawes, but it was only generally taken up in the wider musical community in the later 1640s and 50s, when John Hingeston, Christopher Gibbons, Christopher Simpson and others contributed to it.

During the Commonwealth Oxford was probably the leading (and is certainly the best-documented) musical centre in England, and it is clear that the violin suddenly became acceptable in serious musical circles there in the late 1650s. Our eyewitness, Anthony Wood, wrote that gentleman in private meetings

> play'd three, four, and five parts all with viols, as treble-viol, tenor, counter-tenor and bass, with either an organ or virginals or harpsicon joy'nd with them: and they esteemed a violin to be an instrument only belonging to a common fidler, and could not indure that it should come among them for feare of making their meetings seem to be vain and fidling.[8]

In the University there was little or no formal instruction in music at the time, but William Heather stipulated in his founding bequest of 1627 that the 'Master of Musick' and two boys should meet every Thursday afternoon in the Music School 'to receive such company as will practise Musick, and to play Lessons of three Parts, if none other come', and he provided viols for the purpose. The Music School ceased to function during the Civil War, but the organist William Ellis later established a weekly meeting in his house; when Wood visited it at the beginning of 1656 he listed some eighteen amateurs and professionals who played viols, lute and keyboard, but not the violin. John Wilson, professor from 1656 to 1661, directed and played the lute in Ellis's meeting until, in 1657, he refurbished and reopened the Music School; the bills of his expenditure mention a harpsichord, an organ and viols, but no violins.[9]

Things changed rapidly in 1657–8 following the visits of two famous violinists, the court musician Davis Mell and the German virtuoso Thomas Baltzar. Wood taught himself the violin by ear, tuning it in fourths like a viol, and later took lessons from several professional musicians in Oxford; but it was only after he heard Mell and Baltzar that he realized the potential of the instrument. When Mell played at Ellis's meeting in the spring of 1657 the opinion was that he had 'a prodigious hand on the violin'; no-one 'could go beyond him'. But when Baltzar arrived in July 1658 'they had other thoughts of Mr Mell, who though he play'd farr sweeter than Baltsar, yet Baltsar's hand was more quick and could run it insensibly to the end of the finger-board'. Soon, 'viols began to be out of fashion and only violins used, as treble violin, tenor and bass violin', and when Wood analysed a meeting at Ellis's house in March 1659, five out of the seventeen amateurs now played the violin, though one still held it between his knees. At the same time Wilson and his successor Edward Lowe, professor from 1661 to 1682, acquired significant portions of the pre-war court violin repertory for the Music School – some, as we have seen, from the Kirtling collection.[10]

With the Restoration of Charles II in May 1660 London and the court once again became the centre of English musical life; the Oxford music meetings 'began to decay', wrote Wood, 'when the masters of musick were restored to their several places that they before had lost, or else if they had lost none, they had gotten them preferments'.[11] The royal music was initially restored to its pre-war state, and no attempt was made to reform its archaic structure of separate groups of musicians. But change came in the summer of 1660, when the violin band was enlarged to create the 24 Violins. The aim was not just to emulate the French royal orchestra, the 24 Violons du Roi, for it only functioned as a single group on special occasions. Rather, the extra players were needed because the king, though a 'professed lover of musick', really only liked the French orchestral style. 'He had lived some considerable time abroad', North explained, 'where the French musick was in request', and 'could not bear any musick to which he could not keep the time', so his violinists acquired many new duties.[12] They were admitted to the Privy Chamber for the first time, superseding the contrapuntal consorts that had hitherto played there, for Charles had 'an utter detestation of fancys'; they soon replaced the wind players in the Chapel Royal; they took part in the New Year and birthday odes that became a feature of court life during the reign; and they were also lent out to play in London's newly reopened commercial theatres.

Before long the Private Music and the Wind Music effectively ceased to exist, except as sources of places for yet more violinists.

The French influence on English music did not begin in 1660. There were more French musicians at Charles I's court than at Charles II's, and they had a profound influence on English lute music and song in the 1620s and 30s. Furthermore, the English aristocracy had been taught French dances ever since French dancing-masters such as Jacques Bochan, Sebastian La Pierre and Adam Vallet arrived at the Jacobean court. Jeremy Gohory was the court dancing-master after the Restoration, and Pepys admired the result of his teaching one afternoon in April 1669:

> stepping to the Duchesse of York's side to speak with Lady Peterborough, I did see the young Duchess [Princess Mary, the future queen], a little child in hanging sleeves, dance most finely, so as almost to ravish me, her airs were so good – taught by a Frenchman that did heretofore teach the King and all the King's

68. Painting traditionally called 'The Cabal' (attributed to J. B. Medina) but more likely to show members of the King's Private Music in the early 1660s, shortly before they were disbanded

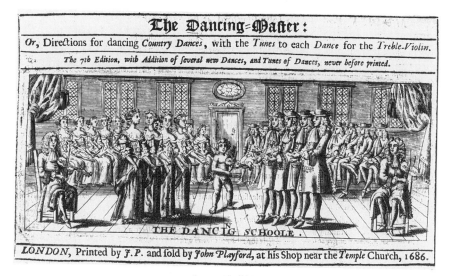

The Dancing-Master:

Or, Directions for dancing *Country Dances*, with the *Tunes* to each *Dance* for the *Treble-Violin*.

The 7th Edition, with Addition of several new Dances, and Tunes of Dances, never before printed.

THE DANCING SCHOOLE.

LONDON, Printed by *J. P.* and sold by *John Playford*, at his Shop near the *Temple* Church, 1686.

69. *Title-page of 'The Dancing-Master' (London: John Playford, 7/1686)*

children, and the Queen-Mother herself, who doth still dance well.[13]

The middle classes mostly learnt to dance at boarding schools or at dancing academies; indeed, dancing-masters such as John Weaver the elder and Josias Priest are known to have run their own schools. 'Dancing is a very common and favorite amusement of the ladies in this country', wrote an Italian visiting London in 1669, 'every evening there are entertainments at different places, at which many ladies and citizens' wives are present, they going to them alone, as they do to the rooms of the dancing masters, at which there are frequently upwards of forty or fifty ladies'. And nothing illustrates better the importance of dancing to Restoration society than the comment of sober John Evelyn, sorrowfully listing the virtues of his daughter Mary after her death in March 1685: she 'daunc'd with the most grace that in my whole life I had ever seene, & so would her Master say, who was Monsieur *Isaac*'.[14]

The skills painstakingly acquired from the dancing-master were exhibited at formal balls, the Restoration equivalent of the pre-war masque, held regularly at court on royal birthdays and during the Christmas season. Eyewitnesses record that they opened with a suite of formal branles, and proceeded by way of corants and other French dances to English country dances. The branle, a four-movement pattern starting with an overture-like entry and ending with a gavotte, was fashionable in England for a fairly short time and was never much used in chamber suites or in the theatre. Thus the surviving examples, such as those by Matthew Locke (a composer for the 24 Violins), are likely to be pieces that were actually played at court balls. They are in four parts, with a single treble, two inner parts and bass, that is, violin, two violas and bass; the 24 Violins changed to the Italianate two-violin scoring in the mid-1670s, as the music that Blow and Purcell wrote for it shows. Dance bands outside the court, by contrast, had used two violin parts before the Civil War, and Pepys danced to 'extraordinary music, two violins and a bass viallin and Theorbo (four hands), the Duke of Buckingham's Musique, the best in Towne' on Twelfth Night 1668.

Matthew Locke effectively became England's leading composer in 1660; Lanier was still Master of the Music, but he and most of the pre-war generation were near retirement. In addition to his post with the 24 Violins, Locke became Composer for the Private Music and organist in the Catholic chapel of Charles II's queen, Catherine of Braganza. He also wrote anthems for the Chapel Royal and was the most distinguished composer of consort music of his generation. Furthermore, his theatrical career reads like a miniature history of the contemporary English stage. During the Commonwealth theatrical performances, of necessity given more or less in private, often took the form of masques. The masque was usually a lavish court entertainment that used speech and music to give aristocratic dancing an allegorical or mythological setting. But when they were written for private houses, as when Milton's *Comus* was given in the Bridgewater household at Ludlow in 1634, there was no need for ostentatious display, and the dramatic and musical elements came to the fore. After 1642 there were no more court masques, so the private offshoot of the form became the mainstream. James Shirley earned his living as a schoolmaster after the theatres were closed, and wrote several masques for his pupils, one of which, *Cupid and Death*, is the only one for which the music has survived complete.[15] It was given in 1653, but the surviving music by Locke and Christopher Gibbons relates to a revival in 1659. Locke broke new ground by setting a number of passages to recitative that are given as speech in the text, in addition to the normal songs, dances and incidental music.

It is usually thought that Locke did this to make *Cupid and Death* more operatic, but it also probably had a good deal to do with attempts to circumvent the Commonwealth ban on stage plays, for the London riding school used in 1659 might have been thought of as a public theatre by the authorities. Locke had been involved in several ventures of this sort over the previous few years. In 1656 William Davenant had his play *The Siege of Rhodes* performed (or at least prepared for performance) at his home, Rutland House, in a version that was apparently set to continuous music. Locke was one

70. Engraving from John Ogilby, 'Fables of Aesop' (1651) showing a masque, possibly on Cupid and Death, the subject of a masque by James Shirley (1653)

of the consortium of composers on that occasion, and he also wrote music in 1658–9 for two more of Davenant's musical entertainments, *The Cruelty of the Spaniards in Peru* and *The History of Sir Francis Drake*. But Davenant, for one, clearly did not regard *The Siege of Rhodes* as a milestone in the history of English opera, for it was given without music after the Restoration, when the theatres were reopened and plays could once again be given.

On his return to England Charles II created a new pattern for London's commercial theatre by granting a monopoly to Davenant and Thomas Killigrew; they formed rival companies under the patronage of the Duke of York and the king. For want of anything else, the new companies began by reviving the old pre-war repertory of plays, but they produced them in a manner that owed more to the masque or Italian opera, which Davenant and Killigrew had both experienced abroad during the Interregnum. Women appeared on the stage in public for the first time, in place of the boys of Shakespeare's time; the theatres were now equipped with changeable scenery and machines; and plays were given with orchestral incidental music and masque-like scenes. Davenant's company proved to be the more musical of the two, and Locke, naturally, worked for it. He wrote songs for a number of the company's productions, including Davenant's adaptations of Shakespeare's *Henry VIII* and *Macbeth*, and in 1675 he published the incidental music he had written the previous year for Shadwell's 'operatic' version of *The Tempest*. Such suites, written for three- or four-part strings and consisting of a 'curtain tune' or overture and seven or more dances played before the play and between the acts, were specially composed and soon became a distinct genre of consort music, especially after the post-humous publication in 1697 of Purcell's *A Collection of Ayres, Compos'd for the Theatre*.

The 1674 production of *The Tempest* was regarded as 'operatic' not because it was set to continuous music – Shakespeare's play remained in mutilated form – but because it had masque-like scenes set to concerted music and, more important, spectacular scenic effects. As such it was the prototype for Shadwell's own *Psyche* (February 1675), with music by Locke, and the series of semi-operas produced by Betterton and Purcell in the 1690s.[16] Semi-opera remained the mainstream of the English musical theatre until it was replaced in the public's affections by Italian opera in the first decade of the eighteenth century. Blow's *Venus and Adonis* (?1682) and Purcell's *Dido and Aeneas* (performed at Priest's school in 1689, but perhaps written earlier) both belong to some extent to the private masque tradition, though they are set to continuous music; both, significantly, call for a large amount of dancing, and neither seems to have been seen in public in the composer's lifetime. But Charles II was personally interested in Italian opera, and made a number of attempts during his reign to establish an opera company in London, though with little success.

Locke was also one of the composers who established a new style of anthem for the Restoration Chapel Royal. The Chapel took some time to re-establish itself after eighteen years of inactivity. Locke himself wrote in *The Present Practice of Musick Vindicated* (London, 1673) that the treble parts had to be taken for over a year with cornetts and men singing in falsetto, 'there being not one Lad, for all that time, capable of Singing his Part readily', and on 14 October 1660 Pepys wrote of hearing 'an anthemne, ill sung' at Whitehall, 'which made the King laugh'. Luckily, the new Master of the Children, Captain Henry Cooke, proved to be an energetic organiser and an excellent trainer; he was responsible for a precociously gifted group of boys that included the future composers Pelham Humfrey,

Michael Wise, John Blow, William Turner, Henry Hall and Henry Purcell.

Thomas Tudway, another of Cooke's boys, wrote in later life that it was Charles II, 'a brisk, & Airy Prince, comeing to ye Crown in ye Flow'r & vigour of his Age', who effectively invented the Restoration verse anthem: he was soon

> tyr'd wth ye Grave & Solemn way, And Order'd ye Composers of his Chappell, to add Symphonys &c wth Instruments to their Anthems; and thereupon Establis[h]'d a select number of his private music, to play ye Symphonys, & Retornellos, wch he had appointed.[17]

The new type of verse anthem differed from the pre-war type in that the instrumental parts were played by violins rather than viols or cornetts and sackbuts, and the idiom, particularly in the instrumental sections, was derived from dance music. Not everyone liked the change: 'instead of the antient grave and solemn wind musique accompanying the *organ*', wrote John Evelyn on 21 December 1662, 'was introduced a Consort of 24 Violins between every pause, after the *French* fantastical light way, better suiting a Tavern or Play-house than a Church'.

Evelyn was exaggerating when he wrote of 'a Consort of 24 Violins' in the Chapel Royal. In fact, apart from such special events as coronations, there were only ever four, five or six violinists assigned at a time to play verse anthems during Charles II's reign, one of whom may have played the theorbo. The chapel at Whitehall was small, so the instrumentalists and the solo singers seem to have been distributed between the organ loft and the 'singing loft', while the choir was placed in decani and cantoris choir stalls at ground-floor level. Thus, all Restoration verse anthems were effectively performed in a polychoral manner, and a few, such as Locke's great 'Be thou exalted Lord', written to commemorate a naval victory over the Dutch in 1666, exploit the layout of the chapel to the full. After Charles II's death in 1685 violins were no longer used regularly in the Chapel, though in James II's reign there was a separate Catholic chapel at Whitehall with a group of instrumentalists. After the accession of William and Mary anthems were normally performed with organ alone, which diminished the splendour of the Chapel but had the effect of making its repertory more readily available to cathedrals and collegiate foundations. In general, provincial choirs were at a low ebb at the time, and relied increasingly on the output of court composers such as Purcell and Blow, transmitted to them through manuscript copies.

The Glorious Revolution and the accession of William and Mary in 1689 was a turning point in English musical life. For over a hundred years the court had employed nearly all of England's leading composers, who between them had either created or imported most of the new musical trends. In 1690 the royal music was reduced in size, and became effectively a part-time institution; henceforth, it seems, its members were mostly required to appear only on special occasions. The change can be clearly seen in Henry Purcell's output. Before, he was largely a court composer, writing anthems for the Chapel, and odes and other secular music for the Private Music. After 1690 he became essentially a theatre composer, and wrote for nearly 50 stage productions in little more than five years. Though he remained a member of the Chapel Royal, he cannot have attended court more than occasionally, especially as he was also organist of Westminster Abbey.

The court musicians made redundant or rendered under-employed by the Glorious Revolution also began to earn their livings by giving concerts. The earliest public concerts in England are usually said to be those instituted by John Banister in his London house in 1672, though similar experiments were made in London in the 1660s, and they were not unlike the Oxford music meetings of the 1650s.

71. String orchestra (probably members of the King's 24 Violins) playing at Westminster Hall during the banquet celebrating the coronation of James II on 23 April 1685: engraving from Francis Sandford, 'The History of the Coronation of . . . James II' (London, 1687)

72. Henry Purcell:
portrait (1695) by John
Closterman

Banister probably started his concerts because he and his fellow musicians were not receiving regular wages from a court beset by financial crisis. Things were so bad in December 1666, John Hingeston told Pepys, that 'many of the Musique are ready to starve, they being five years behindhand for their wages', and that the court harper Lewis Evans 'did the other day die from mere want'; a month earlier the wind player John Gamble was four and three quarter years in arrears of salary, had 'lost all he had by the late dreadful fire', and had contracted a debt of £120 'for which one of his securities is now sent prisoner at Newgate'.[18] Banister could apparently call on many of his court colleagues for his concerts, since a pamphlet-cum-programme, *Musick; or, A Parley of Instruments, the First Part* (London, 1676), for those given in December 1676 mentions a vast and exotic array of instruments, including a band of 20 violins (who also played for a ball), viols, lutes, citterns, theorbos, guitars, harps, harpsichords, organs, recorders, pipes, flutes, flageolets, cornetts and sackbuts; he even offered anyone 'that hath a desire to have any New Songs or Tunes' the services of one of the royal composers.

All the early public concerts were held in makeshift premises such as taverns, schools (Banister's 1676 concerts were given at his school in Little Lincoln's Inn Fields) and dancing academies. Some of them, such as the meeting held at the Castle Tavern in Fleet Street in the 1680s, or the remarkable series run by the coal merchant Thomas Britton at his premises in Clerkenwell from 1678 until his death in 1714, mixed amateur and professional performers. The Castle Tavern series eventually evolved into the professional concerts at York Buildings off the Strand – London's first purpose-built concert room. Concerts at the time, and for at least another century, normally mixed vocal and instrumental solos with concerted items. Much of the repertory, inevitably, was taken from existing genres. Thomas Britton's concerts, if his library is any guide, consisted largely of English consort music – originally composed for the home or the theatre – as well as collections of imported Italian and German sonatas – mostly written for church use.[19] In England they proved to be ideal material for public concerts. The sonata was also popularised in England by the many foreign instrumentalists who were beginning to arrive in England, attracted by London's booming musical life. In particular, two of the musicians involved in the York Buildings concerts in the 1690s, the German harpsichordist Gottfried Keller and the Moravian bass viol player Gottfried Finger, wrote and published many sonatas for exotic combinations of recorders, oboes, trumpets and strings. Their mixture of tunefulness and virtuosity was just what was required by a public that was becoming accustomed to listening to music rather than playing it.

The other genre that proved to be particularly suitable for public concerts was the ode. Originally developed to celebrate the New Year and royal birthdays at court, the ode came into its own as a genre of concert music, particularly in the annual celebrations of St Cecilia's day given most years from 1683 to 1703 by the Musical Society at Stationers Hall, and in the annual degree ceremonies at Oxford. The early odes are modest in scale and scoring, and resemble contemporary verse anthems. But Purcell's *Hail, bright Cecilia* of 1692 lasts about 45 minutes, has spectacular solos and massive choral writing, and uses a full orchestra of trumpets, drums, recorders, oboes, bassoon, strings and continuo. In the 1690s St Cecilia odes and court birthday odes were often repeated in ordinary public concerts, and new odes were written for concert use on subjects ranging from the untimely death of Henry Purcell to the Peace of Ryswick. It was, in effect, the beginning of the later English choral tradition, and it kept elements of the Purcellian style alive for much of the next century.

How musical, then, was English society in the second half of the seventeenth century? The examples of Samuel Pepys, John Evelyn or Roger North should not lead us to suppose that music was important to more than a small proportion of the educated population, or that more than a few households practised domestic music on a high level. Nor does the matchless presence of Henry Purcell mean that the period did not produce its fair share of bad music. But an astonishing number of Purcell's contemporaries wrote at least a little music that is worthy of him. And England's new-found role as a world commercial power created the conditions that began to attract distinguished musicians from all over Europe, who were only too happy to adopt the English musical style. Most important, perhaps, music was still a natural mode of expression and recreation for members of England's elite, from the king downwards. A century later, England's politicians and intellectuals were mostly taken up with literature, and music for them was well on its way to becoming little more than an accomplishment for young ladies.

NOTES

[1] *Records of English Court Music*, ed. A. Ashbee, iii (Snodland, Kent, 1988), 115–16; Public Record Office [PRO], SP 16/489 (107), SP 16/490 (18).

[2] P. Scholes, *The Puritans and Music in England and New England* (Oxford, 1934), 233.

[3] PRO, SP 29/36, no. 39; Scholes, *The Puritans*, 282–3.

[4] Scholes, *The Puritans*, 137–49; L. Hulse, 'John Hingeston', *Chelys*, xii (1983), 28–9.

[5] *Roger North on Music*, ed. J. Wilson (London, 1959), 294; see also 10–11.

[6] *The Diary of Samuel Pepys*, ed. R. C. Latham and W. Matthews, x (London, 1983), 275–9.

[7] *Diary*, ed. Latham and Matthews, vii (London, 1972), 271.

[8] J. D. Shute, *Anthony à Wood and his Manuscript Wood D 19(4) at the Bodleian Library, Oxford* (diss., International Institute of Advanced Studies, Clayton, Missouri, 1979), ii, 99.

[9] R. Poole, 'The Oxford Music School and the Collection of Portraits formerly Preserved there', *Musical Antiquary*, iv (1912–13), 151–2; Shute, *Anthony à Wood*, ii, 96–7; B. Bellingham, 'The Musical Circle of Anthony Wood in Oxford during the Commonwealth and Restoration', *Journal of the Viola da Gamba Society of America*, xix (1982), 6–70.

[10] Shute, *Anthony à Wood*, ii, 94–5, 99, 100; P. Holman, 'Thomas Baltzar (?1631–1663), the "Incomparable Lubicer on the Violin"', *Chelys*, xiii (1984), 3–38.

[11] Shute, *Anthony à Wood*, ii, 103.

[12] *Roger North on Music*, ed. Wilson, 299.

[13] *Diary*, ed. Latham and Matthews, ix (London, 1976), 507.

[14] ibid, ii (London, 1970), 212; *The Diary of John Evelyn*, ed. E. S. de Beer (London, 1959), 797.

[15] Text and music are edited by B. A. Harris in *A Book of Masques in Honour of Allardyce Nicoll* (Cambridge, 1970), 371–403, and E. J. Dent in Musica Britannica, ii (London, 1951, 2/1965).

[16] The music for *The Tempest* and *Psyche* is in *Matthew Locke: Dramatic Music*, ed. M. Tilmouth, Musica Britannica, li (London, 1986).

[17] C. Hogwood, 'Thomas Tudway's History of Music', *Music in Eighteenth-Century England*, ed. idem and R. Luckett (Cambridge, 1983), 25.

[18] *Diary*, ed. Latham and Matthews, vii (London, 1972), 414; *Calendar of State Papers, Domestic Series, of the Reign of Charles II*, ed. M. A. Everett Green, vi: *1666–7* (London, 1864), 245.

[19] The contents of Britton's library are known from a sale catalogue, now lost but reprinted in J. Hawkins, *A General History of the Science and Practice of Music* (London, 1776), ii, 792–3.

BIBLIOGRAPHICAL NOTE

Politics

For surveys of the politics of the period, see *Bibliography of British History: Stuart Period, 1603–1714*, ed. G. Davies (London, 1928, 2/1970), and *Restoration England,*

1660–1689, ed. W. L. Sachse, Bibliographical Handbooks (Cambridge, 1971). The best and most recent survey of the music of the period is *The Seventeenth Century*, ed. I. Spink, Blackwell History of Music in Britain, iii (Oxford, 1992); also very useful is J. Caldwell, *The Oxford History of English Music*, i: *from the Beginnings to c.1715* (Oxford, 1991). However, the accounts in C. Burney, *A General History of Music* (London, 1776–89), ed. F. Mercer (London, 1935), and J. Hawkins, *A General History of the Science and Practice of Music* (London, 1776), are still valuable and contain much original source material. P. Scholes, *The Puritans and Music in England and New England* (Oxford, 1934), revolutionized the study of its subject and is still unsurpassed. J. Harley, *Music in Purcell's London: the Social Background* (London, 1968), is also useful, though it is based largely on secondary sources. Roger North was the best contemporary observer, and *Roger North on Music*, ed. J. Wilson (London, 1959), is the standard edition, though it is only a selection; two volumes of a replacement, both ed. M. Chan and J. C. Kassler, are *Roger North's Cursory Notes of Musicke (c. 1698–c. 1703): a Physical, Psychological and Critical Theory* (Kensington, NSW, 1986) and *Roger North's The Musicall Grammarian 1728* (Cambridge, 1990).

Historians tend to think of the court as an arm of government rather than as a cultural centre, but there is much to be learnt from G. E. Aylmer's classic *The King's Servants: the Civil Service of Charles I 1625–1642* (London, 1961, 2/1974), and his sequel, *The State's Servants: the Civil Service of the English Republic 1649–1660* (London, 1973); R. Sherwood, *The Court of Oliver Cromwell* (London, 1977), is also useful. We need an Aylmer for the Restoration , but J. M. Beattie, *The English Court in the Reign of George I* (Cambridge, 1967), is useful for later developments. *The English Court: from the Wars of the Roses to the Civil War*, ed. D. Starkey (London, 1987), is a stimulating and provocative volume on the background. *The History of the King's Works*, ed. H. M. Colvin (London, 1963–82), and *The London Encyclopaedia*, ed. B. Weinreb and C. Hibbert (London, 1983, 2/1987), deal with topographical matters. There is no overall history of the royal music at present, but the most important source material is in *The Old Cheque-Book or Book of Remembrance of the Chapel Royal*, ed. E. F. Rimbault, (London, 1872), and in the admirable volumes ed. A. Ashbee: *Records of English Court Music*, i–iii (Snodland, Kent, 1986–8), and v (Aldershot, 1991). Two recent studies of court musical institutions are D. Baldwin, *The Chapel Royal, Ancient and Modern* (London, 1990), and P. Holman, *Four and Twenty Fiddlers: the Violin at the English Court 1540–1690* (Oxford, 1993).

Church music

This is surveyed in two companion volumes: P. le Huray, *Music and the Reformation in England 1549–1660* (London, 1967, 2/1978), and C. Dearnley, *English Church Music 1650–1750* (London, 1970); the former is much the more penetrating. N. Temperley, *The Music of the English Parish Church* (Cambridge, 1979), is one of the best books about English music, so it is maddening that only the text was put into paperback in 1983, since it needs to be read with the volume of music examples. Biographies of church musicians are dealt with in W. Shaw, *The Succession of Organists of the Chapel Royal and the Cathedrals of England and Wales from c. 1538* (Oxford, 1991), and D. Dawe, *Organists of the City of London, 1666–1850* (Padstow, 1983). There are accounts of the musical life of most cathedrals and collegiate foundations, many of them by local historians; two recent ones that stand out are N. Wridgway, *The Choristers of St. George's Chapel* (Slough, 1980), and S. Eward, *No Fine but a Glass of Wine: Cathedral Life at Gloucester in Stuart Times* (Wilton, 1985).

The most useful account of Oxford musical life is B. Bellingham, 'The Musical Circle of Anthony Wood in Oxford during the Commonwealth and Restoration', *Journal of the Viola da Gamba Society of America*, xix (1982), 6–70, though it will be superseded in part by P. Gouk, 'Music in Seventeenth-Century Oxford', when the

History of the University of Oxford, iv: *1603–1688* appears. Much of the source material comes from the writings of Anthony Wood, whose references to music have been edited complete in J. D. Shute, *Anthony à Wood and his Manuscript Wood D 19(4) at the Bodleian Library, Oxford* (diss., International Institute of Advanced Studies, Clayton, Missouri, 1979). A similar edition of John Aubrey's writings on music is urgently needed.

Theatre

The best general books are L. Hotson, *The Commonwealth and Restoration Stage* (Cambridge, Mass., 1928); A. Nicoll, *A History of Restoration Drama 1660–1700* (Cambridge, 4/1952); R. Leacroft, *The Development of the English Playhouse* (London, 1973, 2/1980); and R. D. Hume, *The Development of English Drama in the late Seventeenth Century* (Oxford, 1976). *The London Stage 1660–1800*, i: *1660–1700*, ed. W. Van Lennep (Carbondale, 1965), is an invaluable theatrical calendar. Much of the material in E. Boswell, *The Restoration Court Stage (1660–1702)* (Cambridge, Mass., 1932, 2/1966), relates to music. C. A. Price, *Music in the Restoration Theatre* (Ann Arbor, 1979), is the standard work on music in the theatre, through E. J. Dent, *Foundations of English Opera* (Cambridge, 1928), and D. Arundell, *A Critic at the Opera* (London, 1957), are still useful, the latter mainly as a collection of source material. E. Harris, *Henry Purcell's 'Dido and Aeneas'* (Oxford, 1987), is stimulating if controversial; it needs to be read in the light of subsequent articles in *Early Music*.

A new book is badly needed on London's early concerts. At present it is a choice between R. Elkin, *The Old Concert Rooms of London* (London, 1955), affectionate but unscholarly, and M. Tilmouth, *Chamber Music in England, 1675–1720* (diss., U. of Cambridge, 1959–60), excellent but rather inaccessible. W. H. Husk, *An Account of the Musical Celebrations on St. Cecilia's Day* (London, 1857), and R. McGuinness, *English Court Odes 1660–1820* (Oxford, 1971), cover particular areas of the repertory. The three main sources of documentary material are 'A Calendar of References to Music in Newspapers published in London and the Provinces (1660–1719)', ed. M. Tilmouth, *RMARC*, i (1961) [with an index in ibid, ii (1962), 3–15]; *The Diary of John Evelyn*, ed. E. S. de Beer (Oxford, 1955; one-vol. ed. 1959); and *The Diary of Samuel Pepys*, ed. R. C. Latham and W. Matthews (London, 1970–83); an essay by R. Luckett – ibid, x, 258–82 – is by far the best short account of Restoration musical life.

Domestic music

This is patchily covered. I. Spink, *English Song: Dowland to Purcell* (London, 1974, 2/1986), and J. Caldwell, *English Keyboard Music before the Nineteenth Century* (Oxford, 1973), are useful surveys, but E. H. Meyer, *English Chamber Music* (London, 1946, rev. 1982 with D. Poulton as *Early English Chamber Music*), is badly out of date, even in the revised edition. For recent research one has to go to periodicals, particularly *Chelys* (the Journal of the English Viola da Gamba Society) and *Early Music*. The same is true of lute music and the *Lute Society Journal* (latterly *The Lute*); M. G. Spring, *The Lute in England and Scotland after the Golden Age, 1620–1750* (diss., U. of Oxford, 1987), deserves to be published. The guitar, cittern and gittern are well covered by J. Tyler, *The Early Guitar* (London, 1980), and J. M. Ward, 'Sprightly & Cheerful Musick: Notes on the Cittern, Gittern and Guitar in Sixteenth- and Seventeenth-Century England', *The Lute Society Journal*, xxi (1979–81) [whole vol.]. The organ is covered by C. Clutton and A. Niland, *The British Organ* (London, 1963), and M. Wilson, *The English Chamber Organ: History and Development 1650–1850* (Oxford, 1968), but both are rather out of date. G. Cox, *Organ Music in Restoration England: a Study of Sources, Styles and Influence* (New York and London, 1989) is valuable. Music printing is surveyed by D. W. Krummel, *English Music Printing 1553–1700* (London, 1975), and C. L. Day and E. B. Murrie, *English Song-Books, 1651–1702: a Bibliography* (London, 1940). The best introductions to popular music are W. Chapell, *The Ballad Literature and Popular Music of the Olden Time* (London, 1855–9), and C. M. Simpson, *The British Broadside Ballad and its Music* (New Brunswick, 1966).

The fruits of important research also appear in composer studies, such as M. Lefkowitz, *William Lawes* (London, 1960); F. B. Zimmerman, *Henry Purcell, 1659–1695: an Analytical Catalogue of his Music* (London, 1963); idem, *Henry Purcell, 1659–1695* (London, 1967, 2/1983); R. E. M. Harding, *A Thematic Catalogue of the Works of Matthew Locke* (Oxford, 1971); C. A. Price, *Henry Purcell and the London Stage* (Cambridge, 1984); P. Dennison, *Pelham Humfrey* (Oxford, 1986); and A. Ashbee, *The Harmonious Musick of John Jenkins*, i: *The Fantasias for Viols* (Surbiton, 1992).

Chapter XV

Spain

LOUISE K. STEIN

With Spain, it is futile to attempt to set a date for the beginning of the Baroque period in music. The principal genres of both secular and sacred music in early seventeenth-century Spain continued traditions and techniques established by the final decades of the previous century. Spanish music did not go through a Mannerist phase, nor did a particular musical publication, a specific controversy or the work of any composer around the turn of the century represent a challenge to the late Renaissance aesthetic. Changes in the generalized musical language came about gradually, and a characteristically Spanish seventeenth-century style was not fully realized until towards 1650, although the early years of the century did witness shifts in the focus and social context of Spain's musical life.

While the seventeenth century was a Golden Age for Spanish culture, music held a subsidiary, even a subservient place, next to theatre and the visual arts, in terms of private and ecclesiastical patronage, public financial support, commercial appeal, and influence in contemporary society. One obvious symptom of its lesser status is that Spanish music from this period survives largely in manuscript copies. A few theoretical and practical manuals, especially for organ, harp or guitar, were published, but it would seem that few composers sought to publish their works, printers found little market for the sale of music, and the public was largely illiterate in musical notation. The absence of musical publications is particularly striking when compared with the large number of printed literary anthologies, of poetry, the most popular plays, and short novels, evidently demanded by literate middle- and upper-class readers hungry for the latest fashionable writings.

Spanish musicians left behind virtually no accounts of their lives, performances or ideas concerning music, which inhibits easy understanding of music in Spanish society. Yet this lack of historical information is probably a direct result of the musician's place in society and is thus an important statement about how musicians were viewed and how they perceived themselves. Composers and performers were servants and artisans and were generally employed

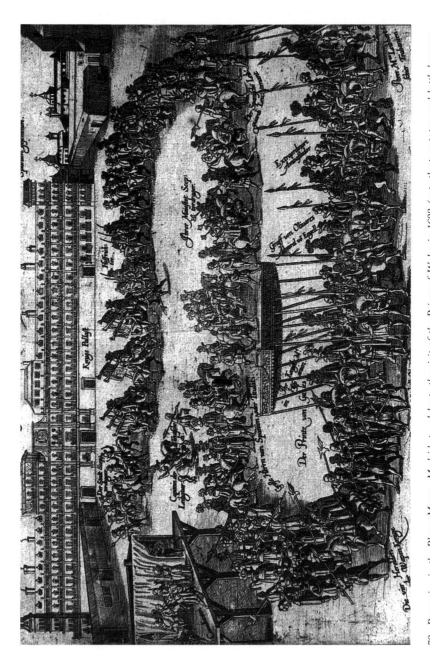

73. *Procession in the Plaza Mayor, Madrid, to celebrate the visit of the Prince of Wales in 1623 (note the trumpeters and kettledrummers, and the temporary stage): engraving*

by the court, the Church or the municipal theatres in the largest cities. Professional composers did not come from the upper reaches of society, and even the best could not rise to that level. The most fashionable and influential of the court composers lived as servants of the crown, with limited social and professional mobility. Generally excluded from high society, professional musicians were not welcomed in the *academias* of the aristocratic intelligentsia, with few exceptions. Even within the Iberian peninsula, only a handful of Spanish composers became famous. Opportunities for individual renown were restricted; for example, the names of composers and performers are rarely given in printed descriptions of royal entertainments or in the accounts of court copyists.

Contemporary Spaniards felt that the death of King Philip II in 1598 signalled the end of an age, one of great monarchs, strong imperial politics and cultural security. Spain had enjoyed a distinguished and productive epoch, as is illustrated by the number and quality of Spanish composers abroad. By the third decade of the seventeenth century, a new politics and a new outlook promoted cultural changes that affected music as they had the other liberal arts. The centrally administered monarchy of the Spanish Habsburgs systematically reduced the power and wealth of the aristocracy and drew the rich and the well-born to the royal court. Cultural patronage was not divided among competitive aristocratic courts with individual musical establishments, and this ensured the supremacy of royal patronage. Once established as the seat of royal power, Madrid, both city and court, became the busiest artistic centre in Spain, so free-lance musicians came there in search of work. The best seventeenth-century composers, writers and painters lived and worked in Madrid. The painter Velázquez, courtier and decorator to the king, painted his masterpieces for Philip IV's residences. The king's pleasure palace, the Buen Retiro, was hastily constructed but exquisitely decorated, and Philip IV amassed perhaps the largest and most impressive of Baroque art collections in Europe. The plays of Lope de Vega and Pedro Calderón de la Barca were written for the busy commercial theatres or *corrales* in Madrid and for the court stages. Because a shift in population density had transformed Madrid into an overcrowded metropolis, much of the countryside was left to illiterate peasants. Some smaller cities and provincial regions became artistically deprived, suffering a decline in the number and quality of musicians, composers, artists and writers, as compared to Madrid. The study of Spanish music in its cultural and social context must therefore emphasize the court and the influence of the monarchy and royal musical institutions on composers and genres of the period.

Spanish composers worked within the fixed social and administrative conventions of a stratified society, and, within a generally homogeneous culture, they seem to have conformed to the aesthetic conventions manifest in the other arts. Spanish music and musical institutions can be seen as representing a cautious mixture of tradition and innovation, devoid of the brilliant strokes of revolutionary genius that characterized, for example, the beginnings of the Baroque period in Italy. This compromise between an older system of musical values and the belated emergence of new techniques is reflected in the organization of musical institutions and in the generic forms and structures of music in the seventeenth century. At first, Spanish composers did not reject the forms and genres that they inherited from an earlier generation; nor do we find experimentation and controversy concerning a new style or a new aesthetic. Throughout the century, composers cultivated a strongly diatonic, contrapuntally structured style and used chromaticism and harmonic daring only for the most extreme instances of word-painting. This cautious approach was paralleled by a lack of speculative, scientifically orientated or philosophical work in music theory. However, some of the new techniques common in Baroque music outside Spain were immediately adapted to Spanish usage. One such was the basso continuo, which may have been accepted as an offshoot of the traditional native practice of polyphonic accompaniment that had already been highly developed for the singing of ballads. The characteristic Spanish continuo ensemble included harps and guitars, the preferred accompanimental instruments in Spain since at least the middle of the sixteenth century. In a sense, then, Spanish continuo practice was a compromise between new techniques and an older tradition.

One manifestation of Spanish conservatism, in music as in literature, painting and drama of the period, is the inclusion of popular and folk elements. The widespread practice of borrowing and recomposition shaped the content of much of the repertory, and, together with the conservation of traditional musical forms and gestures, helped to shape a characteristic musical language, accepted then as the *estilo español*. In songs and villancicos, this national style is evident in the consistent use of borrowed materials, stereotypical musical gestures and conceits, rhythms of popular and folk derivation, and some peculiarly Spanish modes of performance. A conservative Spanish style is heard both in the polyphonic secular songs of the early seventeenth century, many of which use pre-existing tunes, as well as in songs from late in the century which relied on a set of conventional figures of musical rhetoric that were exploited by most composers and transferred from genre to genre.

Towards the end of the century, the fusion of native elements with elements adapted from foreign innovations contributed to the definition of a last phase of a Spanish Baroque style. This third stage of

74. *Three musicians, with a violin and two guitars: painting (1617–23) by Diego Velázquez*

cultural compromise appears first in theatrical music, to a limited degree in the music of the court composer Juan Hidalgo (1614–85) but more essentially in the works of Sebastián Durón (1660–1716) from the last decade of the seventeenth century. It was Durón who was accused by later critics of opening the way for the 'barbarisms' of the Italianate or pan-European style that became synonymous with high culture in the eighteenth century, after the end of the Habsburg era.

While the sixteenth century was a Golden Age for Spanish cathedral music, the seventeenth century reveals a decided shift of emphasis in favour of secular and theatrical music, in line with social and economic change. As the reforming zeal of the Counter-Reformation in Spain calmed, so did the emphasis on religious art and music, since religious institutions, public devotion and hence religious music were in decline. Many *maestros de capilla* of churches and monasteries in smaller cities and towns were unequal to the task of composing large polyphonic works for the most important religious celebrations and wrote to more illustrious *maestros* or friends in large cities to request copies of sacred pieces.[1] The most talented composers of sacred music worked at the royal chapels in Madrid and at the important cathedrals at Avila, León, Saragossa, Segovia, Seville, Toledo, Valencia and Valladolid. Because the *maestros* moved from place to place in search of a more prestigious or remunerative appointment, regional musical traditions with distinctive forms or styles of sacred music cannot effectively be isolated.

A conservative approach to Latin sacred music seems to have been the rule in most Spanish churches and cathedrals, probably because two strong institutions provided the structure within which the *maestros de capilla* worked. They were strictly governed by the *cabildos* (the ruling cathedral chapters), and the place of music was still generally determined by the liturgy established by the Council of Trent. These institutional structures had a restrictive effect on the composition of sacred music. Although the stylistic development of Latin sacred music in Spain has not been thoroughly studied, it appears that the forms demanded by the liturgy (mass, motet, psalm, lamentation) were most often written in the strict, contrapuntal church style or in the polychoral style involving choirs of voices and/or instruments. The legacy of sacred music from the Renaissance was very much alive in Spain in the seventeenth century: sixteenth-century choirbooks (*libros de facistol*) were preserved and mended, and sacred pieces by Renaissance masters were still copied into new collections. In most churches, and in the hands of the less expert composers, the strict *a cappella* style went unchallenged, although the polychoral idiom (a sixteenth-century innovation) became more and more usual in the seventeenth century and was gradually adapted to the freer musical language of the Baroque era. Because instruments (especially wind instruments) had already been used in sacred polyphony in Spanish cathedrals before the seventeenth century, the concerted style of sacred music and the expansion of the polychoral idiom were accepted for settings of both vernacular and Latin sacred texts.

A national spirit and a native musical style closely allied with that of secular music burst forth not in Latin polyphony but in the villancico, a vernacular sacred or devotional work for any number of voices with or without instruments. The villancico encompassed all forms of vernacular religious music in Spain and was the genre that responded most immediately to local traditions, tastes and circumstances. It was cultivated in both large and small churches, used within the liturgy for certain feasts and performed at devotional services, and it was essential to outdoor religious festivals and processions. According to a seventeenth-century Spanish dictionary, villancicos were originally of popular origin, and the newly composed seventeenth-century villancicos drew their inspiration and some material from the popular tradition.[2] The villancico was without a doubt the most widely cultivated genre in seventeenth-century

Spanish music: it was mass-produced and was aimed at a mass audience. The prolific production of sacred works in the vernacular had social causes and function. Even among trained members of the clergy and in some monasteries, a large segment of the religious community (especially in provincial churches) was not proficient in Latin, and this was certainly true of the common people. Vernacular sacred music that included texts in regional languages and dialects, was more immediately effective as comprehensible religious propaganda and more appealing for public celebrations and community devotions. However, proclamations against the use of villancicos in churches reveal a mistrust of them on the part of the clergy. While many villancicos were written in the polychoral style associated with Latin sacred music, the genre also embraced several contemporary secular styles. To some critics, both texts and music sounded too much like secular music and thus not sacred enough. From secular song, villancico composers adopted well-known tunes set in simple polyphony for two to four voices, and the medium of a solo voice with accompaniment, along with the traditional form of strophes (*coplas*) with refrain (*estribillo*) from the *romance*. Theatrical music, especially that performed in the smaller, popular forms of the *entremés, baile* and *mojiganga*, was also an important source, and from it were adopted numerous sung dances such as the *villano, chacona, jácara* and *seguidilla*, and songs that parodied or burlesqued exotic foreign accents. Public theatrical performances and travelling theatrical companies helped to spread popular lore and musical forms, so that many villancico texts contain self-conscious imitations of standard theatrical scenes.

After about 1650, musical forms and styles that had belonged exclusively to the courtly sphere were also drawn into the villancico, beginning with those composed for the royal chapels and for the cathedral at Valladolid.[3] Specific favourite songs from the court plays were included in Christmas or Epiphany villancicos for the chapels, with their texts slightly altered. Towards the end of the century, musical forms such as the recitative and the concerted aria with obbligato instruments were adapted by church composers for use in cycles of villancicos. Because it could function as dramatic music with discrete scenes and characters and because its texts could be narrative, descriptive or dramatic, the villancico obviated the need for other pseudo-dramatic non-staged forms of sacred music, such as the dialogue, oratorio or sacred cantata.

To prevent the abuse of the villancico, it was the rule in most cathedrals that the *maestro* was responsible for composing all the villancicos needed during the church year, that villancicos could not be borrowed from other composers and that each set of villancicos could be performed only once. The composers were usually responsible for writing the texts as well, and the texts therefore are generally not of high literary quality. Even though these rules were broken, the demand for new villancicos impelled each *maestro* into a prolific output, and it also produced a kind of crisis: the genre was over-cultivated. Prone to widespread musical borrowing and recomposition, it became a genre of clichés and sterile gestures, so that by the end of the century villancicos in the traditional Spanish style were altogether predictable.

The institutional conservation of tradition with limited innovation is perhaps most clearly visible in the musical structure of the Spanish royal chapel during the early decades of the seventeenth century. Spain's traditionally strong political relationship with specific areas in Europe – Flanders, Portugal, Milan – and the political inheritance of Philip III's reign is reflected in the personnel of the royal chapel and chamber musicians during his reign. Moreover, the distribution and ranking of the court musicians influenced musical style by contributing to the conservation of the so-called *stile antico* or strict church style. Flemish musicians dominated the chapel as they had since the time of Charles V, although their Spanish peers also filled out the ranks of singers and wind players. The *maestro* of the chapel, the Fleming Mateo Romero (1575/6–1647; originally Matthieu Rosmarin), known as 'El Maestro Capitán', was probably the most respected composer of the early seventeenth century, and ruled the royal musical establishment with an iron hand from 1598 until his retirement at the end of 1633. His political career was extraordinary for a musician; he became Registrar (*Grefier*) to the Order of the Golden Fleece and was nominated by the king for the position of Chaplain of Honour to the Capilla de los Reyes Nuevos in Toledo. It is likely that Romero's control over the chapel musicians was bolstered by his political status, which he would not have attained had he been a native Spaniard who had simply risen through the ranks. His Latin sacred music (masses, motets, psalm settings etc.) written for the royal chapel falls into two broad categories: pieces in the contrapuntal *a cappella* style, and those in the grandiose polychoral style, some of which call for organ accompaniment and additional instruments. These are the two principal types of Latin sacred music that had been cultivated by Romero's teacher and former *maestro* of the chapel, the Flemish composer Philippe Rogier, whose music proved to be the strongest single influence on Spanish sacred music in the early seventeenth century.[4] Romero, as a follower of Rogier, ensured the survival of the traditional sacred styles at court, through his conservative, doctrinaire control of the chapel and choir school. Within a fixed, tradition-bound administrative structure, he represents the arch-conservative side of the royal music, and his was the most powerful force in the dialectic between tradition and innovation.

75. *'La sagrada forma': painting (1685–90) showing Carlos II kneeling before the elevated Sacred Host, surrounded by members of the court, with the choir of the royal monastery of the Escorial and a small organ*

The Early Baroque Era

The tradition of classical polyphony also influenced the secular music performed on important royal occasions during the first four decades of the century – large balls, masques and spectacle plays. None of the music for royal festivals and rituals before 1652 has survived, but the printed *relaciones* or descriptions of these entertainments help us to know what the music was like. From the masque and ball performed by the court at Valladolid to celebrate the birth of Philip IV in 1605 to the antiquated masque and ball called *El nuevo Olimpo* performed by courtiers on Philip's engagement to Mariana of Austria in 1648, ceremonial music for large choirs and loud wind instruments was the mainstay of court entertainments, as it had been of court celebrations in the Renaissance. For instance, in the 1605 masque two choirs in alternation sang staid verses in praise of the new-born prince. These choral hymns of praise were composed by Jean Dufon (known as Juan de Namur), the Flemish assistant choirmaster, who had also been a pupil of Rogier. He is known as a composer of sacred works in five to eight parts and of French chansons, but he is not credited with other pieces set to Spanish texts. The choral music for the masque may have reflected the sixteenth-century Franco-Flemish style in which Dufon was trained and which had been the dominant tradition of the chapel under Philip II. Early in the seventeenth century, the court relied on the types of music that had served the same function for solemn occasions under the greatest of monarchs (Charles V and Philip II) in an earlier Golden Age. The type of music chosen for the Valladolid masque of 1605 accorded with a larger iconography that depicted the dynastic inheritance of the new-born prince. The newly constructed *salón* was decorated with the tapestries depicting Charles V's conquest of Tunis in 1535. Since their completion in 1554, these had been an essential part of court and diplomatic ceremonial for Charles V and Philip II, and 'acquired an almost iconic status' for their descendants.[5] The association between a glorious history, hallowed artistic depictions and a decorous musical aesthetic is not surprising when we remember that royal occasions followed a predetermined set of rules for behaviour and protocol, the *etiquetas de palacio*, which were also inherited from the court of Charles V with only minor alterations.[6] The dignity of the celebration and the image of the monarchy were preserved in a strictly unified display in which the music's function determined its decorous style.

In the last years of Philip III and the early years of Philip IV's reign (1621–65), a lighter Spanish court entertainment, the early spectacle play, was developed for more relaxed celebrations and settings. With texts by courtier poets such as Lope de Vega, Luis Vélez de Guevara and Calderón, such plays were performed (at first by courtiers and later by professional troupes) outdoors during sojourns at country estates and in the royal gardens at Aranjuez or the Buen Retiro. They included descriptive ballads in a traditional style performed with guitar accompaniment, and clearly brought a current popular musical style into the courtly setting. In like manner, Calderón's early court plays, performed in the 1630s and 40s, call for musical techniques already common in *comedia* productions in the public theatres; in fact, they relied even more heavily on current musical styles and conventional theatrical practices by including more songs on traditional or well-known tunes and more accompanied solo singing in general. The king's chamber musicians, both singers and instrumentalists, were charged with providing some of the music for these performances (the song settings, the instrumental dances, the musical interludes between the acts of a play), and in this more flexible medium, without formal ritual and beyond the ruling hand of Mateo Romero, the innovative side of the royal music could flourish.

Beyond the rigid structure and ideology of the royal chapel, new compositional styles were heard at court as chamber music or in the theatres. The favourite entertainment of King Philip III and Queen Margarita was dancing, and for this purpose a strong complement of violinists was maintained at court. Eight violinists (five Spaniards, two Italians and an Englishman) were employed as servants in the queen's household. A group of six violinists from Milan, led by Stefano Limido, were hired for the king's household by the Duke of Lerma just in time for Philip III's wedding in 1599; they probably contributed to the modernization of instrumental practice at the Spanish court. Some years later, they were joined by other prominent foreign musicians, among them the Bolognese lute and theorbo player Filippo Piccinini, hired in 1613, and the English viol and violin virtuoso Henry Butler, who joined the court in 1623. Piccinini was the king's favourite musician and his teacher. Butler, who later became Philip IV's music teacher as well, was accorded special status because he was a foreigner and a gentleman. Philip IV and his brothers regularly played chamber music with Piccinini and Butler, and the king was reputed to be a fine player of the bass viol. We may assume that both of these talented foreigners exercised considerable influence on their fellow musicians because of their closeness to the king, such that instrumental music at court probably included sophisticated styles and new techniques. Piccinini had absorbed the musical traditions of Ferrara, Rome and Turin, and, because his early career in Italy followed a path similar to that of the young Girolamo Frescobaldi, he may have been an essential link between Spain and the new forms and spirit of instrumental music represented by the work of Frescobaldi.[7]

We may speculate that the court instrumentalists, in their capacity as chamber musicians, worked with an enthusiastic patron in a more flexible environment, outside the strict regime of the royal chapel. Through contact with excellent foreign musicians, they were exposed to recent trends and innovations from abroad, even if this exposure did not lead to the wholesale imitation of a foreign musical style. The court's instrumental music may well have been a window to the world, an innovative faction in an otherwise conservative institutional structure. The importance of the foreign musicians is underlined in court records: instrumental music and the teaching of musical instruments (except for guitar, harp and keyboard) were in such decline outside Madrid that Spanish replacements could rarely be found for the leading posts. Players of the theorbo, *lirone*, instruments of the violin family, and transverse flute were still recruited from Italy or France in the later seventeenth century. Throughout the century, string instruments and players were brought from Italy to ensure the quality of the king's music.

Spain, however, produced its own excellent harpists, guitarists and keyboard players, and, not surprisingly, a Spanish style and technique developed in the seventeenth-century repertory for these instruments. Most of the published guitar and harp music dates from the later part of the century. The repertory includes simple dance pieces and sets of variations, arrangements of popular dances, and a few settings based on popular tunes from secular songs. Although the most illustrious of seventeenth-century Spanish composers for the guitar – Gaspar Sanz, Antonio de Santa Cruz, Francisco Guerau – evidently knew the works of Italian and French composers, foreign influence on Spanish guitar music seems to have been slight, and it is undocumented for the harp. Perhaps the most readily identifiable feature of the Spanish style in guitar music is that the separation between the strummed or *rasgueado* style and the plucked or *punteado* style was maintained by Spanish composers throughout the century. In addition, the repertory of pieces based on Spanish dances such as the *jácara*, *marizápalos*, *villano*, *mariona* and *canario* was not replaced or superseded by pieces of a pan-European orientation until the eighteenth century. Because the guitar and the harp were the principal accompanimental and continuo instruments in Spain, Spanish continuo practice also retained the native style until the eighteenth century, and the repertory for guitar and harp was closely aligned with that of secular and theatrical songs.

Seventeenth-century Spanish secular music reacted to and reflected contemporary culture yet had its roots in an older tradition. It presents a fusion of popular or even folk elements with the technical and aesthetic goals of cultivated art music. The polyphonic songbooks or cancioneros preserve only part of what must have been a large repertory of settings of vernacular poetry of a high quality, often well-known texts by the best poets of the day. The repertory of the musical cancioneros parallels that of the printed poetic anthologies called romanceros or cancioneros, which were widely distributed and quite popular, with numerous prints and reprints of this type throughout the century. The availability of the poems in printed sources must have prompted composers to set these texts and ensured that the public knew the texts well. But it is curious that a parallel market for printed musical anthologies seems not to have emerged. Because two or more different musical settings of the same text usually share a core of material (a common tune and characteristic rhythmic figures), it is probably safe to say that these are independent settings of a well-known tune which was closely identified with its text. The repertory of the musical cancioneros is dominated by the court composers, with a lesser representation from composers who held important positions as church musicians in other regions of Spain. Mateo Romero, Juan Blas de Castro (*c* 1560–1631), Alvaro de los Ríos (1580–1623), Gabriel Díaz (1590–1638) and Manuel Machado (1590–1646) were employed by the court in the royal chapels or as chamber musicians. Juan Pujol (*c* 1573–1626) was never connected officially with the court, but for most of his career served at Saragossa and later at Barcelona Cathedral.

That the court and its activities became increasingly the focus of art music is attested to by the content of the last of the cancioneros, the Libro de Tonos Humanos, compiled in Madrid in 1655–6. It contains a repertory of 227 songs (mostly in four parts), some from the first decades of the century (by Romero and Machado) and a second, more contemporary layer of songs by a younger generation of composers, such as Carlos Patiño (1600–75) and Manuel Correa. The later songs show a change in musical style: they are longer, with a more elaborate *estribillo* (or refrain), and they display a closer relationship between text and music, and a preference for triple metre and hemiola rhythms. Many of the songs have fashionable texts by the most active of the court poets.[8] One anonymous song is actually a short scene from the prologue to Calderón's *Fortunas de Andrómeda y Perseo*, a mythological semi-opera given at court in 1653 (*see* fig. 76).

Songs from the two cancioneros most securely connected to the courtly circle, the Libro de Tonos Humanos and the Cancionero de Sablonara,[9] help us to understand the aesthetic of the court composers and the transformation of well-known, popular or 'common' materials into the sophisticated art music appropriate to an élite audience. It is clear that court composers such as Romero, Blas and Patiño were not content merely to provide a well-known tune with a correct harmonization but worked the pre-existing material into a new polyphonic setting.[10] In this way, the songs incorporated what was Spanish, popular and fashionable, yet demonstrated the 'art' of composition. This notion of art is related to the long-standing, continuing practice of instrumental *glosas* (or glosses), both improvised and composed. It is also very much in keeping with the practice of the best poets, who based many of their poems on borrowed material (e.g. popular refrains, stylish conceits) in order to retain a natural flavour and a popular spirit while exhibiting technical sophistication. One of the most successful of the courtier poets, Antonio Hurtado de Mendoza, praised some of Romero's music for a court entertainment as 'combining the crispness of parchment with the sweetness of the guitar',[11] which is to say that the composer infused the true compositional art, polyphony, with the uncontrived, popular native element of the well-known tunes.

This musical practice and aesthetic seem to have developed within a larger cultural shift, when, about the end of the sixteenth century, composers of secular music responded to the same artistic and social impulses that had prompted a major change in literary style and the birth of two new literary genres identified with the revival of interest in native culture (the *romance nuevo* and the *comedia nueva*). A younger generation of writers sought to rid Spanish literature of the all-too-high, classical, artificial tone that had characterized the work of sixteenth-century humanist writers such as Boscán and Garcilaso de la Vega. Informed by a broadly Aristotelian understanding of the relationship between art and reality, they sought to present, reflect or criticize an enhanced representation of the real world, defined as 'the behaviour and life of the citizens and all manner of people . . . all that happens in the world'.[12] Spanish poets, dramatists, artists and musicians exploited popular and traditional lore (themes, characters, modes of address, expressions, refrains and tunes) in order to give their creations a sense of immediacy and verisimilitude.

The songs on well-known texts, the *romance nuevo* and the new theatrical form of the *comedia*, together found an essential public forum in the commercial theatres that were opened in several Spanish cities in the last decade of the sixteenth century and the first of the seventeenth. Vocal music (songs and sung dances) was brought to the theatres as an expressive and structural resource of the *comedia nueva*. The identifiable quality of many of the texts and tunes helped to bring the audience closer to the action on stage, and the simplicity of the musical settings made them appropriate for the level of both performers and audience. Perhaps because of their success in the public theatres, the well-known songs (many of which are preserved in the cancioneros) dominated secular music at least during the first half of the seventeenth century, and stayed in fashion into the eighteenth. The repertory of the cancioneros also influenced vernacular sacred music. For example, there are many songs with devotional texts that are merely slightly altered from their secular originals, and many villancicos inspired by or modelled on secular songs.

The repertory of secular songs composed in the second half of the seventeenth century (surviving mainly in the form of loose manuscript scores and performing parts) is remarkably homogeneous. The style of Juan Hidalgo, court composer of chamber and theatre songs, became the ideal 'modern' style and was consciously emulated by other composers throughout Spain. Because Hidalgo was the best and the most esteemed of the court composers, his music was considered to be of the highest status and in the most refined style, and therefore worthy of emulation. While this courtly style was not imposed on his contemporaries, it filtered down from the elevated domain of the court and became the core of the Spanish national style.

Hidalgo's music and its wide dissemination signalled a readjustment in the relationship between popular music and cultivated art music in the later seventeenth century. The Spanish style became less dependent on materials borrowed from the popular tradition. These were replaced by a characteristic set of stylized but refined musical gestures and figures, appropriate to the images and affects in the equally refined, highly rhetorical poetry of the newer song-texts. The generally consonant, transparent texture of Spanish vocal music of the preceding years was retained, now enriched and further defined through the exploitation of a new set of musical clichés and figures that were appreciated all the more because of their familiarity. Again, what we see is a fusion of tradition and innovation.

Opera, the most innovative and socially significant musical genre to develop in seventeenth-century Europe, was only mildly influential in Spain. Even though some operatic ideals and forms were adopted at court during the Hidalgo epoch, at no time does seventeenth-century Spanish music display the wholehearted assimilation of a foreign style. The first performance of an opera on Spanish soil took place in the early years of Philip IV's reign and is a particularly strong illustration of the Spanish rejection of a wholly foreign genre and musical style. In 1627, the Florentine stage designer and engineer Cosimo Lotti (*d* 1643), eager to further his recent appointment at the Spanish court, planned the presentation of an opera in the Florentine style for the royal family. His idea appealed to the ambitious Florentines installed at the Tuscan embassy in Madrid, and the entire production was planned, supervised and presented by the Florentine delegation. Aware of the virtual rejection of Italian poetry and drama in Spain at the time, they turned to the leading Spanish dramatist, Lope de Vega, for a libretto

76. Stage set by Baccio di Bianco for the celebration scene from the semi-opera 'Fortunas de Andrómeda y Perseo' (libretto by Calderón, music attributed to Juan Hidalgo) performed at the Madrid court in 1653

in Spanish. Lope's text (the only surviving part of the opera), *La selva sin amor*, consists of a prologue and seven scenes written entirely in Italian metres, a metrical scheme unique among Lope's works for the stage. This was because Lope's text, like the earliest Florentine librettos, was based on a pastoral fable of love and disdain and written as the poetic and structural vehicle for continuous recitative, with only a few closed numbers (a trio, some closing refrains, and choruses). According to the diplomatic correspondence between the embassy in Madrid and the Tuscan court, the music was largely composed by Filippo Piccinini, who was drafted in somewhat against his better judgment, since he claimed to be unfamiliar with, and unskilled in, the writing of recitative. Moreover, recitative was completely unknown to the Spanish court musicians. And audiences were unprepared too. Thus opera and recitative had an inauspicious introduction to Spain. Unsurprisingly, the opera seems to have been a failure, an outcome hardly likely to be attributable to Lotti's scenery or Lope's text but rather to Piccinini's presumably inexpert music. After *La selva sin amor*, opera was not heard again in Spain until 1660, and the genre of the idealized pastoral with music was avoided until after 1655. Here we see the Spanish rejection of an imported musical style (recitative) that was not only artificial but the very antithesis of popular native styles; and it was no doubt a misjudgment to present recitative within a theatrical genre – the metrically too regular, idealized courtly pastoral – that was too far removed from the strong verisimilitude of early seventeenth-century Spanish drama.

Because of the problems posed by *La selva sin amor*, and perhaps because of the rigidity of musical traditions in Spain, Philip IV made no attempt to recruit an Italian composer to work with his Italian scenographers on court plays. It would appear that an idealized imported form, pastoral opera, was not considered appropriate to the grandeur of the 'most Catholic king'. The Spanish cultural and political situation demanded a compromise between native and foreign styles in court entertainments, a compromise required if operatic trends were to be received well in Madrid.

After Philip IV's second marriage, to Mariana of Austria, and once the monumental project of the Buen Retiro palace was completed and the court theatres renovated, spectacular dramas were cultivated with renewed interest as the principal court entertainments. The splendour, solidity and political vigour of Philip IV's reign found a worthy symbol in the mature work of Pedro Calderón de la Barca (1600–81), the greatest dramatist of his time, who decided in 1651 to write only plays for the court and religious plays (*autos sacramentales*) for Corpus Christi. In the court plays, the heroic dignity symbolic of royal power was combined with the dramatic flexibility of the earlier spectacle plays and the popular appeal and

77. *Drawing of a tarasca for the 1674 Corpus Christi celebration in Madrid*

verisimilitude of the *comedia*. The music of Calderón's court plays juxtaposed traditional and popular songs with solo songs and recitatives that indicate a generic (but not a stylistic) influence from contemporary Italian opera. In the zarzuelas, lighter plays on pastoral stories, elaborate solo songs, a few sung dialogues and some choruses are woven into a short spoken play. Calderón's *El laurel de Apolo* (1657) was the prototype for this enduring musical-theatrical genre.[13] In the mythological semi-operas, the most exalted genre, dialogues between the gods and dramatic monologues for the gods were performed as recitatives, and their songs to the often uncomprehending mortals are notated mostly in the form of strophic airs, called *tonos humanos* or *tonadas*. Thus, the gods had a special kind of music distinguished from that of the simple mortals, who sang only 'realistic' traditional or well-known songs, with texts largely from the pre-existing repertory of the cancioneros. The only imported type of music consistently used in the mythological plays was recitative, and the circumstances surrounding its adaptation reveal a great deal about the social and cultural roles of music in Spain.

Recitative was brought into the earliest of Calderón's mature mythological plays, *La fiera, el rayo y la piedra* (1652) and *Fortunas de Andrómeda y Perseo* (1653). Both plays were performed with scenery and stage designs by the third of Philip IV's Italian engineers, the Florentine Baccio del Bianco, who had come to Spain in 1651 (*see* fig. 76 above).[14] As with the abortive attempt to introduce recitative to Spain, in *La selva sin amor*, the use of recitative in Calderón's plays was an Italian idea. Baccio del Bianco, formerly in the employ of the Tuscan court at Florence, and the papal legate Giulio Rospigliosi, a poet and opera librettist important in the history of Roman opera under the Barberini family, worked to convince the Spaniards that one could indeed speak in song. According to Del Bianco, the Spaniards claimed never even to have heard of recitative before, and were at first stubborn in their opposition to the idea of acting in song. Through the persistence of Rospigliosi and Del Bianco, recitative became an essential feature of Calderón's mythological plays. Like the Florentine pioneers, the Spaniards finally understood the ideal of speech in song as 'a recitative style, which, being a mixture of declamation and music, was neither really music nor declamation, but rather an intoned consonance, accompanied by the choir of instruments'.[15] Admittedly, the use of recitative in Calderón's plays is an isolated example of grafting an Italianate genre into a decidedly Spanish medium. But in these plays (in essence, semi-operas) the form and the objective of recitative were adapted to the Spanish usage. The recitatives from the Spanish plays are not mere imitations of Italian recitatives (nor are they essentially close in style to the recitative passages from French court plays). Only in the very earliest Spanish examples do we find the static bass line and many repeated notes in the vocal part that were still found in the long recitative narratives and dialogues of Roman opera. In general, Spanish recitative is not as freely expressive in its declamation, harmony, dissonance treatment or rhythm as Italian recitative of the same period.

For some 40 years, Calderón's zarzuelas and semi-operas dominated the court stages (they were frequently revived), along with plays in a similar vein by his followers. But recitative was avoided in most of the plays written by other dramatists, and it was only infrequently employed in zarzuelas too. Thus, even after the introduction of recitative in 1652, Italian operatic influence on the music of the Spanish court plays was minimal.

In 1660 two operas with texts by Calderón and music by Hidalgo, *La púrpura de la rosa* and *Celos aun del aire matan*, were perfomed at court. The only Spanish operas from before the eighteenth century, they were produced for specific, momentous occasions with a definite political purpose. They were written to commemorate two related events, the signing of the Peace of the Pyrenees, the long-awaited truce between France and Spain after 35 years of war, and the marriage of the Spanish princess María Teresa to Louis XIV. Probably through diplomatic and intelligence reports, the Spaniards learnt that the French were planning to celebrate the events by performing at court Italian operas specially commissioned by Cardinal Mazarin. Not wishing to be outdone, and eager to display its own elegance, the Spanish crown commissioned its own operas. By depending on artists in his own employ, Philip IV could ensure that the entertainments would not only be appropriate to the occasion but would contain the required political message.

Hidalgo's score for *La púrpura de la rosa* has not survived, but we do have music for voices and continuo for the three acts of *Celos aun del aire matan*. The score includes all the forms commonly found in semi-operas and zarzuelas, and it is stylistically consistent with other Spanish music of the period. Moreover, Hidalgo's solution to the problems posed by having to set three acts in continuous music without spoken dialogue does not depend on any foreign model.

Although he was acknowledged as the leading composer of theatrical music in Spain, Hidalgo's career, financial state and social position at court do not seem to have been greatly affected by his substantial and superior contributions as a composer. He was never promoted to an administrative post in the musical establishment, nor was he awarded an honorary or 'political' position in the king's chamber. He was not, therefore, the social or administrative equal of men like Calderón, Baccio del Bianco or Rospigliosi. He was paid small amounts for his work on specific productions, and from time to time he successfully petitioned the crown for additional remuneration, since his work on the court plays was additional to his duties as harpist in the royal chapel. Although he enjoyed a high reputation among musicians, his name does not appear in any of the descriptive accounts of the performances, nor is it cited in Del Bianco's letters. We know little of his ideas about music, his knowledge of foreign musical styles or his musical education. Because of his inferior social standing and position at court, and perhaps also because he lacked the refined formal literary education of his non-musical colleagues, Hidalgo was entirely subservient to the dramatist and the stage designer in general artistic decisions. On at least two important occasions, he followed the advice or instructions of his non-musical superiors. It was the exhortations of Del Bianco and Rospigliosi that brought about the introduction of recitative into the court plays. In 1656 Del Bianco persuaded Hidalgo to compose a lament 'more or less in the Italian style' for the climactic scene of Luis de Ulloa's pastoral play *Pico y Canente*. In style and technique the lament ('Crédito es de mi decoro') eschews the musical devices essential to the Italian lament and is not Italianate.[16] Hidalgo worked under the supervision of the Italian stage designer, but the advice he received was that of a non-musician and it did not fundamentally alter his technique or his approach to composition. Although he was obliged to include recitative in 1652 (and possibly in six subsequent plays) and a lament in 1656, he was never forced to change his musical idiom or to adopt a foreign musical language. The definition and realization of the style and content of individual pieces in the court plays were his responsibility, but his impact on the structure and function of the theatrical genres was probably negligible.

Whether we consider the early seventeenth-century polyphonic songs of Romero, the villancicos and sacred works of Patiño or Cristobal Galán (*c* 1630–84) or the theatrical airs and recitatives of Hidalgo and Durón, it is debatable how far the term 'Baroque' (in its usual musical connotation) may be applied to seventeenth-century Spanish music. Nevertheless, a distinctly Spanish seventeenth-century style developed in the works of these composers, which reveals an aesthetic of restraint, structural clarity, subtle rhetorical eloquence and direct expression. The generalized style and aesthetic were a response to the role of art music in Spanish culture and, especially, the place of music in society: musicians were subject to a rigid set of social, administrative and artistic conventions, and music itself was accorded a lesser status compared with painting and literature (perhaps because it was less useful as a tangible symbol or emblem of religious or political power). While Spaniards were familiar with foreign developments, they did not feel obliged to emulate or imitate them, and so the style of Spanish music in this epoch also responded to the cultural and political position of Spain in Europe. In music, Spain maintained her national character, remaining clearly separated, but not isolated, from other countries.

NOTES

[1] Documented in M. Querol, 'Corresponsales de Miguel Gómez Camargo', *Anuario musical*, xiv (1959), 165–78; and J. López-Calo, 'Corresponsales de Miguel de Irízar', ibid, xviii (1963), 197–222, and xx (1965), 209–33.

[2] See S. de Covarrubias Orozco, *Tesoro de la Lengua Castellana o Española según la impresión de 1611, con las adiciones de Benito Remigio Noydens publicadas en la de 1674*, ed. M. de Riquer (Barcelona, 1943), s.v. 'Villanescas', 1009.

[3] On the presence of theatrical songs in the villancicos composed for Valladolid by Miguel Gómez Camargo, see C. Caballero, 'Nuevas fuentes musicales de *Los celos hacen estrellas* de Juan Vélez de Guevara', *Música y teatro*, ed. L. García Lorenzo, Cuadernos de teatro clásico, iii (Madrid, 1988), 119–55; and idem, *Música profana y teatral del Barroco en la catedral de Valladolid* (in preparation).

[4] On Rogier and Romero, see P. Becquart, *Musiciens néerlandais à la cour de Madrid: Philippe Rogier et son école (1560–1647)* (Brussels, 1967).

[5] J. Brown and J. H. Elliott, *A Palace for a King: the Buen Retiro and the Court of Philip IV* (New Haven and London, 1980), 148.

[6] ibid, 31; J. E. Varey, 'La mayordomìa mayor y los festejos palaciegos del siglo XVII', *Anales del Instituto de Estudios Madrileños*, iv (1969), 145–68.

[7] Piccinini came from a family of well-known lutenists who had served the Este court at Ferrara until 1597. After the dissolution of Alfonso II's court, Filippo and his older, more famous brother Alessandro were in the musical service of the Bentivoglio family in Rome, and Filippo briefly served Cardinal Pietro Aldobrandini before accepting a position with the Savoy court in Turin (1609–12). See A. Newcomb, 'Girolamo Frescobaldi 1608–1615: a Documentary Study', *Annales musicologiques*, vii (1964–77), 111–58; F. Hammond, *Girolamo Frescobaldi* (Cambridge, Mass., and London, 1983).

[8] On the court poets, see G. A. Davies, *A Poet at Court: Don Antonio Hurtado de Mendoza (1586–1644)* (Oxford, 1971).

[9] Copied in Madrid by the court copyist Claudio de la Sablonara in 1624 or 1625, this source is the subject of R. A. Pelinski, *Die weltliche Vokalmusik Spaniens am Anfang des 17. Jahrhunderts. Der Cancionero Claudio de la Sablonara* (Tutzing, 1971); and *Cancionero musical y poético del siglo XVII recogido por Claudio de la Sablonara*, ed. J. Aroca (Madrid, 1916).

[10] Twelve secular songs by Patiño are transcribed in *Las obras humanas de Carlos Patiño*, ed. D. Becker (Cuenca, 1987); for a study of Blas, see L. Robledo, *Juan Blas de Castro (ca. 1561–1631): vida y obra musical* (Saragossa, 1989).

[11] Hurtado de Mendoza did not name Romero in his description of a performance of the Count of Villamediana's play *La gloria de Niquea* (composers are never named in connection with court plays in this period), but he refers to the 'maestro de capilla'; A. Hurtado de Mendoza, *Fiesta que se hizo en Aranjuez a los años del Rey Nuestro Señor D. Felipe IIII* (Madrid, 1623), f.15v.

[12] Covarrubias, *Tesoro*, s.v. 'Comedia', 341–2. Lope de Vega's *Arte nuevo de hacer comedias en este tiempo* (Madrid, 1609) contains a similar statement (lines 50–54), which translates roughly thus: 'The true art of writing plays, as all types of poetry, proposes to imitate the actions of men and portray the customs of its time'.

[13] The first zarzuela was written for performance at the Zarzuela Palace, a royal hunting lodge in the wooded outskirts of Madrid, so that the name of the palace was identified with the new genre. The word 'zarzuela' comes from 'zarza', meaning bramble bush; hence its association with the rustic retreat and with rustic or pastoral settings and characters.

[14] Information concerning Baccio del Bianco from M. Bacci, 'Lettere inedite di Baccio del Bianco', *Paragone*, xiv (1963), 68–77; P. D. Massar, 'Scenes from a Calderón Play by Baccio del Bianco', *Master Drawings*, xv (1977), 365–75; L. Bianconi and T. Walker, 'Dalla *Finta pazza* alla *Veremonda*: storie di Febiarmonici', *RIM*, x (1975), 379–454, esp. 452–3.

[15] Quoted from the rubrics in the presentation manuscript, preceding the appearance of the

The Early Baroque Era

deities in Act 1 of Calderon's *Fortunas de Andrómeda y Perseo* (Harvard U., Houghton Library, MS Typ. 258H, f.22*v*).

[16] The lament is studied and transcribed in '*La plática de los dioses*: Music and the Calderonian Court Play', chap.2 of P. Calderón de la Barca, *La estatua de Prometeo*, ed. M. R. Greer with a study of the music by L. K. Stein (Kassel, 1986), 49–59, and in L. K. Stein, *Songs of Mortals, Dialogues of the Gods: Music and Theatre in Seventeenth-Century Spain* (Oxford, 1993), 274–82.

BIBLIOGRAPHICAL NOTE

Historical-political background

Two books and an essay by J. H. Elliott can be recommended: *Imperial Spain 1469–1716* (London, 1963), *The Count-Duke of Olivares: the Statesman in an Age of Decline* (New Haven and London, 1986) and 'Philip IV of Spain, Prisoner of Ceremony' in *The Courts of Europe: Politics, Patronage and Royalty 1400–1800*, ed. A. G. Dickens (London, 1977), 169–89. So too can two studies by H. Kamen: *Inquisition and Society in Spain in the Sixteenth and Seventeenth Centuries* (Bloomington, 1985) and *Spain in the Later Seventeenth Century 1665–1700* (London, 1980); and a further valuable study: J. Lynch, *Spain under the Habsburgs*, ii: *Spain and America 1598–1700* (Oxford, 2/1981).

Literature and the visual arts

For an overview of the literature of the period, see R. O. Jones, *A Literary History of Spain*, ii: *The Golden Age, Prose and Poetry, the Sixteenth and Seventeenth Centuries* (London, 1971). More specific studies include N. D. Shergold, *A History of the Spanish Stage from Medieval Times until the End of the Seventeenth Century* (Oxford, 1967), H. J. Chaytor, *Dramatic Theory in Spain: Extracts from Literature before and during the Golden Age* (Cambridge, 1925), and G. A. Davies, *A Poet at Court: Don Antonio Hurtado de Mendoza (1586–1644)* (Oxford, 1971).

On the visual arts, two fine studies are J. Brown, *Velázquez Painter and Courtier* (New Haven and London, 1986), and idem and J. H. Elliott, *A Palace for a King: the Buen Retiro and the Court of Philip IV* (New Haven and London, 1980).

Music

The standard work is J. López-Calo, *Historia de la música española*, iii: *Siglo XVII* (Madrid, 1983). See also L. K. Stein, *Songs of Mortals, Dialogues of the Gods: Music and Theatre in Seventeenth-Century Spain* (Oxford, 1993); and idem, 'Opera and the Spanish Political Agenda', *AcM*, lxiii (1991), 125–67.

A representative sampling of seventeenth-century Spanish sacred music is available in the following anthologies: *Música barroca española*, iii: *Polifonía policoral litúrgica*, ed. M. Querol, Monumentos de la música española, xli (Barcelona, 1982); and *Polifonía aragonesa*, i: *Obras de los maestros de las capillas de música de Zaragoza en los siglos XV–XVII*, ed. P. Calahorra (Saragossa, 1984); ii: *Obras de los maestros de música de la Colegial de Daroca en los siglos XVI y XVII*, ed. idem (Saragossa, 1985); iii: *Obras de los maestros de la Catedral de Albarracín (Teruel) de los siglos XVI–XVIII*, ed. J. M. Muneta (Saragossa, 1986). See also *Carlos Patiño: Obras musicales recopiladas*, i, ed. L. Siemens Hernández (Cuenca, 1986). For a selection of villancicos, see *Música barroca española*, iv: *Villancicos polifónicos del siglo XVII*, ed. M. Querol, Monumentos de la música española, xlii (Barcelona, 1982).

Chapter XVI

Mexico

STEVEN BARWICK

In 1523 the first Franciscan friars to reach Mexico landed at what is now Veracruz to begin their monumental task of converting the Indians to Christianity. They found a people subdued by battle, yet one in whose lives music and dance played a highly important role. The reports of early missionaries tell of the wide use of music, in war, sacrificial ceremonies and funeral rites as well as Montezuma's dinner music.

What we know of pre-conquest music in Mexico has come from the researches of archaeologists, ethnomusicologists and early historians, but no written music of the period survives. Some scholars have collected melodies from Indian groups which may still contain some of the elements of their ancestors' music, while studies of pre-conquest instruments and figurines of musicians playing instruments uncovered in archaeological digs have led to valuable conclusions about the country's earliest music. Much information about the prominent place music played in the lives of the aborigines has come from examining early Indian codices in which musicians are pictured and from accounts of chroniclers who lived in Mexico immediately after the conquest.

Evidence that some features of Mexico's pre-conquest music remained constant for centuries came to light about 40 years ago with the discovery of wall paintings on an eighth-century temple at Bonampak, in the Chiapas jungle. In the Instituto Nacional de Antropología at Mexico city one can see full-scale reproductions colour of these paintings showing instruments still in use when Cortés arrived in the sixteenth century. Essentially the same instruments were used by Mayan, Aztecan and other ethnic Indian groups, although their names varied according to the language spoken.[1] Chief among these instruments was the *huehuetl*, a cylindrical wooden drum standing on legs and varying in size up to a metre in height, with an animal hide stretched across the top. It was capable of producing two notes commonly a fifth apart and was played by beating with the hands. The *teponaztli*, again a hollowed-out cylinder but played with mallets, could also produce two pitches. It had two lateral incisions on top and a rectangular opening on the opposite side. Carvings on some of these archaeological instruments have revealed, often in detail, how and where they were used. Other Indian instruments of the period included various sorts of rasps, rattles, flutes (clay, reed or bone) and conch-shell trumpets. Another type of trumpet made of clay or wood was tubular in shape and up to two feet in length. This type appears in the Bonampak paintings, where warriors in battle scenes are shown blowing on trumpets longer than an arm. No string instruments were used in pre-conquest Mexico.

Early colonial accounts of what the aborigines' music sounded like vary from one chronicler to another. One of the early conquerors in Cortés's army, Bernal Díaz del Castillo, wrote in his *Historia verdadera de la conquista de la Nueva-España* of his contact with Aztec music:[2]

> As we were retreating we heard the sound of the trumpets from the great Cue, which from its height dominates the whole city [the great Cue was the principal sacrifical temple, and stood on the exact spot where now rises the Cathedral of Mexico City]. We heard also a drum, a most dismal sound indeed it was . . . as it resounded so that one could hear it two leagues off, and with it many small tambourines and shell trumpets, horns and whistles. At that moment . . . they were offering the hearts of ten of our comrades and much blood to the idols that I have mentioned . . .
>
> Again there was sounded the dismal drum of Huichilobos. There sounded also many other shells and horns and things like trumpets and the sound of them all was terrifying . . . The Mexicans offered great sacrifice and celebrated festivals every night and sounded their cursed drum, trumpets, kettle drums and shells, and uttered yells and howls. Then they sacrified our comrades . . .

While this description might represent a pre-missionary impression of music in a particularly horrifying event, another point of view comes from Toribio Motolinía, who was one of twelve Franciscans who arrived in Mexico in 1524 and whose writings were among the earliest to speak of the Indians. The following extract from his *Memoriales* addresses the situation after the missionaries had exerted their influence:[3]

> One of the main happenings everywhere in this country were the festivals of song and dance, which were organized not only for the delight of inhabitants themselves, but more especially to honor their gods, whom they thought well pleased by such service . . . it was the custom in each town for the nobility to maintain in their own houses choirs of singers, amongst whom some were composers of new songs and dances. Composers skilled in fashioning songs and ballads were everywhere in great demand. Among singers, those with good bass voices were the most sought after for the

frequent private ritual observances held inside the houses of the nobility.

Singing and dancing usually enlivened the principal fiestas occurring every twenty days, and also less important fiestas . . . when a battle victory was celebrated, or when a new member of the nobility was created, or when a chieftan married, or when some other striking event occurred, the singing masters composed new songs especially for the occasion.

The earliest missionary to Mexico, Fray Pedro de Gante (?1480–1572), found a way to win over the Indians, who at first fled from contact with the priests and did not take kindly to the new faith. This skilled teacher's method is recorded in the sixteenth-century Códice Franciscano:[4]

By the grace of God I began to understand them and to see how they must be won. I noted that in their worship of their gods, they were always singing and dancing before them. Always, before a victim was sacrificed to the idol, they sang and danced before the image. Seeing this and that all their songs were addressed to the gods, I composed very solemn songs regarding the law of God and the faith . . . Then when Christmas time drew near, I invited every one from a radius of twenty leagues to come to the festival of the Nativity . . . So many came that the *patio* would not hold them all, and they sang, the very night of Nativity, 'Today is born the Redeemer'.

The success of which Gante spoke began after he had spent about three years in Texcoco, where he learnt the Náhuatl language and started a school. In 1524, a year after his arrival, twelve Franciscans arrived, and after that scarcely a year passed without the appearance of more missionaries – more Franciscans, Dominicans (1526), Augustinians (1533).[5] Representatives of the newly formed Jesuit order entered Mexico in 1572, and the Carmelites followed in 1585. The Indians assimilated European cultural traits in an amazing manner. They participated in the musical activities of the church and were adept at making and playing instruments.

In December 1527 Cortés returned to Castile and took with him some Indians, who displayed their abilities to the court of Charles V and then to Pope Clement VII. The next year Juan de Zumárraga (1468–1548) was appointed the first Bishop of Mexico, and Mexico City Cathedral was founded. Within two years the Sunday services were sung by an Indian choir which had been trained at the San Francisco school opened near the cathedral and directed by Gante. As early as 1532 he wrote to the emperor to say that Indian singers trained in his school were so accomplished that they could perform creditably in the imperial chapel. His statement is believable inasmuch as he originally came from Ghent, where he would have known the work of the great Flemish masters of the Renaissance.[6]

In the mission schools, Indians learnt not only how to sing and play instruments but also how to copy music that the bishop had obtained from Spain and to build instruments. The Franciscan missionary and writer Juan de Torquemada wrote in his *Monarquía indiana* (1615) that there was no single instrument used in churches that Indians in the larger towns had not learnt to make and play. He stated that it was no longer necessary to import instruments from Spain but that organs, installed in nearly all the churches administered by the orders, were constructed under the supervision of Spanish builders. In the same document Torquemada gave the following testimony:[7]

> Nowadays every town of one hundred population or more contains singers who have learned how to sing the Offices, the Mass, Vespers, and are proficient in polyphonic music; competent instrumentalists are also found everywhere. The small towns all have their supply of instruments, and even the smallest hamlets, no matter how insignificant, have three or four Indians at least who sing every day in church. Especially is this true in the provinces of Michoacán and Jalisco.

Finally, Torquemada spoke of the Indians' creativity in the European idiom:

> With this I conclude: Only a few years after the Indians began to learn the chant, they also began to compose. Their villancicos, their polyphonic music in four parts, certain masses and other liturgical works, all composed with adroitness, have been adjudged superior works of art when shown Spanish masters of composition. Indeed the Spanish masters often thought they could not have been written by Indians.

Ironically, the friars' success in cultivating Indian musicians had gone too far by the middle of the sixteenth century. Probably many Indians enjoyed exemption from taxation and also a special prestige among their people by virtue of their profession. The authorities sought to curtail their number, and the Dominican Alonso de Montúfar, Archbishop of Mexico from 1551 to 1572, called a church council meeting in 1556 to deal with the matter. The council's printed provisions tell us much about the musical environment of the time:[8]

> The great excess in our archdiocese of musical instruments, of chirimías, flutes, viols, trumpets, and the great number of Indians who spend their time in playing and singing obliges us to apply a remedy and to place a limit on all this superabundance. We there-

fore require and order that from henceforth trumpets shall not be played in churches during divine service, and require that no more be bought; those which are already in possession of the churches shall be used only in outdoor processions, and not as accompaniment for the liturgy. As for the chirimías and flutes, we require that they be stored in the principal towns and only distributed for use in the villages on festival days of their patron saints; and as for viols and other instruments, we request that these too be no longer used; we urge all the clergy to install organs everywhere so that indecorous and improper instruments may be banished from the church. The organ is the correct instrument for use in the church, and we wish its use to become universal in Mexico.

We charge all clergy in our archdiocese and all other clergy in Mexico residing outside our archdiocese but under our spiritual jurisdiction, carefully to limit the number of singers so that no more than are necessary shall continue to spend their time simply in singing. Those who are permitted to continue must be able to sing plainchant intelligently. They shall sing polyphonic music only when their singing conforms to standards which we consider acceptable.

Philip II reinforced the Mexican council's provisions in 1561 with a cedula ordering a reduction in the number of Indians permitted to work as musicians, but not all of the proposed restrictions were effective, and the proliferation of Indian musicians continued.

It was into this developing abundance of Indian musicians that Bishop Zumárraga first introduced choirbooks and hired musicians from Spain for the enrichment of his cathedral. Juan Xuárez, a canon of the cathedral, had been in Mexico since 1530, and he was assigned to teach young Indian choristers polyphonic singing, thus bringing music training more directly into the cathedral itself. In 1539 he was appointed *maestro de capilla* of the cathedral in Mexico City, and one Antonio Ramos was appointed cathedral organist.

The responsibilities of the choirmaster included composing, the selection of repertory, teaching the choirboys and preparing the musicians for the many services. Each cathedral eventually had one choirmaster, responsible to the cathedral chapter (*cabildo*), which supervised all the cathedral's activities. When a musician needed to be appointed, the chapter determined the job description and salary. The minutes (*actas*) of cathedral chapters remain as a valuable source of information about music and musicians in the Mexican cathedrals. Applicants for the post of choirmaster were carefully screened, and they had to demonstrate their ability at composition through serious competition.

As far as is known, no works by this first *maestro de capilla* in New Spain survive. Xuárez was succeeded in 1556 by Lázaro del Álamo, who had been a singer in the cathedral for two years. Although his music, too, has not survived, his work is mentioned in the *Túmulo imperial* of 1560 by Francisco Cervantes de Salazar, a description of an elaborate ceremony in memory of Charles V in which Álamo directed his own compositions as well as some double-choir antiphonal music by Morales. Álamo was followed in 1570 by the Spaniard Juan de Victoria, from Burgos, who, after four years, was summarily dismissed. He was replaced in 1575 by the Spaniard Hernando Franco (1532–85), the leading composer of sixteenth-century New Spain, who retained the position until his death.[9]

Franco probably emigrated to New Spain in 1554 but is first mentioned only in 1573, as *maestro de capilla* of Guatemala Cathedral. It was possibly an improvement in salary that prompted his move to Mexico. Construction of a new cathedral had begun in 1573. The choir was designed, in the style of Spanish cathedrals, with seating on opposite sides, which facilitated the type of antiphonal performance common at the time. Franco's major works, a set of sixteen *Magnificat* settings in the eight modes, were written for such performance. Six of the twelve verses of each *Magnificat* were sung in plainsong, alternating with six in polyphony. This is largely in four parts; although there are occasional three-part verses, and an expansion to six parts, containing two-part canons, for the concluding 'Sicut erat' verses. The music survives (without the lost third-tone settings) in a handsome manuscript dating from 1611 in Mexico City. Franco also wrote a number of other works, including hymns, responsories and psalms. All his music shows that he was a master of his craft, who established a tradition for his successors to follow.[10]

While the polyphony of Franco and other composers discussed below was widely used in cathedral services, most liturgical music consisted of plainchant. Great collections of manuscripts of chant survive in various cathedral archives, and, with the advent of printing in Mexico in 1540 (over 200 books were published during the sixteenth century), at least thirteen volumes containing plainchant portions of the Mass and Offices as well as ritual directions appeared between 1556 and 1589. These books, containing the first music printed in the New World, provided material for use in Indian missionary parishes as well as in cathedrals and in smaller churches. Only a few copies of these volumes can be found today in scattered locations such as the British Library and libraries in Mexico, Chile and the United States. Print runs could have been as high as 1000 copies. This to some extent verifies the claims of the missionary chroniclers Mendieta and Torquemada that there was an astounding development of Indian choirs in sixteenth-century Mexico, for a single copy, placed on a choristers' lectern, was large enough to be read by an entire choir.[11]

There were comparatively few Spanish choral singers, and these only in the larger cathedrals, but immigrants from Spain continued to be appointed as choirmasters in the important cathedrals. In 1576 Franco's eventual successor, Juan Hernández (1545–1600), updated a *Graduale Dominicale* and according to the title-page composed some of the chants in the volume. He was clearly aware of the latest decrees of the Council of Trent. It has been tentatively suggested that he can be identified with the composer Juan de Lienas, but Lienas appears to have been a somewhat later composer of church music found in Mexican sources outside cathedral archives, chief among them the anthology known as the manuscript of the Convento del Carmen.[12]

Hernández was followed in 1625 by Antonio Rodríguez Mata, who had already figured in the cathedral's musical activities for some time. In the same year an English traveller in the New World, the Dominican Thomas Gage, wrote of the religious music he had heard in Mexico City, declaring the performances so exquisite that he could say that people were 'drawn to their churches more for the delight of the music than for any delight in the service of God'. A disaster that greatly affected the musical life of the capital struck in 1629, when floods caused tremendous destruction and death and forced 27 000 inhabitants to flee. More than 30 000 Indians died, and, according to reports from Archbishop Manso de Zúñiga to Philip IV, of 20 000 Spanish families only 400 remained.[13]

The next significant choirmaster-composer was Francisco López Capillas (c1612–74), who served from 1654 to 1674 and was the first natire Mexican to hold the post. He has been called the 'most profound and prolific composer of Masses in Mexican history'[14] and is represented in four of the nine choirbooks of polyphony in the Mexico City archive, two of which are devoted to his works alone. His masses and a set of eight *Magnificat* settings show his mastery of the *stile antico*, which survived in Mexico as a vehicle for formal religious music as late as the mid eighteenth century.

López Capillas's successor was Antonio de Salazar (c1650–1715), who became *maestro de capilla* in 1688. He had served with distinction at Puebla Cathedral, whose archives include such representative works by him as six Latin hymns and a *Magnificat*; his name also appears on the title-pages of four villancico cycles by the poetess Sor Juana Inés de la Cruz, which were published and performed in Puebla. In Mexico City he continued to be as productive as he had been at Puebla; he was also concerned about the condition of the cathedral's musical patrimony, and he recovered missing books of polyphony and had them repaired and safely stored. A *Te Deum* by him was performed in cathedral ceremonies in 1701–2, as were several four-voice hymns; these are in two sections, the first by Salazar, the second by his pupil Manuel de Zumaya. Salazar's polychoral motets are outstanding. His *O sacrum convivium*, for example, contains typical Baroque features. The two four-part choirs are treated brilliantly, and the use of imitation, antiphonal effects, dotted rhythms and marked contrasts show him breaking away from the *stile antico*. In the last quarter of the seventeenth century instrumental music also flourished at Mexico City Cathedral; an orchestra of fifteen included strings, woodwinds and brass. In 1695 a great new organ, built in Madrid, was installed, and about 40 years later a second organ, still in the cathedral, was added.

Manuel de Zumaya (*c*1678–1756) had substituted for the ailing Salazar for several years before 1715, when he became *maestro de capilla* on the latter's death. He had become the cathedral organist by about 1700 and cultivated literary interests to the extent that he could publish an original play, *El Rodrigo*, in 1708. A versatile composer, he wrote not only polyphonic church music but also villancicos with continuo and ensemble accompaniment, which were tantamount to short solo cantatas. He also composed the first opera to be produced in North America. When a new viceroy, the Duke of Linares, arrived in January 1711, Zumaya was commissioned to translate Italian opera librettos and to write new music for them. On a libretto by Silvio Stampiglia, Zumaya's opera *Parténope* was produced in May that year, apparently successfully; only the libretto has survived.[15] Zumaya resigned his post in 1739 and moved to Oaxaca.

In addition to Mexico City other important artistic centres in early colonial Mexico included Puebla de los Angeles (founded in 1531), Oaxaca and Morelia (formerly Valladolid). Archives at Morelia contain principally eighteenth-century works, but the holdings of cathedrals and other sources in Oaxaca and especially Puebla have music from earlier periods as well. The Puebla Cathedral archive houses the richest collection of sixteenth- and seventeenth-century polyphony in the New World. This collection and those in Mexico City and Oaxaca contain not only works by composers living in Mexico but also many volumes of music (both printed and manuscript) of European composers such as Morales, Guerrero and Palestrina. Shipping inventories and cathedral chapter records attest to the presence of this repertory from as early as the middle of the sixteenth century. During the seventeenth century Puebla rivalled Mexico City in size, wealth, culture and fame. Its cathedral was dedicated in 1649, and the city had about 30 other sumptuous churches and monasteries. Puebla also produced a native school of renowned painters and a group of literary figures including the above-mentioned nun Juana Inés de la Cruz, one of the finest poets in Spanish letters. In 1646 the first public library in the New World was founded at Puebla with the donation of a collection of 5000 volumes by Bishop Juan de Palafox y Mendoza, a patron of the arts.[16]

The succession of choirmasters at Puebla can be traced from Pedro Bermúdez, who was born in Granada. His term of office lasted only three years (1603–6). Both he and his successor, Gaspar Fernández (c1566–1629), had served in Guatemala City before moving to Puebla, and examples of their works can be found in both of these cities as well as in Oaxaca. Bermúdez's *Salve regina* settings, mass and other works show a keen feeling for expressive harmonic devices and a mastery of the contrapuntal style. Fernández displays not only ability in that style but also a special talent for the villancico. Written for Puebla Cathedral between 1609 and 1620, some 250 villancicos survive at Oaxaca, with texts in Spanish, Portuguese and Tlaxcalan, an important early repertory of vernacular polyphony containing picturesque effects.

Juan Gutiérrez de Padilla (c1590–1664) followed Fernández as Puebla's *maestro de capilla* in 1629 and served until his death. Born in Málaga, his early training was in Andaluciá, where in 1616 he became the *maestro* of Cádiz Cathedral. He lived in the New World from at least 1622. He has been called the most important composer in seventeenth-century Mexico, worthy of being ranked with Spaniards of the time such as Juan Pujol, Mateo Romero and Carlos Patiño.[17] His compositions in the Puebla Cathedral archive include four double-choir masses, a *missa ferialis* and a Passion for four voices, a number of hymns, lamentations and motets for from four to six voices, other works for eight voices, and seven villancico cycles for Christmas.

Under Padilla's direction, cathedral music flourished as never before in Puebla. He had full charge of the music for the elaborate fourteen-day dedication ceremonies of the cathedral in 1649, which included performances of sacred and secular festival music for voices and instruments. His choir in 1651 consisted of twelve adults and fourteen choirboys, together with numerous instrumentalists and assistants, such as López Capillas, who served with him until his move to Mexico City in 1654. His double-choir music remained basically within a type of *stile antico* polyphony using imitative and antiphonal devices and often skilfully alternate polyphonic and homophonic textures. In his masses *Ave regina* and *Ego flos campi* he achieved overall formal unity by using motto phrases and adopting cyclic principles.

The texts of Padilla's villancicos include imitations of various dialects, and the music includes folk elements; the works had additional genre designations such as *negrilla*, *calenda*, *gallego* or *jácara*. By the middle of the century the polyphonic villancicos were very popular and were written for such festive occasions as Corpus Christi, Christmas and saints' days. A later *maestro*, Miguel Matheo de Dallo y Lana (c1650–1705), was also well known even beyond Mexico for his villancicos, and he produced at least four cycles to texts by Juana Inés de la Cruz, as well as Latin polyphonic works, after his appointment in 1688.[18]

While the history (sometimes sketchy) of sacred music in Mexico in the sixteenth and seventeenth centuries can be drawn from compositions – both manuscript and printed – surviving in cathedral archives, other religious institutions, private collections and libraries, as well as from cathedral chapter minutes, secular and non-liturgical sacred music is less well documented. Clearly, music was used widely outside the Church, but significant records are available only for that composed for religious functions. Spectacular non-liturgical events such as ceremonies of welcome for new dignitaries or grandiose acts of mourning for deceased sovereigns such as Charles V (*d* 1558) and Philip II (*d* 1598) are particularly well documented.[19] Little plays treating various religious subjects were popular in the sixteenth century, and the music for these developed in line with that for the Church. Early missionaries used them for religious instruction as well as for devotional purposes, and the Indians participated in the performances and contributed music for some of them. Two *chanzonetas* – hymns to the Virgin with Náhuatl texts – from the end of the sixteenth century could be examples of such music, probably written by an Indian, Hernando Franco, who had taken his sponsor's name at baptism.[20]

During the seventeenth century the villancico style adopted typically Baroque formal patterns, and more instruments were used. Religious and secular elements are frequently mixed in these pieces, some of which are especially interesting for their negro-dialect texts and other 'Black' stylistic features. It is not surprising that such characteristics were present in these compositions, for Blacks had been singing in church choirs and providing musical entertainments outside the church for some time.

Although purely instrumental music was cultivated, there are few extant examples of it. But we do have a mid-seventeenth-century cittern instruction book (*Método de cítara*) in tablature by Sebastián de Aguirre. It consists mainly of dances such as the *pavana*, *pasacalle*, *gallarda*, *branle*, *panamá*, *zarabanda* and *minute*. The book also contains two Indian *tocotines* (a dance with singing, popular during the colonial era) and a *portorrico de los negros* and other *portorricos* as well as an early example of an instrumental version of a *corrido*, a well-known Mexican ballad-type folksong.[21]

Many aspects of music in sixteenth- and seventeenth-century Mexico, both sacred and secular, remain to be explored but such music and documentation as we have gives a lively picture of a flourishing tradition deriving from the Old World with an admixture of indigenous elements from the New.

NOTES

[1] R. Stevenson, *Music in Aztec and Inca Territory* (Berkeley and Los Angeles, 1968), 19; for a detailed description and historical discussion of Aztec instruments, see pp.30–86. See also S. Martí, *La música precortesiana – Music before Cortés* (Mexico City, 1971, rev. 2/1978 by G. Nilsson as *Música precolombina – Music before Columbus*).

[2] Cited from R. Stevenson, *Music in Mexico: a Historical Survey* (New York, 1952), 4.

[3] Cited from Stevenson, *Music in Aztec and Inca Territory*, 97.

[4] Cited from S. Braden, *Religious Aspects of the Conquest of Mexico* (Durham, North Carolina, 1930), 155.

[5] ibid, 136.

[6] G. Béhague, *Music in Latin America: an Introduction* (Englewood Cliffs, New Jersey, 1979), 7.

[7] Cited from Stevenson, *Music in Mexico*, 67, 68.

[8] ibid, 63; from *Constituciones del arcobispado . . . de Tenuxtitlan Mexico* (Mexico, 1556), f.xxxiii (chap.66).

[9] Béhague, *Music in Latin America*, 6–8.

[10] *The Franco Codex of the Cathedral of Mexico*, ed. S. Barwick (Carbondale, 1965), pp.vii–viii.

[11] For a detailed discussion of music prints in sixteenth-century Mexico and the important volume *Liber in quo quatuor passiones Christi Domini continentur* (1604) by Juan Navarro, see Stevenson, *Music in Aztec and Inca Territory*, 172–95.

[12] Béhague, *Music in Latin America*, 11. See *El Códice del Convento del Carmen*, ed. J. Bal y Gay (Mexico City, 1952).

[13] *Two Mexico City Choirbooks of 1717: an Anthology of Sacred Polyphony from the Cathedral of Mexico*, ed. S. Barwick (Carbondale, 1982), pp.xii–xiv.

[14] R. Stevenson, 'López Capillas, Francisco,' *New Catholic Encyclopedia*, viii (1967), 986.

[15] *Two Mexico City Choirbooks*, ed. Barwick, pp.xiv–xv.

[16] A. R. Catalyne, 'Music of the Sixteenth to Eighteenth Centuries in the Cathedral of Puebla, Mexico', *Yearbook for Inter-American Musical Research*, ii (1966), 75–9.

[17] See A. R. Catalyne, *The Double-Choir Music of Juan de Padilla, Seventeenth-Century Composer in Mexico* (diss., U. of Southern California, 1953).

[18] Béhague, *Music in Latin America*, 17–26; facsimiles of manuscripts of Padilla's music from the Puebla Cathedral archive are reproduced on pp.19, 24 and 25.

[19] Stevenson, *Music in Aztec and Inca Territory*, 199–204.

[20] ibid, 204–19, including transcriptions of the two Náhuatl pieces; facsimiles of these pieces first appeared in print in G. Saldívar, *Historia de la música en México (épocas pre-cortesiana y colonial)* (Mexico City, 1934), 102–5.

[21] Béhague, *Music in Latin America*, 61. For more information about the role of Blacks in colonial music in Mexico, see E. Russell and R. Stevenson, sleeve-notes to *Blanco y Negro: Hispanic Songs of the Renaissance from the Old and New World*, Klavier Records (1975), and Saldívar, *Historia*, 219–26.

BIBLIOGRAPHICAL NOTE

An excellent survey of early music in Mexico may be found in G. Béhague, *Music in Latin America: an Introduction* (Englewood Cliffs, New Jersey, 1979). Both sacred and secular music of the colonial period are treated concisely but authoritatively. Music examples contribute to a clear understanding of the text, and the bibliographical notes after Chapter 1 are well chosen. R. Stevenson, *Music in Aztec and Inca Territory* (Berkeley and Los Angeles, 1968) is especially valuable for more detailed pre-colonial and early colonial information. The portion dealing with Mexico occupies about two-thirds of the book, and the inclusion of transcriptions of two sixteenth-century Aztecan apostrophes to the Virgin illustrates a type of Indian composition often cited in the writings of early chroniclers. There is also a 30-page bibliography.

The pioneer works in the field are M. Galindo, *Naciones de historia de la música mejicana* (Colima, 1933), and G. Saldívar, *Historia de la música en México (épocas pre-cortesiana y colonial)* (Mexico City, 1934). The latter is divided into three sections – 'Indigenous Music', 'European Music in Mexico' and 'Popular Music' – and

The Early Baroque Era

Saldívar made good use of his privileged access to both governmental and ecclesiastical archives. S. Barwick, *Sacred Vocal Polyphony in Early Colonial Mexico* (diss., Harvard U., 1949), the first extensive study of the subject in English, has a separate volume of transcriptions from sources in Mexico City and Puebla.

G. Chase, *The Music of Spain* (New York, 1941, 2/1959), in the chapter 'Hispanic Music in the Americas', and R. Stevenson, *Spanish Cathedral Music in the Golden Age* (Berkeley and Los Angeles, 1961), speak of the transplantation of Spanish sacred music to the New World, and they are useful in studying the European background of the period. For a serious and comprehensive study of what early missionaries found in Mexico when they used music in converting the Indians, C. Braden, *Religious Aspects of the Conquest of Mexico* (Durham, North Carolina, 1930), is worthwhile. S. Marti, *La música precortesiana – Music before Cortés* (Mexico City, 1971, rev. 2/1978 by G. Nilsson as *Música precolombina – Music before Columbus*, is a 95-page, beautifully and generously illustrated monograph on Aztec instruments.

R. Stevenson, *Music in Mexico: a Historical Survey* (New York, 1952), is an important early study, although the author has updated his material elsewhere over the years. L. B. Spiess and E. T. Stanford, *An Introduction to Certain Mexican Musical Archives* (Detroit, 1969), contains valuable bibliography, lists of sources and composers and a music supplement of transcriptions and photographs by Stanford. Because more information concerning music in colonial Mexico has been slowly uncovered for some time now, one finds the most recent data in articles in periodicals such as the *Yearbook for Inter-American Musical Research*, the *Latin American Music Review*, the *Inter-American Music Review* (see especially ix, (1987)), the *Hispanic American Historical Review*, *The Americas*, *Anales* (of the Instituto Nacional de Antropología e Historia) and the *Musical Quarterly*. The writers include R. Stevenson, L. Brothers, A. R. Catalyne, E. T. Stanford, G. Chase and S. Barwick. Pertinent material can also be found in the *Cambridge History of Latin America*, ii, ed. L. Bethell (Cambridge, 1984), and in the *Cambridge Encyclopedia of Latin America and the Caribbean*, ed. S. Collier and T. Skidmore (Cambridge, 1992)

The following volumes consist of early colonial sacred music from Mexico in modern transcriptions:

El Códice del Convento del Carmen, ed. J. Bal y Gay (Mexico City, 1952); *The Franco Codex of the Cathedral of Mexico*, ed. S. Barwick (Carbondale, 1965); *Christmas Music from Baroque Mexico*, ed. R. Stevenson (Berkeley and Los Angeles, 1974); *Latin American Colonial Music Anthology*, ed. idem (Washington, DC, 1975); and *Two Mexico City Choirbooks of 1717: an Anthology of Sacred Polyphony from the Cathedral of Mexico* (Carbondale, 1982). Also, A. R. Catalyne, *The Double-Choir Music of Juan de Padilla, Seventeenth-Century Composer in Mexico* (diss., U. of Southern California, 1953), includes copious transcriptions.

Chronology

The Early Baroque Era

MUSIC AND MUSICIANS	POLITICS, WAR, RULERS
1600 *Euridice*, pastoral opera by Jacopo Peri (1561–1633) and Giulio Caccini (*c*1545–1618), given for wedding of Maria de' Medici and Henri IV of France, Florence. *Rappresentatione di Anima, et di Corpo* by Emilio de' Cavalieri (*c*1550–1602) performed before the Collegio Sacro, Rome. G.M. Artusi publishes criticisms of Monteverdi's contrapuntal licence in his madrigals.	**1600** Henri IV, having divorced Margaret of Valois, marries Maria de' Medici.
1601 Claudio Monteverdi (1567–1643) appointed *maestro di cappella* at Mantua. Luzzaschi publishes virtuoso madrigals composed for the ladies of Ferrara. Thomas Morley (*c*1557–1602) issues *The Triumphes of Oriana*, madrigals honouring Elizabeth I.	**1601** The Earl of Essex leads a rebellion against Queen Elizabeth I; he is tried for treason and executed.
1602 Cavalieri (*c*52) dies, Rome. Caccini publishes *Le nuove musiche*, Florence. First book of madrigals by Salamone Rossi (1570–*c*1630) (with unfigured bass) and *Cento concerti ecclesiastici* by Lodovico Viadana (*c*1560–1627) (with continuo) published, Venice.	**1603** Death of Queen Elizabeth I; accession of James VI of Scotland as James I of England. Amnesty in Ireland.
1604 Caccini family in Paris at the invitation of Maria de' Medici. Incorporation of the Company of Musicians in London. *Lachrimae or Seaven Teares* by John Dowland (1563–1626) published, London. *50 pseaumes de David*, polyphonic Psalter setting by Jan Pieterszoon Sweelinck (1562–1621), published, Amsterdam.	**1604** 'False Dmitry' defeated by Tsar Boris of Russia (*d* 1605).
1605 Monteverdi replies to Artusi's criticisms in his fifth book of madrigals. The Ottoneum (first German court theatre) opens in Kassel.	**1605** Death of Pope Clement VIII; election of Leo XI who dies, followed by Paul V. Discovery of Gunpowder Plot.
1606 Edmund Hooper (*c*1553–1621) appointed first organist at Westminster Abbey. Joachim Burmeister (1564–1629) defines musical-rhetorical figures in *Musica poetica*, published in Rostock.	**1606** Peace of Vienna between Habsburgs and Hungary.
1607 Monteverdi's *Orfeo* performed at the Mantua court. His brother's further response to Artusi printed in Monteverdi's *Scherzi musicali*. Viadana publishes second book of *Concerti ecclesiastici*, with *Missa dominicalis* (earliest liturgical monody), Venice.	

LITERATURE, PHILOSOPHY, RELIGION	SCIENCE, TECHNOLOGY, DISCOVERY	FINE AND DECORATIVE ARTS, ARCHITECTURE
1600 William Shakespeare (1564–1616) writes *Hamlet* (–1601).	**1600** Foundation of the English East India Company.	
	1601 Johannes Kepler (1571–1642) becomes court astronomer and astrologer to Emperor Rudolf II.	
1602 Persecution of Protestants in Hungary and Bohemia and violent recatholicization of Lower Austria (–1603).	**1602** Galileo Galilei (1564–1642) discovers the laws of gravitation and oscillation.	
	1603 Beneho de Goes sets out for India in search of Cathay, through eastern Turkestan.	**1603** Carlo Maderno (1556–1629) completes the façade of S Susanna, Rome.
	1604 French settlement in Novia Scotia.	
1605 Miguel de Cervantes Saavedra (1547–1616) publishes *El Ingenioso Hidalgo Don Quixote de la Mancha*. Publication of *The Advancement of Learning* by Francis Bacon (1561–1626). Ben Jonson (1572–1637) writes *Volpone*.		
1606 Shakespeare writes *King Lear* and *Macbeth*.		
		1607 John Thorpe (*fl*1570–1610) begins Hatfield House (–1611).

The Early Baroque Era

MUSIC AND MUSICIANS	POLITICS, WAR, RULERS
1608 Girolamo Frescobaldi (1583–1643) appointed organist at St Peter's, Rome. The royal printer Ballard issues his first collection of lute airs, Paris.	**1608** Protestant Union of German Princes formed under Christian of Anhalt and Frederick IV of the Palatine.
1609 Heinrich Schütz (1585–1672) studies with Giovanni Gabrieli (*c*1555–1612) in Venice. Caterina Assandra, a nun, publishes concertato motets in Milan. Francis Tregian begins compiling MS collections of English and Italian music (one became *The Fitzwilliam Virginal Book*) in a London prison (–1619).	**1609** Truce agreed between Spain and United Provinces.
1610 Giovanni Paolo Cima (*c*1570–1625) publishes *Concerti ecclesiastici* (containing violin and trio sonatas), Milan. Viadana publishes *Sinfonie musicali à 8*, Venice. Instrumental *Fantasies* by Eustache Du Caurroy (1549–1609) published, Paris.	**1610** Assassination of Henri IV of France; succeeded by Louis XIII (aged 9).
1611 Lucia Quinciani's *Udite lagrimosi spirti* (first known solo monody by a woman composer) published, Venice.	**1611** Death of Charles IX of Sweden; succeeded by Gustavus II.
1612 Gabrieli (*c*57) dies Venice. Giovanni de' Bardi (78) dies, Florence. Hans Leo Hassler (47) dies, Frankfurt. Michael Praetorius (*c*1591–1621) publishes *Terpsichore* (containing French dances), Wolfenbüttel.	**1612** Death of emperor Rudolf II; succeeded by his brother Matthias. Death of Henry, Prince of Wales.
1613 Gesualdo (*c*52) dies, Gesualdo; Artusi (*c*73) dies, Bologna. Monteverdi succeeds Gabrieli at St Mark's, Venice. *Parthenia or the Maydenhead of the First Musicke that ever was printed for the Virginalls* published, London.	**1613** Marriage of Princess Elizabeth, daughter of James I, to Frederick V, Elector Palatine. Michael Romanov elected Tsar of Russia.
1614 Adriano Banchieri (1568–1634) founds Accademia dei Floridi (later Accademia dei Filomusi), Bologna.	**1614** Civil war in France (also 1615). French settlements in north America prevented by Virginian colonists.
1615 Congregazione dell'Oratorio at S Barbara founded in Bologna. Frescobaldi publishes *Toccate e partite d'intavolatura di cembalo*, Rome.	
1616 Johann Hermann Schein (1586–1630) appointed Kantor of the Leipzig Thomaskirche. Johann Staden (1581–1634) publishes *Harmoniae sacrae* (early German sacred concertos), Nuremberg.	**1616** Cardinal Richelieu (1585–1642) first appointed to French government.

LITERATURE, PHILOSOPHY, RELIGION	SCIENCE, TECHNOLOGY, DISCOVERY	FINE AND DECORATIVE ARTS, ARCHITECTURE
1608 Publication of *Characters of Virtues and Vices* by Joseph Hall (1574–1656).	**1608** The Dutch Johann Lappershey (*c*1570–*c*1619) invents the telescope. Quebec founded.	**1608** El Greco (1541–1614) paints *View of Toledo*, *Golgotha* and the *Assumption* (–1613).
1609 The English Baptist Church founded in Amsterdam by John Smith and Thomas Helwys.	**1609** Henry Hudson (*d* 1611) discovers Hudson's Bay (–1610).	**1609** Francesco Mochi sculpts *The Annunciation* in Orvieto Cathedral.
	1610 Galileo describes his astronomical discoveries in *Sidereus nuncio*.	
1611 Publication of *The Authorized Version of the Bible*.		**1611** The *Descent from the Cross* (–1614) painted by Peter Paul Rubens (1577–1640).
1612 Publication of *The White Devil* by John Webster (*c*1580–1625). Shakespeare writes *The Tempest*.		**1612** *The Vision of Father Simon* painted by Francisco Ribalta (1550–1628).
1613 Francis Beaumont (1584–1616) and John Fletcher (1579–1625) write *The Knight of the Burning Pestle*.		**1614** Santino Solari begins Salzburg Cathedral (–1628), an early manifestation in Austria of the Italian Baroque. El Greco paints *Betrothal of the Virgin*.
1614 Translation of the *Odyssey* by George Chapman (1559–1634) begun (–1615; the *Iliad* was completed in 1611).		
1615 Cervantes writes part ii of *Don Quixote*.	**1615** Willibord Snell (1591–1626) establishes the technique of trigonometrical triangulation for cartography.	**1615** Salomon de Brosse (1565–1626) begins work on the Palais de Luxembourg, Paris. Inigo Jones (1573–1652) appointed surveyor of the king's works.
1616 Shakespeare (52) dies, Stratford-on-Avon; Cervantes (69) dies, Madrid. Collected edition of Jonson's works published, the first of its kind.	**1616** Galileo refuses to teach the Copernican system despite Inquisition threats.	**1616** Gianlorenzo Bernini (1598–1680) sculpts *Apollo and Daphne*. Jones designs the Queen's House, Greenwich.

The Early Baroque Era

MUSIC AND MUSICIANS	POLITICS, WAR, RULERS
1617 *Affetti musicali* by Biagio Marini (*c*1587–1663) published, Venice. Schein publishes *Banchetto musicale*, Leipzig. *La délivrance de Renaud* (ballet with music by Mauduit, Guédron, Boësset and Bataille) performed in Paris.	**1617** Treaty of succession between Austrian and Spanish Habsburgs. War between Sweden and Poland.
1618 Caccini (*c*73) dies, Florence. Descartes completes his *Compendium musicae* (pubd 1650). Praetorius publishes second part of *Syntagma musicum* (on musical instruments).	**1618** Rebellion in Bohemia, followed by 'defenestration of Prague'; beginning of Thirty Years War. Walter Raleigh executed.
1619 Pierre Guédron (*c*1570–1619) appointed *surintendant* of music at the French court. *Teatro armonico spirituale* by Giovanni Francesco Anerio (*c*1567–1630), a vernacular oratorio with obbligato instruments, performed at the Oratorio di S Filippo Neri, Rome. Schütz publishes *Psalmen Davids*, Dresden.	**1619** Archduke Ferdinand deposed as King of Bohemia and Frederick V of Palatinate installed; Ferdinand elected Holy Roman Emperor. First American representative assembly meets, Jamestown.
1620 Mogens Pederson (*c*1583–1623) publishes *Pratum spirituale* (early polyphonic settings of Danish texts) in Copenhagen. Manuel Rodrigues Coelho (*c*1555–*c*1635) publishes *Flores de musica* (earliest known Portuguese instrumental music) in Lisbon.	**1620** Battle of the White Mountain in which Catholic League forces defeat Frederick of Bohemia; Catholicism imposed (also in Palatinate and Béarn).
1621 Praetorius (*c*50) dies, Wolfenbüttel; Sweelinck (59) dies, Amsterdam.	**1621** Expiry of twelve-year truce between the United Provinces and Spain; war resumes and engulfs Central Europe, involving all major powers.
1622 *Hashirim asher lish'lomo* (Songs of Solomon) by Salamone Rossi (1570–*c*1630) published in Venice by Leo da Modena, whose preface defends polyphony in the synagogue.	**1622** Edict of Nantes confirmed, guaranteeing religious freedom for Huguenots.
1623 William Byrd (80) dies, Stondon Massey, Essex; Thomas Weelkes (47) dies, London.	**1623** Death of Pope Gregory XV; election of Urban VIII (Maffeo Barberini), who inclines towards the French anti-Habsburg policy.
1624 Monteverdi uses *stile concitato* in *Combattimento di Tancredi e Clorinda* (pubd 1638), given in Venice.	**1624** Richelieu appointed president of the Council of Ministers; from 1629 he was chief minister and effectively ruler of France.
1625 John Coprario (*c*1575–1626) appointed composer-in-ordinary to Charles I. *La Liberazione di Ruggiero dall' isola d'Alcina*, opera by Francesca Caccini (1587–*c*1640), given in Florence.	**1625** Death of James I of England; succeeded by his son Charles I, who marries Henrietta Maria, sister of Louis XIII. Parliament refuses to finance war with Spain.
1626 Coprario (*c*50) dies, ? London; John Dowland (*c*59) dies, London. Formation of the Vingt-quatre Violons du Roi in Paris.	**1626** Defeat of the Protestant Christian IV of Denmark at Lutter by the Catholic League under Count Tilly, leaving North Germany open to the League. Huguenots revolt.

LITERATURE, PHILOSOPHY, RELIGION	SCIENCE, TECHNOLOGY, DISCOVERY	FINE AND DECORATIVE ARTS, ARCHITECTURE
1617 Martin Opitz founds a literary society, Fruchtbringende Geselleschaft, Heidelberg.	**1618** English West African Company founded, establishing settlements in the Gambia and Ghana.	**1617** Guido Reni (1575–1642) paints *The Deeds of Hercules* (–1621). Gerard van Honthorst (1590–1656) paints *Christ before the High Priest*.
1618 The Marquise de Rambouillet founds the first Paris literary salon (–1650).	**1619** Johannes Kepler (1571–1630) publishes *Harmonices mundi*. Dutch colony founded at Batavia, Java.	**1619** Jones begins the Banqueting House, Whitehall (–1622).
	1620 Pilgrim Fathers leave Plymouth in the *Mayflower*. Black slaves first imported into America. Cornelius Drebbel (1572–1634) constructs a thermometer and demonstrates the first submarine.	**1620** Bernini sculpts *Neptune and the Triton*; Diego Velazquez (1599–1660) paints *The Water-Seller*; Honthorst paints *The Concert*.
1620 Francis Bacon's *Novum organum scientiarum*, a work of philosophy of science, published.	**1621** Refraction discovered by Snell.	**1621** Anthony Van Dyck (1599–1641) paints *Rest on the Flight to Egypt*. Bernini sculpts *The Rape of Proserpina*.
1621 The first English newspaper, *Corante*, founded (–1641).	**1624** New Amsterdam (later New York) founded by the Dutch. First English settlement in India. Henry Briggs (1561–1631) publishes *Arithmetica logarithmica*, improving on John Napier's method of constructing logarithms (1614). Publication of *Introductionis in universam geographiam* by Philipp Cluver (1580–1622), the founder of historical geography.	**1622** Rubens begins 25 vast canvases on the life of Maria de' Medici for the Palais de Luxembourg.
1622 Benedictine University of Salzburg founded.		
1623 First folio edition of Shakespeare's plays published.		**1623** Velazquez becomes court painter to Philip IV of Spain.
1624 Lord Herbert of Cherbury (1583–1648), forerunner of English Deism, publishes *De veritate*.		**1624** Frans Hals (*c*1581–1666) paints *The Laughing Cavalier*. Building of the Wallenstein Palace, Prague (–1629), an early example of Baroque building in Central Europe. Bernini erects a daringly original baldacchino under the dome of St Peter's, Rome, a symbol of the richness and grandeur of the Baroque era (–1633).
1625 Honorat de Beuil, Seigneur de Racan (1598–1670), writes the pastoral comedy *Bergeries*.	**1625** Sanctorius (1561–1636) demonstrates the use of a thermometer to measure body temperature in studying disease.	
	1626 Jardin des Plantes, Paris, founded as a physic garden by Louis XIII's royal physician Guy de la Brosse.	

The Early Baroque Era

MUSIC AND MUSICIANS	POLITICS, WAR, RULERS
1627 Carlo Farina (*c*1600–*c*1640) publishes a quodlibet for violin, *Capriccio stravagante* (imitating other instruments and animals), Dresden. Schütz's *Dafne* (probably the earliest German musical work for the stage) performed for the Dresden court in Torgau.	**1627** Albrecht von Wallenstein, commander of the imperial forces, and Tilly, subdue Holstein, Schleswig and Jutland and take control of Mecklenburg and Pomerania. Richelieu besieges La Rochelle, centre of Huguenot rebellion.
1628 Alfonso Ferrabosco the younger (*c*52) dies, London; John Bull (*c*65) dies, Antwerp. Schütz returns to Venice to study with Monteverdi.	**1628** Gustavus II Adolphus of Sweden, alarmed by the Catholic threat, enters the Thirty Years War and relieves the siege of Danzig. Fall of La Rochelle
1629 Sigismondo d'India (*c*47) dies, ?Modena. Virgilio Mazzocchi (1597–1646) appointed *maestro di cappella* at the Cappella Giulia and Giacomo Carissimi (1605–74) at the Jesuit Collegio Germanico, Rome. Schütz publishes *Symphoniae sacrae*, Venice. Lope de Vega's *La selva sin amor* (earliest known Spanish sung drama) performed at the Coliseo del Buen Retiro in Madrid.	**1629** Peace treaties between Christian IV and Emperor Ferdinand II and between Sweden and Poland. Charles I dissolves Parliament after its resolutions demanding parliamentary rights and its rejection of the king's excise taxes, beginning 12 years of personal rule.
	1630 Gustavus II marches into Germany. Wallenstein is replaced by Tilly.
1630 Alessandro Grandi (*c*52) dies; Bergamo; J. H. Schein (66) dies, Leipzig.	
	1631 Magdeburg is brutally sacked by the imperial army. War of Mantuan Succession ends and Ferdinand II appoints the Duke of Nevers, betrothed to Louis XIII's sister, giving France a foothold in Italy.
1631 Margherita Basile becomes the first female singer in the Viennese Hofkapelle. Giovanni Valentini (*c*1582–1649) publishes *Canone nel modo Salomonis* for 96 voices, Rome.	
1632 *Il Sant'Alessio* by Stefano Lardi (*c*1586–1639), the earliest known musical setting of a historical subject, inaugurates the opera house, Quattro Fontane, at the Palazzo Barberini, Rome (possibly 1631).	**1632** Battle of the Lech: Gustavus II Adolphus defeats Tilly, enters Munich and defeats Wallenstein at Lützen, where he dies; succeeded by his daughter, Christina.
1633 Perl (71) dies, Florence; Jehan Titelouze (*c*70) dies, Rouen. Schütz appointed Hofkapellmeister in Copenhagen. Carlos Patiño becomes first Spaniard to serve as court *maestro de capilla* at Madrid.	**1633** League of Heilbronn formed by the south German Protestants, with Sweden and France. Swedish forces defeated at Steinau by Wallenstein. Death of Archduchess Isabella of the Netherlands, which are now ruled from Spain.

LITERATURE, PHILOSOPHY, RELIGION	SCIENCE, TECHNOLOGY, DISCOVERY	FINE AND DECORATIVE ARTS, ARCHITECTURE
1627 F.G. Quevedo y Villegas (1580–1645), a great writer of Spain's Golden Age, publishes his picaresque novel *Historia de la vida del Buscon*.	**1627** Kepler publishes *Tabulae rudolphinae*, used to calculate the positions of the planets.	**1627** Francesco Maria Ricchino (1583–1658) builds the Collegio Elvetico, Milan, an early example of a concave façade.
1629 Publication of the *Confessio fidei*, authorized by Cyril Lucar, Patriarch of Constantinople, reinterpreting the Eastern Orthodox faith in Calvinistic terms. Ferdinand II passes edict restoring to the Catholic Church property secularized in 1555.	**1628** William Harvey (1578–1657) publishes his discovery of the circulation of the blood.	**1628** Simon Vouet (1590–1649), court painter to Louis XIII and leading French artist, paints *Time Conquered*.
1630 Tirso de Molina (1583–1648) writes *El burlador de Sevilla*, the first dramatization of the Don Juan legend.		**1629** Daniel Mytens (c1590–1647), Anglo-Dutch artist, introduces a new elegance and grandeur into English portraiture with *The First Duke of Hamilton*.
1631 The masque *Chloridia* ends the collaboration of Ben Jonson and Inigo Jones (1573–1652) with a quarrel over the priority of literature and the visual arts. Friedrich von Spee (1591–1635) denounces the prevalent persecution of witches.	**1630** John Winthrop (1588–1649) sails from England as Governor of 'the Company of Massachusetts Bay in New England' and settles in Boston.	**1630** Georg Petel (c1601–1634) carves his major sculpture, the *Ecce homo*, for Augsburg Cathedral.
1632 Philip Massinger (1583–1640), a leading dramatist of the post-Shakespearian era, writes *The Maid of Honour*, after Boccaccio. Lope de Vega Carpio (1562–1635) writes *La Dorotea*, a major novel in dialogue.	**1631** Members of the Dutch West India Company settle on the Delaware River.	**1631** Baldassare Longhena (1598–1682) begins Maria della Salute, Venice with a vast dome anchored to an octagonal base by huge Baroque scrolls. Jones designs the first London square, Covent Garden (–1633), modelled on those he had seen in Italy.
1633 Publication of the *Poems* of John Donne (1572–1631), greatest of the 'metaphysical poets' (who include Herbert, Crashaw, Marvell, Vaughan, King, Traherne and Cowley). William Laud (1573–1645) becomes Archbishop of Canterbury.	**1632** Foundation of the Observatory at Leyden University; University Botanic Garden established at Oxford.	**1633** After the invasion of Lorraine by Richelieu, Jaques Callot (c1592–1635) produces a series of etchings *Les grandes misères de la guerre*. Jacob van Campen (1595–1657) begins his masterpiece, the Mauritshuis, The Hague, on a Palladian plan with a Dutch hipped roof. Pietro da Cortona (1596–1669) begins the *Allegory of Divine Providence and Barberini Power* for the Barberini Palace, Rome.

The Early Baroque Era

MUSIC AND MUSICIANS	POLITICS, WAR, RULERS
1634 Amsterdamsche Musijck Kamer founded. William Lawes (1602–45) and Simon Ives (1600–62) contribute music to the London performances of Shirley's *The Triumph of Peace*, most spectacular of all English masques. Henry Lawes (1596–1662) collaborates with Milton on *Comus* at Ludlow Castle.	**1634** Swedish defeat at Nördlingen marks the recovery of the Catholic cause; imperial troops conquer Württemberg and Franconia.
1635 Schütz returns to Dresden. Frescobaldi publishes *Fiori musicali*, Venice. Louis XIII provides words, music and choreography for the *Ballet de la Merlaison*, given at Chantilly.	**1635** Peace of Prague between Emperor Ferdinand II and Elector Johann Georg of Saxony. Conflict continues with France and Sweden allied against Spain and the Empire.
1636 Marin Mersenne issues first of four volumes of *Harmonie universelle*. Schütz publishes first volume of *Kleine geistliche Concerte*, Leipzig. Butler publishes *The Principles of Musik*, London.	**1636** France invaded by Austrians in Franche-Comté and Burgundy and by a Spanish army in Picardy. Ferdinand II dies; succeeded by his son Ferdinand III (–1657). Spain loses Artois to the French.
1637 Mazzocchi and Marco Marazzoli (*c*1605–62) collaborate on comic opera, *Chi soffre speri*, Rome. *L'Andromeda* by Francesco Monelli (1594–1667) inaugurates the Teatro S Cassiano, the first public opera house in Venice.	
1638 Monteverdi publishes *Madrigali guerrieri et amorosi*, Venice. Schütz's *Orpheus und Euridice* performed at Dresden.	**1638** Bernhard of Saxe-Weimar (1604–39), Swedish commander, defeats the Bavarians and captures Breisach, a turning-point in the Habsburg–Bourbon power struggle.
1639 Landi (*c*55) dies, Rome. André Maugars writes an open letter from Rome comparing French and Italian performing practices. *Le nozze di Teti e di Peleo* by Francesco Cavalli (1602–76) given, Venice.	**1639** War between Scotland and England forces Charles I to recall parliament.
1640 Monteverdi's *Il ritorno d'Ulisse in patria* given, Venice. The *Whole Booke of Psalmes* (first book in English printed in the New World) published in Cambridge, Massachusetts.	**1640** Under João IV Braganza, Portugal becomes independent of Spain, to be allied with France against her. Death of Elector Georg Wilhelm of Brandenburg; succeeded by his son Friedrich Wilhelm, the Great Elector (–1688). Elections in England for the Long Parliament, in session until 1653.
1641 *La finta pazza* by Francesco Sacrati (1605–50) inaugurates the Teatro Novissimo, Venice. The Palais Royal theatre built in Paris. Gioanpietro del Buono publishes the earliest harpsichord sonatas, Palermo.	
1642 Schütz returns to Copenhagen as Hofkapellmeister. Monteverdi's *L'incoronazione di Poppea* given in Venice.	**1642** Outbreak of Civil War in England between Royalist and Parliamentary forces. Death of Richelieu; Cardinal Mazarin (1602–61) becomes prime minister, ruling France until his death.

LITERATURE, PHILOSOPHY, RELIGION	SCIENCE, TECHNOLOGY, DISCOVERY	FINE AND DECORATIVE ARTS, ARCHITECTURE
1634 First performance of the Oberammergau Passion Play, in gratitude for deliverance from plague. Jean Mairet (1604–86) writes *Sophonisbe*, the first French play to conform to the rules of tragedy.	**1634** Jean Nicolet lands at Green Bay and explores Wisconsin. First English settlement at Cochin, Malabar.	**1634** Nicholas Poussin (*c*1593–1665), greatest French artist of the 17th century, in paintings such as *The Worship of the Golden Calf* (*c*1635), moves to a more austere classicism. Cortona builds SS Martina e Luca, Rome (–1650), the first great, homogenous Baroque church.
1635 Pedro Calderón de la Barca (1600–81) writes *La vida es sueño*, displaying the typical Spanish Baroque themes of worldly disillusion and the vanity of earthly things. Richelieu founds the Académie Française to perfect the French language (Dictionary compiled 1639–94).		
	1637 René Descartes (1596–1650) in *La géométrie*, introduces the notions of constant and variable and demonstrates that the properties of curves could be expressed algebraically.	**1638** Van Dyck paints *Charles I on Horseback* (*c*1638); his paintings of Stuart court personalities profoundly influenced English portraiture. Francesco Borromini (1599–1667) builds the ingenious S Carlo alle Quattro Fontane, Rome (–1641), a miniature on an oval plan.
1637 René Descartes (1596–1650) writes the *Discours de la méthode*, demonstrating his philosophical system. Pierre Corneille (1606–84) writes *Le Cid*, introducing in French drama the new theme of conflict between duty or honour and passion. The new Laudian Prayer Book causes a riot when used in Edinburgh.	**1638** Galileo publishes *Discorsi e dimostrazioni matematiche intorno a due nuove scienze*, containing the laws of the fall in vacuum and the idea of force as a mechanic agent.	**1639** Claude Lorrain (1600–82), celebrated for his ideal landscapes, paints *Seaport at Sunset*, commissioned by Urban VIII.
1640 The *Augustinus* of Cornelius Jansen (1585–1638) published, a treatise on grace and human nature based on the anti-Pelagian works of Augustine (condemned in 1653 by Innocent X).	**1639** Gérard Desargues (1593–1662) publishes the *Brouillon projet*, dealing mainly with conic sections and originating projective geometry. Jeremiah Horrocks (*c*1617–1641) records observations of the transit of Venus which he had predicted.	**1641** Jacques Sarrazin (1588–1660) executes the eight caryatids on the Pavillon de l'Horloge at the Louvre. Simon de La Vallée (*d* 1642) designs the Riddarhaus, Stockholm, one of the first Scandinavian buildings in the classical style.
1641 Luis Vélez de Guevara (1579–1644) writes a picaresque and satirical novel, *El diablo cojuelo*. John Evelyn (1620–1706) begins his *Diary*, an invaluable record of the era (–1706).	**1642** Abel Tasman (*c*1603–1659) embarks on the most ambitious Dutch exploration in the southern hemisphere, discovering Tasmania and New Zealand but unaware he had circumnavigated Australia.	**1642** Rembrandt van Rijn (1606–69) paints *The Night Watch*, the culminating work of the Dutch tradition of civic-guard portraits. François Mansart (1598–1666), the first great exponent of French classicism in architecture, builds Maisons-Lafitte (–1646), near Paris.

The Early Baroque Era

MUSIC AND MUSICIANS	POLITICS, WAR, RULERS
1643 Marco Gagliano (60) dies, Florence; Frescobaldi (59) dies, Rome; Monteverdi (75) dies, Venice. Cavalli's *Egisto* performed in Venice (in Paris 1646). Johann Andreas Herbst (1588–1666) publishes *Musica poetica* (first composition manual in German), Nuremberg.	**1643** Death of Louis XIII; succeeded by Louis XIV (aged 5). French troops under d'Enghien (Condé) defeat the Spanish at Rocroi.
1644 Giovanni Rovetta (*c*1595–1658) succeeds Monteverdi at St Mark's, Venice. Barbara Strozzi (1619–*c*1665) publishes *Il primo libro de madrigali*, Venice. The last church organs in London ordered destroyed by Puritan Parliament.	**1644** Royalist forces under Prince Rupert of the Rhine (1619–82) defeated at Marston Moor by Oliver Cromwell (1599–1658). Death of Pope Urban VIII; election of Innocent X (Giambattista Pamphili).
1645 William Lawes (43) dies, Chester. Sacrati's *La finta pazza* (1641) performed at court in Paris.	**1645** Cromwell and New Model Army defeat Royalists at Naseby; Royalist Oxford surrenders (1646).
1646 Orazio Benevoli (1605–72) appointed *maestro di cappella* of the Cappella Giulia, Rome. Jean-Baptiste Lully (1632–87) and Luigi Rossi (*c*1597–1653) arrive in Paris.	**1647** Electors of Bavaria and Cologne break their neutrality to support Emperor Ferdinand III.
1647 Rossi's *Orfeo* given (in Italian, with French prologue and ballets), Paris. Queen Christina of Sweden engages six French musicians to perform ballets at Stockholm court.	**1648** Peace of Westphalia ends the Thirty Years War, with Sweden, France and Brandenburg making territorial gains and independence of the Netherlands, German states and Swiss cantons guaranteed. The first fronde in Paris, led by Parlement against the absolutist government of Mazarin, ends in uneasy alliance. In England, Cromwell repulses the Scots.
1648 Italian musicians flee Paris during the Fronde. Lully founds the Petit Violons. Schütz publishes the monumental *Geistliche Chor-Musik*, Dresden. Henry Lawes publishes *Choice Psalmes*, London.	
1649 *Orontea* by Antonio Cesti (1623–69) given in Venice.	**1649** Trial and execution of Charles I; England declared a Commonwealth. Cromwell brutally represses Irish resistance.
1650 Pierre Corneille, Dassoucy and Giacomo Torelli collaborate on *Andromède* at the Petit Bourbon in Paris. Kircher publishes compendious *Musurgia universalis*, Rome.	**1650** Fronde of the Princes, a series of uprisings (–1653); fear of anarchy enables Louis XIV and Mazarin to strengthen central government.
1651 Louis XIV dances role of the Sun in Benserade's first ballet, *Cassandre*, at the Palais Royal, Paris.	**1651** Charles II, son of Charles I, crowned king of Scotland but is defeated by Cromwell at Worcester and flees to France; end of English Civil War.
1652 Henri Du Mont (1610–84) publishes *Cantica sacra* (first printed collection of *petit motets*), Paris.	**1652** First Anglo-Dutch War (–1654), after Navigation Act aiming at trade monopoly for English ships.

LITERATURE, PHILOSOPHY, RELIGION	SCIENCE, TECHNOLOGY, DISCOVERY	FINE AND DECORATIVE ARTS, ARCHITECTURE
1643 Molière (Jean-Baptiste Poquelin, 1622–73) founds the Illustre Théâtre in Paris (tours the provinces, 1645–58).	**1644** Evangelista Torricelli (1608–47) invents the mercury barometer.	**1643** Longhena designs the double staircase for the monastery of S Giorgio Maggiore, Venice.
1644 Antoine Arnuald (1612–94), with *Apologie de M. Jansenius*, becomes acknowledged leader of the Jansenists.	**1645** A group of scientists, including Boyle, Williams and Watt, begin to meet regularly in London and Oxford, leading to the foundation of the Royal Society (1662).	**1645** Bartolomé Esteban Murillo (*c*1617–1682) establishes himself as the leading painter in Seville with 11 paintings on the lives of Franciscan saints. Bernini works on the celebrated *Ecstasy of St Theresa*, aiming to fuse sculpture, architecture and painting into a magnificent whole (–1652).
1646 Jean de Rotrou (1609–50), to be Corneille's only serious rival, writes the tragedy *Saint Genest* on a theme from Lope de Vega.		
1647 The Westminster Confession becomes the definitive statement of Presbyterian doctrine in the English-speaking world.	**1647** Johannes Hevelius (1611–87) describes his discoveries about the moon.	**1646** Alessandro Algardi (1598–1654) works on the relief *Pope Leo driving Attila from Rome* (–1653).
1648 George Fox (1624–91) founds the Friends of Truth, later the Society of Friends, or Quakers.	**1648** Publication of *Ortus medicinae* by Johannes Baptista van Helmont (1579–1644), with the results of his medical research including his invention of the word 'gas' for carbon monoxide. *Mathematical Magick* by John Wilkins (1614–72) brings new scientific ideas to a wider audience.	**1648** Gerard Terborch the Younger (1617–81) paints *The Swearing of the Oath of Ratification of the Treaty of Münster*.
1649 Descartes publishes *Les passiones de l'âme*, attempting to reconstruct philosophy and to deduce the existence of God.		**1650** Jean de La Vallée (1620–96) completes his father's Riddarhaus and builds the Oxenstierna Palace in Stockholm, introducing the Roman *palazzo* style. Georges de la Tour (1593–1652) paints *The Denial of St Peter*, showing his style as the most personal and poetic of the Caravaggesque painters.
1650 Jeremy Taylor (1613–67) publishes the first of two devotional treatises, *The Rule and Exercise of Holy Living* and *Holy Dying* (1651), expressions of Anglican spirituality. Publication of *The Tenth Muse Lately Sprung up* by the American Anne Bradstreet (*c*1612–1672).	**1651** William Harvey describes his advances in embryology.	
1651 Thomas Hobbes (1588–1679) publishes *Leviathan*, an attempt to base a theory of human conduct on science.	**1652** The German Scientific Academy, Naturae Curiosi, founded at Schweinfurt. Dutch trading station established at the Cape of Good Hope.	**1651** Jacob Jordaens (1593–1678), the leading figure painter in Flanders paints *The Triumph of Frederick Hendrik* for the Huis ten Bosch, near The Hague.

MUSIC AND MUSICIANS	POLITICS, WAR, RULERS
1653 L. Rossi (*c*55) dies, Rome. Lully appointed Louis XIV's *compositeur de la musique instrumentale*. Teatro Malvezzi opens in Bologna. Masque *Cupid and Death*, with music by Matthew Locke (*c*1621–1677), given in London.	**1653** Cromwell becomes Lord Protector of England, Scotland and Ireland.
1654 Samuel Scheidt (66) dies, Halle. Christina of Sweden's Roman palace becomes an important musical venue. *Le nozze di Peleo e di Teti* by Carlo Caproli (*c*1617–*c*1693) given, Paris. Cesti's *La Cleopatra* inaugurates the Komödienhaus, Innsbruck. Playford publishes *A Breefe Introduction to the Skill of Musick*, London.	**1654** Abdication of Christina of Sweden, who converts to Catholicism (1655).
1655 Inauguration of the Festival of Sons of the Clergy, London, giving rise to annual music festivals in England.	**1655** Sweden and Brandenburg fight over Poland and Prussia, which is ceded to the Great Elector by the Treaty of Labiau.
1656 Carissimi appointed *maestro di cappella del concerto di camera* by Christina of Sweden, in Rome. Davenant's *Siege of Rhodes* (earliest English opera, music by several composers) given, London.	**1656** France and England at war with Spain (–1659); Dunkirk and Gravelines retaken in 1658.
1657 Maurizio Cazzati (*c*1620–1677) appointed *maestro di cappella* at S Petronio, Bologna. *La Tancia* by Jacopo Melani (1623–76) inaugurates the Teatro della Pergola, Florence. Cesti's *La Dori* given, Innsbruck. Kerll's *L'Oronte* inaugurates the Munich court opera house.	**1657** Death of Emperor Ferdinand III; succeeded by his son Leopold I, elected Holy Roman Emperor in 1658.
1658 René Ouvrard (1624–94) publishes *Secret pour composer en musique*, Paris.	**1658** Formation of Rhenish League under French protection, after Louis XIV's failure to win the imperial election, to balance Habsburg power in Germany. Cromwell dies; succeeded as Lord Protector by his son Richard (1626–1712).
1659 Christopher Simpson publishes *The Division-Violist*, London.	**1659** Resignation of Richard Cromwell; Commonwealth re-established by the Rump Parliament. Peace between Spain and France, with French territorial gains; marriage arranged between Louis XIV and daughter of Philip IV.
1660 Cavalli's *Xerse* (1654) given at the Louvre, Paris, as part of the wedding festivities for Louis XIV and Maria Theresa of Spain. Schütz's *Historia der . . . Gerbuth . . . Jesu Christi* performed in Dresden. Matthias Weckmann (*c*1617–1674) founds Hamburg Collegium Musicum. Juan Hidalgo (*c*1614–1685) and Calderón de la Barca collaborate on *Celos aun del aire matan* (the earliest surviving Spanish opera) in Madrid.	**1660** Restoration of Charles II to the English and Scottish thrones, after his promise of an amnesty, liberty of conscience (short-lived) and respect for changes in land ownership.

LITERATURE, PHILOSOPHY, RELIGION	SCIENCE, TECHNOLOGY, DISCOVERY	FINE AND DECORATIVE ARTS, ARCHITECTURE
1653 Izaak Walton (1593–1683) publishes *The Compleat Angler*, including folklore, songs, poems and anecdotes.	**1653** Giovanni Riccioli (1598–1671) publishes *Almagestum novum astronomiam*, with observations on the moon; he and Francesco Maria Grimaldi (1618–63) perfect the pendulum for the measurement of time.	**1653** Façade of S Agnese, Rome, by Borromini, one of his most typical compositions (–1657).
1654 Friedrich von Logan (1604–55) publishes *Salomon von Golaw*, satirical epigrams.		**1655** Alonso Cano (1601–67), sculptor, painter and architect, completes *Immaculate Conception*, a polychrome wooden statue.
1655 Emanuele Tesauro (1592–1675) writes *Il cannocchiale aristotelico*, a treatise on literary theory. Sir William Dugdale (1605–86) publishes *Monasticon anglicanum*, on the history of medieval monasteries and churches (further volumes, 1661, 1673).	**1654** Francis Glisson (1597–1677) describes the human liver. Blaise Pascal (1623–62) completes his treatises on geometry and physics, continues his studies in arithmetic and combinatorial analysis, and begins the calculus of probability.	**1656** Jan Vermeer (1632–75) paints *The Procuress*, marking the transition of his style from the early to middle phase. Velazquez paints *Las Meniñas*, his most complex essay in portraiture (including a self-portrait).
1656 Blaise Pascal (1623–62) writes his 18 *Lettres provinciales*, aiming to expose the immoral casuistry of the Jesuits in contrast to the rigorous Jansenist morality.	**1655** John Wallis (1616–1703) publishes *Arithmetica infinitorum*, discussing curves.	**1657** Louis Le Vau (1612–70) designs his master-piece, the château of Vaux-le-Vicomte (–1661). The gardens were laid out by Le Nôtre and the interior decorated by Lebrun, their first collaboration. Bernini works on St Peter's Square, Rome (–1670).
1657 Completion of the London Polyglot Bible containing Hebrew, Greek, Latin, Syriac, Arabic and Persian texts, and the Samaritan Pentateuch. John Amas Comenius (1592–1670) publishes his educational work, *Didactica magna*.	**1657** Foundation of the Accademia del Cimento in Florence. **1658** Johann Rudolph publishes *Opera omnia chemica* and *De natura salium*, describing sodium sulphate.	**1658** Pieter de Hooch (1629–84) paints *The Courtyard of a House in Delft*, a masterpiece of Dutch genre painting.
1660 Samuel Pepys (1633–1703) begins his *Diary* (–1669), covering the Restoration, Plague and Fire of London, and social and political information. John Dryden (1631–1700) establishes himself as Stuart court poet with *Astraea redux*; with the reopening of the London theatres, closed since 1642, he begins to write plays.	**1660** Robert Boyle (1627–91) publishes *New Experiments Physico-Mechanicall*.	**1660** Poussin paints his last great series of pictures. *The Four Seasons* (–1664), the basis of Lebrun's academic doctrine and to be enormously influential. Jacob van Ruisdael (c1628–1682), greatest of Dutch landscape artists, paints *The Jewish Cemetery* (c1660), contrasting man's transitory existence with Nature's power of renewal.

MUSIC AND MUSICIANS	POLITICS, WAR, RULERS
1661 Lully appointed *surintendant de la musique de la chambre* by Louis XIV and the soprano Anne de La Barre the first female *ordinaire de la musique de chambre*. Locke appointed 'private composer-in-ordinary', 'in the wind music' and 'for the violin band' by Charles II. Davenant's *The Siege of Rhodes* inaugurates Duke's Theatre, London. Christiaan Huygens publishes mathematical basis for dividing the octave into 31 parts, in *Novus cyclus harmonicus*, The Hague. Rudbeck founds an orchestra, the Akademiska Kapellet, at the University of Uppsala.	**1661** Death of Mazarin; start of Louis XIV's personal rule, with Colbert (1619–83) his financial and economic adviser.
1662 Marazzoli (*c*58) dies, Rome; Henry Lawes (66) dies, London. The *Ceremoniale parisiense* (forbidding use of instruments other than the organ in church services) authorized by the Archbishop of Paris.	**1662** Marriage of Charles II to Catherine of Braganza, whose dowry includes Tangier and Bombay; Charles sells Dunkirk to France.
1663 The first Theatre Royal, in Drury Lane, opens in London.	**1663** The Turks under Mohammed IV declare war on Leopold I; they advance through the Balkans until defeated at Vienna in 1683.
1664 Johann Heinrich Schmelzer (*c*1620–1680) publishes *Sonatae unarum fidium* (earliest German collection of violin sonatas), Nuremberg.	
1665 Christopher Simpson (*c*1605–1669) publishes *The Principles of Practical Musick* (later *A Compendium of Practical Musick*), London.	**1665** Death of Philip IV of Spain; succeeded by his cousin Charles II. Second Anglo-Dutch war (–1667), with James, Duke of York, commanding the English fleet.
1666 The Accademia Filarmonica founded in Bologna. Cesti's *Nettunno e Flor festeggianti* (Leopold I contributes an aria), performed in Vienna.	**1666** Great Plague of London, followed by the Great Fire, which in five days destroys most of the City, including St Paul's Cathedral.
1667 Johann Jakob Froberger (50) dies, Héricourt. The Dresden opera house opens.	**1667** Thirteen Years War between Russia and Poland ends, with Smolensk and Kiev ceded to Russia. War of Devolution: the French threaten the Dutch Republic, which allies itself with England and Sweden.
1668 Cavalli appointed *maestro di cappella* at St Mark's, Venice. Blow appointed organist of Westminster Abbey, London. Cesti's *Il pomo d'oro* given in Vienna in celebration of a royal wedding. Melani's operatic satire on absolutism, *Il Girello* (prologue by Stradella), given, Rome. Bacilly publishes *Remarques curieuses sur l'art de bien chanter*, Paris.	

LITERATURE, PHILOSOPHY, RELIGION	SCIENCE, TECHNOLOGY, DISCOVERY	FINE AND DECORATIVE ARTS, ARCHITECTURE
1663 Charles de Saint-Denis, Sieur de Saint-Evremond (1613–1703), writes *Réflexions sur les divers génies du peuple romain*, a pioneer work in making the study of ancient manners and mentality a part of history. Andreas Gryphius (1615–64) writes *Horribilicribifax*, a satire on the Thirty Years War.	**1662** The Royal Society receives its royal charter.	**1662** Philippe de Champaigne (1602–74) paints his famous *Ex-voto de 1662*, commemorating his daughter's recovery from paralysis.
1664 Armand de Rancé (1626–1700) reforms the monastery of La Trappe to the rule of Reformed Cistercians, based on the original spirit of Cîteaux (known later as Trappists). *La Thébaïde*, the first tragedy by Jean Racine (1639–99), produced by Molière. Molière writes *Le Tartuffe*.	**1665** Publication of experiments by Grimaldi explaining the diffraction of light. Giovanni Domenico Cassini (1625–1712) computes the configurations of the four satellites of Jupiter discovered by Galileo (–1668). Richard Hooke (1635–1703) publishes *Micrographia*, comparing the spreading of light vibrations to that of waves in water.	**1663** Charles Lebrun (1619–90) becomes *premier peintre du roi*, director of the Gobelins factory and director of the Académie. Christopher Wren (1632–1723) designs his first building, the Sheldonian Theatre, Oxford.
1665 Francois de La Rochefoucauld (1613–80) publishes *Maximes*, a tour de force of 500 gnomic sentences analysing human motive.		**1664** Cano designs the façade of Granada Cathedral (*c*1664), the first masterpiece of Spanish Baroque. Hals paints group portraits of the *Regents* and *Regentesses of the Old Men's Alms Houses* (*c*1664), the culmination of his career.
		1665 Vermeer paints *The Lacemaker* (*c*1665), one of the most exquisite of his serene images of domestic life.
1666 Colbert founds the Académie des Sciences in Paris.	**1666** Gottfried Wilhelm von Leibniz (1646–1716) writes *De arte combinatoria*, elaborating a new system of symbolic logic.	**1666** Peter Lely (1618–80) paints one of his most splendid portraits, *Lady Byron*; court painter since 1661, he introduced a modified Baroque style to England.
1667 John Milton (1608–74) publishes *Paradise Lost*, his greatest poem and the first important original non-dramatic work in blank verse in English.	**1667** The French National Observatory founded.	**1667** Claude Perrault (1613–88) begins the east front of the Louvre, one of the supreme master-pieces of the Louis XIV style. Guarino Guarini (1624–83) builds Turin Cathedral, with an unprecedented cone-shaped dome.
1668 Jean de la Fontaine (1621–95) publishes 12 books of *Fables* (–1694), drawn from Eastern, classical and modern sources.	**1668** Anthony van Leeuwenhoeck (1632–1723), Dutch microscopist, confirms Malpighi's discovery of blood capillaries.	**1668** Jan Steen (*c*1635–1679) paints *Twelfth Night*, a large canvas in which life is treated as a comedy of manners.

377

The Early Baroque Era

MUSIC AND MUSICIANS	POLITICS, WAR, RULERS
1669 Cesti (46) dies, Florence; Simpson (*c*64) dies, London. Pierre Perrin and Robert Cambert (*c*1627–1667) granted royal patents to establish 'Académies d'Opéra' in Paris.	**1669** After 21-year siege, Venice surrenders Crete to the Turks.
1670 Cavalli's *Scipione affricano* (1664, prologue by Stradella) inaugurates the Teatro Tordinona, Rome.	**1670** Secret Treaty of Dover between Louis XIV and Charles II, who in return for a subsidy breaks alliance with Holland.
1671 Lully and Molière (with Quinault and P. Corneille) present their only *tragédie-ballet*, *Psyché*, at the Palais des Tuileries, Paris. *Pomone*, by Cambert, given in Paris.	**1671** Emperor Leopold I signs treaty with France, promising neutrality if France attacks Holland providing that Louis XIV does not invade Spain or the Empire.
1672 Schütz (87) dies, Dresden; Jacques Champion de Chambonnières (*c*70) dies, Paris. Lully acquires ownership of the Académie Royale de Musique, ends partnership with Molière and begins new one with Quinault: *Les fêtes d'Amour et Bacchus* given, Paris. John Banister (*c*1625–1679) presents first known concerts where admission is charged, in London. Hidalgo collaborates with Guevara on *Los celos hacen estrellas* (earliest surviving zarzuela with music) in Madrid.	**1672** William of Orange elected Stadholder of Holland. Third Anglo-Dutch War (–1674): English defeated at Texel in 1673 and withdraw from conflict.
1673 Charpentier and Molière collaborate on *Le malade imaginaire*, Lully and Quinault on the first *tragédie en musique*, *Cadmus et Hermione*, in Paris. Locke publishes *Melothesia* (keyboard music with earliest instructions for realizing figured bass) in London.	**1673** Emperor Leopold I forms alliance with the Dutch and declares war on France.
1674 Carissimi (68) dies, Rome. Pelham Humfrey (*c*27) dies, Windsor. Lully's *Alceste* performed in Paris. A new Theatre Royal, Drury Lane, opens in London.	**1674** John Sobieski elected King of Poland after defeating the Turks at Korzim in 1673. Triple Alliance of Austria, Holland and Spain, later joined by the papacy and Brandenburg, against France.
1675 Locke and Giovanni Battista Draghi (*c*1640–1708) compose music for Shadwell's English version of Lully's *Psyché*. Staggins and Crowne collaborate on masque, *Calisto*, at Whitehall, London.	**1675** Turenne's death and Condé's retirement bring an end to French military victories and expansion.

LITERATURE, PHILOSOPHY, RELIGION	SCIENCE, TECHNOLOGY, DISCOVERY	FINE AND DECORATIVE ARTS, ARCHITECTURE
1669 William Penn (1644–1718), imprisoned in the Tower of London, writes *No Cross, No Crown*, soon a classic of Quaker practice. Jacques-Bénigne Bossuet (1627–1704) delivers his first great funeral oration on Henrietta Maria.	**1669** Kircher publishes *Ars magna scienda*, designed to teach all disciplines systematically. Marcello Malpighi (1628–94), pioneer in embryology and comparative anatomy, publishes the first full account of an insect's structure; Jan Swammerdam (1627–80), in the same field, publishes a history of insects. Hennig Brand discovers phosphorus (*c*1669). Nicolaus Steno (1638–86) publishes *De solido*, a treatise on fossils, founding the science of geology.	**1669** Le Vau begins, with Le Nôtre and Lebrun, to transform the hunting-lodge at Versailles into the grandest palace in Europe. Rembrandt paints two self-portraits, last of a series (1629–).
1670 Baruch Spinoza (1632–77), Dutch Jewish philosopher, publishes *Tractatus theologico-politicus*, developing purely rationalist religious ideas.		**1670** Pedro Roldan (1624–1700) executes his greatest sculpture, the reredos for La Caridad, Seville (–1675), polychromed by J. de Valdes Leal (1622–90). Liberal Bruant (*c*1635–1697) builds the Hôtel des Invalides (–1677), Paris, with arcaded courts of a Roman gravity.
1671 William Wycherley (1641–75) writes his first two plays, *Love in a Wood* and *The Gentleman Dancing Master*, embodying acute social criticism, particularly of marriage and sexual morality.	**1671** Leibniz begins work on his calculating machine.	**1671** Pierre Puget (1620–94) begins the *Milo of Crotona* (–1682) for Versailles.
1672 The Synod of Jerusalem, the most important modern Council of the Eastern Church, repudiates the movement towards accommodating Calvinism.	**1672** Otto von Guericke (1602–86) describes his invention of the vacuum pump. Isaac Newton (1642–1726) establishes the existence of coloured rays in white light. Jacques Marquette and Louis Joliet explore the River Missouri near modern Chicago (–1673).	**1672** Willian van der Velde (1611–93) and his son (1653–1707) settle in England and paint maritime scenes.
	1673 Christiaan Huygens (1629–95) solves the problem of the compound pendulum and states the laws of centrifugal force. Leibniz works towards the discovery of the differential and integral calculus (–1675).	**1673** Edward Pierce (*c*1635–1695) executes a marble bust of Sir Christopher Wren.
1674 Nicolas Malebranche (1638–1715) publishes his pantheistic *La recherche de la vérité*.	**1674** John Mayow (1641–79) describes respiration and recognizes *physici*, the existence of oxygen.	**1674** Baciccio (Giovanni Battista Gaulli, 1639–1708) paints the illusionist *Adoration of the Name of Jesus* (–1679) on the ceiling of Il Gesu, Rome, and the nave vault, a masterpiece of illusionist decoration.
1675 Philipp Spener (1635–1705) publishes *Pia desideria*, aimed at fostering a revival in German Protestantism (later known as the Pietist movement).	**1675** Royal Observatory, Greenwich, founded, with John Flamsteed (1646–1719) as Astronomer Royal.	**1675** François Girardon (1628–1715) begins the Richelieu monument in the church of the Sorbonne, Paris. Wren begins St Paul's Cathedral (–1709).

379

Index

Index

Baker family, 311
Balifre, Claude, 221
Ballard, 7, 223–5
  Pièces pour violon à quatre parties, 228
Ballard, Robert, 230
ballet, 9, 16, 17, 175–6
Ballet de Flore, 240
Ballet de l'impatience, 240
Ballet de la Galanterie du temps, Le, 228
Ballet de la naissance de Venus, 240
Ballet de la Nuit, Le, 233, *233*
Ballet de la Prospérité des armes de France, Le, 232
Ballet de Tancrède, 232
Ballet des arts, 240
Ballet des ballets, 240
Ballet des muses, 240
Ballet des quatre saisons, 242
Ballet des saisons, 240
ballets de cour, 176, 222, 227, 228, 230, 231–4,
  232, *233*, 240, 245
balli, 17
Baltzar, Thomas, 313
Banchieri, Adriano, 53, 107, 108–9, 113
  Cartella musicale, 109
  Organo suonarino, L', 109
Banister, John, 311, 320–1
  Musick; or, A Parley of Instruments . . ., 321
Baraillon, 264
Barberini family, 59–60, 62, 64, 67, 71, 72
Barberini, Antonio, 49, 59, 60, 62
Barberini, Francesco, 49, 59, 60
Barberini, Maffeo *see* Urban VIII, Pope
Barberini, Taddeo, 60, 62
Barcelona, 339
Bardi, Giovanni de', 127–9, 131–2, 134, 142
  Amico fido, L', 127
  *Discorso mandato a Caccini sopra la musica
    antica e'l cantar bene*, 128, 132
  Mascherata del Piacere e del Pentimento, 134
  Nuove musiche, Le, 127
  Pellegrina, La, 132, 133, *134*
Bardi, Pietro, de', 128
Bargagli, Girolamo
  Pellegrina, La, 132, *133, 134*
Barley, William, 288
Barnard, John
  First Book of Selected Church Musick, The, 292
Baroque, 2
Bartolaia, Lodovico
  Inganni di Polinesso, Gl', 153
  Sidonio, Il, 153
Basile, Adrian, 30
Bassano family, 311
Bassano, Giovanni, 78, 85
basso continuo, 7, 9–12, 30, 129, 291, 330
Bataille, Gabriel, 224
Bati, Luca, 131, 142
Bavaria, Electress of, 169
Beauchamp, Pierre, 240, 245, 264
Beaujoyeulx, Balthasar de

Circé, ou Le ballet comique de la Royne, 231–2
Beaumont and Fletcher
  Knight of the Burning Pestle, The, 272
Bella, Stefano della, *15*, *44*
Benevoli, Orazio, 64
Benserade, Isaac de, 222, 232, 240
  Fêtes de l'Amour et de Bacchus, Les, 243, 244,
    262
  Triomphe de l'Amour, Le, 245
Bentivoglio family, 347n7
Benvenuti, Giovanni, 112
Berain, *264*
Bergen, C., *167*
Bergerotti, Anna, 227, 231, 250
Berlin, 214
Bermúdez, Pedro, 357
Bernhard, Christoph, 178, 193
  Geistlicher Harmonien I. Teil, 193
  Geistreiches Gesangbuch, 172, 173
  *Opernballett von der Wirckung der sieben
    Planeten*, 177, *177*
Bernini, Gian Lorenzo, 59, 60, *61*
Bertali, Antonio, 152
  Inganno d'amore, L', 153
  Magia delusa, La, 153
Berthod, Blaise, 231
Bertoli, Giovanni Antonio, 152
Betterton, Thomas, 318
Beys, Charles de, 235
Bezzi, Tomaso, *97*
Bianco, Pietro Antonio, 148
Blas de Castro, Juan, 339
Blow, John, 316, 319
  Venus and Adonis, 318
Boccaccio, Giovanni, 62
Bochan, Jacques, 314
Boësset, Antoine, 224, 227, 248
  Ballet de la Douanière de Billebahout, 232
Boësset, Claude Jean-Baptiste de, 248
Boësset, Jean-Baptiste de, 227, 240, 248
Boethius, 283
Bologna, 4, 103–20, *105*
  academies, 104, 107, 115
  Accademia dei Filaschisi, 107
  Accademia dei Filomusi, 107
  Accademia dei Floridi, 107
  Accademia dei Gelati, *114*, 115
  Accademia Filarmonica, 107, 108, 109, 110
  cantatas, 117
  commedia dell'arte, 115
  Concerto Palatino della Signoria, 106, 111,
    113
  concertos, 112
  Madonna della Galliera, 117
  madrigals, 115
  masses, 113–14
  motets, 117
  music publishing, 109, 117–18
  opera, 114–16
  Oratorians, 117

The Early Baroque Era